Reimagining Characters with Unreal Engine MetaHuman Creator

Second Edition

AF717635

Learn the complete MetaHuman production pipeline using Unreal Engine 5.7

Brian Rossney

<packt>

Reimagining Characters with Unreal Engine MetaHuman Creator

Second Edition

Copyright © 2026 Packt Publishing

All rights reserved. No part of this book may be reproduced, stored in a retrieval system, or transmitted in any form or by any means, without the prior written permission of the publisher, except in the case of brief quotations embedded in critical articles or reviews.

Every effort has been made in the preparation of this book to ensure the accuracy of the information presented. However, the information contained in this book is sold without warranty, either express or implied. Neither the author, nor Packt Publishing or its dealers and distributors, will be held liable for any damages caused or alleged to have been caused directly or indirectly by this book.

Packt Publishing has endeavored to provide trademark information about all of the companies and products mentioned in this book by the appropriate use of capitals. However, Packt Publishing cannot guarantee the accuracy of this information.

Portfolio Director: Rohit Rajkumar
Relationship Lead: Neha Pande
Project Manager: Sandip Tadge
Content Engineer: Anuradha Joglekar
Technical Editor: Tejas Mhasvekar
Copy Editor: Anuradha Joglekar
Indexer: Hemangini Bari
Proofreader: Anuradha Joglekar
Production Designer: Alishon Falcon
Marketing Owner: Nivedita Pandey

First published: December 2022
Second edition: July 2026

Production reference: 1130726

Published by Packt Publishing Ltd.
Grosvenor House
11 St Paul's Square
Birmingham
B3 1RB, UK.

ISBN 978-1-80602-469-8
www.packtpub.com

To my mother, Gaby, for her unwavering inspiration. To my wife, and to my children, Eoin and Isabella, for their support, encouragement, and understanding throughout this journey. Finally, to my sister Aileen and to all my friends who checked in on my progress, thank you for your encouragement and belief in me.

- Brian

Foreword

When Brian's first book on the MetaHuman Creator landed, it filled a gap the industry badly needed filled. Digital humans had, until then, been the preserve of studios with the budgets to build them from the ground up. Brian's achievement was to take that process apart and hand it back to filmmakers, in plain language, without losing any of the craft that makes a character believable. Rather than simply explaining the software, he showed readers how these tools could be applied within a real production environment.

This new edition does something harder: it keeps pace with a tool that hasn't stood still. Since the first book, MetaHuman has moved from a promising shortcut to a genuine production pipeline, and the workflows around it have grown in step. Clothing and hair grooms, once among the most stubborn technical obstacles to a convincing digital human, now have chapters of their own. And the addition of external tools and plugins reflects something I think is genuinely important: MetaHuman was never meant to be used in isolation, and this book treats it that way.

I've had the pleasure of working alongside Brian on productions where Unreal and MetaHumans sat right at the center of the previs and virtual production process, and what struck me each time was how little separation there is between how he teaches and how he actually works. He isn't writing about theory he's read up on. He's writing about problems he's solved, on set and in the edit, under the same time and budget pressures the rest of us are working under. That's a rare thing in technical publishing, and it's the reason this book earns its place.

What I appreciate most, reading through this new edition, is that it doesn't simply update the previous book for the sake of keeping pace with new software releases. Every new chapter feels purposeful, addressing the questions artists naturally began asking as they became more ambitious with MetaHuman. Whether it's creating believable clothing, developing convincing hair, improving performance capture, or extending Unreal Engine through complementary tools, Brian has focused on the areas that genuinely help artists move from experimentation to production. That's the mark of an author who's still listening to his readers after the first edition shipped.

The barrier to entry for high-end digital character work keeps falling, and that's good news for our industry. It means studios and solo creators competing for the same audience are increasingly working from the same toolkit, and the differentiator becomes what it always should have been: taste, craft, and storytelling. Brian's book doesn't just teach you the buttons to press. It teaches you to think like a production artist, which is a far more durable skill. Those are lessons that remain valuable long after individual software features have evolved.

Whether this is your first introduction to MetaHuman or you're returning to build on the foundations of the first edition, you're in very capable hands. I'm delighted to introduce this updated edition, and I have no doubt it will help a new generation of filmmakers and digital artists discover what's possible when great technology is combined with thoughtful, practical guidance.

John Kennedy

VFX Supervisor & Co-Founder, Elephant Goldfish

Contributors

About the author

Brian Rossney is a filmmaker, VFX supervisor, and creative director with more than 27 years of experience across film, television, games, and virtual production. He specializes in real-time filmmaking with Unreal Engine, MetaHumans, virtual cinematography, and digital character workflows. Brian has worked as a consultant with studios across Ireland, the United Kingdom, mainland Europe, and the United States, contributing to feature films, television productions, animation, and games. His recent work includes previs for *Wednesday Season 3* using Unreal Engine and MetaHumans.

Brian has lectured at Dublin City University and Galway Film Centre and is the author of the first edition of *Reimagining Characters with Unreal Engine MetaHuman Creator*. Through Red Spider Studios, he continues to write, direct, and produce original films while exploring how real-time technology and artificial intelligence are reshaping the future of filmmaking.

I would like to thank my family for their patience, support, and understanding while I spent countless hours working on this second edition.

I would also like to thank the team at Packt Publishing for making this second edition possible. My sincere thanks go to Sandip Tadge for managing the project, Anuradha Joglekar for her guidance and support as the Content Engineer, Neha Pande for her support as the Relationship Lead, and Deepak Jadhav for his valuable feedback as the Technical Reviewer. Finally, thank you to the entire Packt team for their support throughout the writing and production of this book.

About the reviewer

Deepak Jadhav is an experienced software professional with an extensive background in game development, project management, and extended reality. He has worked on immersive AR and MR solutions across different industries, with expertise in game programming, game engines such as Godot, Unity, and Unreal, and AI system implementation for enterprise applications. He also brings experience in real-time systems, digital twins, and cross-functional team leadership, supported by a master's degree in game development and project management and a bachelor's degree in computer technology.

Table of Contents

Chapter 10: Using a Webcam and Audio for Facial Motion Capture 249

Chapter 11: Advanced Rendering with the Level Sequencer 269

Chapter 14: External Tools and Plugins for MetaHuman Workflows 341

Chapter 15: Unlock Your Exclusive Benefits 357

Other Books You May Enjoy 362

Index 365

Preface

When I wrote the first edition of this book, MetaHuman Creator was still a standalone application accessed through Quixel Bridge. While it was already capable of producing impressive digital humans, many of the workflows were still evolving and often required artists to move between multiple applications to complete even relatively straightforward tasks.

Since then, Epic Games has transformed the MetaHuman ecosystem. MetaHuman Creator is now fully integrated into Unreal Engine, the animation pipeline has matured considerably, and many workflows have become faster and more streamlined. These developments are the reason for this second edition. Every chapter has been reviewed and updated for Unreal Engine 5.7, with revised workflows, updated techniques, and new chapters that reflect the way MetaHumans are created in production today.

During the final stages of writing this second edition, Epic Games announced Unreal Engine 5.8, introducing exciting additions to the MetaHuman ecosystem, including full-body Mesh to MetaHuman workflows, improved markerless performance capture, and powerful crowd generation tools. While these new features continue to expand what is possible, they build upon the same core principles covered throughout this book. The workflows presented here remain highly relevant and provide the foundation needed to understand not only Unreal Engine 5.7, but future versions of the MetaHuman ecosystem as it continues to evolve.

Rather than focusing on individual tools or isolated features, this book follows the same progression you would typically use on a real production. You'll begin by creating and assembling a MetaHuman before moving on to clothing, body animation, facial motion capture, cinematic sequencing, lighting, and rendering. Finally, you'll extend your workflow using professional applications such as Blender, Maya, Houdini, and a range of third-party tools that are commonly used in production. By the end of the book, you'll have developed a solid understanding of the complete MetaHuman production pipeline.

One of my goals while writing this book was not simply to explain which buttons to press, but to explain why particular workflows are used and where they fit within a professional production pipeline. Software will continue to evolve, interfaces will change, and new features will be introduced, but the underlying principles remain the same. Once you understand those principles, adapting to new versions of Unreal Engine and MetaHuman Creator becomes a much easier process.

I hope this second edition gives you the confidence to move beyond simply creating digital characters and begin using them as part of complete productions. Whether you're producing a short film, developing a game, working in virtual production, or simply exploring digital humans for the first time, I hope the workflows and techniques covered throughout this book help bring your own characters to life.

Who this book is for

This book is intended for filmmakers, game developers, technical artists, animators, and digital content creators who want to create realistic digital humans using Unreal Engine and MetaHuman Creator. Whether you're completely new to MetaHumans or returning from the first edition, you'll learn practical, production-ready workflows for character creation, body animation, facial motion capture, rendering, and cinematic production. A basic familiarity with Unreal Engine is recommended, but no previous experience with MetaHuman Creator is required.

What this book covers

Chapter 1, Getting Started with Unreal, introduces Unreal Engine 5.7 and MetaHuman Creator, guiding you through installation, project setup, and the tools required to begin creating digital humans.

Chapter 2, Creating Characters in the MetaHuman Interface, explores the MetaHuman Creator interface and demonstrates how to design and customize realistic digital characters.

Chapter 3, Assembling the Character, covers assembling your MetaHuman, downloading assets, and preparing your character for use inside Unreal Engine.

Chapter 4, Diving Into the MetaHuman Blueprint, introduces Blueprints and explains how they control character behavior, animation, and skeletal workflows.

Chapter 5, Clothing Our MetaHuman, demonstrates clothing workflows using Fab and Marvelous Designer, including garment fitting and cloth simulation.

Chapter 6, Retargeting Mixamo Animations, explains how to import and retarget third-party body animation onto your MetaHuman.

Chapter 7, Adding Motion Capture with DeepMotion, shows how to generate your own body performances using markerless motion capture and apply them within Unreal Engine.

Chapter 8, Using the Level Sequencer, introduces Unreal Engine's cinematic timeline, Control Rig, and animation editing tools.

Chapter 9, Using an iPhone for Facial Motion Capture, demonstrates professional facial performance capture using Live Link Face, Take Recorder, and MetaHuman Animator.

Chapter 10, Using a Webcam and Audio for Facial Motion Capture, presents an alternative facial animation workflow using a standard webcam and Unreal Engine's Audio to Animation tools.

Chapter 11, Advanced Rendering with the Level Sequencer, focuses on cinematic lighting, cameras, animation management, and producing high-quality final renders.

Chapter 12, Using the Mesh to MetaHuman Plugin, explains how to create MetaHumans from custom meshes and scanned faces using the MetaHuman Identity workflow.

Chapter 13, Applying Hair Grooms, demonstrates how to create, import, and simulate custom hair grooms using Blender.

Chapter 14, External Tools and Plugins for MetaHuman Workflows, explores additional professional applications and plugins that extend MetaHuman

To get the most out of this book

- To follow the workflows in this book, you'll need a computer capable of running Unreal Engine 5.7.
- Some chapters require additional software such as Blender and Marvelous Designer, while others make use of an iPhone with a TrueDepth camera or a standard webcam for facial motion capture.
- An internet connection is recommended for downloading Unreal Engine, plugins, MetaHumans, and supporting assets.

Download the color images

Your purchase includes a color, DRM-free PDF copy of this book, ideal for viewing color images, screenshots, and diagrams. Refer to *Free benefits with your book section* at the end of the *Preface* to unlock your PDF copy.

Conventions used

There are a number of text conventions used throughout this book.

Bold: Indicates a new term, an important word, or words that you see on the screen. For instance, words in menus or dialog boxes appear in the text like this. For example: "The **Hair & Clothing** tab includes **Hair (Grooms)** menu, with a variety of presets."

> **Note**
>
> Warnings or important notes appear like this.

> **Tip**
>
> Tips and tricks appear like this.

Get in touch

Feedback from our readers is always welcome.

General feedback: If you have questions about any aspect of this book or have any general feedback, please email us at `customercare@packt.com` and mention the book's title in the subject of your message.

Errata: Although we have taken every care to ensure the accuracy of our content, mistakes do happen. If you have found a mistake in this book, we would be grateful if you reported this to us. Please visit `http://www.packt.com/submit-errata`, click **Submit Errata**, and fill in the form.

Piracy: If you come across any illegal copies of our works in any form on the internet, we would be grateful if you would provide us with the location address or website name. Please contact us at `copyright@packt.com` with a link to the material.

If you are interested in becoming an author: If there is a topic that you have expertise in and you are interested in either writing or contributing to a book, please visit `http://authors.packt.com/`.

Subscribe to Game Dev Assembly!

We are excited to introduce **Game Dev Assembly**, our brand-new newsletter dedicated to everything game development. Whether you're coding, designing, animating, or managing a studio, we've got insights, trends, and expert advice to help you create, innovate, and thrive. Sign up now and get exciting benefits.

`https://packt.link/gamedev-newsletter`

Join our community on Discord

Join our community's Discord space for discussions with the authors and other readers:

`https://packt.link/unrealengine`

Free benefits with your book

This book comes with free benefits to support your learning. Activate them now for instant access (see the "*How to Unlock*" section for instructions).

Here's a quick overview of what you can instantly unlock with your purchase:

How to Unlock

Scan the QR code (or go to `packtpub.com/unlock`). Search for this book by name, confirm the edition, and then follow the steps on the page.

UNLOCK NOW

Note: Keep your invoice handy. Purchases made directly from Packt don't require one

Share your thoughts

Once you've read *Reimagining Characters with Unreal Engine MetaHuman Creator, Second Edition*, we'd love to hear your thoughts! Scan the QR code below to go straight to the Amazon review page for this book and share your feedback.

https://packt.link/r/1806024691

Your review is important to us and the tech community and will help us make sure we're delivering excellent quality content.

Part 1

Getting Started with Unreal

In this first part of the book, you'll build a solid foundation in Unreal Engine 5.7 and MetaHuman Creator. You'll learn how MetaHuman Creator has evolved into an integrated part of Unreal Engine, install and configure the tools needed for production, and explore the MetaHuman Creator interface in depth.

You'll then create, customize, assemble, and prepare your first MetaHuman for animation, while gaining an understanding of the Blueprint that drives your character inside Unreal Engine.

By the end of this part of the book, you'll have a production-ready MetaHuman and the knowledge needed to confidently continue through the animation and performance workflows covered in the rest of the book.

This part of the book includes the following chapters:

- *Chapter 1, Getting Started with Unreal*
- *Chapter 2, Creating Characters in the MetaHuman Interface*
- *Chapter 3, Assembling the Character*
- *Chapter 4, Diving Into the MetaHuman Blueprint*

1

Getting Started with Unreal

Welcome to the second edition of *Reimagining Characters with Unreal Engine's MetaHuman Creator*. The **MetaHuman Creator** has come a long way since its first release. In my previous book, it was available in Unreal Engine version 5.0 via **Quixel Bridge** and now in Unreal Engine version 5.7, it comes built in. But that isn't the only reason for this second edition. MetaHumans have hit the industry of games design and animation with force and have become a recognizable industry standard, with more and more artists and studios implementing MetaHumans into their pipelines. At the time of writing the first edition, Netflix's *In Vaulted Halls Entombed* was in its early stage of production, with MetaHumans being central to the character production.

The focus of this edition is to get users up to speed on the new features of MetaHuman, to introduce new users to MetaHumans with a focus on getting all users production ready. Some readers may have the hardware such as an iPhone to create bespoke MetaHuman versions of themselves walking and talking and others may have no hardware other than a computer capable of running Unreal, but both will learn how to create and animate talking MetaHumans for their games and animation projects. This book will cover techniques and efficient methods tried and tested in real production environments.

In the first chapter of this book, you will learn about what Unreal Engine is, what it is used for, and how you can start working with it. You will then learn how to set up an account with Epic Games and download Unreal Engine, before using the same account details to download Bridge, which is the application needed to start creating MetaHuman characters.

By the end of this chapter, you will be proficient in installing and setting up these applications on a Windows machine.

We will cover the following topics:

- What is Unreal Engine?
- What are MetaHumans?
- Setting up Unreal Engine and the MetaHuman Creator

> Note
>
> **Download the PDF version of this book**
>
> Your purchase includes a DRM-free PDF copy of this book, the code bundle, and a range of exclusive benefits. To unlock everything, follow the *Free benefits with your book* section in the *Preface*.

Technical requirements

Before we get started, I must remind you that this book is about extremely high-quality 3D characters so it's important you understand this before setting up Unreal and risk being disappointed because of technical issues. This is because Unreal Engine, like any 3D graphics tool, requires a powerful machine; much of this power comes from the graphics cards.

As a result, if you want to enjoy the real-time experience of working in Unreal, you'll need a computer that can handle the best settings and display a MetaHuman character in real time. Otherwise, you'll experience a very sluggish machine with a tendency to crash a lot, and nobody wants this. To complete this chapter, you will need an internet connection and the following minimum hardware specifications:

- Operating System: Windows 11
- RAM: 16 GB DDR5-4800MHz (RDIMM, ECC)
- Quad-core Intel or AMD, 2.5 GHz or faster
- DirectX 11 or 12 compatible graphics card with the latest drivers

The screen grabs you will see in the pages of this book are from my own machine, which is configured as follows:

- Windows 10 64-bit
- 128 GB RAM
- 1 TB GB SSD (OS drive)
- 4 TB SSD (data drive)
- NVIDIA GeForce RTX 3090
- 20-Core i9 10-900k @ 3.7 GHz

If you're using a modern Apple Silicon Mac, Unreal Engine performs significantly better than in previous releases and many MetaHuman workflows are now supported. However, Windows still provides the most complete experience, particularly for advanced MetaHuman Animator workflows and DirectX 12-dependent features.

I'd also like to point out that there are solutions out there that will allow you to test on powerful machines. For the most part, they will get you through all the chapters of this book, except for live facial motion capture and any live body motion capture that may be featured. Therefore, if you're on a budget, I suggest you look at some cloud computing solutions such as the following: `paperspace.com`.

> **Note**
>
> On a cloud machine, you still won't be able to do any live motion capture, as this requires a direct interface or shared network with your machine. However, you could take advantage of the higher specification of the cloud machine for experimenting with render and lighting settings and pre-recorded motion capture.

At this point, you may be getting needlessly worried. However, I personally tried using the tools mentioned in this book on a lower-spec machine and, for the most part, I was able to work through it using very low render settings. However, I was just not able to do any live motion capture at all. Instead, I was only able to rely on library motion capture or iPhone facial capture recordings I made myself—so if you plan to learn now and invest in a newer, faster machine later, this book is certainly still for you.

What is Unreal?

Put simply, **Unreal Engine** is a game engine. There are many other game engines out there, but Unreal Engine is one of two that are the leading ones in the field of game development, the other being Unity. Had the people of Unity come up with MetaHumans, this book would have a slightly different title!

Unreal Engine is an incredibly powerful tool used for displaying graphics in real time. It was originally built for a PC-based first-person shooter game called 'Unreal' and developed by Epic Games in the mid- to late 1990s. In its earlier years, Unreal Engine was capable of rendering frames at rates as high as 60 fps on the CPU, giving the user a real-time experience.

However, there were many limitations, such as the frame size, limits on how many triangles could be displayed at any given time, and the complexity of the math behind the lighting. The end results were graphics that were not photorealistic but were a significant improvement on other game engines.

As GPUs improved over time, so did Unreal, as it was able to migrate a lot of its mathematical computations over to the GPU. As a result, the engine was able to rely on hardware that was specifically designed to calculate 3D rendering faster, and many features were developed to introduce photorealistic lighting solutions that were previously only available on traditional CPU path-traced solutions found in film and TV.

Path-traced or ray-traced rendering solutions involved very complex mathematics that would trace photons from the pixel of the final render through the CGI camera and around the scene. This tracing was incredibly time-consuming and required a lot of processing power just to deliver a single image. Therefore, conveying a sense of motion or real time was impossible for photorealism.

Due to very recent innovations, Unreal Engine is now being used to generate photorealistic renders in real time, and we can see the result of that in Disney's "The Mandalorian." The companies behind the real-time environments, StageCraft and Industrial and Light & Magic, worked together to create LED backgrounds that displayed the output of scenes within Unreal Engine. In addition to supplying a photorealistic background, the LED backgrounds would also light the real actors, adding even more realism.

I expect that if you are a complete newbie to all of this, you may be scratching your head thinking: *What does a game engine like Unreal do?* More generally, it is a software application designed for building games that render graphics in real time. For games, Unreal is used for the creation of the following:

- User functions
- Game logic
- Environment design
- Animation
- Real-time rendering of what the user sees

Be it input from a mouse click, an Xbox controller button, or an Oculus headset, this user input affects how and when characters move and what is being displayed at any given time.

Ultimately, this book is only about getting you up and running with your own characters and animating them how you want them to be animated even if you don't have an art background or character animation background. So, gaming, and game development knowledge isn't required. Exciting stuff? I think so.

Next, let's think a little more about how we are going to create those characters.

What are MetaHumans?

MetaHumans are very complex characters that have the capability of looking photorealistic and moving realistically. They are templates to be edited by users and artists. The editing of the character templates used to take place on a web browser but now with Unreal Engine 5.7, this all takes place inside the Unreal Application on your machine and allows the user to see their character design being displayed in extreme realism.

A lot of the development of **MetaHuman Creator** is around real-time rendering. Typically, the shading of skin for CGI characters involves a substantial amount of CPU processing, particularly for high-detail areas, such as subtle reflections, pores, and tiny hair or fuzz. The MetaHuman skin shaders are designed to work in real time within Unreal Engine by harnessing recent technological hardware advances, such as real-time raytracing in NVIDIA RTX cards.

In addition to photorealistic skin shaders, MetaHumans have a network of bones and blend shapes that allow for incredibly intricate and powerful facial puppeteering, as well as the ability to be combined with facial and body motion capture, all in real time within Unreal.

Now that you have a good understanding of Unreal Engine and MetaHumans, we will get the software up and running on your system so you can start using Unreal in the next chapter.

Setting up Unreal and the MetaHuman Creator

Before we can start using Unreal Engine and MetaHumans, we need to do some setup. In upcoming sections, we will do the following:

- Create an Unreal account
- Download and install Unreal Engine 5.7
- Launch Unreal Engine 5.7
- Bridge
- Boot up MetaHuman Creator

So, let's get started.

Creating an Epic account

To get started with Unreal, the first thing you need to do is create an Epic account. To do this, follow these instructions:

1. First, navigate to the Epic Games website: `https://www.epicgames.com/`.

Note

Depending on your region, don't be surprised if the URL changes to something like the following: `https://www.epicgames.com/store/en-US/` (you're still in the right place).

2. Once on the Epic Games website, you can navigate to the Unreal Engine link. Alternatively, just use the following URL: `https://www.unrealengine.com/`.
3. In the right-hand corner, click **Sign In** (even though you don't have sign-in credentials, you must still click on this)
4. You'll see a list of ways you can sign in, including using your email account with a bespoke password or just simply linking other social media or gaming credentials to Epic Games. Assuming this is your first account and you're not signed in, select **Don't have an Epic Games account? Sign Up**:

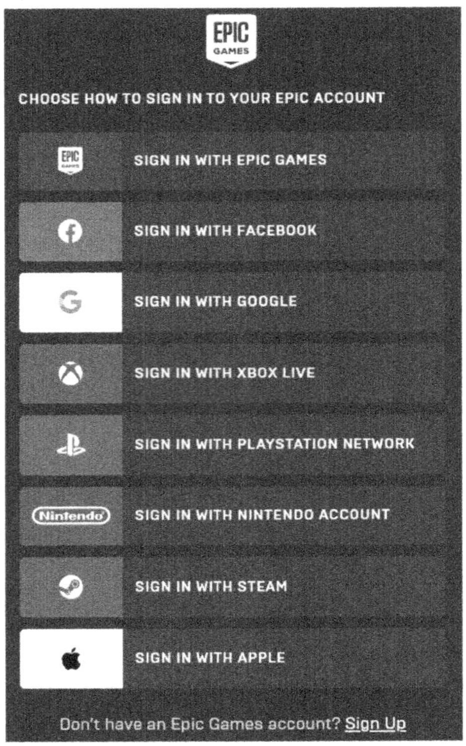

Figure 1.1: Different sign-in methods

5. On the next page, you will be asked for your name, surname, username, and email, and to designate a password for your email. You can opt to receive additional emails, but you will need to read the terms and conditions and tick that you have done so.

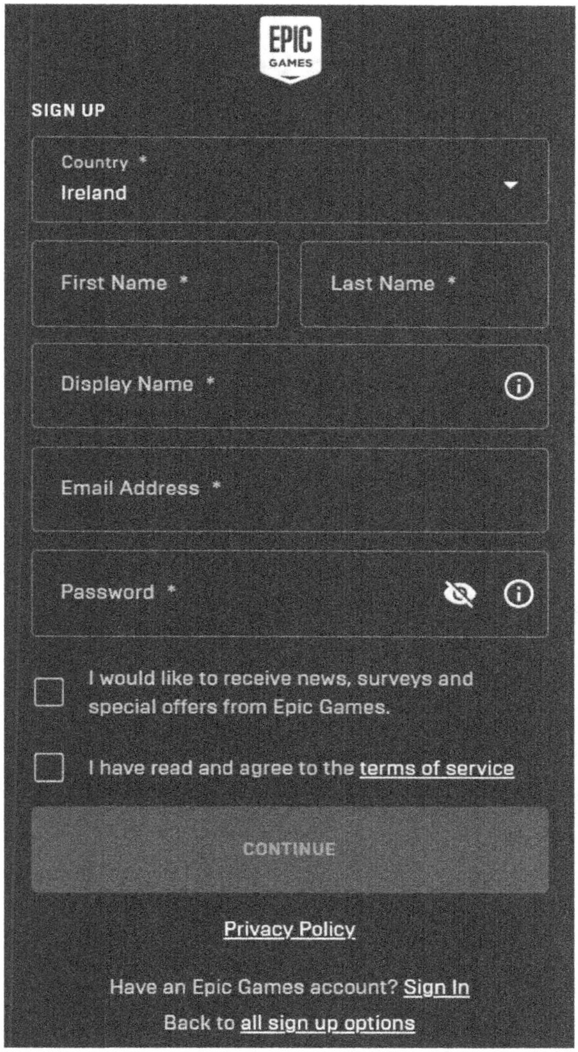

Figure 1.2: Signing up for Epic

6. Once you have done this, a link will be sent to your designated email for verification. When you click on this link, you'll have successfully created an account. You'll need to be logged in whenever you plan to use the engine.

Next, we need to download and install Unreal Engine 5.7.

Downloading and installing Unreal Engine 5.7

Using your Unreal account, we need to download and install Unreal Engine 5.7. The application you are about to install is the **Epic Games Launcher**. This is where you install the engine and gain access to other features related to the engine, such as updates, plug-ins, scripts, models, and a host of many other assets. To do this, follow these steps:

1. Once you have successfully signed into Epic, you'll see a page shown in *Figure 1.3* (the page may vary, as the screenshot is the latest marketing material from Epic at the time of print). Click on **Get Unreal Engine**.

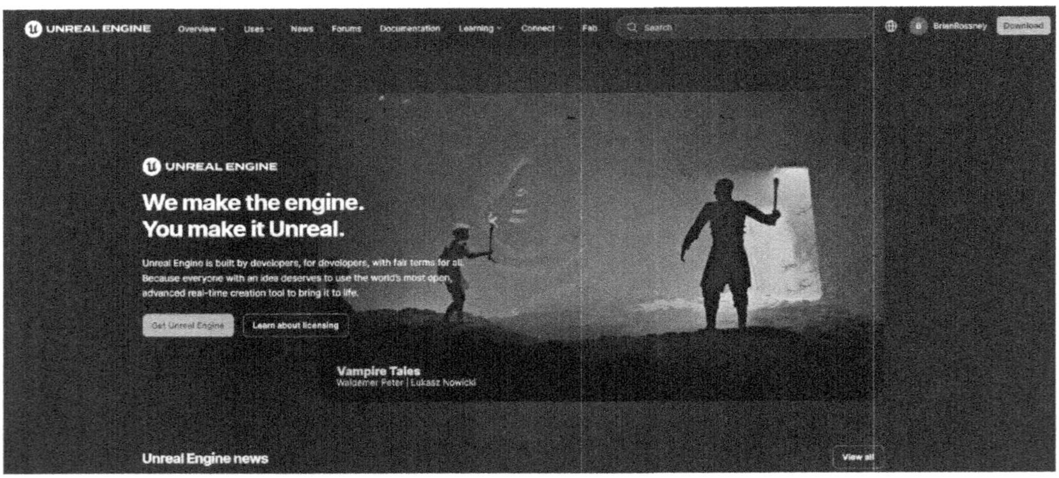

Figure 1.3: Epic splash screen

In the top right corner, you will see your name, as well as the **Download** button. Don't do anything just yet.

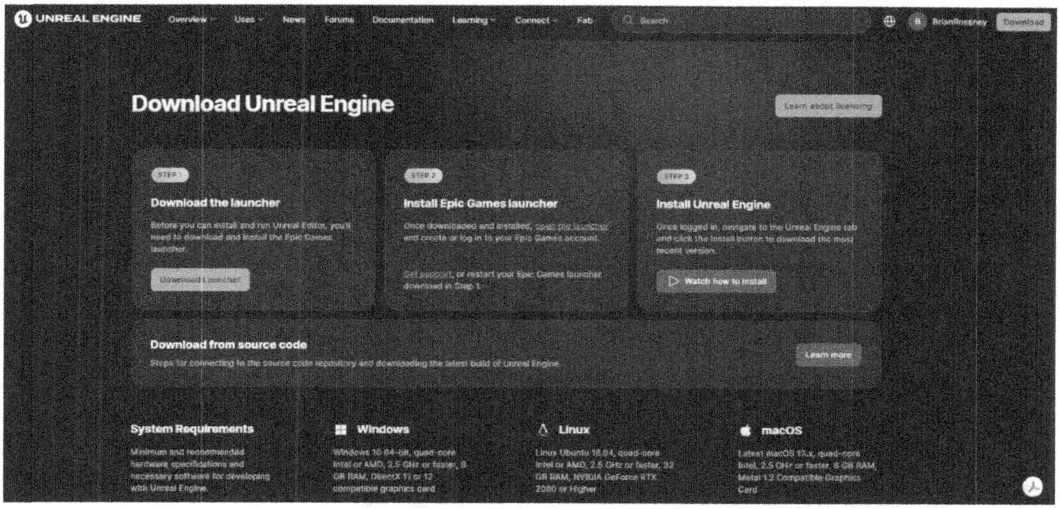

Figure 1.4: Download Unreal Engine Steps page

Epic have created a simple step-by-step guide and have even added a video tutorial in *step 3*. Ultimately, what you need to do first is install the **Unreal Launcher**, which works as a hub to access the various versions of Unreal and many additional assets.

2. When you've watched the video in *step 3*, click on **Download Launcher**.
3. Now, choose where you want to download the installer, which will be called something similar to `EpicInstaller013.0.0.enterprise.msi`. It's a Windows installer package and can be saved anywhere on your machine. You only need this file for the installation process

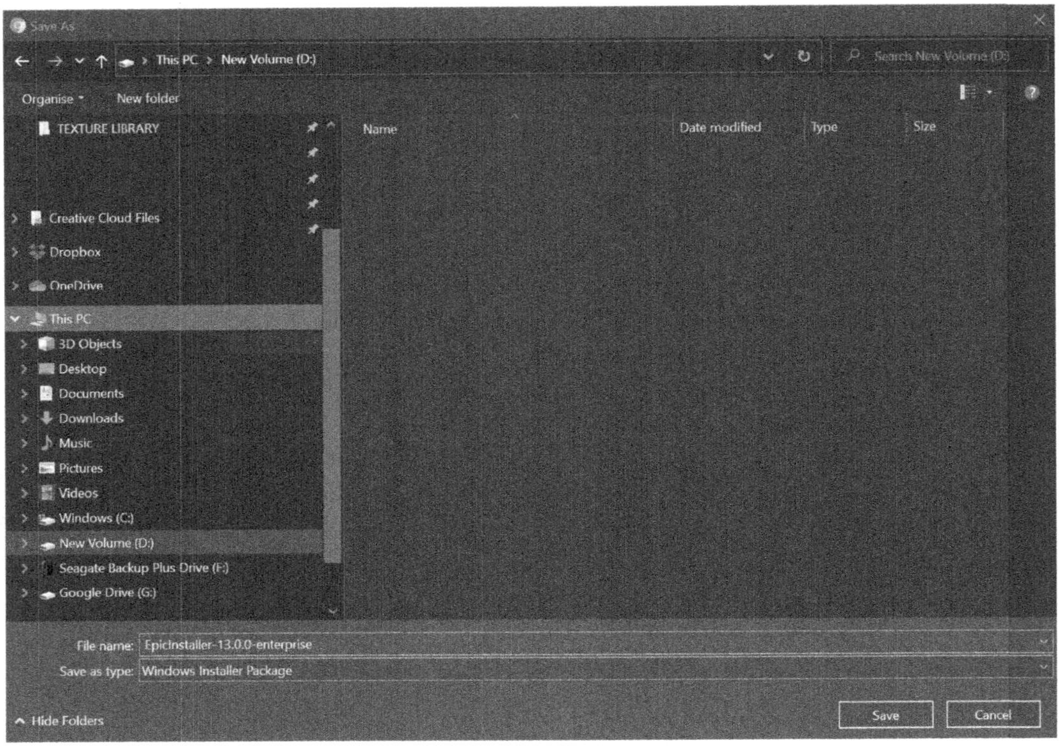

Figure 1.5: Downloading the installer

4. When you have found a suitable place, hit **Save**.
5. Once downloaded, double-click the file and it will run:

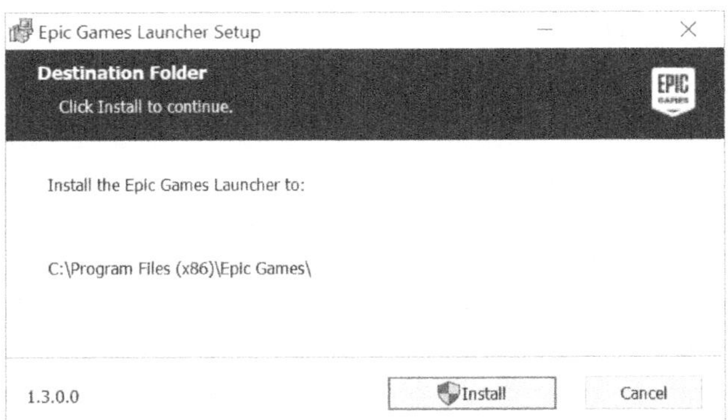

Figure 1.6: The Epic Games Launcher

6. Now, you can click **Install**.

When the installer has finished, you'll see an icon titled **Epic Games Launcher** on your desktop. Clicking on this will open the launcher (note that it could take a few minutes to open the first time). Typically, it doesn't open full screen, but when it does, it looks something like this:

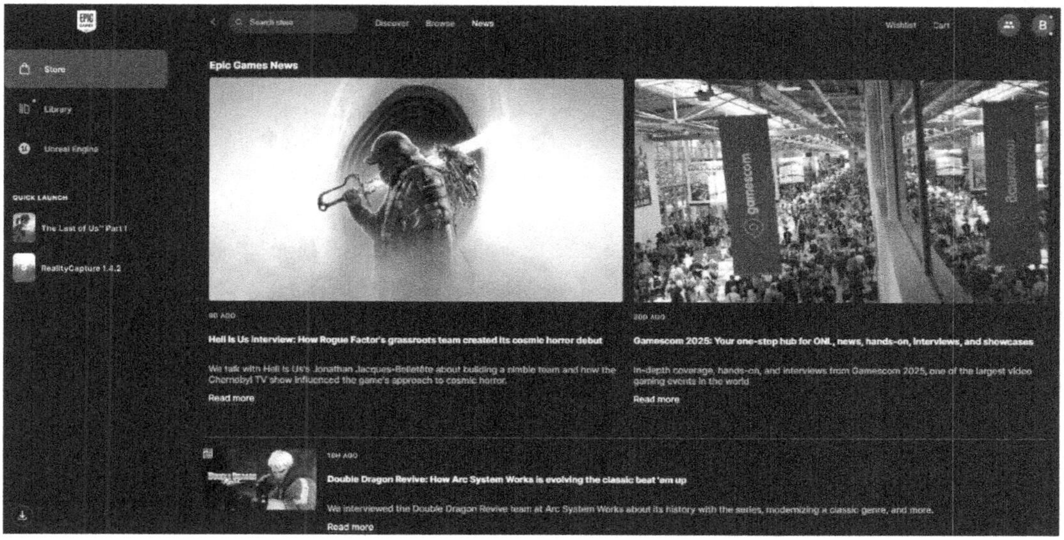

Figure 1.7: The Epic Games Launcher application

From here, you'll see the Epic Games logo on the top left, and under it are:

- Store: This is where you can buy games
- Library: Access to games you've purchased, all the Unreal-related assets, including project files you've created, and access to all available versions of the Unreal Engine
- Unreal Engine: A more direct way to install the engine

Click on Unreal Engine, and you will see on the top right **ENGINE VERSIONS** with a **+** sign.

Figure 1.8: Engine versions

Click on the **+** icon, and as soon as you do, you'll see an install badge appear. It will show the most recent version available, but if for some reason you only see a version lower than 5.7, use the drop-down arrow and choose 5.7 or higher and hit **Install.**

As soon as you do that, you will see your installation options.

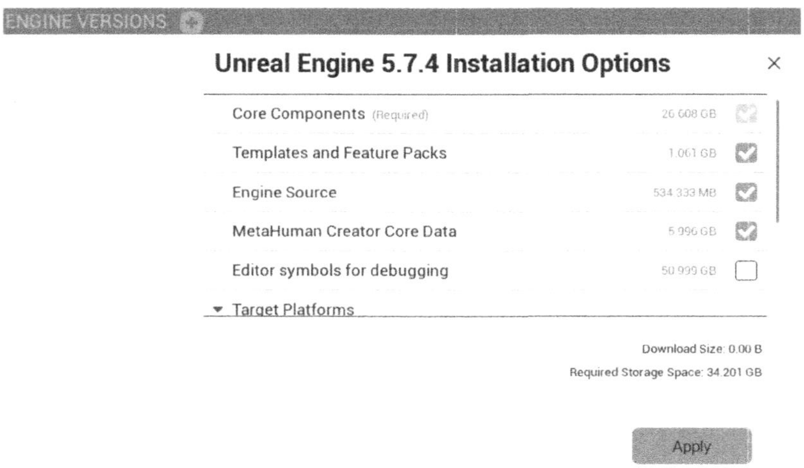

Figure 1.9: Unreal Engine installation options

Scroll down until you see **MetaHuman Creator Core Data** and tick that box. This is a very important step to get MetaHumans working. If you forget this step, just click the drop-down menu next to **Launch** as shown in *Figure 1.8*, and you'll see the options menu to install the missing core data. After ticking that box, hit Apply, and the launcher will continue with the installation.

The installation does take a while, so you may want to come back to this.

- As soon as the installation is finished, the install badge will change from gray to blue and **Install** will be replaced with **Launch**.

In the next section, we will launch UE5.7!

Launching UE 5.7

For the rest of this book, we'll assume you have installed UE 5.7. There may be updates by the time this book goes to print, but they will be minor. I'm writing this book using Unreal Engine version 5.7 Preview. After you have followed all of the previous instructions and the installer has finished installing, you will see **Launch** appear; this indicates that Unreal Engine is ready to go.

Click **Launch** (making sure you have installed UE 5.7 or above).

Next, you'll see a small splash screen as Unreal Engine initializes. This could take a few minutes the first time it runs. Eventually, it will lead to the following interface:

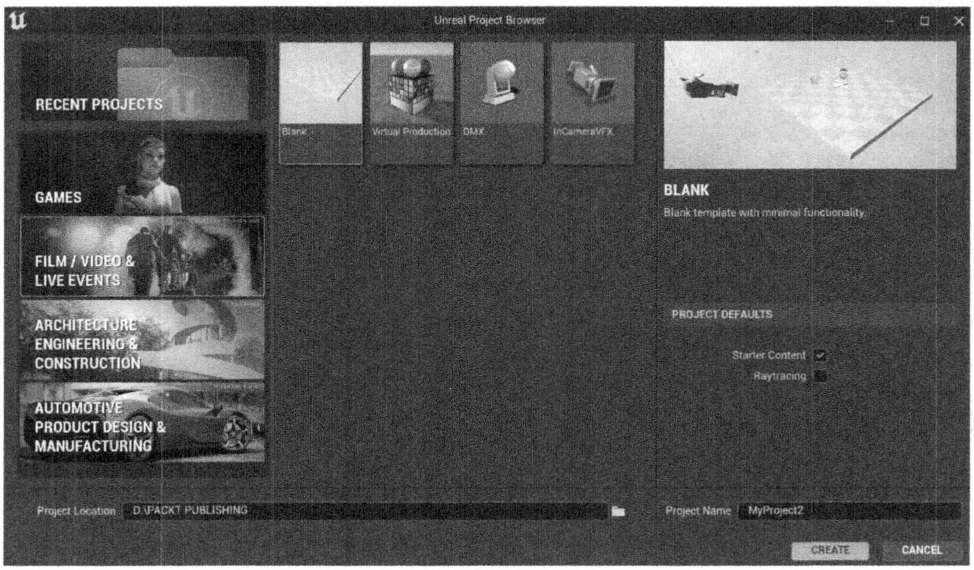

Figure 1.10: Unreal Project Browser

On the left-hand side, you'll see a column listing the following:

- **RECENT PROJECTS**
- **GAMES**
- **FILM / VIDEO & LIVE EVENTS**
- **ARCHITECTURE ENGINEERING & CONSTRUCTION**
- **AUTOMOTIVE PRODUCT DESIGN & MANUFACTURING**

Each one of the listings gives you templates to choose from. Each template will automatically load certain settings and enable various preinstalled plugins required for that nature of work.

Because we are just interested in **FILM / VIDEO & LIVE EVENTS**, when we click on that, we get to choose from a small number of templates related to that type of work:

- **Blank**
- **Virtual Production**
- **DMX**
- **InCameraVFX**

This is what the screen will look like:

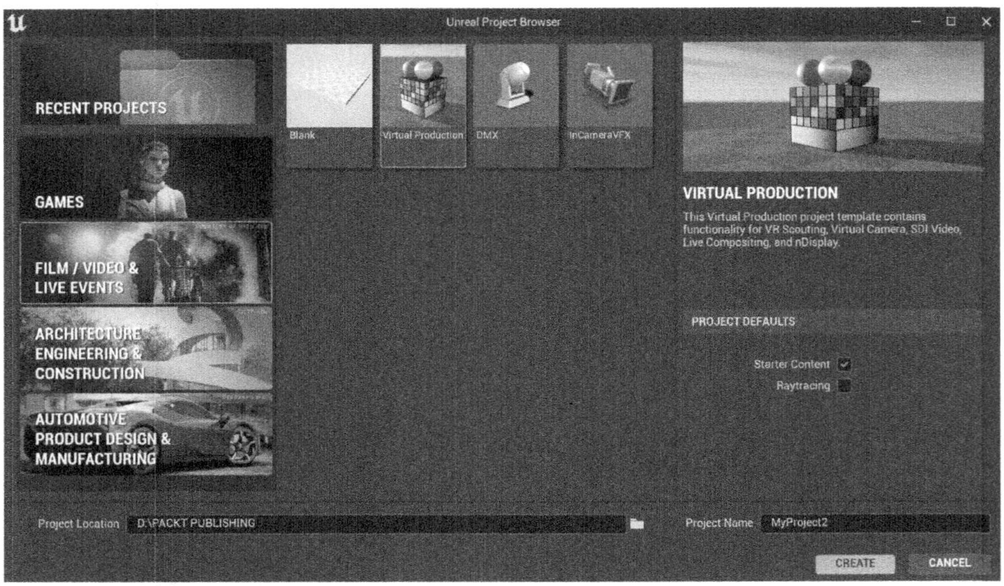

Figure 1.11: Virtual Production template

> **Note**
>
> If you happen to have a lower-specification machine that doesn't support raytracing, it's wise to keep **Raytracing** to the default **Off** mode. You can always enable it again in **Project Settings** at a later stage.

From this list, we're just going to focus on the **Virtual Production** sub template. Then, we need to choose our new project location and create a project title. For my project, I'm going to create a folder titled `BusStop`, and it will be in the D drive. The project folder will be `Bus_Stop_SC_01`. You can name your project file whatever you like.

Feel free to save your files to whatever directory you wish but be advised that it is best practice to avoid the C drive where your operating system is stored.

You'll see a splash screen again, and you will be prompted that the project is loading. This will take a minute or two depending on your machine's specifications. After this, you may get a number of pop-ups:

- You may get a dialog box just as earlier, warning you that a plugin isn't designed to work in UE5.7 and asking whether you still want to proceed. Choose **Yes** if that happens again.
- You also may get asked whether you want to update the project. Choose **Yes**. This will just take a second or two to update.
- Finally, you will be asked whether you want to manage plugins. You can choose **Yes** and then close the plugin window if that happens. You can also choose **No** and enable the plugins later as you import your character into the engine, but I do recommend selecting **Yes** at this point.

That's it! We now have the engine up and running.

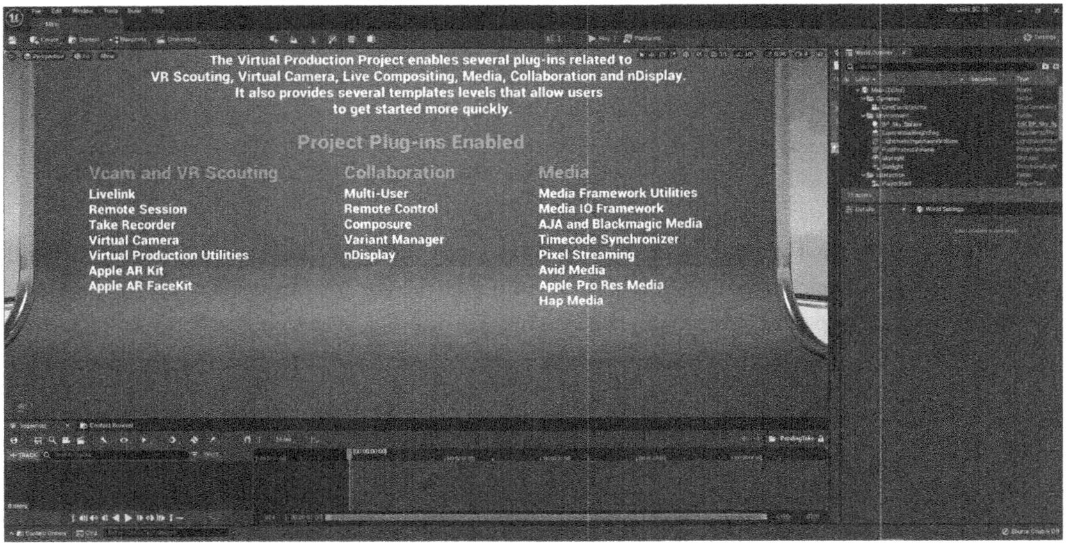

Figure 1.12: The Unreal Engine interface

Next, it's time to install Quixel Bridge.

Bridge

In the previous edition of the book where I was using Unreal Engine version 5.0, Bridge was a standalone application that allowed you to bring in 3D assets from `Quixel.com`, including MetaHumans that would have been created on their online platform.

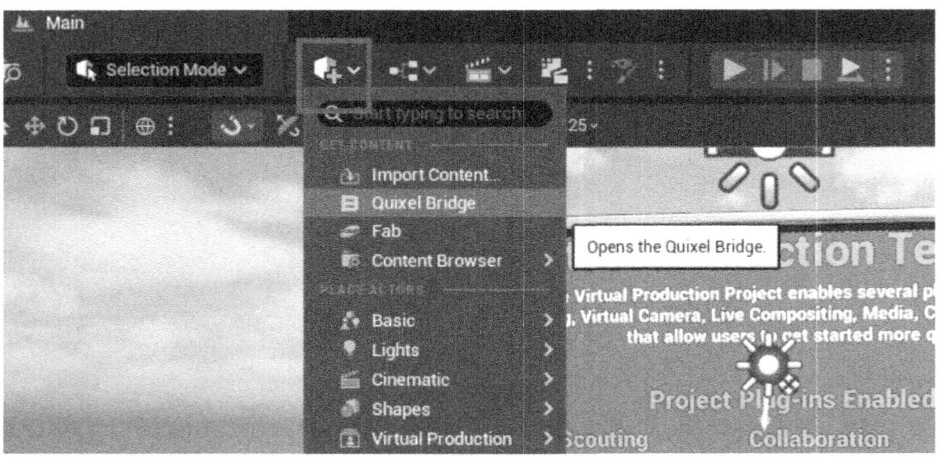

Figure 1.13: Quixel Bridge

Bridge is built into Unreal Engine 5.7 and comes pre-installed.

That being said, we still need to sign into it when we first use it. To first sign in, we can just use the **Add to Project** tool as highlighted in *Figure 1.13*. Here we can see an option to open **Quixel Bridge**.

When **Quixel Bridge** app opens, click on the profile button on the top right and sign in using your Epic Games credentials you created earlier.

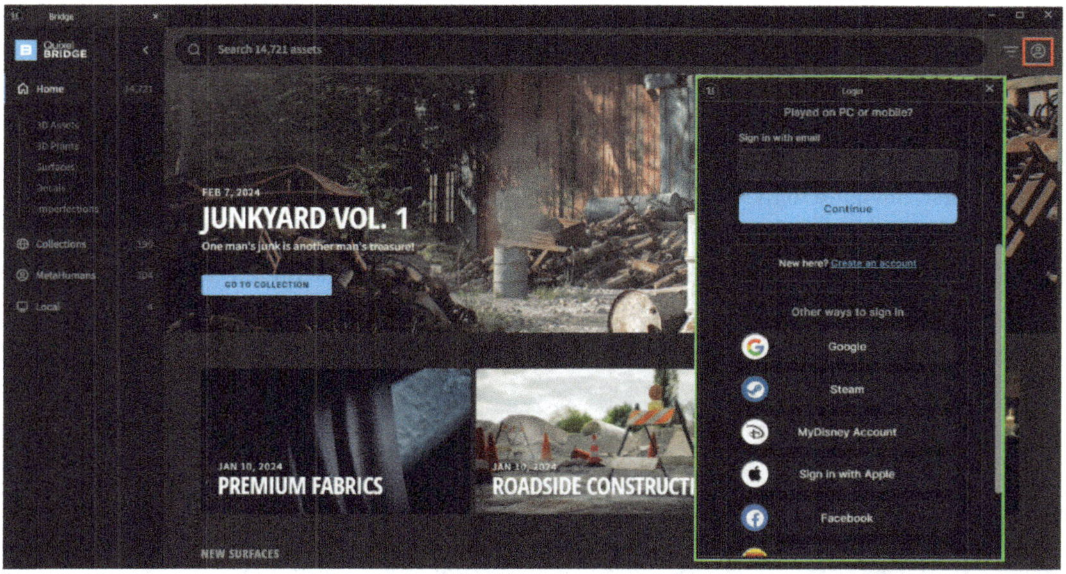

Figure 1.14: Quixel Bridge Interface

Because we signed in with the same credentials used for the installation of Unreal Engine, Bridge will function in the background whenever we need it for MetaHuman authoring, so feel free to close the bridge app and go back to Unreal Engine.

Booting up the MetaHuman Creator

Before we begin, it's worth noting that MetaHuman Creator requires a number of plugins that are installed in different locations within Unreal Engine. We'll enable all of the required plugins first and then restart Unreal Engine before creating our first MetaHuman asset. This is a one-time setup process and won't need to be repeated for future projects.

To create a MetaHuman, we need to ensure that the MetaHuman plugins are enabled. Unfortunately, installing the **MetaHuman Core Data** doesn't automatically do that for us, so we need to head over to **Edit** | **Plugins**.

The required MetaHuman plugins are split across two categories within the Plugins window, so we'll enable both sets before restarting Unreal Engine.

1. First, navigate to INSTALLED | MetaHuman. Here you'll find the MetaHuman Animator Depth Processing plugin. Enable it by ticking the checkbox.
2. When you click on **MetaHuman**, you'll see we have just one plugin titled **MetaHuman Animator Depth Processing** to install here. Tick the box.

Figure 1.15: The MetaHuman Animator Depth Processing plugin

3. Next, scroll down to the Built In section and locate MetaHuman again. Here you'll find several additional MetaHuman plugins. Enable each one before restarting Unreal Engine when prompted.

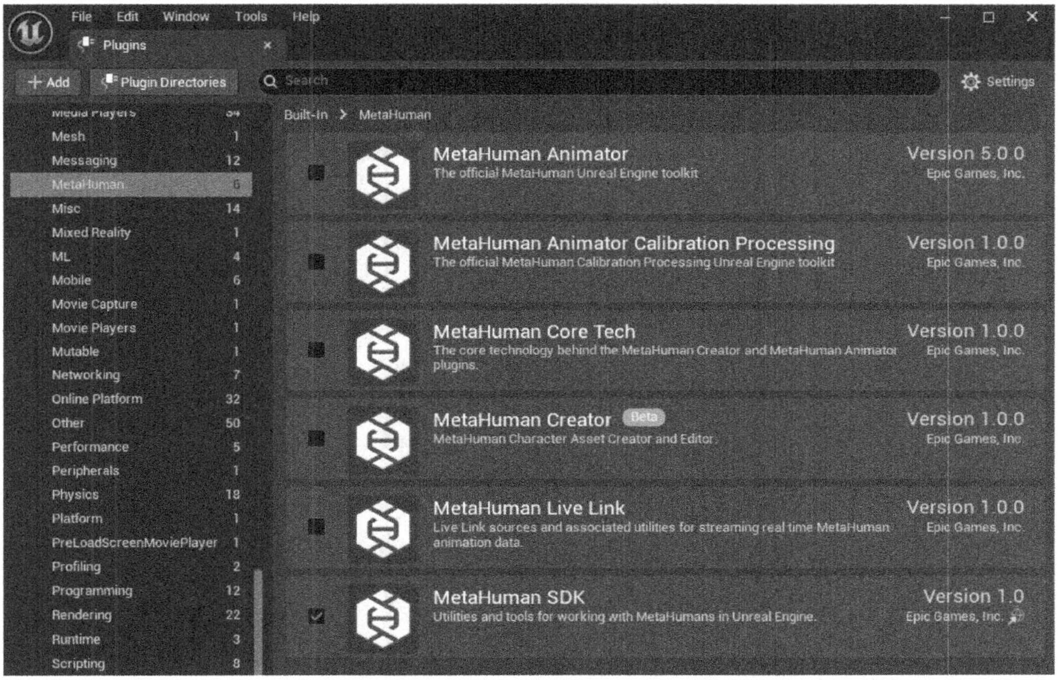

Figure 1.16: MetaHuman Plugins

4. After Unreal Engine has restarted, we're finally ready to create our first MetaHuman asset. Open the Content Browser, right-click, and search for MetaHuman Character.
5. Search for MetaHuman and click on **MetaHuman Character**. This will create an asset right in your content browser.

6. Name it `MyMetahuman` and double-click on it to open the asset

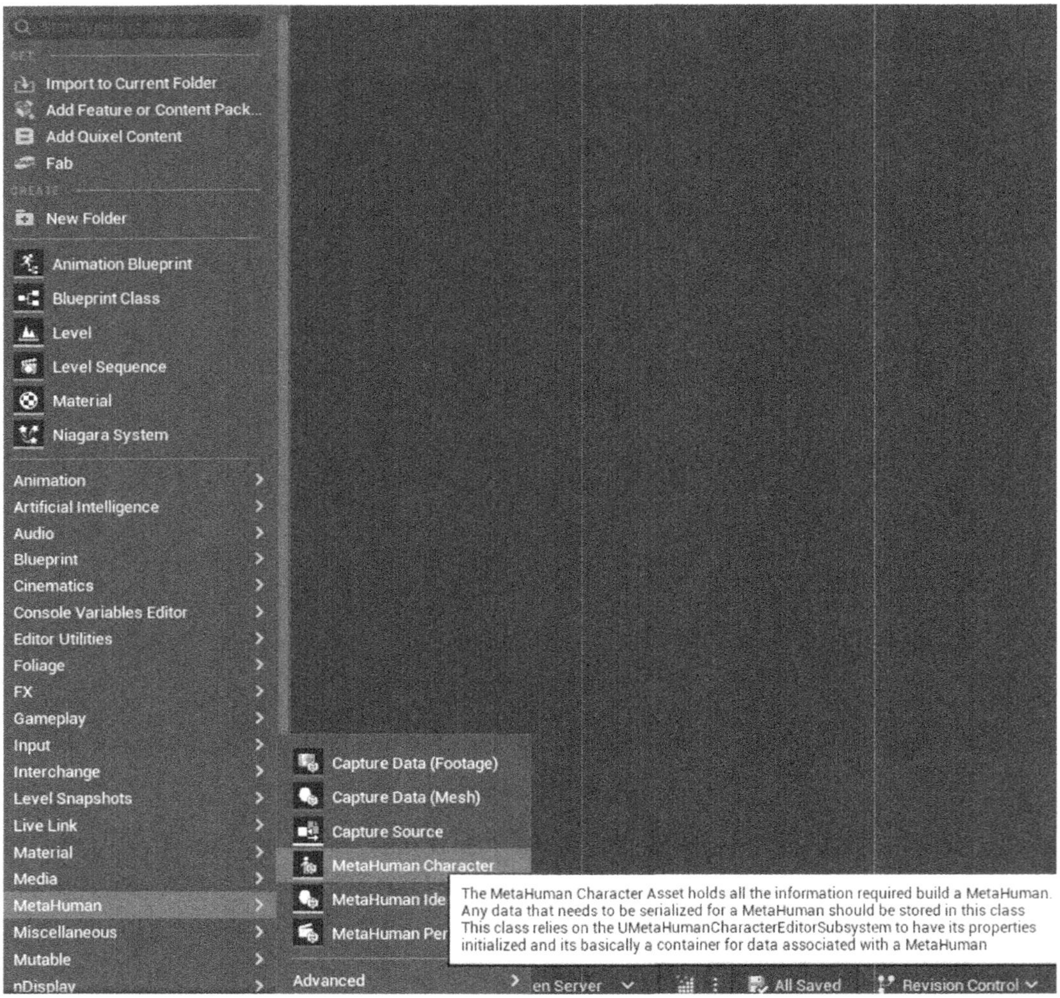

Figure 1.17: MetaHuman Character

7. The first time you create a MetaHuman Character asset, Unreal Engine may detect additional supporting plugins that haven't yet been enabled. If prompted, select Enable, allow Unreal Engine to restart, and then reopen the `MyMetaHuman` asset.

8. Go ahead and restart, and when you come back, double-click on the `MyMetahuman` asset you just created in the **Content Browser**

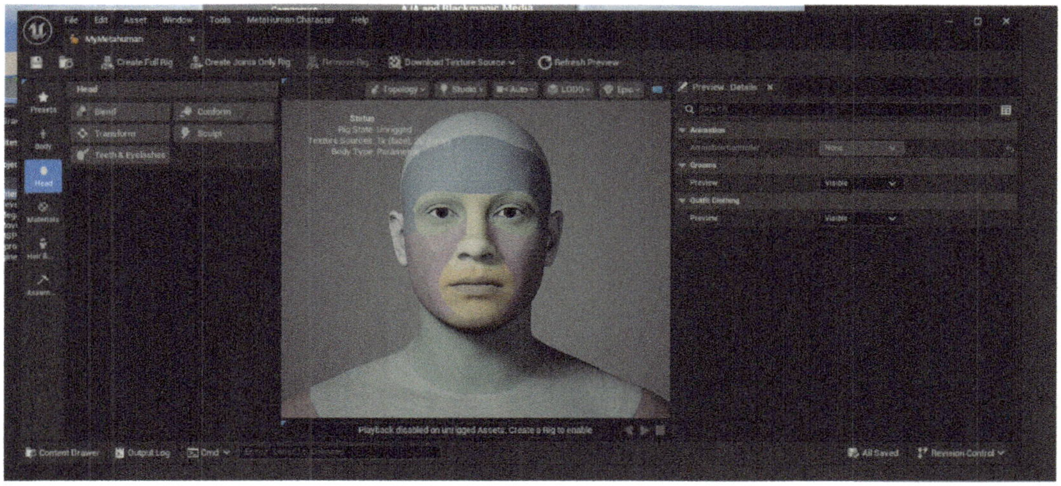

Figure 1.18: MetaHuman Character Interface

Once you have followed all steps, you'll see the **MetaHuman Creator** application, where you get to create your very own MetaHuman.

Summary

In this chapter, you've learned what Unreal is, what MetaHumans are, and what software applications you need to create MetaHumans.

The next chapter is entirely about the MetaHuman Creator session. While there are a lot of features, you will find that the application is very intuitive, and, in many ways, what you have learned in this chapter is much more complicated than what's to come. In fact, you're going to find the next chapter quite enjoyable!

2

Creating Characters in the MetaHuman Interface

In *Chapter 1*, you learned how to install the **Epic Games Launcher** and the UE5 engine. You learned that **Bridge**, which used to be a separate application, now runs under the hood, preinstalled into the engine.

This chapter will cover everything you need to know about the **MetaHuman Creator (MHC)** that is now built into the engine, where all the character designing takes place. We will look at all the editable features of the many MHC templates, including the face, hair, body, blend, move, and sculpt parameters and the best practices of when to use each attribute within the character design phase.

The primary goal of this chapter is to get you accustomed to the interface and accustomed to the character design potential. Secondly, it will also provide notes on how to implement the same design tools for a more acutely focused design process.

In addition to the various tools and preset editors, you will become familiar with learning just how MHC has become the best in the class of photorealist character design, as we delve into some of the science around skin shaders.

So, we will cover the following topics:

- Starting up the MetaHuman Creator
- Editing our MetaHuman
- Using the Move and Sculpt Tools
- Editing Materials

Technical requirements

We will continue from the last chapter, so you will need UE5 along with a reliable internet connection. A stable internet connection is required as there are some backend processes.

Introducing MetaHuman Character

In *Chapter 1*, we installed all the MetaHuman-related plug-ins, which would require a restart. After the restart, we created a MetaHuman. However, I'd like to recap the first couple of steps after you have installed the engine.

Follow these steps to create a MetaHuman character:

1. Create a new or existing Unreal Project
2. Navigate to the **Content Browser** and *right-click* to see a menu
3. Scroll down until you see **MetaHuman** and choose **MetaHuman Character**
   This will create a **MetaHuman Character Asset** for you to create your first MetaHuman and return to whenever you want to make further edits.

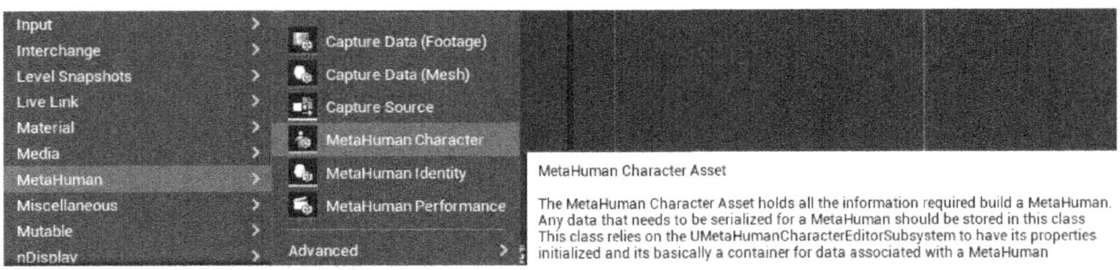

Figure 2.1: Creating the MetaHuman Character Asset

4. Once you click on **MetaHuman Character**, ensure to give it a name you'll remember. You will need to come back to this asset.

Once named, double-click on the asset to boot up the MHC.

> **Note**
>
> Your MetaHuman design is stored inside the MetaHuman Character Asset in the Unreal Content Browser. Changes are saved as part of your Unreal project, so saving the project also preserves your MetaHuman session. You can return to this asset at any time and continue editing.

Next up, the MetaHuman interface.

Navigating the MetaHuman interface

In *Figure 2.2*, I've highlighted the five key areas you'll be using in the MHC interface.

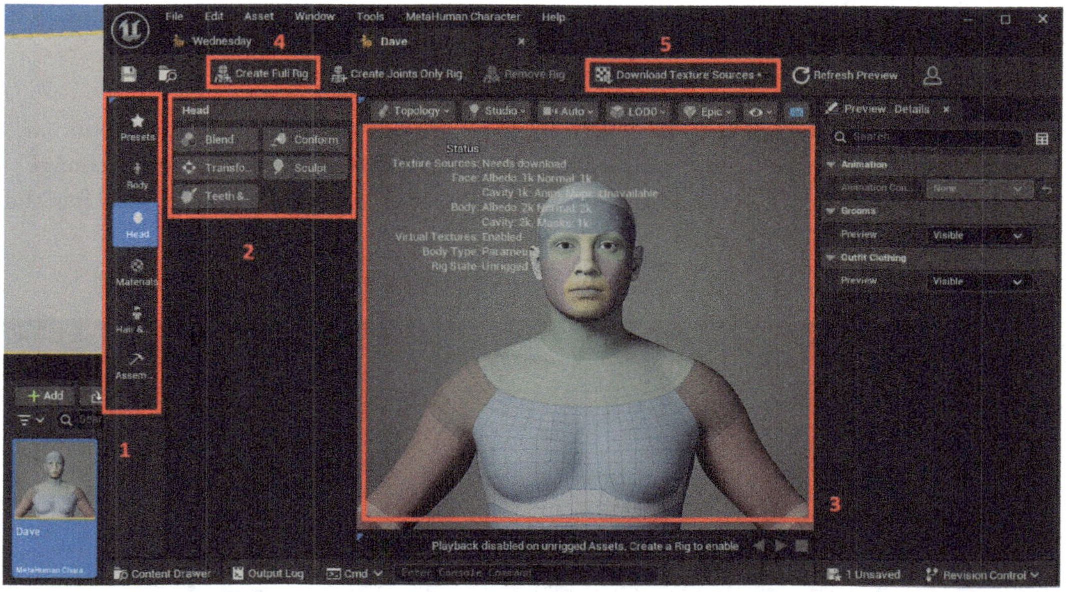

Figure 2.2: The MHC Interface

We will briefly go through the various sections here now and revisit them again in more detail later in the chapter, once you've got to grips with editing your character.

Let's take a look at these main areas one by one.

Tools menu

The left vertical strip is the **Tools** menu (*1* in *Figure 2.2*). You can see by default that the head is selected. It is made up of six components:

- **Presets**
- **Body**
- **Head**
- **Materials**
- **Hair & Clothing**
- **Assembly**

In this chapter, we will focus primarily on the Head and Materials tools. The **Body and Hair & Clothing** tools are covered in the next chapter once we have established the facial design, while Assembly is covered later when we prepare the finished MetaHuman for use inside an Unreal Engine project.

Depending on which tool you choose, the toolset (*2* in *Figure 2.2*) will change as it is a contextual menu.

To get started, let's dive into **Presets**, which is the star-shaped icon at the top of the **Tools** bar. As soon as you click on that, the character will be presented with skin, but the biggest change to the interface is the thumbnails of all the presets. *Double-click* on a thumbnail to view it in the **Viewport**.

In *Figure 2.3*, you can see I chose the **Bruce** preset. He looked like he could be a *Dave*.

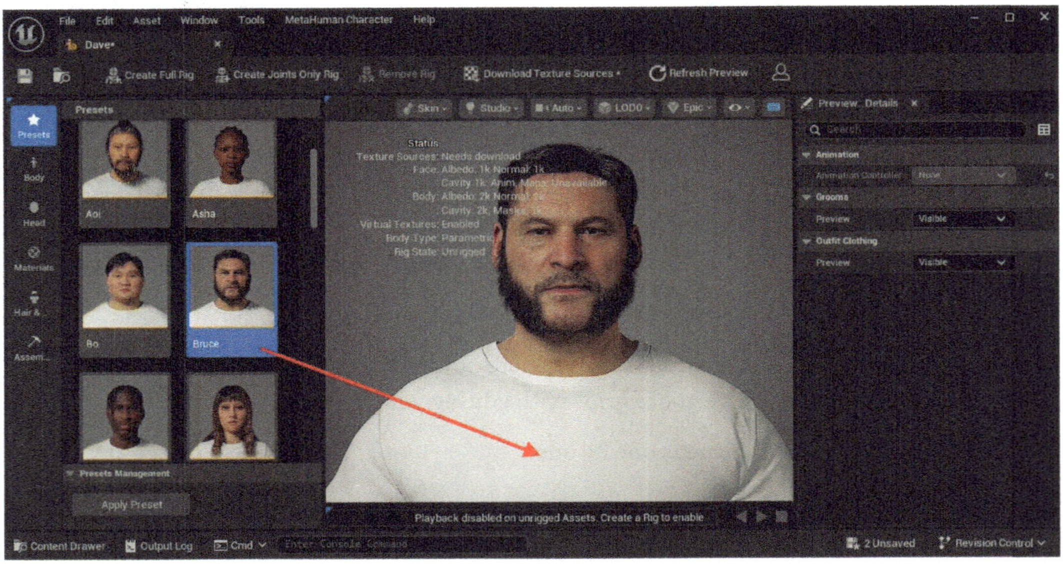

Figure 2.3: Choosing a Preset

Note

Picking the template

By this stage, you will have had two opportunities to choose a template. If you already have a clear character in mind, such as an elderly male, it makes little sense to begin with a young Caucasian female template.

While you can usually adjust features such as ethnicity, changing gender is far more restrictive because some templates have limited editing capabilities. For the best results, choose a template that already matches the intended age and gender of your character before you begin your session.

Viewport

The **Viewport** (*3* in *Figure 2.2*) is where you can view your character from any angle, change the surface between the default **Topology**, **Skin**, or **Clay** surface, or change lighting and quality.

In the **Viewport**, you can inspect the preset using the following commands for **Camera Navigation**:

- **Orbit/Rotate**: Hold *left mouse button* (*LMB*) and drag
- **Pan/Move**: Hold *middle mouse button* (MMB) and drag
- **Zoom**: Hold *right mouse button* (*RMB*) and drag (or just use the Mouse Wheel)

Tip

Select your MetaHuman and press *F* to focus your camera on them first. This sets the perfect pivot point for orbiting.

Create full rig

You will find this option on the upper toolbar as marked by *4* in *Figure 2.2*.

This feature allows us to animate the character by creating a **MetaHuman Skeleton** and binding it to the mesh of the character. It also allows us to preview animation without leaving the MetaHuman Creator application. We will come back to this option in the Test Animating Our MetaHuman section.

Download textures

Finally, to the right of **Create Full Rig**, you have **Download Texture Resources** (*5* in *Figure 2.2*); this allows you to download and apply all the texture maps for the body and head of your character, which is typically one of the last steps required.

Now that you know how to navigate the five most used areas of the MHC interface, let's look at some other useful settings.

Environment & Quality toolbar

You'll have noticed that directly above the **Viewport** is another toolbar where you have options to change the **Skin**, **Lighting**, **Camera Angle**, **Level of Detail**, and **Render Quality**.

Changing the skin

Switching between skin types is helpful to relieve your system of processing power or to remove skin characteristics that might be distracting from the overall form of the character.

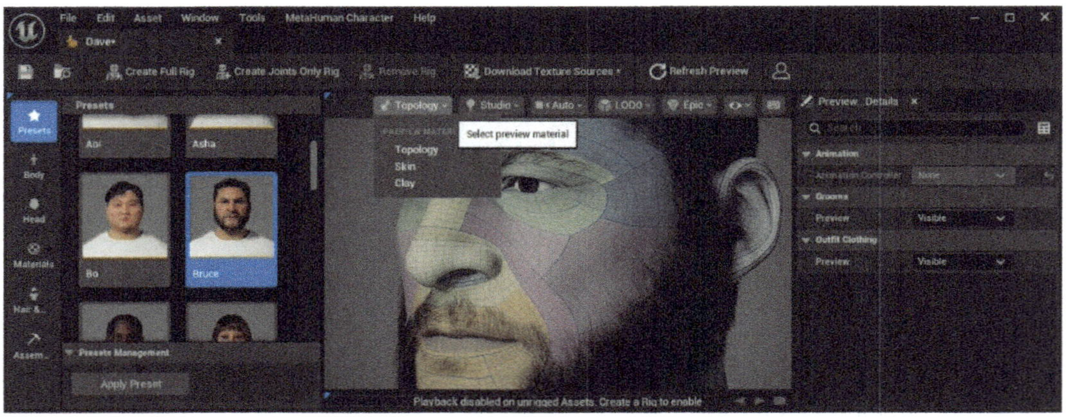

Figure 2.4: Changing the Skin Preview

Lighting

Next are the lighting settings. By default, **Studio** is selected, but you can switch between all the various lighting presets which utilize HDR imagery to light the scene. You can rotate these HDRI environments to inspect how the skin and overall shape interact with the various lighting setups. In addition, as you can see from *Figure 2.5*, you have the option to load small **Unreal Engine Level Maps** to light the scene.

The key difference is that the lighting preset environments are lit by HDRIs, and the custom environments are lit by the UE sky.

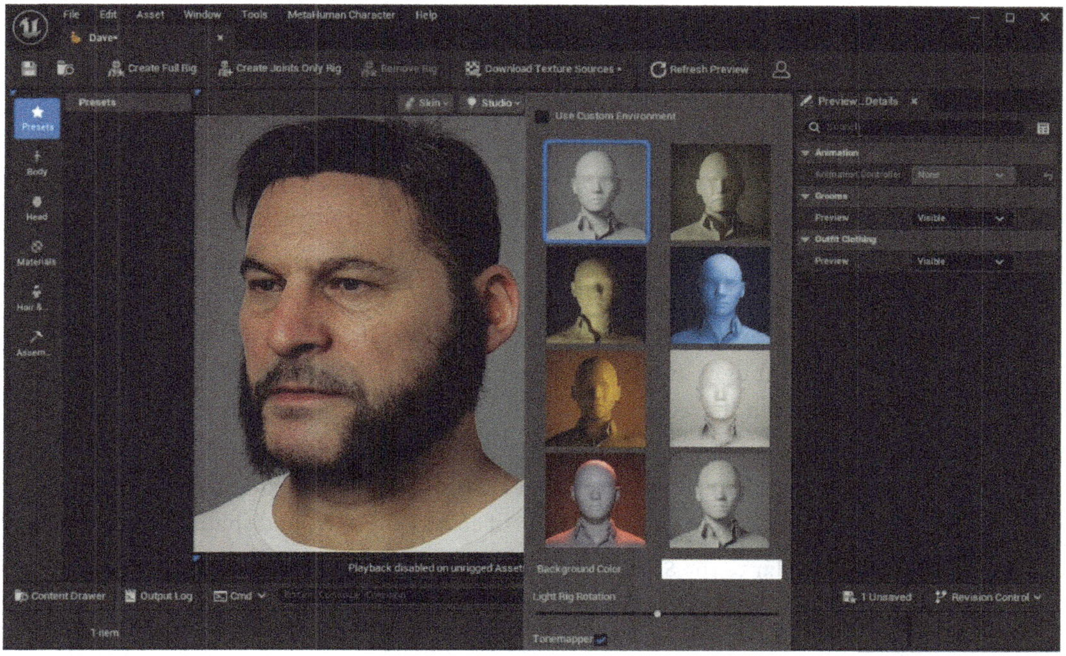

Figure 2.5: Lighting Environments

> **Note**
>
> **Image-based lighting**
>
> In most of MHC's lighting setups, **image-based lighting** is used. Put simply, an image-based light is a sphere that has an image on the inside, which is used as a light source for the entire scene. This gives us a very realistic lighting result and is also a process used within Unreal. To understand image-based lighting in the real world, take a large piece of paper, hold it close to your computer monitor, and play a video full-frame. Make sure all your lights are off and your computer screen is at full brightness. You'll see that the screen is now lighting the piece of paper, with the video influencing both intensity and color. The more reflective the paper, the more obvious the lighting influence is to the eye.

Now, if you click **Studio**, as shown in *Figure 2.5*, you'll see several lighting setups, which will help you design toward a particular scene you have in mind.

Let's go through each option:

- **Studio** (the default setting): A lighting setup made of a small number of soft lights to mimic soft photography lighting. This is the default lighting rig.
- **Indoor**: This preset consists of lighting that utilizes an image rather than a set of lights (as explained; this is known as *image-based lighting*). In this case, it is an image of an interior, captured at an angle of 360 degrees, giving us realistic lighting from every angle. This preset allows users to see their characters with the level of contrast typical of when a subject is lit from a window and reflective ambient light.
- **Outdoor**: Another example of an image-based light, allowing the user to see the effects of outdoor ambient light but also the harshness of direct sunlight and the resulting shadows cast on the character's skin.
- **Silhouette**: An important and overlooked feature when it comes to character design is to see the character in a silhouette. It gives us the ability to see the shape of the character quickly without the distraction of color, reflective, and shadow features.
- **Split**: While similar to the **Studio** light preset, **Split** gives us high contrast and is a great way of measuring the translucency of the characters' skin due to the intensity of the key light or main light. In this preset, we have a split of a high intensity key light to complete darkness. It is a great way to showcase both realism and extreme lighting and to determine both the realism and style of light falling off from intense light to darkness. The areas between the high intensity lighting and shadow, particularly on skin, is known as **roll-off**, a commonly used term by cinematographers.
- **Fireside**: Similar to **Split**, we get high contrast; however, we get the gradual fall-off and attenuation typical of fire. In addition, we get the tonality typical of fire from orange to deep blue. Most importantly, **Fireside** lets users control how light fades into shadow and the skin's level of detail, offering a subtler effect than the Split preset, which highlights surface details more distinctly.
- **Moonlight**: Similar to **Fireside**, we are presented with vibrant tones, in this case blue moonlight. However, it is a much more ambient light with less intensity from any one angle.
- **Tungsten**: While not completely representing the tonality of a common tungsten lamp, it does allow us to see how the skins tone would respond to a tungsten lamp. A lighting preset like this could determine how much detail in freckles would be lost or gained in a similar scenario.
- **Portrait**: A very handy preset as it can double as an indoor and outdoor light to determine how our characters skin behaves. For example, by rotating the scene light using the *left mouse button + L*, or using the **Light Rig Rotation** slider as seen in *Figure*

2.5, we can mimic a window with daylight lighting without the distraction found in the background image that comes with the indoor lighting preset.

- **Red Lantern**: Similar to **Fireside**, we have strong red hues to work with, but we have the advantage of seeing much more intensity without the deep blue background. This allows us to work with a more dramatic lighting setup in mind.

Camera framing

Next to the **Lighting** tab is the **camera framing** drop down menu. This menu comes with four presets, which you can overwrite. For instance, if you are happy with your custom **Body** framing and then choose the **Face** preset, the next time you choose **Body**, it will revert to your custom framing.

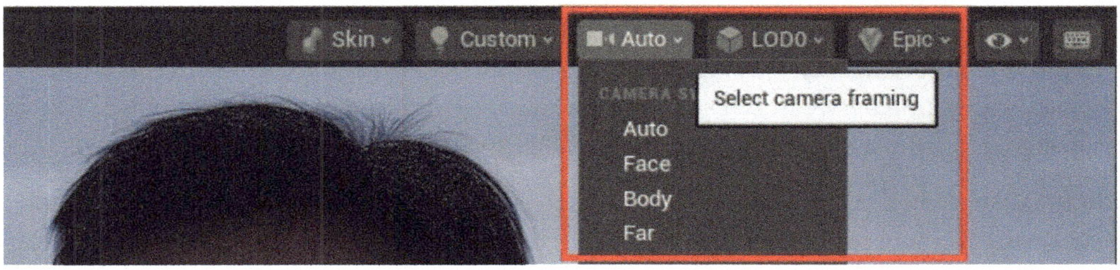

Figure 2.6: Camera framing presets

This is a handy feature when you are working with reference images as you can line up each of your four presets to correspond to your reference material.

Level of detail

Level of Detail (LOD) is the generation of multiple meshes and texture maps based on one source object. Each mesh and map will have varying amounts of detail.

The purpose of **LOD** is engine optimization. As one of the design principles of a game engine is real-time rendering, LOD helps this by reducing the number of triangles in a mesh or pixels in a texture map when not needed. LOD works on the principle of changing the complexity of a mesh based on camera distance. The further away the camera is from an object, the less detail is required without breaking the illusion of realism.

For example, a close-up shot of a MetaHuman's face would require the best quality possible. In this case, we would need to be looking at the original Mesh and texture maps. In general, the original Mesh for an MHC is about 35,000 triangles and made up of texture maps as big as 8,000 pixels in width. It would be a vast waste of resources to be rendering this kind of data if it wasn't necessary.

A good exercise to see for yourself how effective LOD is on your character is to go to the viewport and look through the Face camera. You can do this by simply pressing *1* on your keyboard. This gives us a close-up of the character. From there, we can choose from all the various LODs, from LOD 0 right down to LOD 7.

You'll notice that you are limited to just LOD 0 until you hit the **Create Full Rig** button at the top. See *Figure 2.2* at the beginning of this chapter.

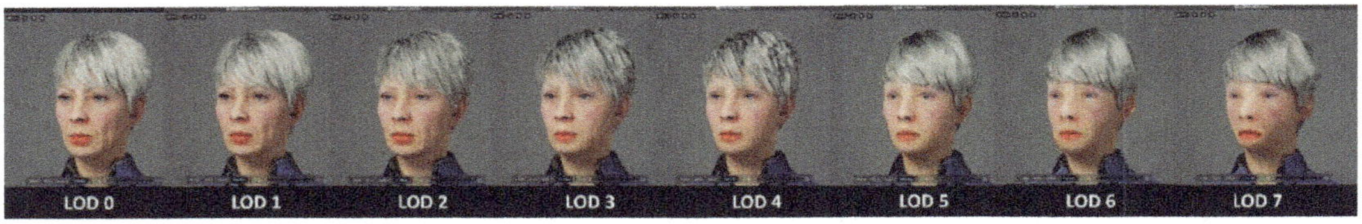

Figure 2.7: LOD 0 to 7

We can push this illustration further by using the **Far** camera; you can do this by pressing 6 on the keyboard. Unfortunately, this is as far as we can go back with the camera in the MHC. However, by toggling between LOD 6 and 7, we can see a difference. This is because LOD 6 and 7 are designed to be used when the camera is even further back.

If you toggle between LODs 3 and 4, you won't see much of a difference. Therefore, it would be a clear waste of resources to display LOD 0, which is around 350,000 triangles and 8k texture maps. Without LOD, computers would never be able to handle multiple characters, let alone crowds.

In LOD settings, you'll see that the only option we have is to choose **Always Use Hair Cards**.

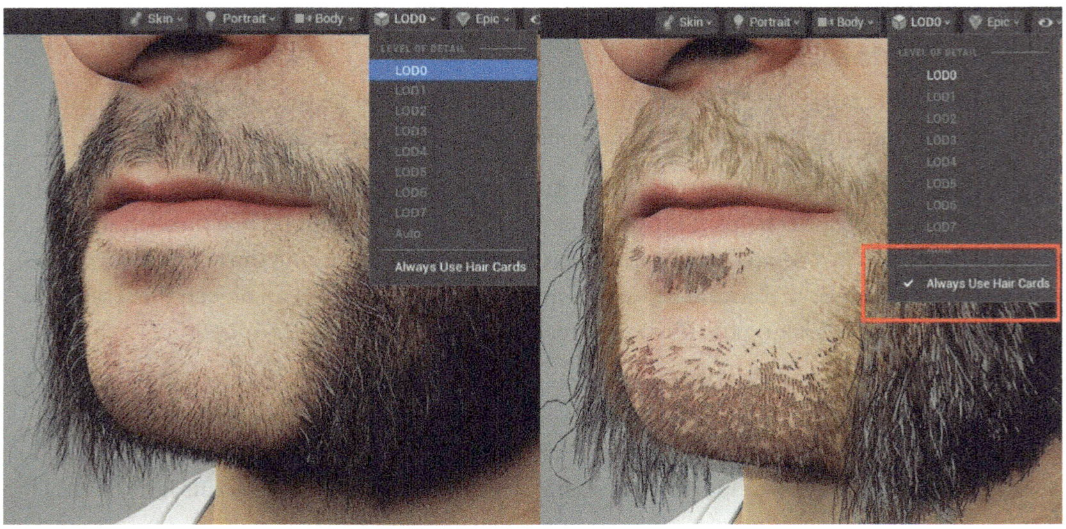

Figure 2.8: Always Use Hair Cards option in LOD settings

The rest of the LODs settings are ghosted out and that's because we need to rig the character first. Choose hair cards to improve performance.

Finally, for this section, let's look at render settings.

Render quality

MHC has three options to choose from when it comes to render quality:

- **Medium** (this is the default setting)
- **High (Ray-Traced)**
- **Epic- (Ray-traced)**

If you choose the **Highest** quality with **Raytraced** settings, this won't have any impact on your machine because the processing of the high-quality render is all done on the cloud. However, the feature is a useful indicator of the result you will get when you use the highest settings under a similar lighting setting.

The differences between the render settings are subtle. You may notice that the quality under the hair intensifies depending on the quality you use. They are there only to give you an indication of what your character would look like should you provide a similar setting, using the corresponding render quality settings that come with the Unreal Engine.

With the knowledge of all MHC menus under our belt, let's move on to the next steps: animating and editing our MetaHuman.

Test animating our MetaHuman

Although we now have applied all the presets we wanted, you'll notice that our MetaHuman isn't moving. MHC has some built-in animations for both the body and face to preview the character in motion. However, it needs a rig to be able to move. For this, we need to click on the **Create Full Rig** button (*4* in *Figure 2.2*). This will take a minute or two to load:

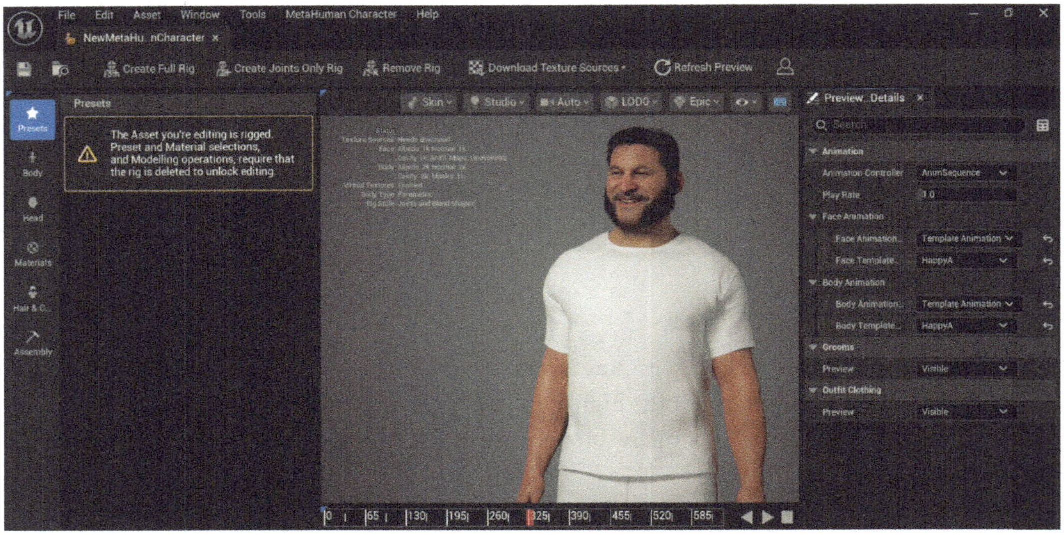

Figure 2.9: Animation Preview

At the bottom of the screen, you will see player controls. On the right, you'll see a **Preview... Details** panel.

We're just going to look at the **Face Animation** and **Body Animation** sections, both of which contain identical lists, but you can mix and match the options as you please.

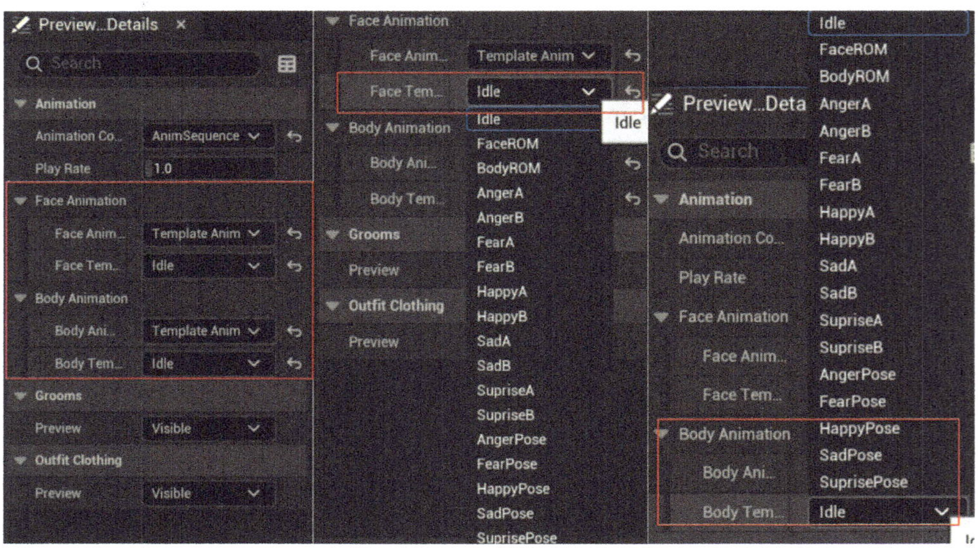

Figure 2.10: Preview...Detail panel

The animation presets I tend to use most are **Idle**, **BodyROM**, and **FaceROM**:

- **Idle**: Provides a small range of motion, which is suitable for a background character
- **FaceROM**: Provides a full range of motion for the face, where the animation is extreme enough to effectively show any potential issues that may come up should your project require close up facial animation
- **BodyROM**: Provides animation extreme enough to show any potential issues, where there is a lot of body motion

In addition to just previewing preset animations, we can also preview our own animations, but we'll do that later when we cover motion capture. As shown in *Figure 2.9*, it is possible to set the visibility of both the **Grooms** and **Outfit Clothing** on the character.

Just to reiterate, to preview animation, we need to create a full rig and to edit the character we need to remove the rig. It is perfectly normal to recreate the rig for animation as often as you like.

Because we're about to start editing our character, click on **Remove Rig**.

As soon as you do that, you'll see most of the options disappear from the **Preview...Details** panel except for the **Grooms** and **Outfit Clothing**, which are essential for character design.

> **Note**
>
> MHC gives a **range of motion (ROM)** designed to give you an idea of how your character will look animated. It is not a definitive debugging tool for all possibilities of what could go right or wrong when you add in your own animation.

If you are familiar with 3D character design in the traditional sense, character design must take the full range of motion into account to work effectively. The model or mesh must allow for the desired type of movement. On a very basic level, the animation must not alter the mesh of the character where parts of the character intersect with other parts. For example, a very thin person can walk in a way where their hands can be closer to their sides; effectively, their wrist bones can come very close to their hip bones during a stride. However, this wouldn't be the same for somebody larger, even with the same type of stride and range of motion.

With all that said, the fidelity of MHC characters does a lot of this calibration. So, what would have been very laborious for someone working in Maya, 3ds Max, or Houdini to account for varying ranges of motion, this is done automatically in an MHC session.

We will come back to some of this later in *Chapter 4*, when we introduce animation to the MetaHuman character within Unreal, but in short, you can push the attributes of characters as much as you want without finding any unusable oddities within any given range of motion during the MHC session.

In the section, we have launched our MetaHuman session and are getting familiar with the interface that we will be spending most of our time designing the character in.

In the next section, we will start editing our MetaHuman, beginning with the face. This section will be split into a number of subsections to coincide with the layout of the MHC Interface.

Editing our MetaHuman

Now it's time to edit our MetaHuman. If you're used to working with MetaHumans with Unreal Engine 5.5 or earlier, you'll notice some significant differences. Some functions have been rearranged and recategorized.

Most notably, editing has been rearranged so that any recoloring of the **Head** and **Body** is now done in the **Material Editor**; this includes skin, teeth, makeup, and eyes. To start editing, ensure you have clicked on **Remove Rig**. Once the rig is removed, we can click on **Head** and then **Blend**, as shown in *Figure 2.10:*

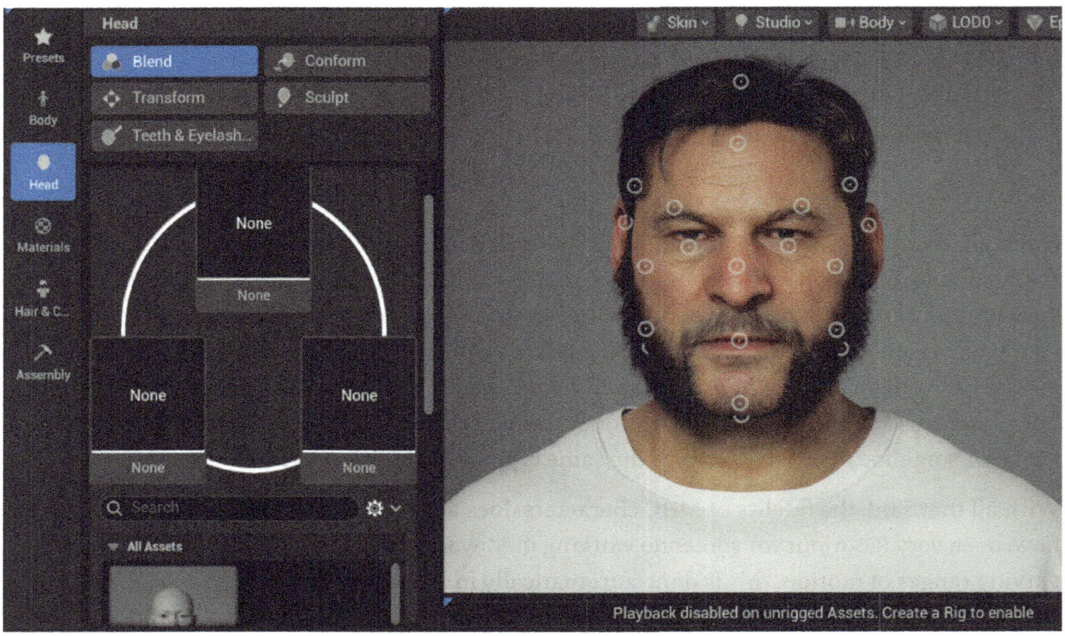

Figure 2.11: Head Blend mode

Blend

We will first look at the Blend function. Put simply, Blend allows us to blend the facial features of your chosen template with other existing templates by dragging and dropping characters from the All Assets box into the **Blend Preset Selection** box, as shown in *Figure 2.12*. This is a great starting point as it is a very intuitive process. For example, we may have selected a male character from our template, but we would like to make him look a little more feminine or perhaps look older. Taking that second example, we can target the nose and blend just the nose with that of an older character template. When using Blend, a white circular manipulator will appear in the viewport on your character's face so you can click and drag it toward the direction of whichever blended character you want to pull features from.

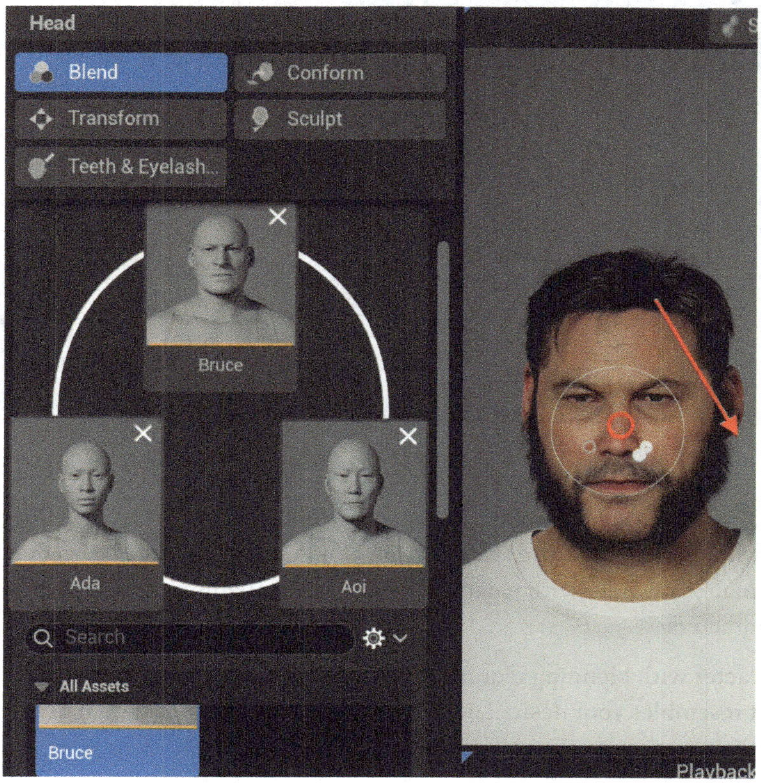

Figure 2.12: Blending Presets

In *Figure 2.12*, I have dragged two other characters and put the original Bruce on top so that I can always use him as a baseline. I've put Ada on the bottom left to make him slightly more feminine and African and put Aoi on the bottom right to make him more Asian and masculine. By clicking on the white manipulator, I dragged it in the direction of the arrow, which refers to Aoi's direction from Bruce. So now Bruce has Aoi's nose.

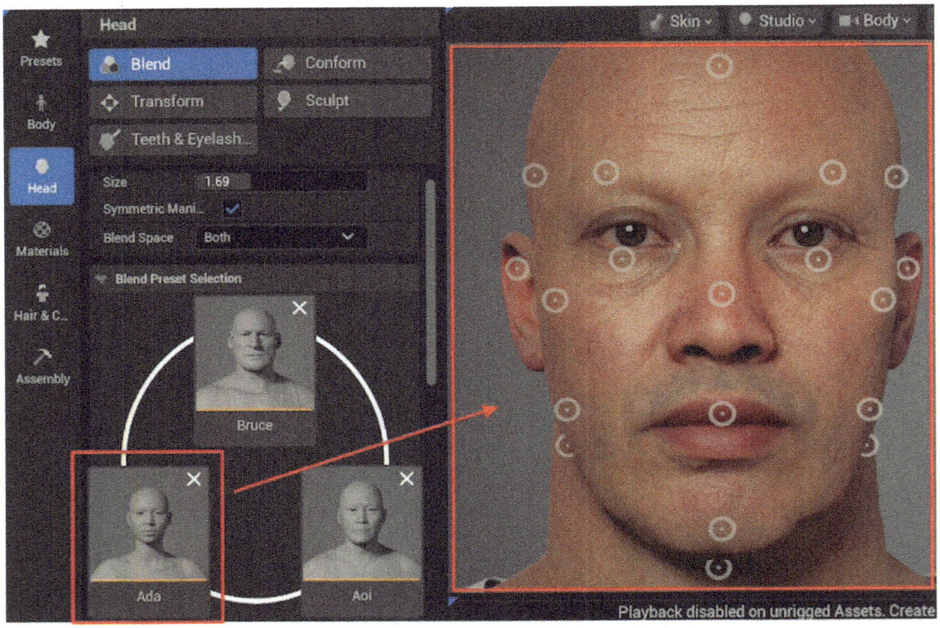

Figure 2.13: Manipulators

In *Figure 2.13*, I've increased the manipulator size to 1.69 so that you can see them better. I also dragged every manipulator toward the direction of Ada so now Bruce has become a dead ringer for Ada, only male, and older with paler skin. With a little planning, you can create whole families of characters.

Editing a character with blending requires a little planning. It's best practice to choose a character that resembles your desired design as much as possible and then use the **Blend** option to get the template as close to your imagined design.

Conform

If you are designing a character based on the likeness of reference material such as a **Mesh Capture** or **Manual Sculpture**, **Conform** will wrap the MetaHuman mesh around the incoming mesh. The steps involved in this process are far too complex for this chapter but will be covered in *Chapter 11* near the end of this book. It is an exciting new feature that allows users to have their exact likeness replicated as a 3D character.

Transform

I'm not going to lie, but I think I may have gotten carried away with *Figure 2.12*. However, I think it makes a strong point that the **Transform** tool allows you to take the manipulators further than the **Blend** tool can.

You can see that I used a second tool. The first is the standard **Transform** tool, while the second is **Transform** in **Screen Space**, which allows you to keep on pushing the manipulators. The third is **Rotation** and the last is **Scale**.

To get stronger values of transformation, you need to work in increments. In *Figure 2.14*, I edged the ear outwards repeatedly as moving it in one go only got me so far.

The rotation and scale values have far less movement than the transformation tool. While this might not be great for non-realistic characters, they are incredibly powerful for realistic characters.

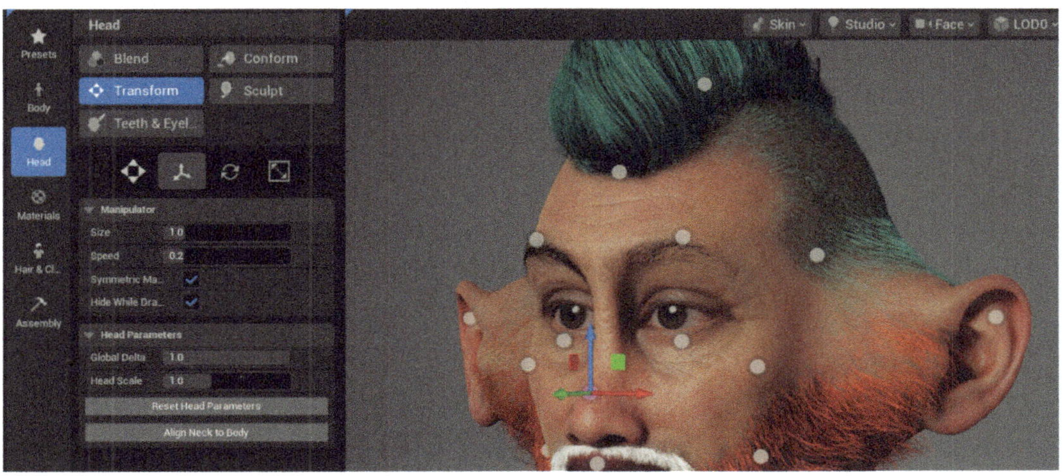

Figure 2.14: Transform tool

If, like me, you lack self-control and have gone too far, there is the convenient **Reset Head Parameters** button as shown in *Figure 2.15*. Also, **Head Scale** editing is located right above it and is also available in the **Sculpt** tool which we will look at next.

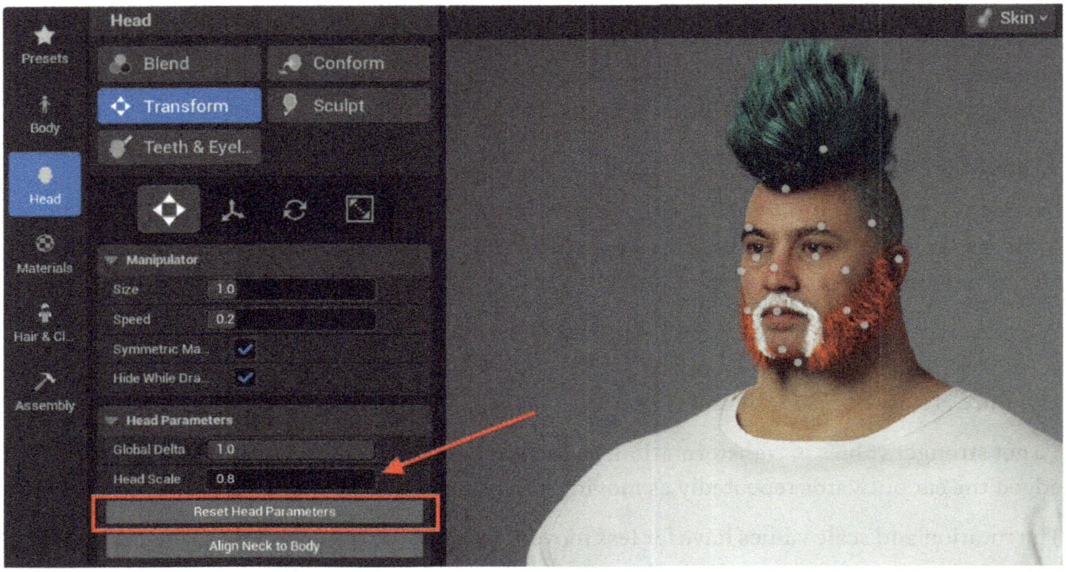

Figure 2.15: Reset Head Parameters and Head Scale

If you have gone too far with the head editing, you can always hit *Ctrl* + *Z* on your keyboard to undo. If you want to just reset a certain portion, this is where the Blend tool comes back in again, as you can always blend select manipulators back to the original without affecting everything you've been editing with the **Transform** tool.

Sculpt

Sculpt works slightly differently from the **Transform** tool. Firstly, you can't move manipulators to the same extent, but they also move slightly differently.

For example, if you were to look at the ear, there is only one **Transform** manipulator as seen in *Figure 2.14*. However, in *Figure 2.16*, you'll see more sculpt manipulators around the ear.

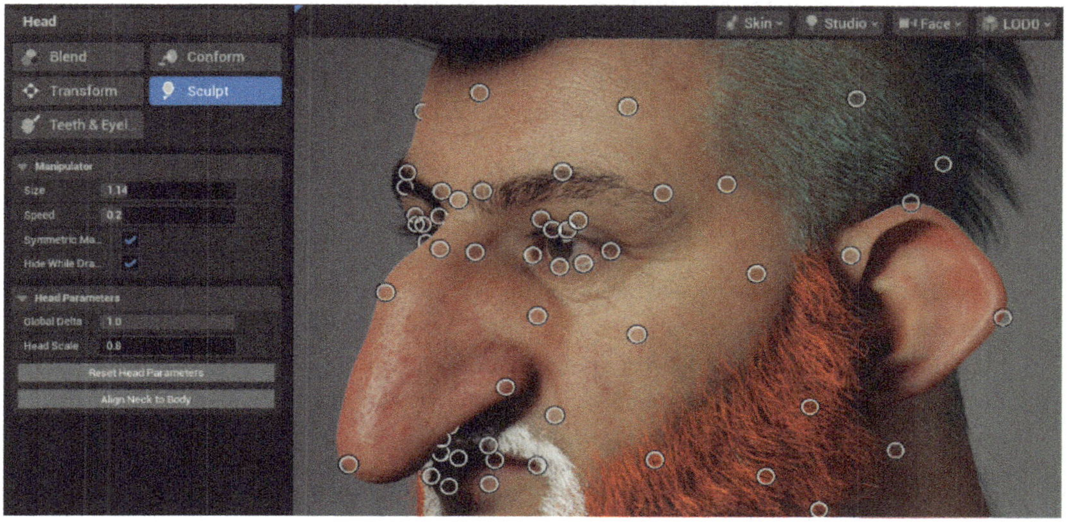

Figure 2.16: Sculpt tool and Manipulators

In fact, it's arguable that there are four manipulators in the ear area using **Sculpt**: the lower one is a grounding or pinning manipulator, and the upper manipulators can be used to define the shape of the ear, whereas the **Transform** tool can only define its position.

This is important to note because these tools are designed to operate separately yet harmoniously. In other words, you need both for full creative control.

As soon as you think you have pushed or pulled a manipulator as far as it can go, switch back to **Transform**, make a slight adjustment and come back to Sculpt. You'll see you've gained a little more wiggle room.

Manipulator

We have only brushed on the **Manipulator** section, which can be seen on the left in *Figure 2.15*. We know we can change the size to make them more visible. But we can also change their sensitivity by changing the **Speed** value. We also have the very important option of unchecking **Symmetric Manipulation**, which I advise using for very subtle changes upon the final stages of design for realistic character design.

> Note
>
> **Asymmetry and Realism**
>
> **Asymmetry** is heavily overlooked in the creation of realism when it comes to digital character design. Because humans don't have identical sides of the face, it is very important to introduce some level of asymmetry, no matter how subtle. CGI characters, historically, have suffered from what is known as the **uncanny valley,** and much of this uncanniness is due to the presence of perfect symmetry which doesn't exist in nature.

Teeth & Eyelashes

In the context of the **Head**, we have the **Teeth & Eyelashes** tool to edit the shape and organization of the teeth with a lot of control compared to other character authoring tools. We'll see a further **Teeth & Eyelashes** in the **Material** tool, but this section is dedicated only to the placement and configuration of the teeth meshes.

Click on **Teeth & Eyelashes**, ensuring you're in **Head** mode and notice the jaw opens automatically just like a well-trained dental patient.

Depending on your personal preference, the MHC offers you a visual and value-based means to edit the teeth, the former being visual sliders for you to grab, and the latter being a drop-down list with contextual value sliders. See *Figure 2.17*:

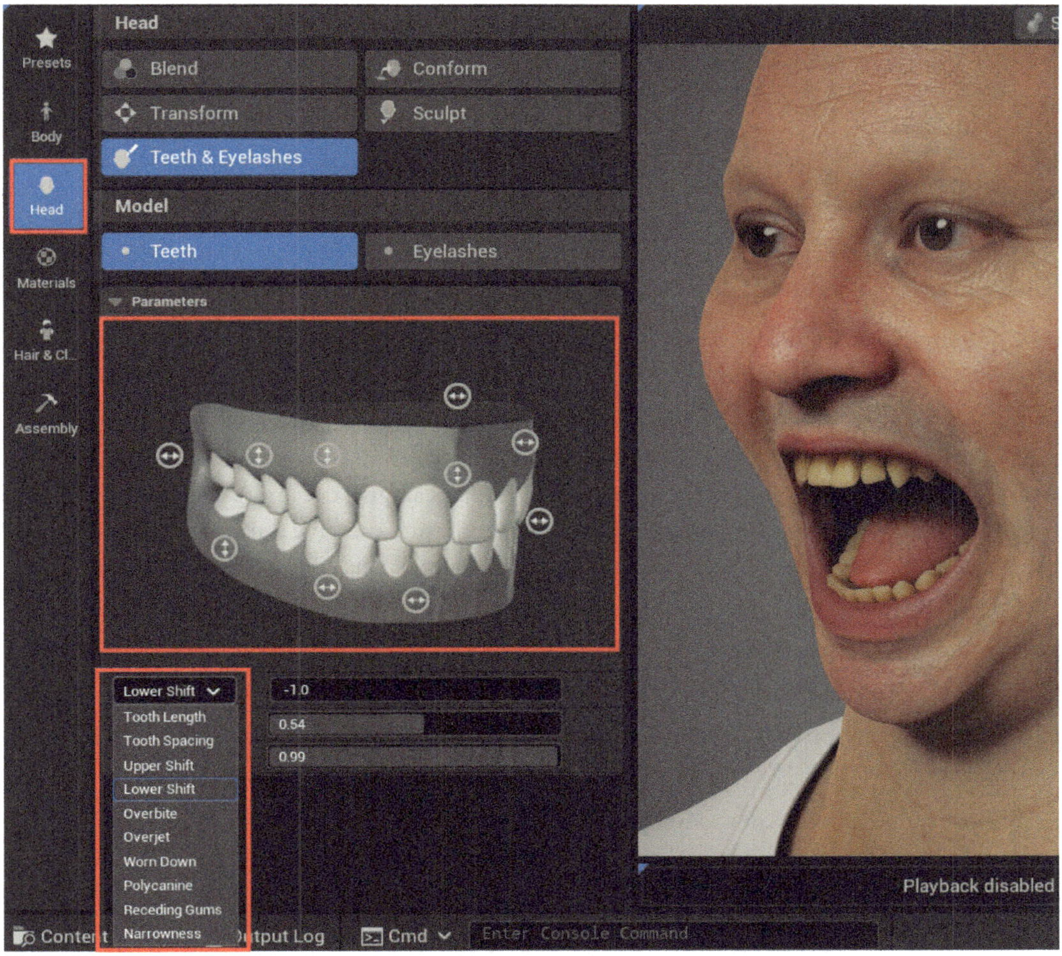

Figure 2.17: Teeth

In *Figure 2.17*, I've already made some edits to the teeth. In the drop-down list, you'll see the first on the list is **Lower Shift**. The slider to the right of that is the intensity.

The next slider is **Variation**, and the last slider is **Jaw Open**, which doesn't edit the teeth in any way but just allows us to see more or less of the teeth.

> **Note**
>
> For a perfect set of teeth, the value for each slider would be set to the default of 0.

While the visual slider is good, it only allows us to edit the intensity of any feature such as **Lower Shift** or **Tooth Length**. It doesn't give us any control over the variation.

My personal preference is just to stick to the lower sliders where I can go through the list editing both intensity and variation in one place.

Additionally, if you want to reset for a perfect smile, you can just go through the list methodically and zero both intensity and variation.

If you are making dramatic changes, it is worth previewing the **Facial ROM** as the teeth do have a significant impact on the overall expression of your character. A major consideration would be how much gum or overbite exists. An overbite can give the impression of an undeveloped jaw and a naive expression, while an underbite can give the impression of an overdeveloped jaw and a stern expression. Of course, a lot of this is subjective but certainly worth consideration.

To wrap up this section on teeth, I would like to emphasize how important teeth editing is to overall character design, and that it is frequently overlooked.

In the previous version of MHC, the material shading for editing color and plaque buildup was featured in this section. We will cover that when we get to the material section shortly.

Let's move onto the Eyelashes to wrap up the head editing tool. As soon as you engage the **Eyelashes** tool, ensure you have selected Visible in the Grooms Preview drop-down menu over in the **Preview Details Panel**.

If you can't see the **Preview Details Panel**, navigate to **Windows** at the top and tick **Preview Details Panel** to see it.

There isn't a lot to do when it comes to editing the eyelashes in the **Head** tool other than choosing from a small group of presets:

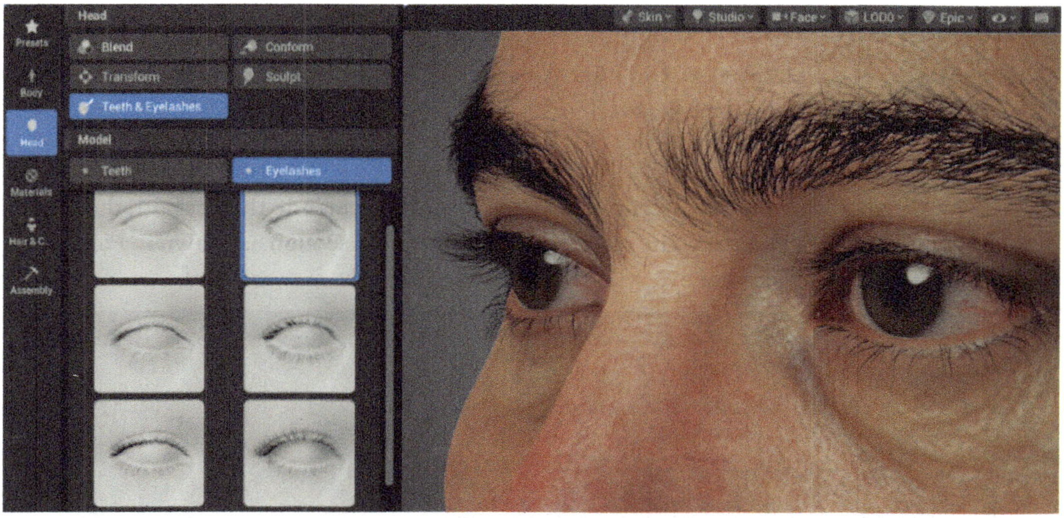

Figure 2.18: Eyelashes

In this section, we've covered all the physical attributes for editing the head. Next, we will look at materials where we have control of the skin, eyes, makeup, and teeth.

Applying materials

Materials describe how a surface looks and reacts to light once it is rendered on screen. While the mesh defines the shape of a MetaHuman, materials determine its visual qualities, such as color, texture, shininess, translucency, and surface detail. In MetaHuman Creator, materials are built from a combination of texture maps and shader settings that work together to produce realistic skin, eyes, teeth, and makeup in real time. Understanding how these materials function is essential, as small adjustments can have a significant impact on realism, performance, and how a character holds up under different lighting conditions. In this section, we will focus on applying and adjusting materials to refine the final appearance of the MetaHuman.

Materials and skin

Click on **Materials and Skin**. Here you'll see we have control over the **Skin**, **Freckles**, **Accents**, **Texture Sources**, and **Texture Override**.

Skin

Within the **Skin** parameters, we can edit the skin tone, and we can't do this for both the face and body separately. To edit the **Skin Tone**, click into the **Color** section as shown in *Figure 2.18* and choose your desired skin tone. It will instantly affect both the face and body.

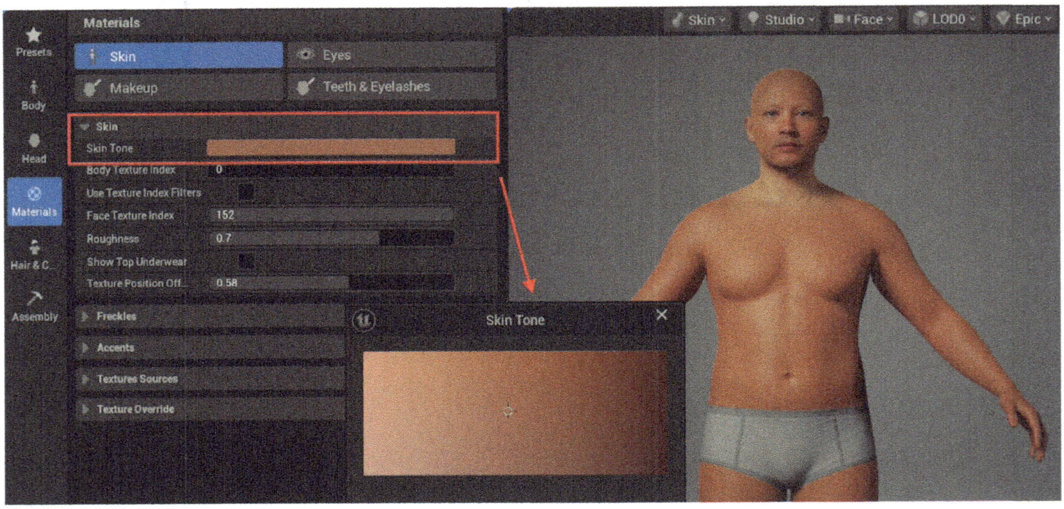

Figure 2.19: Skin Tone Editing

Below **Skin Tone**, you will see the **Body Texture Index**, which provides up to *8* different skin types, rather than the progression of skin types from young to old. While it does feel a little random, there are enough options to choose from, so it is worth being patient and taking the time to familiarize yourself with various skin types. Under the hood, so to speak, are texture maps, particularly **Normal** and **Displacement** maps as well as **Diffuse** maps offering an array of wrinkles, sagging skin, and blemishes.

The same goes for the **Face Texture Index**, but this has substantially more to choose from given that in most cases only the face will be seen. Unlike the **Skin Tone**, we can edit body and face textures independently.

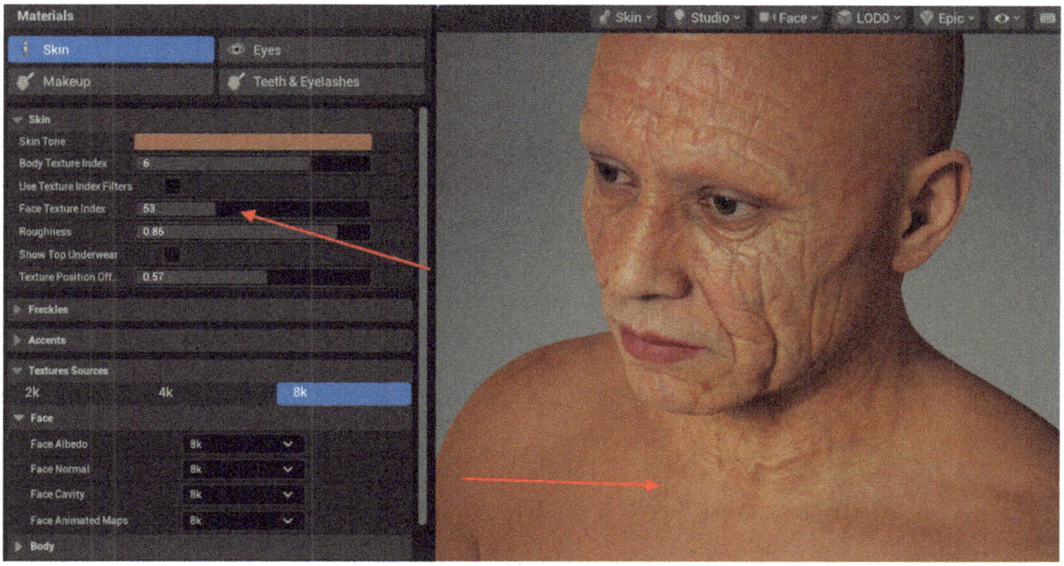

Figure 2.20: Skin texturing

In *Figure 2.20*, I have chosen a body texture Index of 8 and a face texture index of 53. You can see a very subtle blend between the different textures between face and body.

Between the **Body Texture Index** and the **Face Texture Index** is **Use Texture Index Filters**, which is meant to override or change the intensity of the result, but at the time of writing it isn't functional. Epic continues to update MetaHuman Creator regularly, so it is worth checking the latest release notes to see whether this functionality has been enabled in newer versions.

Below the **Face Texture Index** is the **Roughness Intensity**, which adjusts the shininess of the skin. The more roughness, the less shiny the skin. With roughness set to 0, the skin will reflect the surrounding environment and not just react to light sources in the same way a specular surface would.

> Note
>
> **Roughness**
>
> In CGI, the word "roughness" is a common term used to describe how shiny or reflective a surface is. We know that if a surface is rough, light isn't bounced back in as much of a direct way as that of a smooth surface such as a mirror. On skin, a smooth surface could be due to the oiliness of the surface, and this gives us a more realistic effect. Rarely do we get a completely rough surface on skin without the help of foundation makeup. Another factor that introduces roughness in skin is the micro hair follicles on the surface of the skin which are barely visible to the human eye but are factored into the final model.

In the **Skin** settings, we also have an option to show or hide the **Top Underwear**, and there is a **Texture Position Offset** control, which at the time of writing isn't functional.

It is worth noting that choosing the value of the **Face Filter index** creates massive differences before we even get to the other parameters such as **Freckles** and **Accents**.

Freckles

While offering just four presets, from freckle-free to intense freckles, we also get **Density**, **Strength**, **Saturation**, and **Tone shift** to play around with to offer subtle variations.

The freckle-free preset gives us no freckles at all if we don't want any. Using the first preset, **Density** gives us a small amount of freckles even if we set the value to 0. **Strength** controls the visibility of the existing freckles and **Saturation** controls the amount of color. A value of 0 will give us unrealistic gray freckles, whereas a value of 100 will give us realistic yet very vibrant freckles. **Tone shift** provides a variety of different saturation and intensity levels without bringing any freckle to a complete gray.

The presets differ more in the freckle scale and intensity with the intense freckles preset being quite large indeed.

It can be difficult to judge the freckle patterns on darker skin tones, so it is worth popping back to the **Skin Tone** editor to temporarily shift the skin tone to a paler version of your intended skin tone when needed.

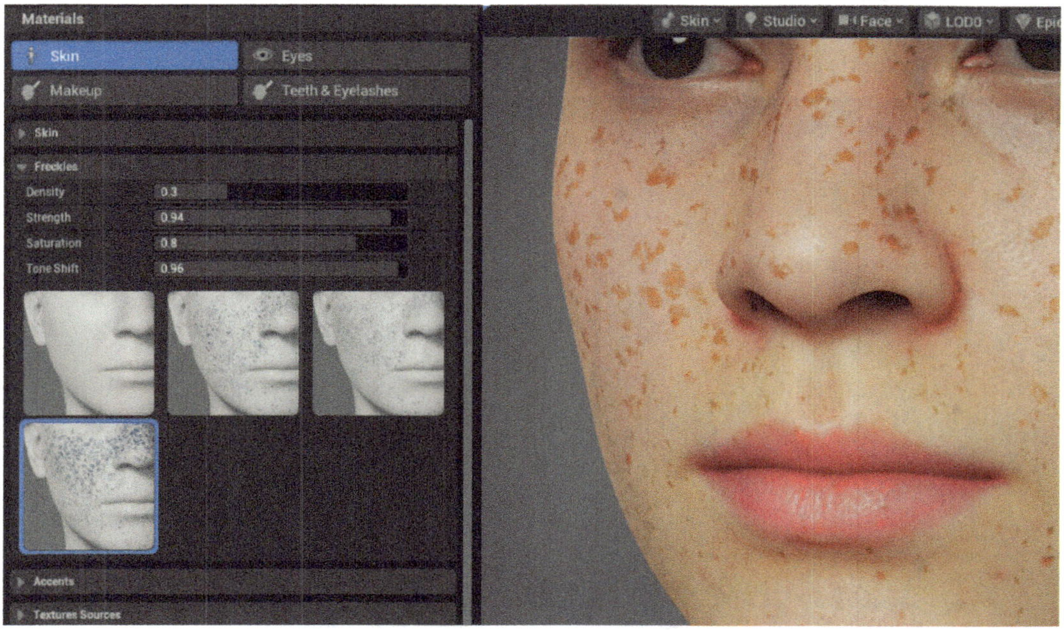

Figure 2.21: Freckles

Accents

Put simply, accents allow us to put tonal changes around the face around the top of the head, forehead, under the eyes, cheeks, lips, and chin.

While in most cases, this complements the underlying skin tone, extreme accents don't work well under all skin tones. For the most part, the use of accents is a great way to add realism when used subtly as they break up the unnatural flat tone.

Another use of accents is to produce a youthful look, particularly around the cheeks or to create a sunburn effect.

For control, we are given sliders for **Redness**, **Saturation**, and **Lightness**. By default, all values are set in the middle at 0.5.

For example, for a tired look we can isolate under eyes by selecting the shape under the eyes from the graph and reduce both the Saturation and Lightness and play around with the redness. It is a subtle effect but can become more obvious on certain skin tones.

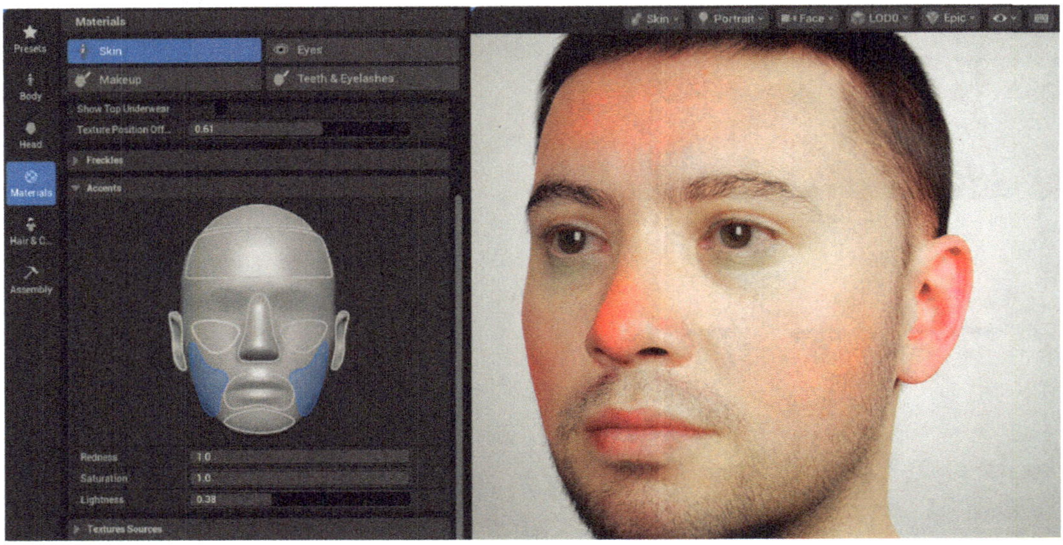

Figure 2.22: Accents

Texture Sources

By default, the textures are low resolution 2K textures. They're fine for games, but a 2K texture on a face wouldn't hold up on a close-up for cinematic projects. However, the smaller resolution requires less computer power, which is fine for editing. As soon as you are ready, you can choose your desired texture size by using the **Texture** tool within materials below the **Accent** tool as seen in *Figure 2.23:*

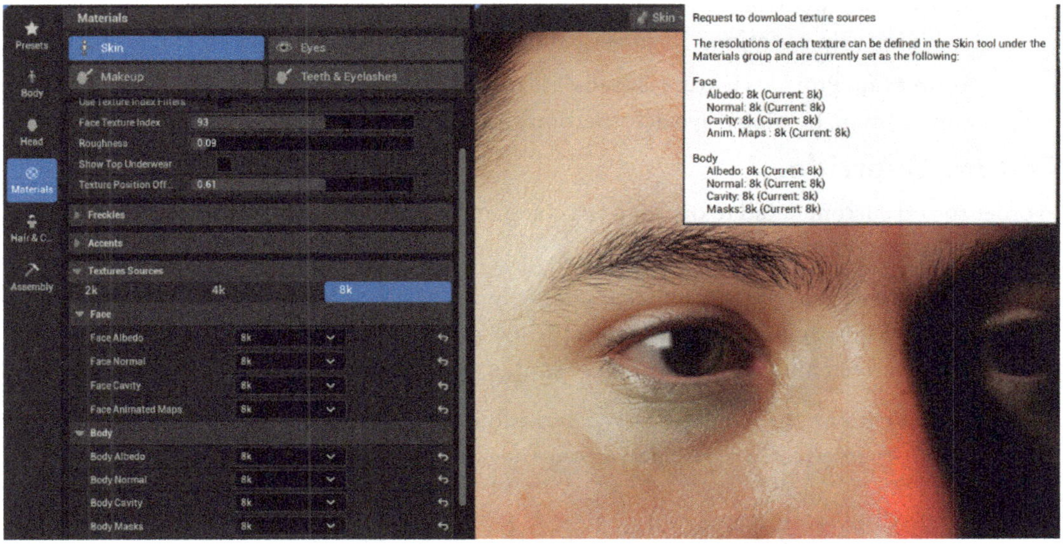

Figure 2.23: Texture sources

In *Figure 2.23*, I chose 8K textures and clicked on the **Download Texture Sources** button on the top. It took nearly 5 minutes for those 8K body and face textures to download and map onto the model.

When first loaded, your character may look very much void of detail initially but as soon as you start orbiting or panning around your viewport, the 8K texture will appear with incredible detail.

At any point, you can hover your mouse over the **Download Texture** button, and it will show you what the current assigned texture size is. In my case, I've confirmed that I have selected and successfully downloaded and loaded the 8K textures marked as (current 8K).

Before moving onto the next section, note that both face and body contain **Albedo**, **Normal**, **Cavity**, **Masks**, and **Anim Maps**.

- **Albedo Map**: Defines the base skin or surface color of the MetaHuman, free from lighting, shading, or shadow information
- **Normal Map**: Stores high-resolution surface detail from the MetaHuman scan, allowing skin pores, wrinkles, and folds to react correctly to light
- **Cavity Map**: Accentuates fine facial creases and micro-details in the MetaHuman, reinforcing depth in areas such as wrinkles and skin folds

- **Masks Map**: Controls how different material layers behave across the MetaHuman, including skin variation, roughness, and subsurface response
- **Anim Map**: Provides texture-based data that supports facial animation in the MetaHuman, helping drive deformation and expression detail

Texture Override

In order to add custom detail to our maps or completely override them, we can use the **Texture Override** feature.

For instance, say we have crafted our character to look like a little cartoon which would in turn make the photorealistic skin texture unsuitable. We'd need something far more solid looking so we could swap out all our maps with very simple textures.

To do this, just click on the + marked in red in the following figure:

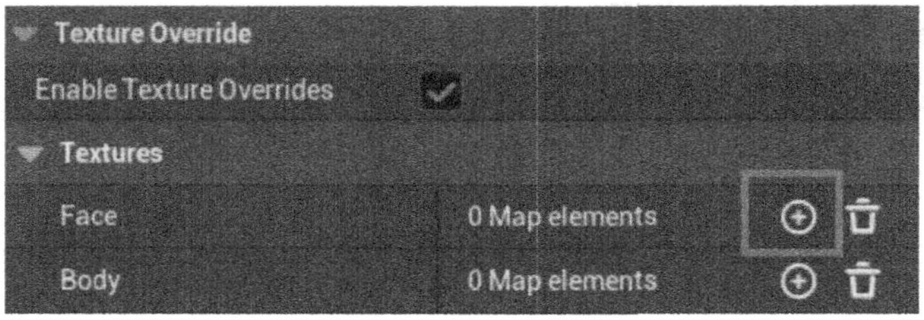

Figure 2.24: Texture Override

This will open up a new slot for you to pick a texture map of your choosing.

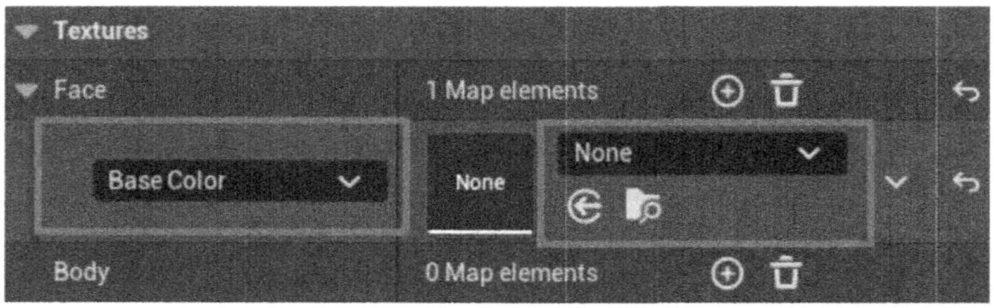

Figure 2.25: Texture Override map

Note that you have a drop-down list for which type of texture you want to override.

For a cartoon-like character, you could create simple texture maps using a constant color for the base color and a plain color for a normal map. Some familiarity with how normal maps work would help.

For custom texturing, the steps are a little more involved and also require the final step of assembling the character, which in turn creates a `MetaHumans` folder that gives us access to the texture maps so we can edit them.

For example, if we want to paint a tattoo onto the base color (Albedo) map for the face, we need to assemble the character first and then find the base color texture map. But don't worry, we'll come to that in *Chapter 4*. Next up is the **Eyes**.

Eyes

Unsurprisingly, there are a lot of controls for the eyes. However, for most cases, the presets will do just fine.

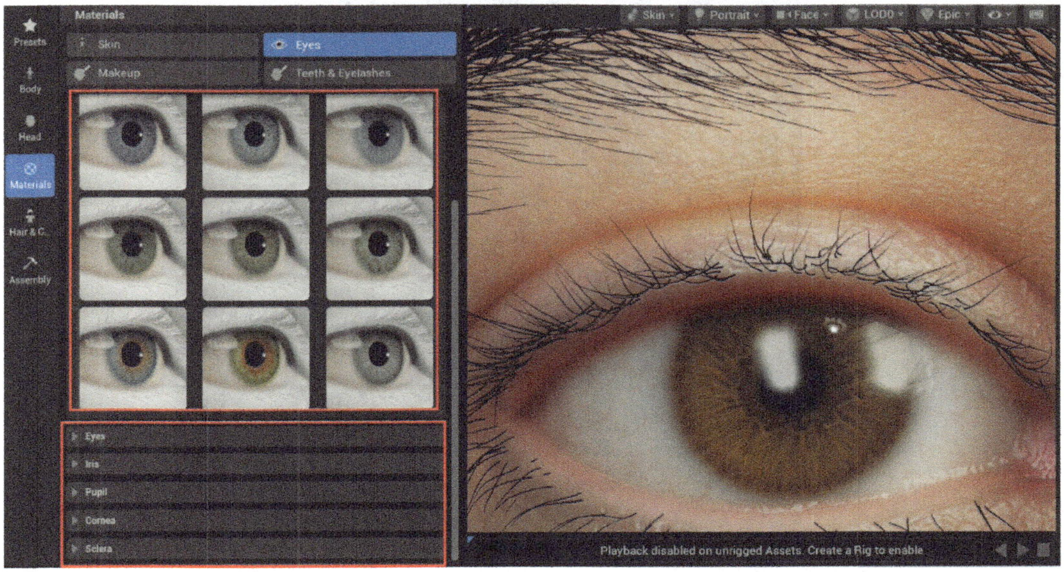

Figure 2.26: Eyes

Under the preset window are five drop-down menus for **Eyes**, **Irish**, **Pupil**, **Cornea**, and **Sclera**.

- **Eyes**: The **Eyes** simply allow us to choose to edit **Both Eyes**, Just the **Left Eye**, or just the **Right Eye**.
- **Iris**: The **Iris** drop down gives us the texture maps options. It also gives us a lot of additional control to color the eye with primary and secondary colors, adding **Shadow details**, which gives us very realistic depth. We can also take it from realistic coloring to more stylized coloring by pushing the saturation and adding a global Tint.

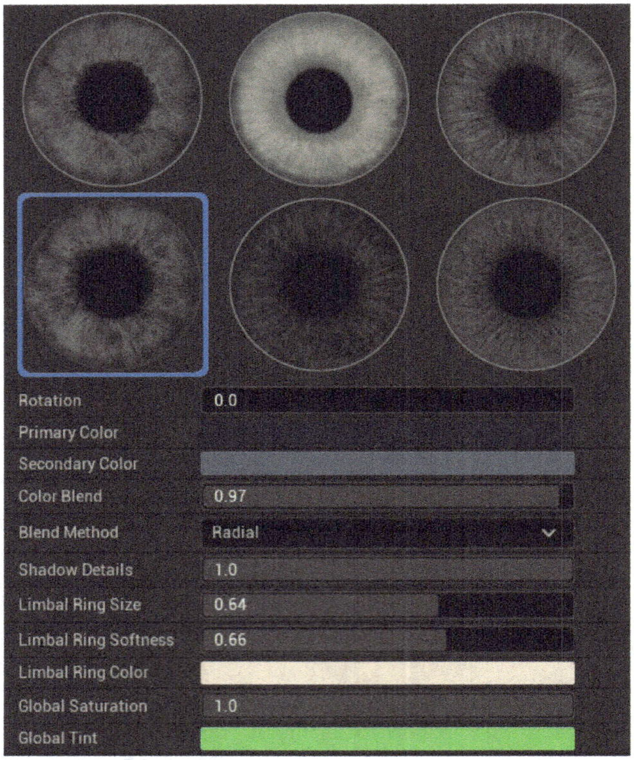

Figure 2.27: Iris

- Pupil: With just the Dilation and Feather sliders available, we can see how the pupil stretches the iris open and closed and the feathering in this case is realistic with all available values

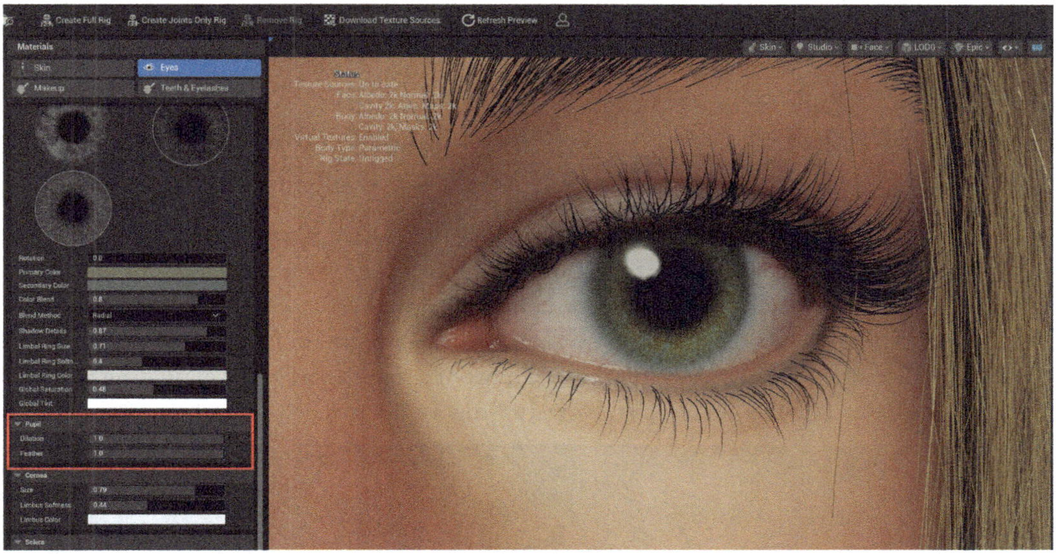

Figure 2.28: Dilation and Feather

The Dilation value won't be permanent after you've Assembled your character. This can be animated for production.

- **Cornea:** Outside of the pupil is the **Cornea** and its size can be edited independently of the pupil's size, as can it's softness using the **Limbus Softness** slider, although too much softness is unrealistic. The **Limbus Color** values effect the outer rim of the **Cornea**.
- **Sclera**: The **Sclera**, or the white part of the eye, is often oversimplified as pure white in CGI, but it's off-white with visible veins.
  The **Dilation** slider allows us to rotate the texture map that gives us vascularity.

Using **Custom Tint** allows us to take total control over the eye, giving it a natural off-white or an extreme color to suggest damage or a vibrant contact lens, perhaps something demonic as it can go full black too.

The **Transmission** spread is a very subtle adjustment to how light gets into the **Sclera**. With a high transmission, it appears that there is a layer of **Sclera** on top of another **Sclera**, giving the overall **Sclera** depth.

Adding a red transmission color for an injury suggested sub-dermal damage, a little more serious than what can be achieved with **Vascularity Intensity** and **Vascularity Coverage** alone.

Vascular Intensity adjusts how visible the outer eye veins are, while coverage sets how far they extend toward the pupil. Higher values result in a veinier appearance.

Makeup

The **Makeup** tool is broken down into four categories: **Foundation**, **Eyes**, **Blush**, and **Lipstick**.

Foundation

Just applied to the face but gradually fading down to the body, the **Foundation** is a powerful tool that gets a realistic makeup effect. Starting with the **Color**, we can play with the intensity. This hides all the pore detail with the chosen color. The **Roughness** slider augments the result found in either a powder or oil-based foundation. We also get the bonus of a concealer, which will directly conceal blemishes and give us even more of a tonally flat result emulating a thick foundation application. Be sure to tick the **Apply Foundation** tick box to apply the foundation.

Figure 2.29: Foundation and Eye Makeup

Eyes

While presenting various presets, we can also edit both primary and secondary colors. Similarly to the foundation, we also get control over **Roughness**, which will augment a glossy or dewy eye pencil look if set to low, or a matte eye pencil finish if set to high. **Opacity** acts in a similar fashion to Intensity in foundation. **Metalness** has a very subtle effect compared to **Roughness** and doesn't really have any impact on how **Roughness** affects the overall shininess of the eye makeup.

Blush

Similar to **Accent**, we get to choose from five presets, the first one being zero blush. The blush effect is limited to just the cheek area and the presets just give us various shapes to work with. We can choose whatever color we want and the intensity. Just like foundation and eye makeup, we can adjust the **Roughness**. For lower roughness values, we get a shinier result that introduces pore detail, therefore bypassing the foundation result in the blush area.

Lips

With even fewer presets, we only get a subtle variation between them, with just the edge line detail changing from a harsh edge line to a soft one. Like the other options, we can edit the **Intensity/Opacity** and **Roughness**, with **Metalness** only giving us a very subtle effect.

Figure 2.30: Blush and Lips

Eyelashes

Like the other **Material** tools, we have sliders to control the overall color, but in this case it is treated as mascara. We can still control the amount of **Melanin** from the original hair color, which is controlled in the hair section, which we will get to in the next chapter. For the most part, you'll get far greater control over the **Eyelash** look in the **Hair** section rather than in the **Materials** section.

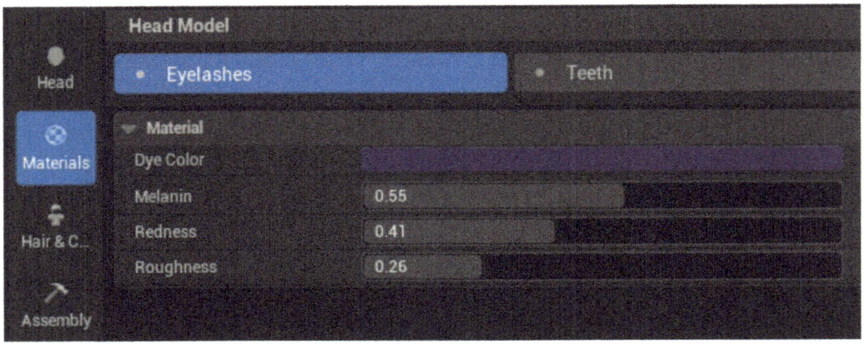

Figure 2.31: Eyelashes

Teeth

Finally, we get to teeth again where we can finalize the look of the teeth. Earlier, I mentioned that we can control the color and intensity of plaque.

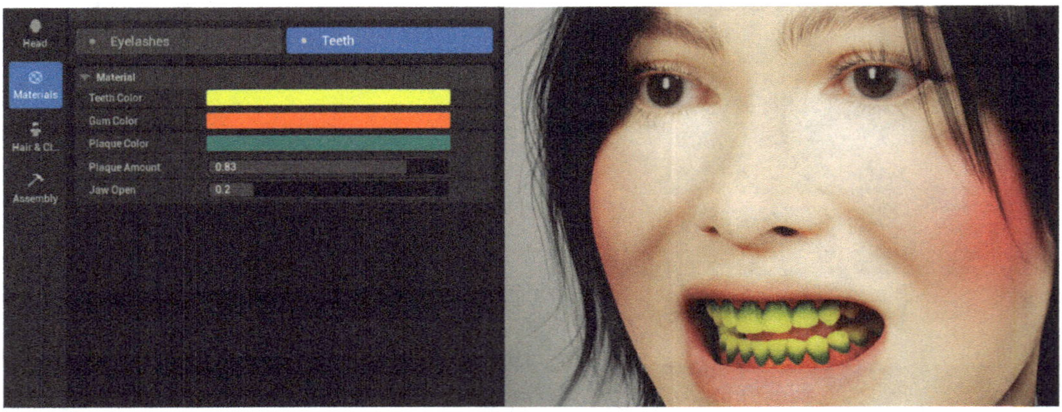

Figure 2.32: Teeth Material

In *Figure 2.32*, I've made the colors very extreme so they could show up clearly in the illustration. You'll see that we have control over the tooth color, which should be an off-white leaning into yellow for realism rather than an unrealistic white. The gum color adds the underlying pinkish color, which is derived from the overall skin tone under the **Skin Parameter**. The plaque color would usually be a gray, and you can change the **Plaque Amount** to your liking. In the earlier **Teeth** parameter under **Head**, we also had the option to open the jaw more to help us without editing. Again, this does not have any impact on the overall character design.

Summary

This chapter introduced the MetaHuman Creator inside Unreal Engine and walked through the complete character creation workflow, from launching a MetaHuman asset to shaping, texturing, lighting, and previewing a fully rigged character. It focused on understanding the interface, choosing the right starting template, navigating the viewport and lighting tools, and using Blend, Transform, and Sculpt to achieve realistic facial structure and asymmetry. The chapter also covered material control in depth, including skin shaders, texture resolution, freckles, accents, eyes, makeup, and teeth, alongside performance concepts such as LODs and render quality.

In the next chapter, we will return to the **MetaHuman Creator** to focus primarily on **Hair** and **Clothing**, but also to cover more on the body. We will then be able to wrap up the editing session by assembling the character to use in an Unreal Engine level.

3

Assembling the Character

In the previous chapter, we covered a lot of the core functions of the **MetaHuman Creator** (**MHC**), including the initial setup, editing the form of the MetaHuman, and its materials. We covered most of the editing parameters except for hair and clothing and the final steps to get the character into the engine.

In this chapter, we will cover the steps from where we left off in *Chapter 2*. Some of these functions will be familiar territory to you, specifically the materials. At the end of the previous chapter, we looked at editing Teeth Materials. Now we are going to look at the hair.

So, we will cover the following topics:

- Hair templates and materials
- Clothing
- Texture downloading
- Rigging
- Assembling
- Opening the character Blueprint

> **Note**
>
> **Download the PDF version of this book**
>
> Your purchase includes a DRM-free PDF copy of this book, the code bundle, and a range of exclusive benefits. To unlock everything, follow the *Free benefits with your book* section in the *Preface*.

Technical requirements

We will be continuing from the last chapter, so you will need UE5 along with a reliable internet connection. A stable internet connection is required as you will be downloading texture files for your MetaHuman which can be large.

Hair templates and materials

You'll remember from *Chapter 2* that we were able to choose templates and then edit those templates. For the hair, we have limited editable parameters. Within the MHC, we are limited to the preset styles. However, don't be discouraged. This isn't a limitation of MetaHuman. For most projects, the built-in presets combined with the material controls provide more than enough variety. Consider creating or purchasing custom hair only when you need a very specific style that cannot be achieved with the existing presets or when matching a real actor or concept design to a MetaHuman, but it requires either acquiring new styles or creating your own using a DCC such as Maya, Houdini, or Blender or an Unreal Engine plugin such as Ornatrix.

With that said, there are plenty of templates in the MetaHuman Creator to choose from to get you started, and with a little tweaking on the material aspects of each hair groom, you can get quite a lot of mileage out of them.

In *Figure 3.1*, you can see I've selected the **Hair & Clothing** tool on the far left. This tab includes menus for various hair types, including the **Hair (Grooms)**, **Eyebrows (Grooms)**, **Eyelashes (Groom)**, and **Mustache (Groom)**, offering a selection of presets under the **All Assets** drop-down.

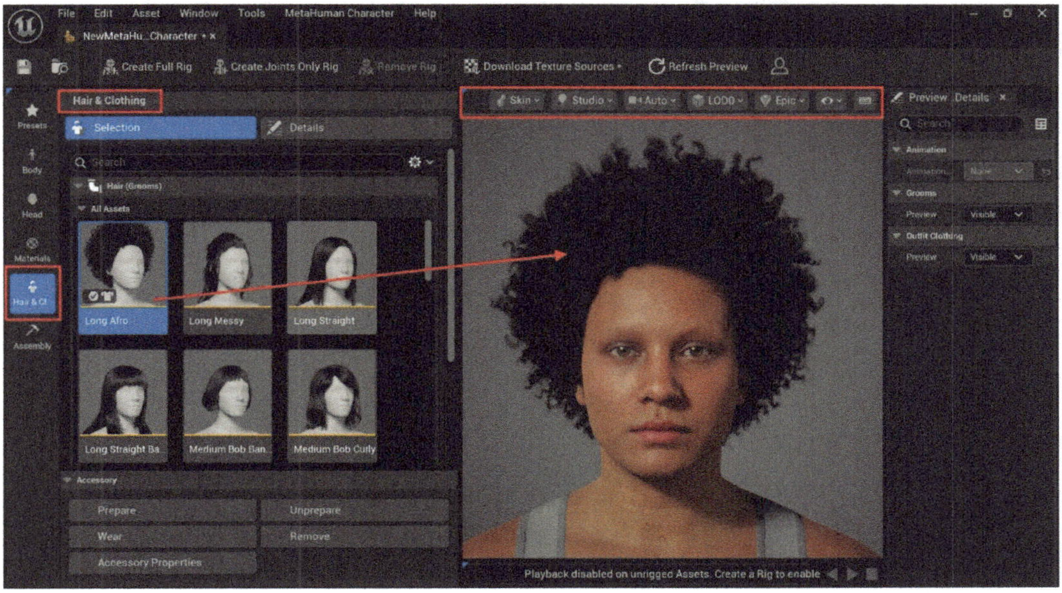

Figure 3.1: Hair & Clothing tab

In *Figure 3.1*, I've also highlighted the visualization controls in red at the top of the **Viewport**. You can see that I'm displaying the **Viewport** with **Epic** settings. If your computer is struggling, click on **Epic** and choose **Medium** instead. This won't affect the final result of your MetaHuman, just the quality that you are previewing in your MHC.

To better understand how the **Hair and Materials** editor works, you need to apply some hair, be it a hair groom (main head hair), eyebrows, eyelashes, beard, or even peachfuzz, before you can edit the details of each.

In *Figure 3.1*, we know we have applied a hair groom not just because we can see it in the **Viewport** but because on the thumbnail under **All Assets**, we have a tick icon and a T-shirt icon. The tick icon represents that it has been applied at some stage and the T-shirt icon represents that it is currently applied.

This system applies to all kinds of hair. If it hasn't been applied, we can't edit the parameters.

If, for whatever reason, you want to remove it altogether, click on **Remove** under the accessory drop down, as illustrated in *Figure 3.2*.

In *Figure 3.2*, I've closed all the drop-down menus to illustrate all the available editors for us to work with from **Hair (Grooms)** down to **Peachfuzz (Groom)**. I've also highlighted the **Accessory** drop-down where **Remove** is located.

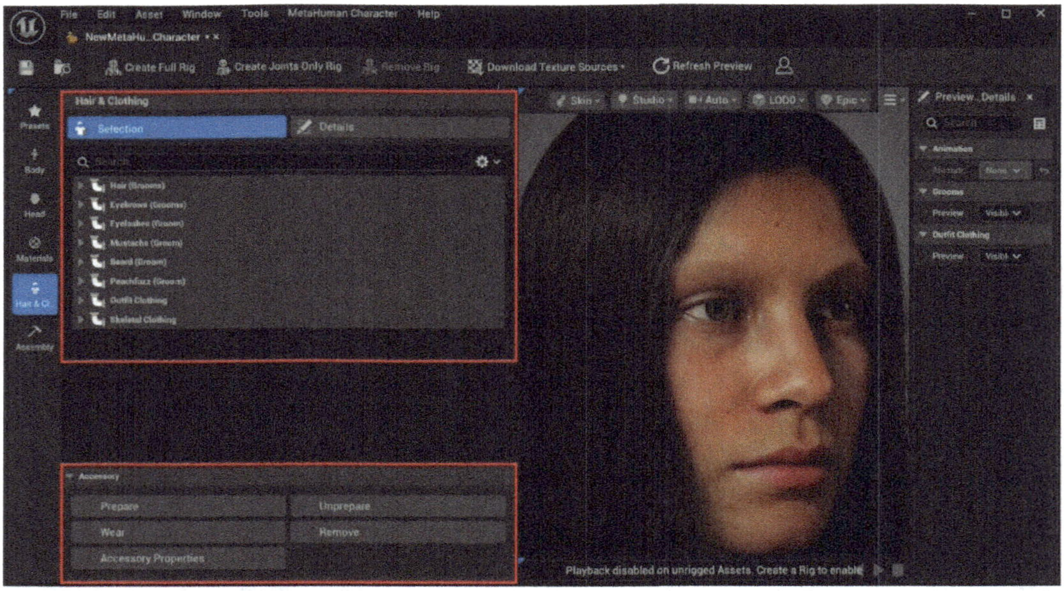

Figure 3.2: Hair & Clothing and Accessory

In *Figure 3.2*, if you look closely, there are no eyebrows yet or any other facial hair for that matter, but we can take a look at those later in the *Eyebrows (Grooms)* section of this chapter. For the rest of this chapter, we will go back and forth between the hair types and the corresponding **Details** tabs.

Let's start with **Hair (Grooms)**.

Hair (Grooms)

The **Hair & Clothing** tab includes **Hair (Grooms)** menu, with a variety of presets. To apply any preset, just *double-click* on the thumbnail. This will not only take a while to apply but it will also use a lot of GPU power to display.

> **Note**
>
> It can take seconds to minutes before the **Hair (Grooms)** is applied and ready to view. This all depends on your hardware.

If your computer is really struggling with previewing hair, you can set **Skin** to **Clay**, which will disable rendering the texture maps, freeing up a little more VRAM.

Some hair grooms use up a little more memory than others depending on their complexity. Scroll through the various templates and *double-click* to assign them.

Note

If you're experiencing preview issues, you can always reduce your render settings inside the MHC or choose the **Always Use Hair Cards** option in the **LOD** drop-down menu. It will significantly free up VRAM, but the quality of the hair will be more of a guide of what your MetaHuman should look like in close-up.

The Details tab of **Hair (Grooms)** lets us edit the look of the hair beyond the basic hair style. I can't stress this enough when I say the **Details** panel is an incredibly powerful editor for getting all sorts of looks and variety from MetaHumans hair and unfortunately it is often overlooked. Some of the settings are obvious, and you might think you've done enough to get the best out of the editor, but I encourage you to play with them all. So, let's go through the settings for the **Hair (Grooms)** in much more detail; rest assured the principles will apply to all the remaining hair types.

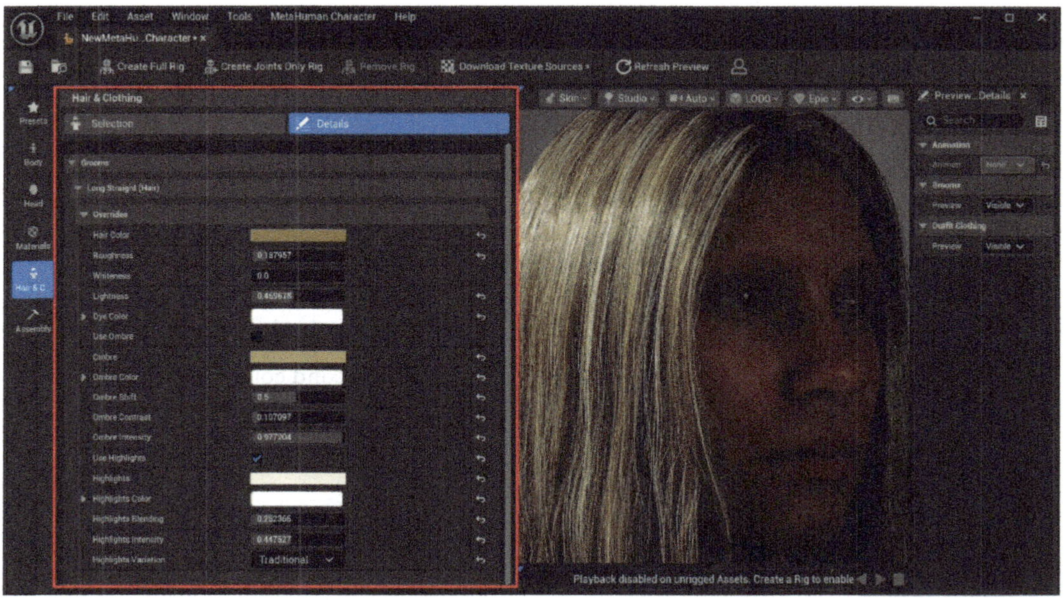

Figure 3.3: The Details panel for Hair (Grooms)

In *Figure 3.3*, I've highlighted the **Details** panel for **Hair (Grooms)**. Notice that the only drop-down menu for **Details** is for the **Long Straight (Hair)**, which I have applied. Had I created eyebrows, there would be an additional drop-down menu available for editing.

You can see straightaway that I've already done some work on the hair and we'll go through the list starting at the top.

In the first quadrant of the panel, we have:

- **Hair Color:** You can lighten the **Hair Color** by clicking on the color to choose from a selection of natural hair colors.
- **Roughness**: It allows you to control the shininess of the hair. I've moved the studio light around to demonstrate the result clearly. Lower values below 2.0 give us an unrealistic look, and we lose a lot of the color information.
- **Whiteness**: Whiteness controls the amount of gray. A complete setting of 1 for Whiteness will give a completely gray result and completely override the hair color above. This function works by increasing the amount of hair follicles that are white. So, from a distance, it looks like you are just fading gray into all the hair, but on close inspection, you'll find that individual hairs are greyer than others, providing you haven't entered extreme values such as 0 or 1.
- **Lightness**: Lightness has a subtle effect when used in most cases. However, when you use higher values of Whiteness the result is more prominent. Arguably **Lightness** is a subset to **Whiteness**.

In the second quadrant, we have:

- **Dye Color**: The **Dye Color** can be achieved by choosing the color picker. However, you can add variations in the dye color itself by choosing a second color from the RGB slider values and editing the opacity of the secondary color.

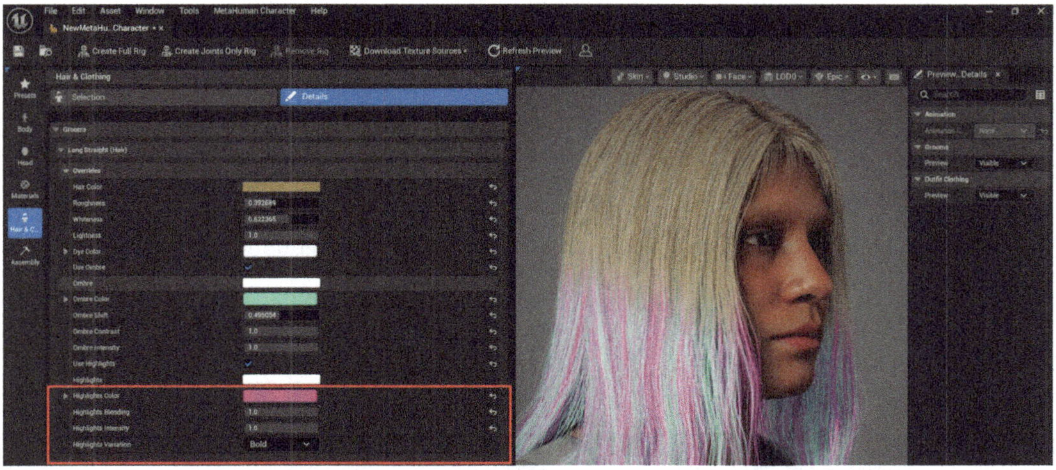

Figure 3.4: Dye Color

From the bottom you can choose from a swatch that is automatically generated the more you edit.

Next up, we have:

- **Use Ombre** and **Ombre**: Ombre defines a graduation of color from the root to the tip of the hair. First, we need to tick **Use Ombre** to use it. Then, under **Ombre**, we can decide to use a natural hair color.
- **Ombre Color**: The lighter the **Ombre** value, the more visible the **Ombre** color will be, as defined in the **Ombre Color** step. To see the full effect of **Ombre Color**, a value of white under **Ombre** will be needed. You can always play with that value to increase or decrease that color effects.
- **Ombre Shift**: The **Ombre Shift** defines height position from root to tip where the **Ombre Color** appears. A value of 0.5 is the halfway mark.
- **Ombre Contrast**: The **Ombre Contrast** controls the blend between the **Ombre Color** and the **Dye**.
- **Ombre Intensity**: Intensity controls the overall effect of the ombre, with a value of 0 meaning no ombre so that just the dye is seen.

Finally, we have:

- **Use Highlights** and **Highlights**: Highlights add lighter strands to the hair, similar to traditional dye techniques such as ombre or streaking. To use them, enable Use

Highlights. The default color picker is limited to natural tones, which keeps the result grounded and realistic.

- **Highlight Color**: For more stylized results, use **Highlight Color**. Unlike the default picker, this allows a full color range. Setting this to pure white effectively removes the visible tint, returning the highlights to a neutral state.
- **Highlight Blending**: Blending works in the same way as contrast does for hair dye.
- **Highlight Intensity**: The intensity will closer match the highlight color when using higher values.
- **Highlight Variation**: Variation will introduce variations in color between follicles or groups of follicles depending on which drop down preset you use which are Bold, Blended, Traditional and Thin.

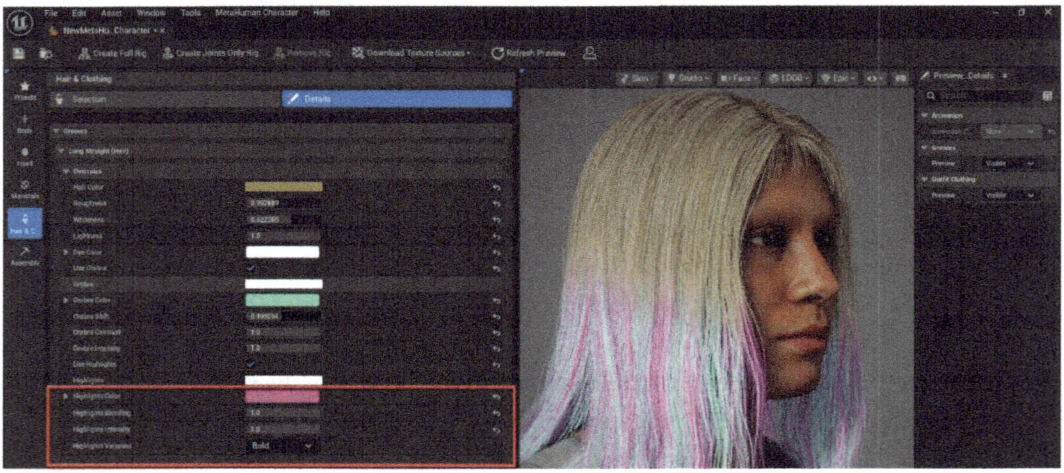

Figure 3.5: Highlights

In *Figure 3.5*,the Bold variation preset is used, making the difference between the pink highlight and the underlying ombre color more pronounced. Note that highlights only affect the ombre region when Use Ombre is enabled.

We've covered all options that are available for the main **Hair (Groom)**, and most of these can be applied to the remaining hair groups as well.

Up next: eyebrows.

Eyebrows (Grooms)

Just like the main **Hair (Grooms)**, we get a selection of preset styles to choose from for **Eyebrows (Grooms)**. From **Hair & Clothing**, go to **the Eyebrows (Groom)** menu, then *double-*

click to apply the eyebrow of your choosing. Remember that if you do not want eyebrows, just use the **Remove** button under **Accessory**.

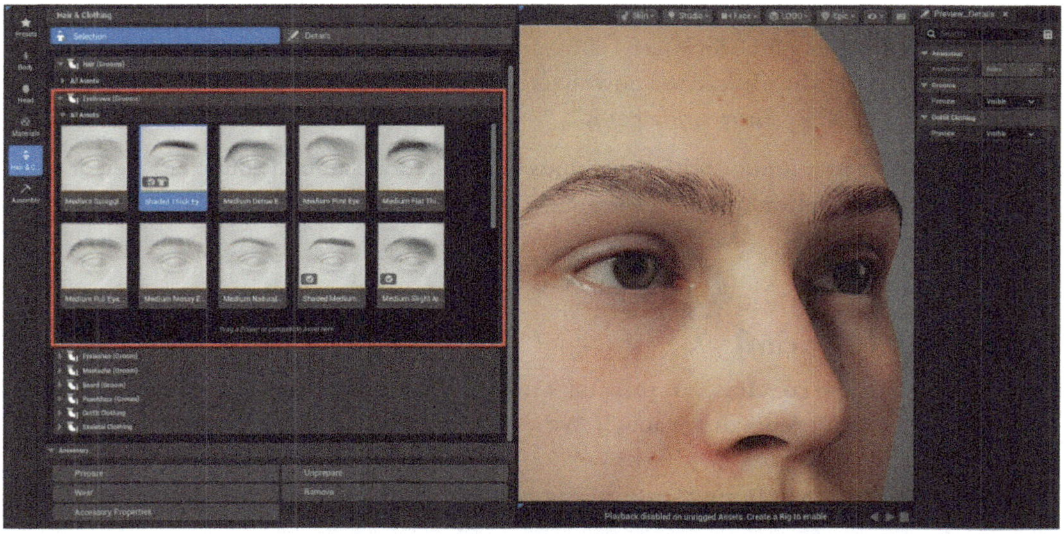

Figure 3.6: Eyebrows (Grooms)

When you're happy with your selections, click on **Details**, and you'll see a very similar **Details** panel to the main **Hair (Groom)**.

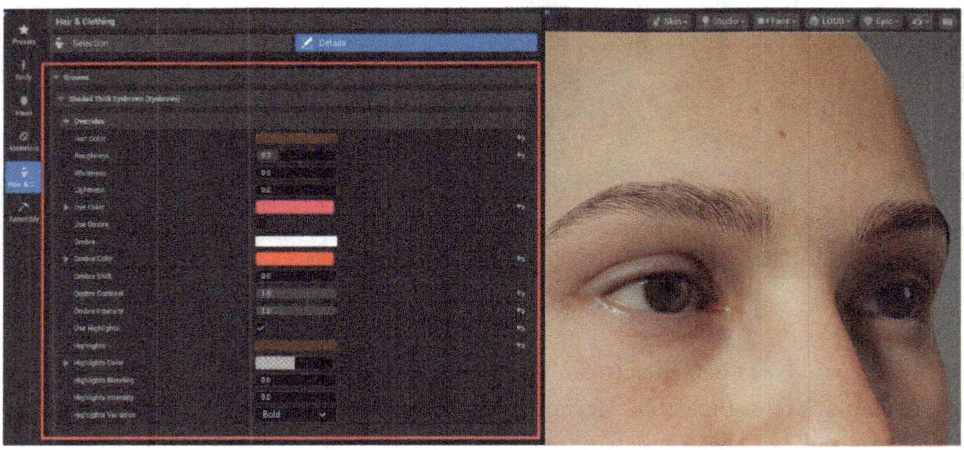

Figure 3.7: The Details panel for Eyebrows (Grooms)

If you compare the **Details** panel of **Eyebrows (Grooms)** in *Figure 3.7* to that of **Hair (Groom)** in *Figure 3.3*, you'll see that they are virtually the same. However, there is a little bit of redundancy for some options, such as the **Ombre Shift**. The size of the **Eyebrow (Groom)** is so small compared to that of the long hair I chose for the head that the **Ombre Shift** has zero effect. However, you'll be pleased to know that the dye works well, so if you want your character to have pink eyebrows, you got it.

I encourage you to play around with the various settings, rotate around your character, or even use the **Light Rig Rotation** tool at the bottom of your **Environment** settings above your **Viewport**.

Next up: eyelashes.

Eyelashes (Groom)

I'm not going to sugar coat this, but there isn't really a lot to eyelashes. We get a few templates to choose from and it's more than enough. We also get a duplicate set of details from the **Eyebrows (Grooms)** section.

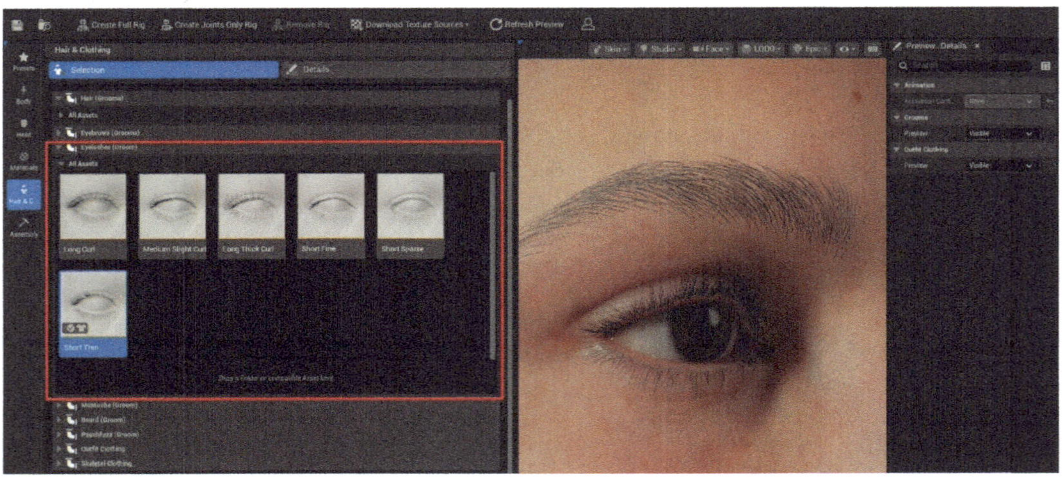

Figure 3.8: Eyelashes

In the **Details** panel for **Eyelashes (Groom)**, only the top quadrant has much of an effect, with **Ombre** having a barely noticeable effect on the end result. The main color does work along with lightness and dye. Dye is much more subtle, and you won't see any results when editing ombre.

Let's move on to mustaches.

Mustache (Groom)

At the time of writing there are just ten presets to choose from under **Mustache (Groom),** but they make a great starting point. Also, at the time of writing, there is one issue with ombre and highlights working effectively despite the length, so don't expect much from the hair coloring of a mustache other than its main color and some greying of the main color along with full control of roughness. The rougher it is, the more prominent the lightness and whiteness effects will be. **Ombre** and **Ombre** shift have no effect on the mustache assets.

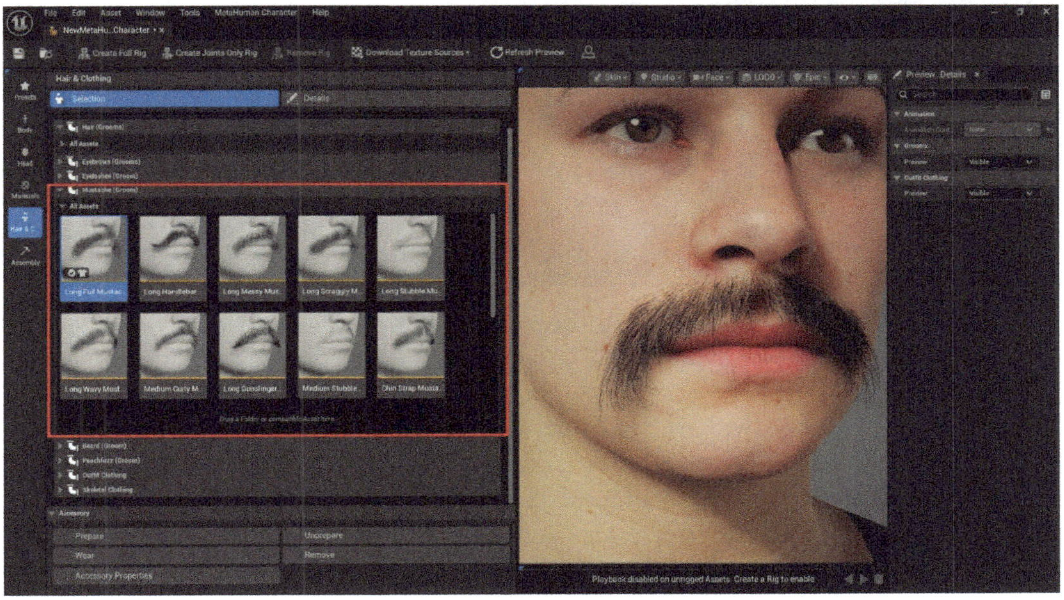

Figure 3.9: Mustache

Without spending any more time on Mustaches, we'll move over to beard hair.

Beard (Groom)

Beard hair falls under the facial hair category. And you'll be pleased to know that because of the available hair length, we gain some of that control back, particularly in the ombre and ombre shift but also more control in the Whiteness and Lightness to the same extent that we had in the main **Hair (Grooms)**. This means we add greys in grouped follicles/strands. This gives us back the salt and pepper look. In addition, the ombre control gives us back that control over the region we want to have a slightly different color, such as around the tips. In addition, we also gain more control over highlights and when combined with the other parameters, we get a very rich and realistic result.

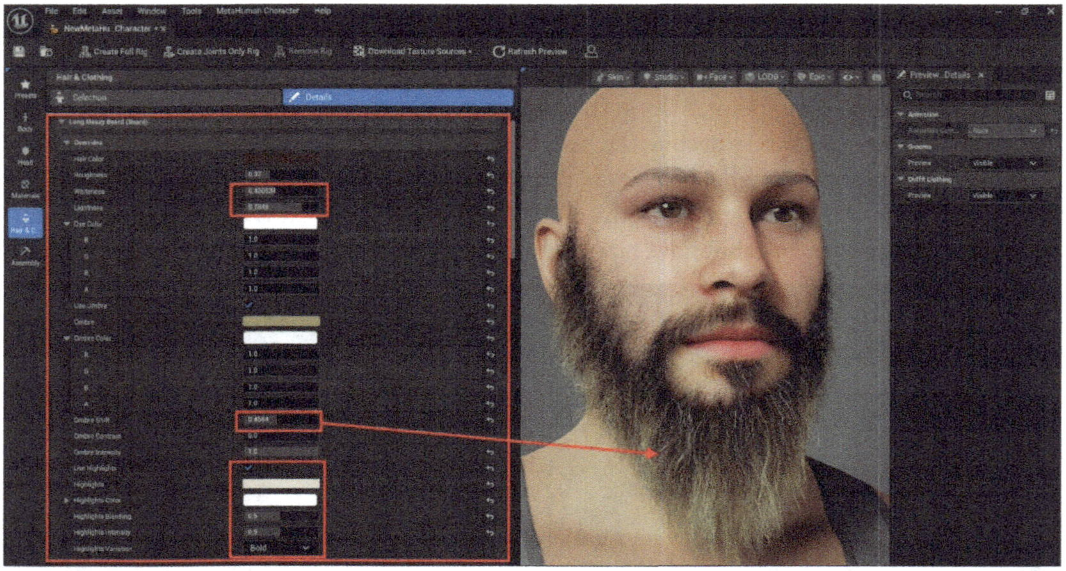

Figure 3.10: Beard (Groom)

Peachfuzz (Groom)

Finally, for the hair section, we have peachfuzz. Something we can completely forget about because it is almost impossible to see. In fact, in *Figure 3.11*, I've had to zoom in dramatically to show the very tiny and thin peachfuzz follicles around the nose. You can see the comparison of thickness next to the mustache hair.

Unsurprisingly, as we've seen with other hairs of diminishing length, we have diminishing editorial control. For peachfuzz, there is no control, no editable attributes in the details panel.

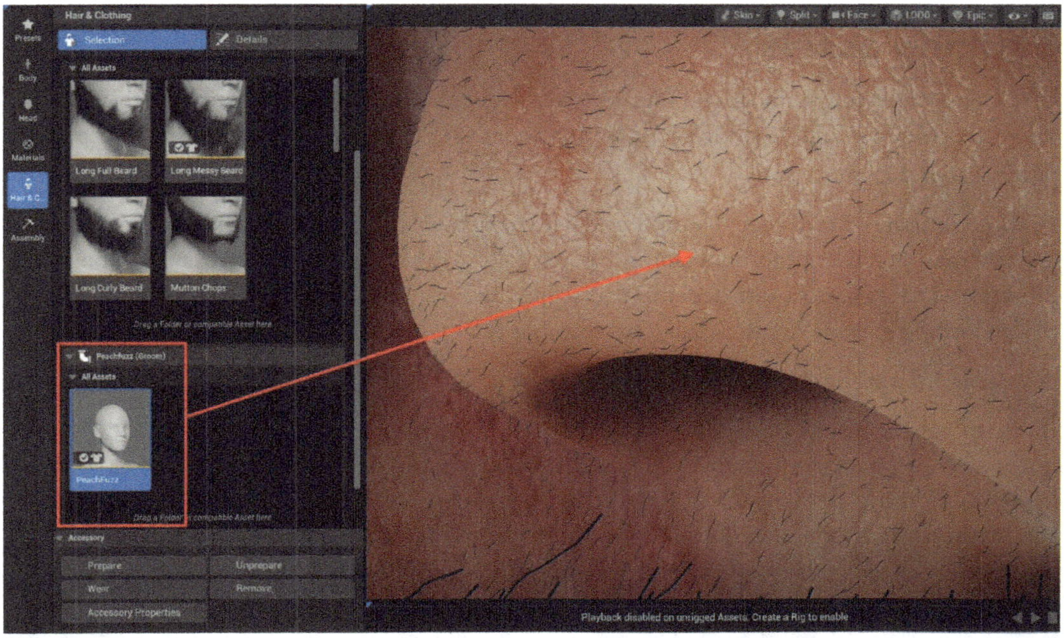

Figure 3.11: Peachfuzz (Groom)

You might ask what the point is in adding peachfuzz if you can't see it. Well, the answer to that is how it reacts to light. There's quite a lot of math involved in how the skin materials and their associated textures react to light, and the Unreal Engine has complex skin shaders and subsurface algorithms built in that MetaHuman's exploit. However, the added layer of peachfuzz gives the skin a photorealistic "roll-off" that would otherwise make the skin appear a little waxy looking under certain lighting conditions. In other words, it's an additional level of realism, albeit a subtle one.

> **Note**
>
> You won't see a difference in how the peachfuzz roll-off effects work until we look at some of the camera raytracing attributes in the Level Sequencer Chapter.

Next up we will look at the clothing assets.

Clothing assets

At the time of writing with Unreal Engine 5.7 Preview, there is only one existing clothing asset. There are readily available clothing assets on `Fab.com` for free, with a fast-growing number of purchasable clothing assets.

For this chapter, we will keep it simple and use the default clothing asset supplied with MetaHuman Creator. Additional clothing packs follow the same workflow but may expose different editable parameters depending on how the asset author configured them. We will cover clothing in more depth in the Clothing chapter.

Let's examine clothing.

Go to the clothing section and *double-click* **WIDefaultGarment** to apply it. You may have underwear on underneath, but this is just a texture map and not geometry. As soon as you apply the clothing asset, which is made up of 3D geometry, a body mask will be applied to hide any texture details underneath such as the underwear.

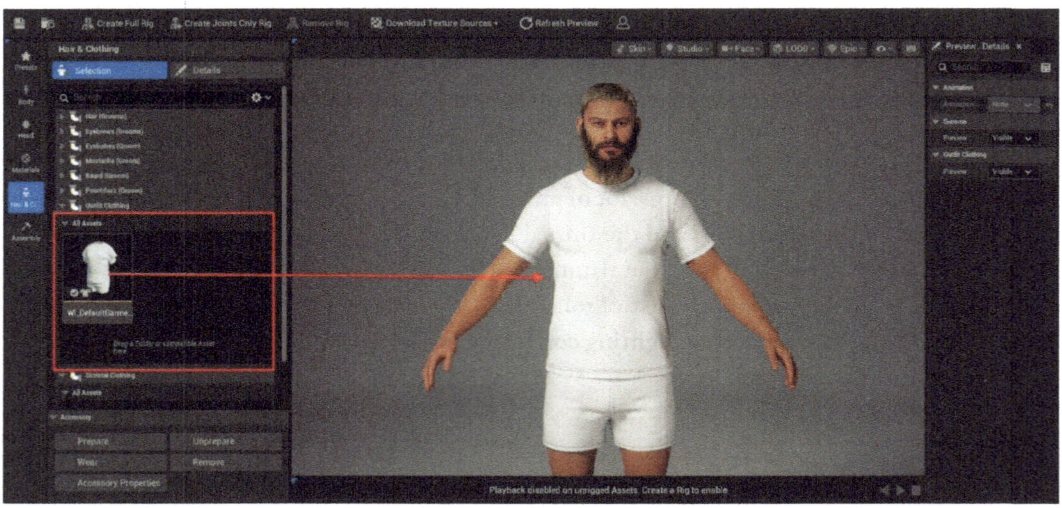

Figure 3.12: Applying the Default Garment

Now, with the default clothing asset applied, let's look at the **Details** panel. You'll be somewhat familiar with the **Details** panel to know what to expect. However, as you purchase MetaHuman clothing, the **Details** panels will change depending on what the clothing author allowed to be editable.

For this chapter, we will only concern ourselves with editing the colors, which in the case of this particular garment collection will be the primary and secondary colors for both the shorts and shirt.

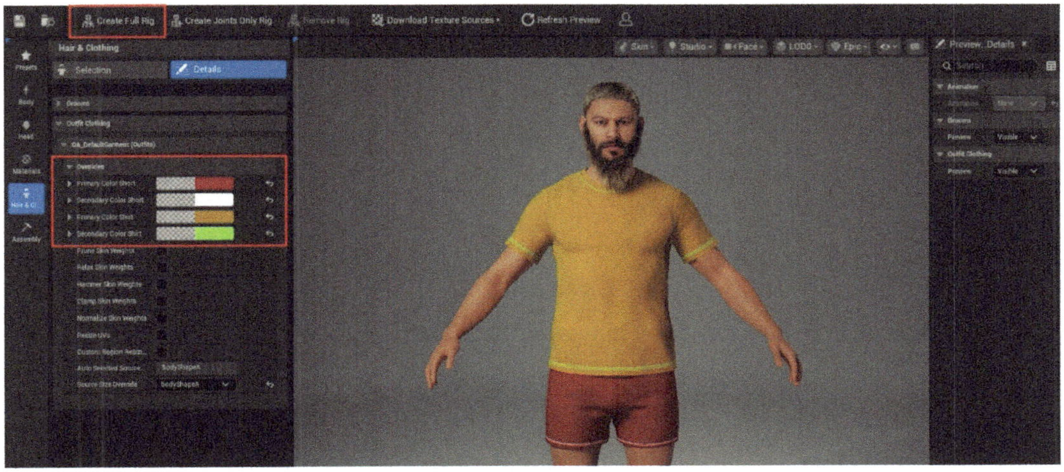

Figure 3.13: Editing the garment colors in the Details Panel

You can see from *Figure 3.13* that I have changed the shorts to red, with the secondary color of white for the stitching to make it stand out. For the shirt, I have selected a mustard color with green stitching.

We don't have any material attributes to edit in the MHC, but if we want, we can edit the material that is applied once the MetaHuman has been assembled. This is because MHC downloads various texture maps such as albedo, roughness, height, and displacement and applies them to an Unreal Engine cloth material, which can be modified in UE or taken to another application such as Photoshop for more detailed editing.

You'll notice a series of options that are disabled by default such as **Prue Skin Weights**, **Relax Skin Weights**, etc. These are attributes designed for external DCC applications such as Maya and are intentionally disabled within the standard MetaHuman Creator workflow. For now, you can safely ignore these options as we'll revisit related concepts in Chapter 5, such as Maya, for editing how the cloth behaves during animation, which is beyond the scope of this book. However, we will look into skin weights throughout this book, particularly in relation to garment skin weight editing in *Chapter 5*. I've also highlighted the **Create Full Rig** button. In order to preview animation with the clothing, you will need to create a full rig. This could take a minute or two.

Note that before you apply your final textures, you'll need to remove the rig. Unfortunately, the process of designing does require creating and removing rigs repeatedly.

> **Tip**
>
> Leave rig creation until the final stages of character design. Complete your hair, clothing, and texture adjustments first, then create a Full Rig once to preview animation before assembling the MetaHuman. This significantly reduces unnecessary rig generation time.

Once you're happy with how your character looks in its new, albeit limited, clothing, click on **Remove Rig** and move onto **Assembly**.

Assembly

Assembly can be broken down into the following sections:

- Assembly Selection: Once in Assembly, under Assembly Selection, you'll see a drop-down list.
    a. By default, we get the **UE Cine (Complete)**. This is the highest setting designed yet optimized for Unreal Engine for cinematic purposes.
    b. The second option is **UE Optimized**, which is designed for performing in games at very high frame rates
    c. The third option is an even more optimized version **UEFN**, specifically for Unreal Engine Fortnite character creation
    d. The last option is **DCC Export**, which is designed with high end cinematic use in applications such as Maya where frame rates aren't a consideration

  For our purposes, we will stick to the default, **UE Cine (Complete)**.
- **Animation**: In the **Animation** section, we just get two options, **AnimBP** and **UAF**, which at the time of writing is an experimental feature we won't be covering. Please ensure **AnimBP** remains selected.
- **Targets**: The **Targets** relate to where we want our character will be saved to. If you leave it at the default settings, a folder called `MetaHuman` will be created within your `Content` folder inside the `Project` folder. Within the `MetaHuman` folder will be the material, textures, meshes, and the MetaHuman Blueprint. You can click the three dots next to the **Root Directory** dropdown to choose a different folder within your Unreal Project.
- Textures: In *Figure 3.14*, I have used the **Textures** dropdown to show what options we can use to override the texture resolution. We have already done this in the **Materials**

section. So, whatever texture resolution you have chosen in the **Materials** section still needs to be downloaded be it 2K, 4K, or 8K. If you're worried that your machine is a low spec, go back to **Materials** and choose 2K. If you have a high-spec machine, 8K will do.

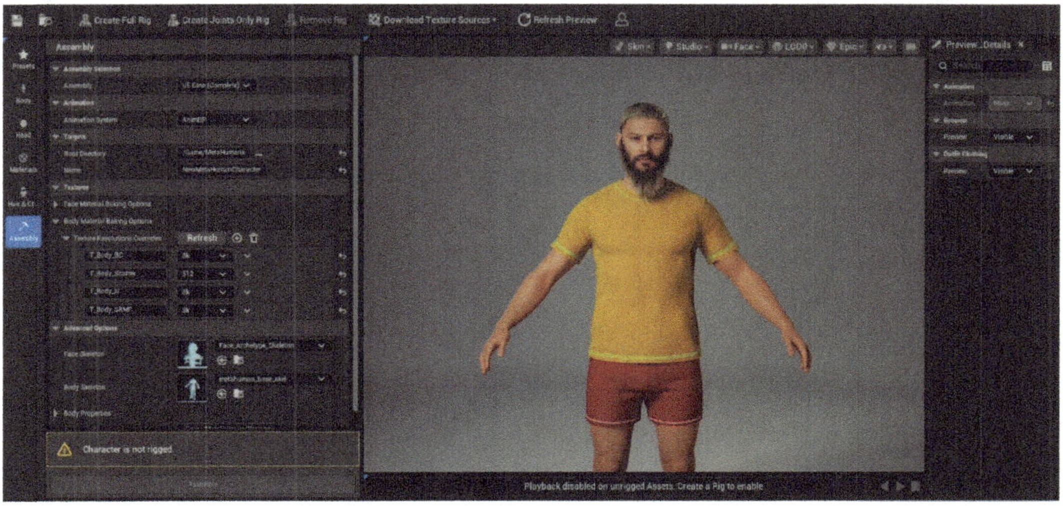

Figure 3.14: Assembling the MetaHuman

Once you're happy with your resolution, by going to **Materials** | **Skin** | **Texture Sources**, click on **Download Texture Sources**.

An alternative way to download the textures is to go to the top tool bar and under **MetaHuman Character**, choose **Download Texture Sources**:

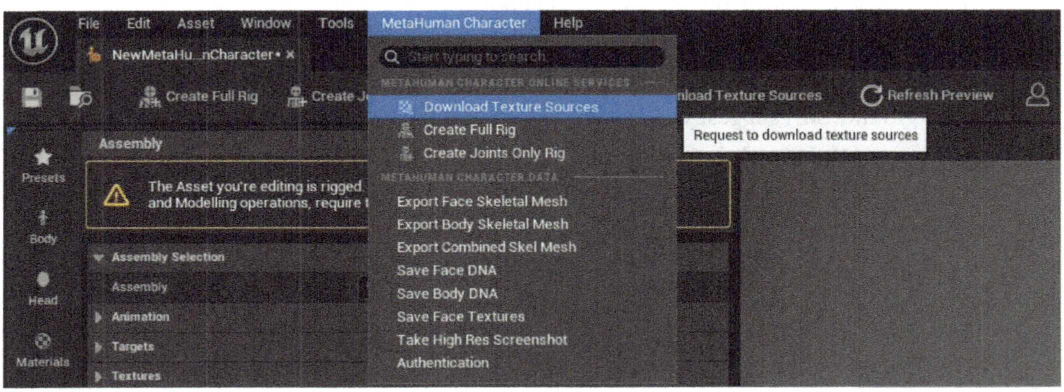

Figure 3.15: Assembling the MetaHuman

This could take a while for the textures to download.

So, with the character rigged and the textures downloaded, you see a green **Assemble** button at the bottom.

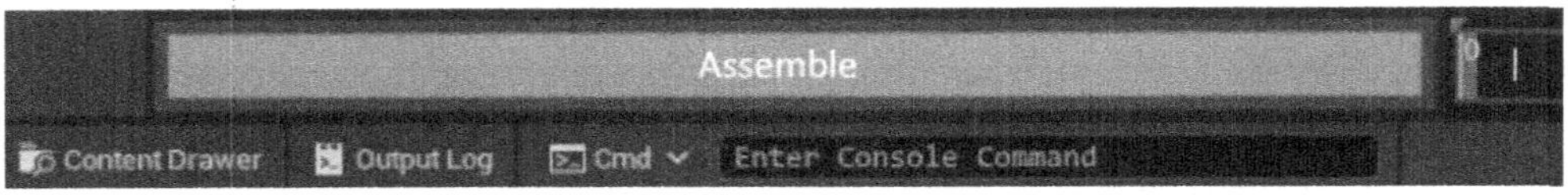

Figure 3.16: Assembly button

When you click Assemble, MetaHuman Creator generates all of the assets required for use inside Unreal Engine, including:

- The character meshes
- Skin weight data
- Materials and textures
- Hair grooms
- A ready-to-use MetaHuman Blueprint

Depending on your hardware, this process may take several minutes; be prepared to wait a while.

Once created, you will get a pop-up on the bottom right of the screen saying **MetaHuman Successfully Created**.

> **Note**
>
> **UE crashing**
>
> If UE crashes at all during the process, it is likely due to memory issues. The MHC itself is already using a considerable amount of VRAM, and you don't need to be looking at the highest quality settings of your MetaHuman while the assembly is taking place in the background. So, I suggest you modify your **Viewport** settings by changing **Skin** to **Topology**, use **Hair Cards** in LOD, or disable **Grooms** and **Outfit Clothing** in the **Preview Details** panel. If that still doesn't work, you may have chosen too large textures for your system process. Make sure you have at least 50GB in both your project drive and/or your C: drive.

If your assembly has been successful, save your MHC (*Ctrl+S*), close it, then go over to your **Content** folder, and *double-click* the `MetaHumans` folder, which was just created. *Left-click* the Blueprint labeled `BP_NewMetaHumanCharacter` (if you haven't renamed it), and drag it into your scene.

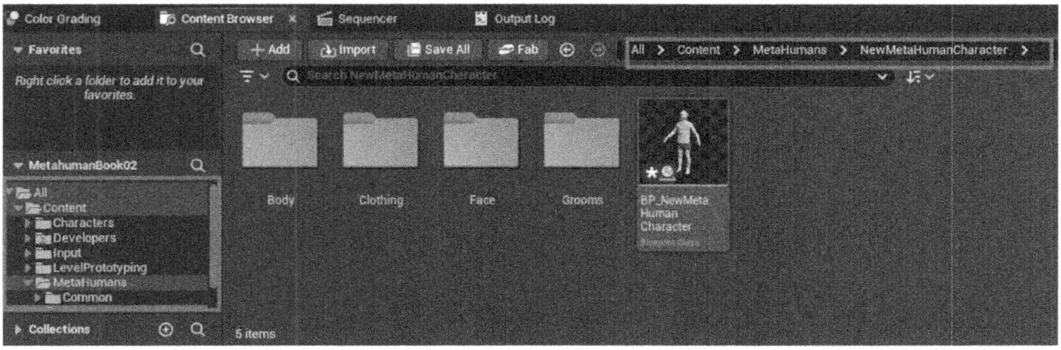

Figure 3.17: MetaHumans Folder

Once you have dragged the MetaHuman into your scene, you can inspect it by navigating in your scene. Ensure you have selected the MetaHuman in your scene and hit *F* to center it. You can navigate through your scene using the following commands:

- *Alt*: Mouse-based camera controls
- *Alt + left mouse button*: Orbit around a point or object
- *Alt + middle mouse button*: Pan the camera side to side and up and down
- *Alt + right mouse button*: Dolly the camera in and out

So, at this point, you've created your MetaHuman.

Summary

In this chapter, we continued from the previous chapter by covering the various hair types and introducing clothing. We also went through the final texturing and rigging, allowing us to assemble the final metahuman, giving us all the assets including the MetaHuman Blueprint, which we added to the scene.

In the next chapter, we will dive into the MetaHuman Blueprint to further explore how we can modify where we left off in the MHC, but more importantly, look at all the functionality that the Blueprint offers now that we have our MetaHuman created.

4

Diving Into the MetaHuman Blueprint

In *Chapter 3*, we assembled a MetaHuman character using the **MetaHuman Creator** (**MHC**) plug-in inside UE5. During the assembly process, a number of folders were created that included assets such as meshes, textures, and materials. Additionally, a Blueprint asset was created for the character. The **Blueprint** is the glue that holds all the assets together.

In this chapter, you will be introduced to Blueprints, including what they are and what they are used for. Using Blueprints, you will learn the first steps required to prepare your MetaHuman for animation, repurposing motion capture data from another character that we will import into a project. We will also look at ways we can further edit the MetaHuman we created.

So, in this chapter, we will cover the following topics:

- What are Blueprints?
- Opening a Blueprint
- Editable features
- Importing and editing skeletons

Technical requirements

To complete this chapter, you will need the technical requirements detailed in *Chapter 1* and the MetaHuman that we imported into UE5 in *Chapter 3*.

What are Blueprints?

So, what on earth is a Blueprint? If that's what you're thinking, I couldn't blame you.

Blueprints are effectively a visual representation of templates written in the C++ programming language. Epic Games could have easily been just created a console within Unreal to let users write C++ code but because not everyone is familiar with the C++ programming language, they created an easy way for artists to edit the relevant code. In addition, for those familiar with C++, Blueprints are a very handy way of creating tools that are relatively easy for artists to use.

The good news is that you don't really need to spend a huge amount of time using them when working on a MetaHumans character and animating them, but they are an integral part of the process and are being used by the engine in the background. It would be good practice for artists to get to grips with the fundamentals of Blueprints as they are a fantastic way of reducing repetitive work; however, it must be said that there are tasks that simply can't be carried out without working with Blueprints.

In terms of functionality with the MetaHumans character, Blueprints essentially hold most of the information relating to the character in one place and we use the Blueprint to make changes to our character. The changes we will make relate to how the character is animated and by the end of this chapter you will be familiar with what areas of the Blueprint you will need to edit to get your characters animated correctly.

You can look at a Blueprint as if it were a driver. Its function is to drive the mesh of your character using a skeleton. It does this by driving the bones, which in turn drives the skin. Because there is a cloth simulation at work, the skin drives the cloth. Because there is also a hair simulation at work, the skin drives the hair. All of this is driven by the Blueprint.

But where does the Blueprint get the initial instructions? Well, the answer is *you*. You tell the Blueprint, what kind of instruction it will use to animate the character and then you point to various animation modes for the Blueprint to use. There are just a couple of different types of animations that can be applied, listed here:

- **Prerecorded data**: This is simply a file that has motion data, usually one file for the face and another file for the body. We can get these files from plenty of resources. We can also use animation files that come with the third person game template in UE5, or create our own files by recording our own motion capture data (we call these **Takes**).

- **Live motion capture data**: The Blueprint gives us the option of using live data that is coming from a piece of hardware, such as:
    a. An iPhone for facial motion capture
    b. Software such as Faceware Studio, utilizing a video camera
    c. Motion Capture Suits also provide us with Live Data via third-party software. The Live Data is information relating to the transformation and/or rotation of bones that is streamed in real-time into the engine.
- **Animation Blueprints**: these are primarily used for game logic, but they can use the same animation file types used in prerecorded data or saved when using Live Motion Capture Data that we would use in traditional 3D animation Film making

Blueprints also allow for new data taken in from the user, such as a player in a game, and will engage a relevant animation file depending on what the player does. For example, if the player runs, the Blueprint will execute the **run** animation file which drives the character to run. That file would usually be in the format of FBX or BVH. The files are referred to as **Assets**.

So, let's look at the Blueprint inside the engine.

Opening a Blueprint

Once you've successfully imported a MetaHumans character into UE5, you'll see a few folders and a file, starting with the BP_, prefix, as seen in *Figure 4.1*. The folder contains all the assets required to display your character.

Figure 4.1: The Blueprint inside the Content Browser

When you *double-click* on the **Blueprint**, this will open your **Character Blueprint**. You will see that the screen is made up of six tabs as seen in *Figure 4.2*:

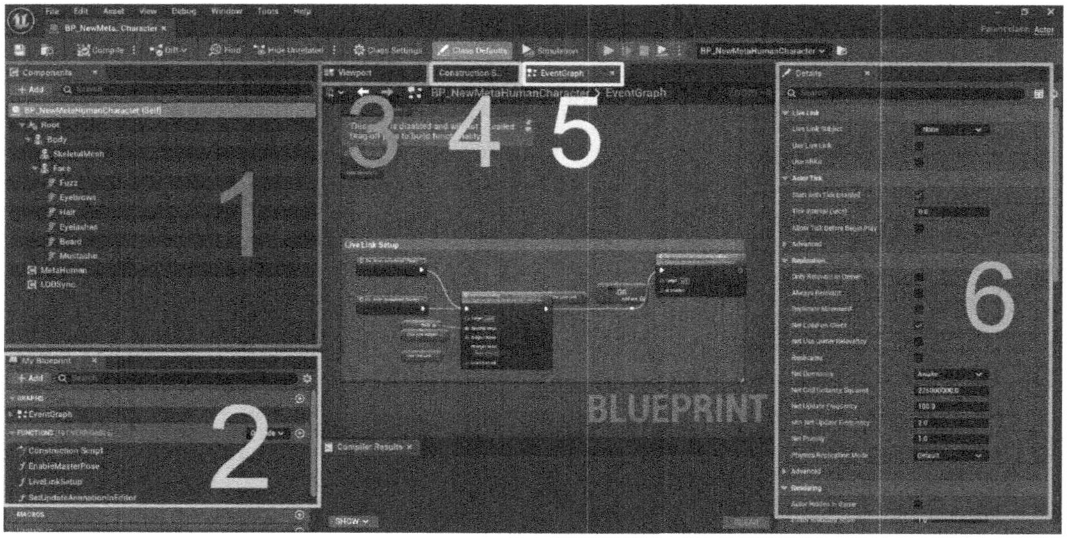

Figure 4.2: Six panels of the Character Blueprint

Let's break down the tabs:

1. **Components**: This is where we can select what part of the MetaHuman we wish to edit. We can also add additional components such as meshes, camera and lights etc. to our MetaHuman.
2. **My Blueprint**: Here, we can see what functional elements are associated with our MetaHuman, such as the ARKit setup which allows for facial motion capture to be directed to our character
3. **Viewport**: This gives us a view of our character without showing use the rest of the level. This comes in handy if we have brought a character into a busy scene and wish to inspect or edit our character without the distraction of a busy environment.
4. **Construction Script**: A construction script allows the engine to read and write data to the Blueprint regardless of which level we are using. In the games world, this is useful as the construction script can hold data such as character health. For the purposes of what we are using our MetaHumans for, we won't need to make any changes to this.
5. **Event Graph**: The event graph contains important information relating to events. An event can be a game starting or the result of pressing a particular key on the keyboard. In terms of MetaHumans, the event graph determines what LOD values should the

character use. For example, if the camera moves far away from the character, that is an event that triggers the character to display an LOD value greater than 0.

6. **Details**: This is where we do most of our editing. It is context sensitive so we will see different information depending on what we have clicked on in the **Component** tab. For instance, the body will give us different parameters to edit than the face.

As we just mentioned, when it comes to editing our characters, we do so in the **Details** pane by editing various assets. Many of these assets are image files, but there are also many editors that allow you to further refine your character. In fact, in some instances, you are given even greater control over many aspects of your character. This additional control can bring even further realism to your character than you could have achieved with the MHC alone.

To see an example of how much extra editing power you have, click on **Face** within the **Component** tab, then *double-click* on one of the **Eye Materials** contained in the **Details** tab. Depending on which eye you choose, it will be labeled as `MI_EyeL_Baked`.

Once you've opened the **Material Editor** for that eye, you can edit certain attributes that weren't available to edit in the MHC. For example, you can edit the **Cloudiness** of the eye and **Ambient Occlusion** within the **Iris**, which adds a lot of depth to the eye, as demonstrated in *Figure 4.3*:

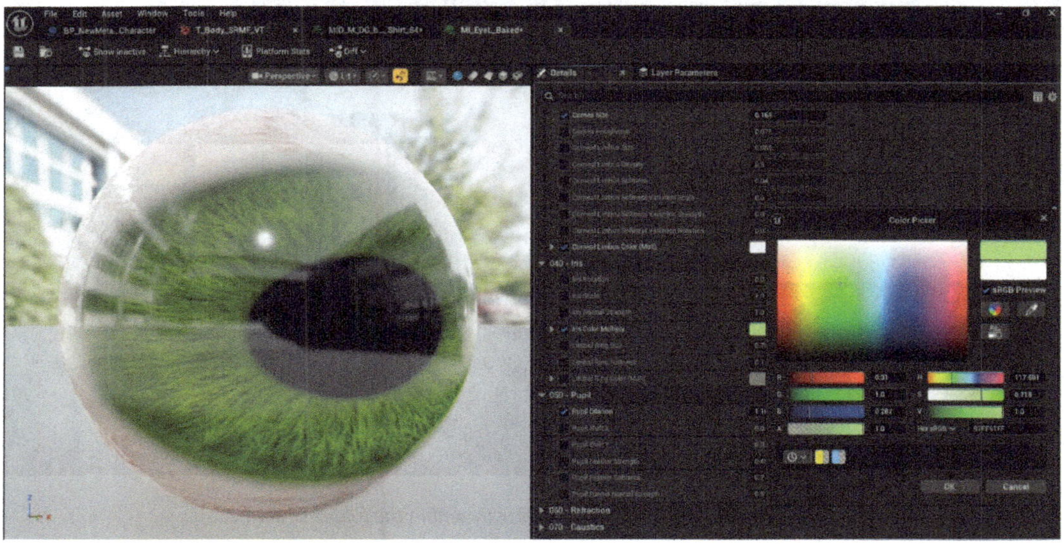

Figure 4.3: Editing the Eye Material

> **Note**
>
> Adding further edits to your character using parameters exclusively available in Blueprints won't affect your original design in the MHC. You will always have a safe backup copy in the MHC.

Just as a reminder, the Blueprint acts like a driver and the characters subfolders act like passengers. While you can access all these components directly through the character Blueprint, you can also gain access by diving into the individual subfolders; there may be occasions where you'd prefer to have multiple folders open at a time, so in many cases, it just comes down to personal preferences.

Using the folder structure to navigate the Blueprint

To show you how to navigate using folders, as seen in *Figure 4.4*, I have gone directly into the `Clothing` folder and *double-clicked* on the `MID_M_DG_bodyShapeA_Shirt_84` asset to change its color.

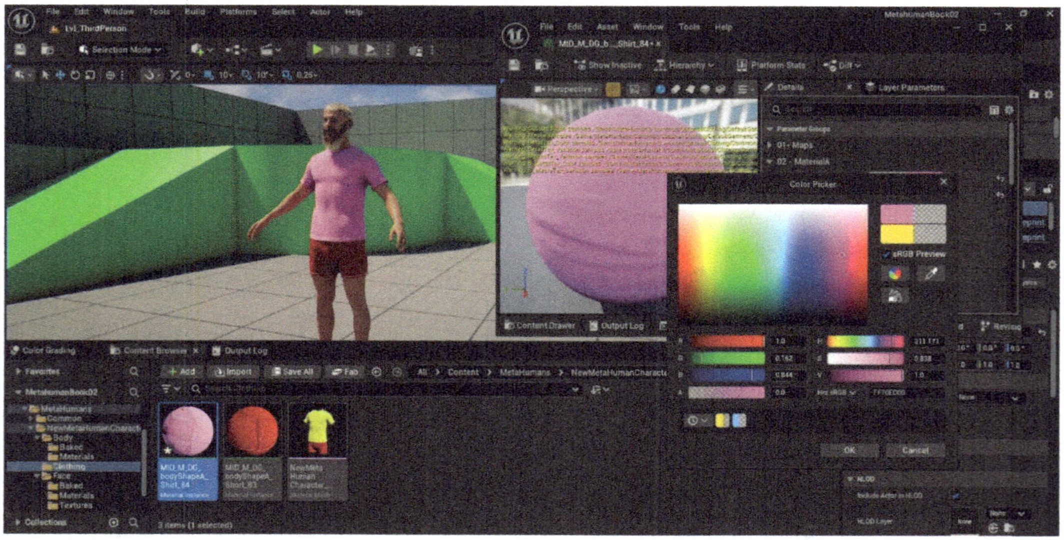

Figure 4.4: Further editing done directly within the folder structure

As you can see, there is even greater control of this particular asset than we would have gotten from just MHC alone; for example, using the color picker tool to change our MetaHuman's hoodie. You may remember from *Chapter 3* that we used the MHC color tools to make such changes.

Navigating around the Blueprint without folders

In *Figure 4.5* you can see that the same edit is taking place, but we are using the characters' Blueprint to edit the same asset. Both methods are equally effective.

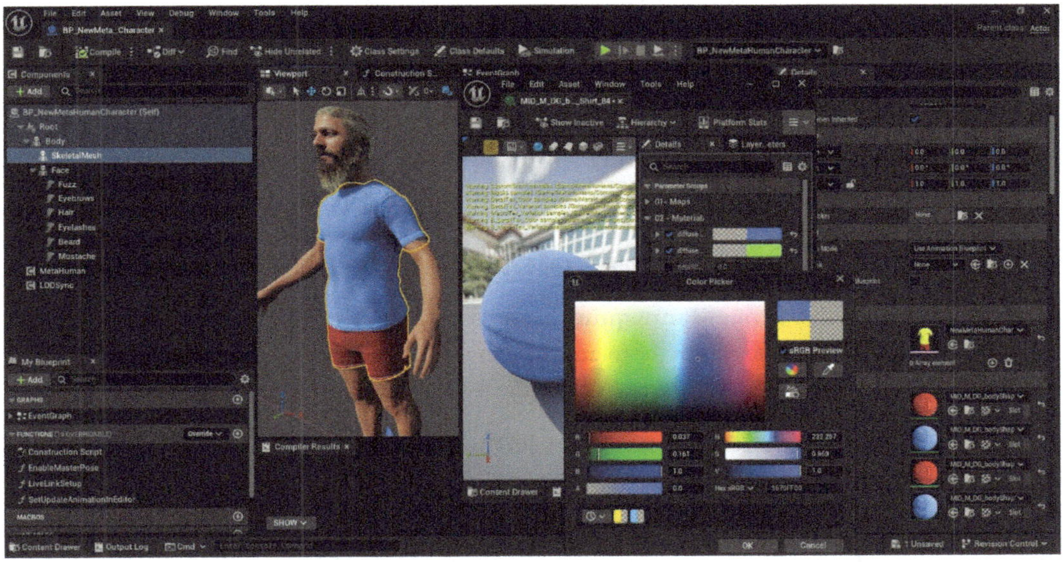

Figure 4.5: Editing a color inside the Character Blueprint

As shown in *Figure 4.5*, you can follow these steps:

1. Select **SkeletalMesh** from the **Component** tab
2. Click on the material element slot, which will open the **Material Editor**
3. Click on the current color, which will open the **Color Picker**, allowing you to change the color

Instead of using the **Components** tab, you can click directly on the character in the **Viewport** to select it.

While there are many additional editors within the Blueprints relating to the appearance of the characters, they are mostly for refining materials. For the most part, the results are subtle, but you can completely change color schemes.

As daunting as this all looks, rest assured that you will only really be editing a tiny section of the Blueprint. At the very least, you will just need to choose what kind of animation you want to drive your character and for repurposing animation from another character, we only need to edit skeletal details.

It makes sense to get up and running with some body animation first. UE5 comes with several starter packs to help us. One of the starter packs is a third-person game, which comes with a **Mannequin** character that is rigged with a skeleton. It also comes with a few animations that we can use to test out our own character.

For the remainder of this chapter, we will look at Blueprints with the view to repurpose the animation from the starter game pack and apply it to our own character in the next chapter.

Importing and editing skeletons

In this section, we will add our **Mannequin** character to our project. Then, to be able to retarget animation from one character to another, the source and target characters both have to have skeletons. We will be looking at both of these skeletons in the following sections.

Adding the mannequin character

To start, we want to use the skeleton of the **Mannequin** character that comes shipped with Unreal. To add it into your project, all you need to do is go to your **Content Browser**, click on the **+ADD** button (*1* in *Figure 4.6*), and choose **Add Feature or Content Pack...** (*2* in *Figure 4.6*):

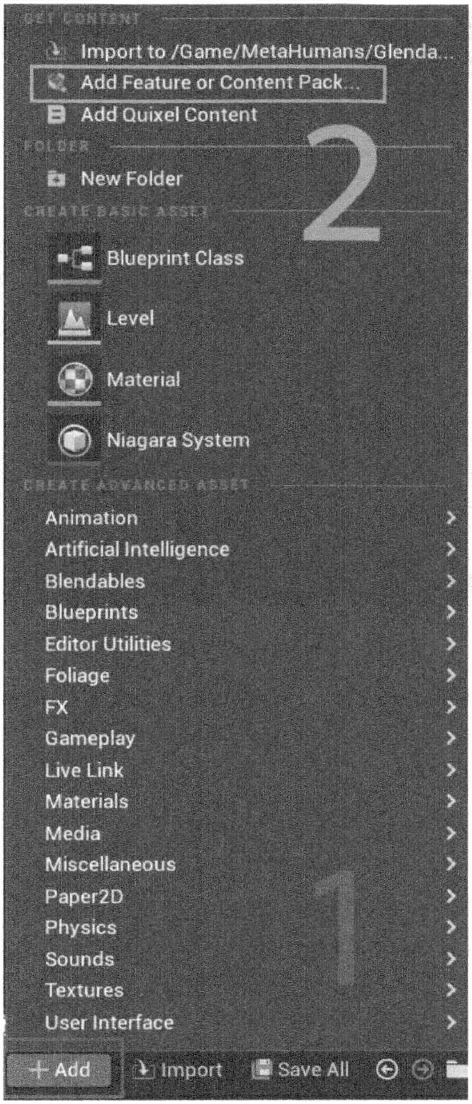

Figure 4.6: Adding a content pack

Once you've clicked on the **Add Feature or Content Pack...**, you'll see a pop-up window where you can choose **Third Person** (*2* in *Figure 4.7*) from the **Blueprint** feature tab (*1* in *Figure 4.7*):

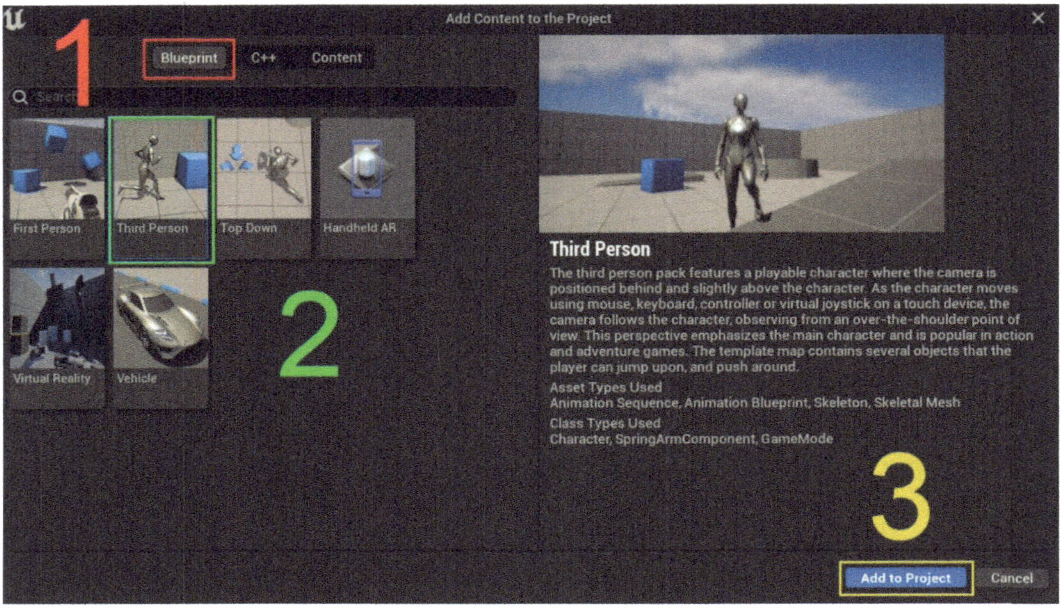

Figure 4.7: Adding content to the project

The reason we choose **Third Person** is because it has a full character, including a mannequin, in the project that we can repurpose. Click on **Add to Project** (*2* in *Figure 4.7*). This will load the project into your **Content Browser**.

You'll notice that there are now two new folders in your Content Browser: `Characters` and `Third PersonBP`.

Prior to Unreal Engine 5.6, we would have had to modify the third person characters so that their associated animation would be compatible with our MetaHuman. Now the process is so much easier.

Animating the character

When we add the **Third Person** pack, it will create many folders, most importantly an `Anims` folder. Navigate to that folder **Content** | **Characters** | **Mannequins** | `Anims`.

The `Anims` folder contains lots of different animations that are compatible with the **Third Person** Blueprint but not compatible with our MetaHumans, at least not yet.

You'll see four additional folders, corresponding to the different types of animation. *Double-click* on **Unarmed** and *right-click* on **MM_Idle.** This is an **Animation Sequence** asset. You can choose any **Animation Sequence** asset you want.

When you *click* on the **Animation Sequence**, you'll see a menu shown in *Figure 4.8*. Choose **Retarget Animations**.

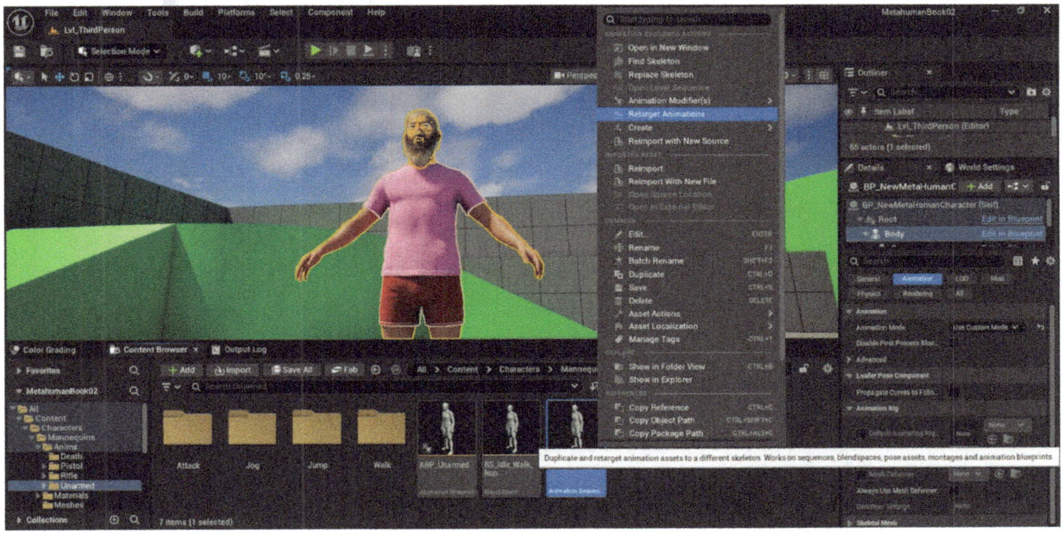

Figure 4.8: The Third Person Blueprint

This will give us an option to create a new **Animation Sequence** that is compatible with our MetaHuman.

When you choose **Retarget Animations**, another window will pop up asking us which **Skeletal Mesh** we want to target.

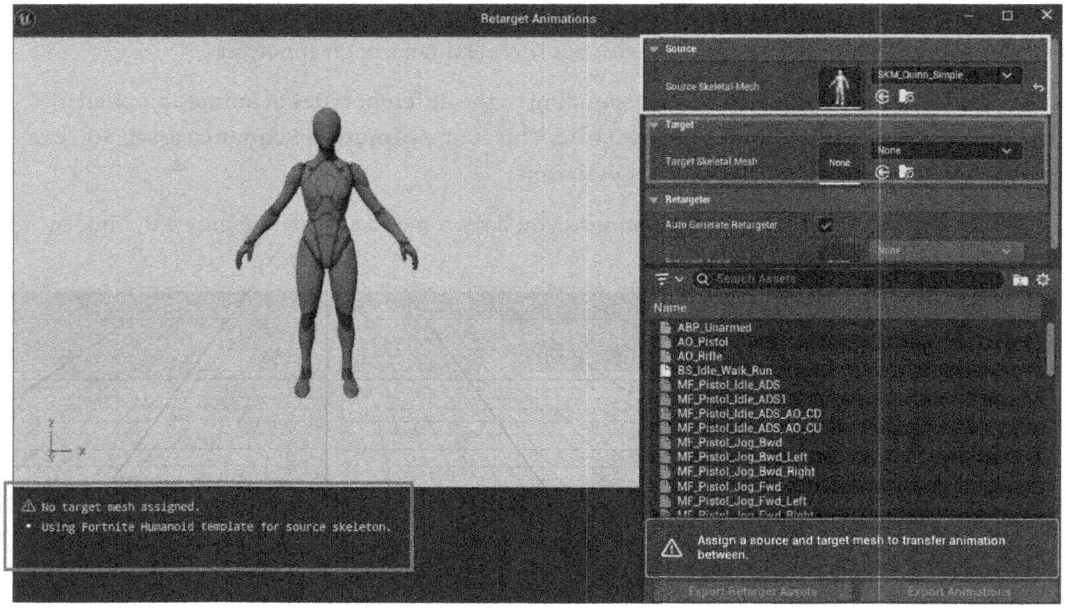

Figure 4.9: Retargeting window

Under **Target**, there is a drop-down menu. This is where we need to choose the MetaHuman skeletal mesh as the target. The **Source** is already selected for us because it was the **Sources Animation Sequencer** we *right-clicked* on earlier. You'll see that the **Source Skeletal Mesh** selection is **SKM_Quinn_Simple**.

Click on the **Target Skeletal Mesh** drop-down list and select the body mesh belonging to your MetaHuman. If you gave your MetaHuman a custom name in *Chapter 3*, the mesh name will reflect that name rather than `SKM_NewMetaHumanCharacterBodyMesh`.

As soon as you select it, a body will appear to the right. Typically, it just shows the arms and legs and not the torso. To test the animation, *click* on any available animation from the list provided in the bottom right as seen in *Figure 4.9*.

The list shows every animation compatible with the source. If the source is transferable to the target, you can apply it and it will automatically play in the Viewport.

Note

If the preview pose appears severely distorted or misaligned, first confirm that you selected the correct MetaHuman body mesh from the Target Skeletal Mesh list. An incorrect target mesh is the most common cause of unexpected retargeting results.

Previous versions of MetaHumans required many additional steps to make Unreal Engine Mannequin animations transferable to MetaHumans. Now the process is largely automatic. For the purposes of this chapter, we are retargeting body animation only. Facial animation follows a separate workflow that will be introduced later when we look at facial motion capture.

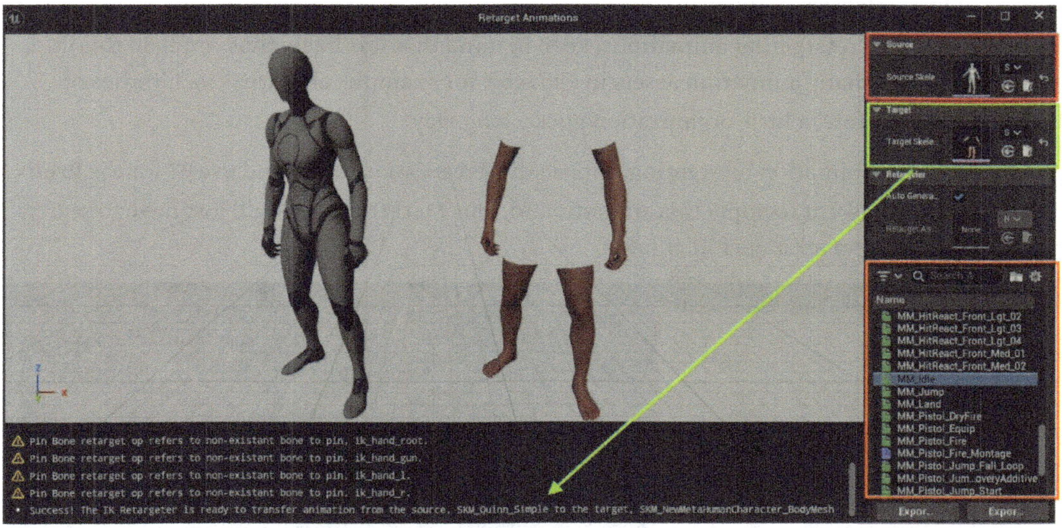

Figure 4.10: Testing Animation

Click on any animation from the list, and *double-click* the animation to preview it in the **Viewport**.

In *Figure 4.10*, I have chosen **MM_Idle**. The MetaHuman on the right now matches the pose of the source on the left and we get a message at the very bottom, which I have pointed to. It reads:

Success! The IK retargeter is ready to transfer animation from the source, `SKM_Quinn_Simple`, to the target, `SKM_NewMetaHumanCharacter_BodyMesh`.

Now that we have tested the animation and we are getting a success message, it is time to export the animation.

Exporting the animation

With your chosen animation still selected from the list, in my case it is **MM_Idle**, *click* on **Export Animations**. A small **Export Animations** dialog box will open.

This allows us to do two things.

1. Choose the destination of our converted animation (the one that is going to work with the MetaHuman).
2. Rename the converted animation so we don't confuse it with the original and can find it using the search tool.

When it comes to retargeting animations, keep in mind that it is likely that you'll do this in large batches, as many animation assets in `Fab.com`, for example, are extensive libraries of animation. Therefore, a little organization goes a long way.

To organize this animation retargeting, choose the `MetaHumans` folder and use `RT` for the **Prefix** so that when you want to apply this animation to your MetaHuman, you'll just have to search for **RT** inside the `MetaHumans` folder later.

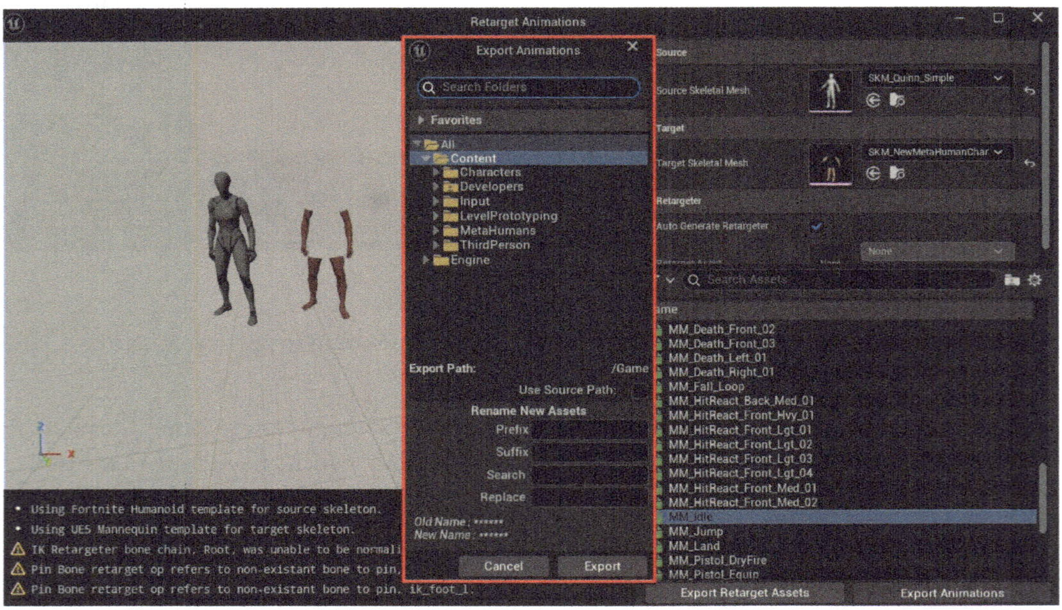

Figure 4.11: Exporting animations

To go one step further with organization, create an `Animations` sub-folder inside the `MetaHumans` folder. This can be done by *right-clicking* on the `MetaHumans` folder, as seen in *Figure 4.11*. You will get an option to create a new folder and name it `Animations`. Next, *double-click* to choose the `Animations` folder as the destination. Now, hit **Export**.

You'll be greeted with a **Batch Export** options. Select **Export** and close the Blueprint. You've successfully retargeted the animation, ready to be assigned.

In the next step, we're going to assign the retargeted animation to the character you placed into your scene. If you haven't done so already, drag your character Blueprint into your scene and make sure it is still selected.

Assigning the retargeted animation to the character

Go to the **Details Panel** on your right. If you can't see it, go to **Window** | **Details** and click **Details 1** to show it.

Next, click **body**. This is where we are going to assign the retargeted animation.

We've already made the retargeted animation compatible with the body; we just haven't assigned it yet.

With the body selected in the **Details** panel, click on the **Animation** button so that our animation options appear at the very top. We want to change the animation mode. By default, it is set to **Use Animation Blueprint**. We want to use our retargeted file, so *click* on the drop-down menu to choose **Use Animation Asset as the Animation Mode**.

As soon as you do that, a thumbnail labeled **None** will appear. This means it is waiting for us to assign an animation asset like the one we just created when we exported the animation.

Earlier, we exported our retargeted animation to `Content` | `MetaHumans` | `Animations`.

So, navigate to `Animations` and *click* on the **RT_MM_Idle** file that we recently exported. We just need to select it.

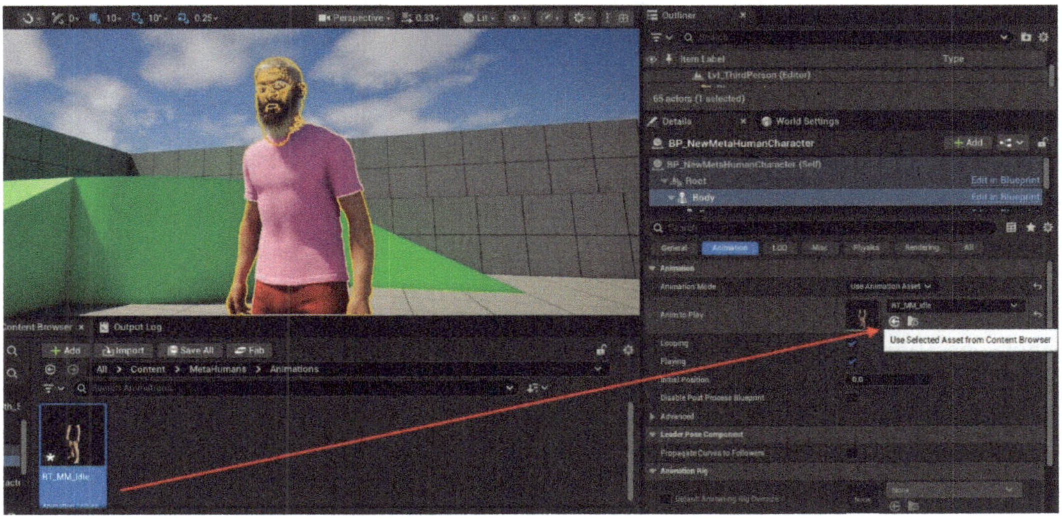

Figure 4.12: Assigning the Animation Sequence to the MetaHuman

Because it's selected, we can just *click* on the **arrow icon** directly beside the **None** thumbnail, and it will assign whatever is selected within the `Content` folder.

As soon as you click it, your MetaHuman will come to life when we run a simulation by using the *Alt* + *S* keys.

I recommend repeating the steps of exporting individual animations and assigning them to the character before moving on to the next chapter.

Minor edits made later in MetaHuman Creator, such as changes to materials, hair, or proportions, will not normally affect previously retargeted body animations because they continue to use the same underlying skeleton.

Also note that you can use any **Animation Sequence** to open the **Retarget Animations** window and change both the source and target meshes as required.

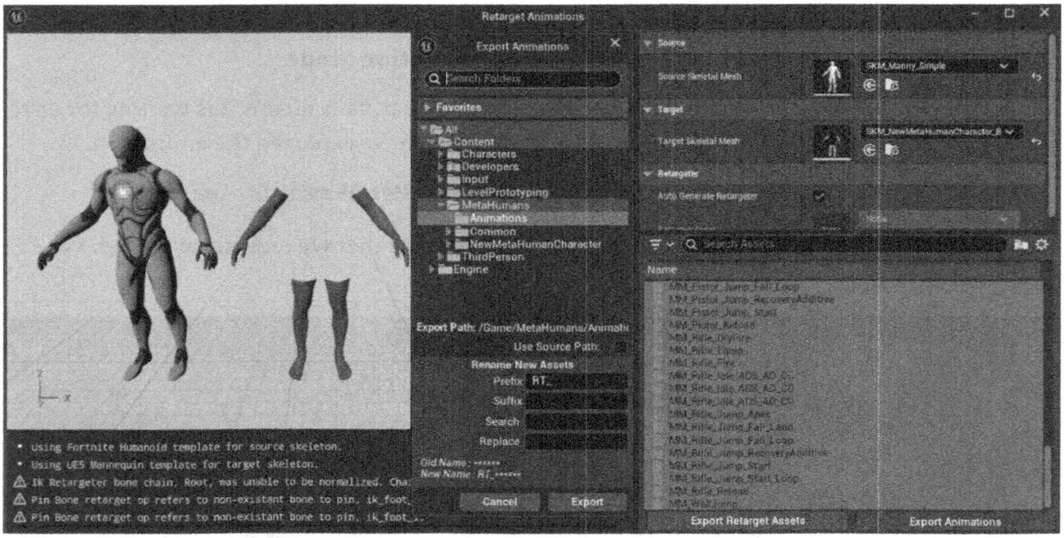

Figure 4.13: Batch Exporting

By Shift-clicking, you can select multiple Animation Sequences and batch export them in a single operation. You can also select every available animation by pressing Ctrl+A. This is particularly useful when retargeting large animation packs downloaded from Fab or other animation libraries.

Summary

In this chapter, we took a brief look at Blueprints and how we can make minor adjustments to the materials. We then focused on how to retarget animations made for Unreal Engine's Manny and Quinn characters and assign them to our character.

In the next chapter, we are going to add clothing to the character using an industry standard 3D garment creator, **Marvelous Designer**. We will create custom clothing that will perfectly fit our characters without any need for 3D modeling.

Part 2

Bringing Your MetaHuman to Life

In this second part of the book, you'll expand your MetaHuman beyond character creation and begin preparing it for real-world animation workflows. You'll learn how to create and integrate clothing, retarget body animation from external sources, generate your own motion capture performances, and refine animation using Unreal Engine's Level Sequencer and Control Rig.

By the end of this part of the book, you'll have the skills needed to animate your MetaHuman with both stock and bespoke performances, giving you the confidence to produce high-quality animated sequences for games, cinematics, and virtual production.

This part of the book includes the following chapters:

- *Chapter 5, Clothing Our MetaHuman*
- *Chapter 6, Retargeting Mixamo Animations*
- *Chapter 7, Adding Motion Capture with DeepMotion*
- *Chapter 8, Using the Level Sequencer*

5

Clothing Our MetaHuman

In *Chapter 4*, we covered the Blueprints of our MetaHuman. If you were new to Unreal Engine, that chapter gave you a pretty good understanding of how Blueprints work at a basic level. By diving into the Blueprints, you were able to edit the look of your MetaHuman without having to reopen the MHC. In real-world practical terms, using Blueprints is an efficient method, as you can see your changes change live within your scene.

In this chapter, you will be introduced to the concept of 3D clothing generation: some simple and fast clothing methods using assets on Fab and Marvelous Designer, which is the industry standard for garment generation and simulation. This chapter tackles a key issue with MetaHumans: how few garments are available within the MHC. We will explore the most efficient way of designing clothing around your bespoke character, minimizing the number of steps and manual work such as modeling and even texturing.

So, in this chapter, we will cover the following topics:

- Getting clothing assets in Fab
- Preparing your MetaHuman for third-party software
- Using Marvelous Designer
- Initial garment fitting
- Cloth simulations

Technical requirements

To complete this chapter, you will need the technical requirements detailed in *Chapter 1* and the MetaHuman that we imported into UE5 in *Chapter 3*.

You will also need a copy of **Marvelous Designer** installed on your PC. For a free 14-day trial, you can install Marvelous Designer from: `https://www.marvelousdesigner.com/product/trial`

> **Note**
>
> This chapter demonstrates an FBX-based workflow that is compatible across multiple versions of Marvelous Designer and Unreal Engine. Recent versions of Marvelous Designer also provide a DNA import workflow and additional USD export options that reduce some of the manual steps shown here. Regardless of the import method, the garment fitting and simulation principles remain the same. The version of Marvelous Designer used in this chapter is Marvelous Designer 2025.1.

You will need to create an account and download Marvelous Designer before progressing to the next section.

Getting clothing assets from Fab

By default, the MetaHuman comes with `WI_defaultGarment`, which is just a white t-shirt and shorts. It is typically wearing this garment by default, and you can use the **Wear** or **Remove** buttons to toggle on and off this garment. Naturally, you will want to bring in alternative clothing, and the most direct way to do this is by acquiring an asset just like the default one, which is a wardrobe asset.

If you were to create your own wardrobe asset, you would first need a **cloth asset**, an **outfit asset**, and then finally a **wardrobe asset**, which you can drag and drop into the **Outfit Clothing** section of the MHC, as highlighted in *Figure 5.1*.

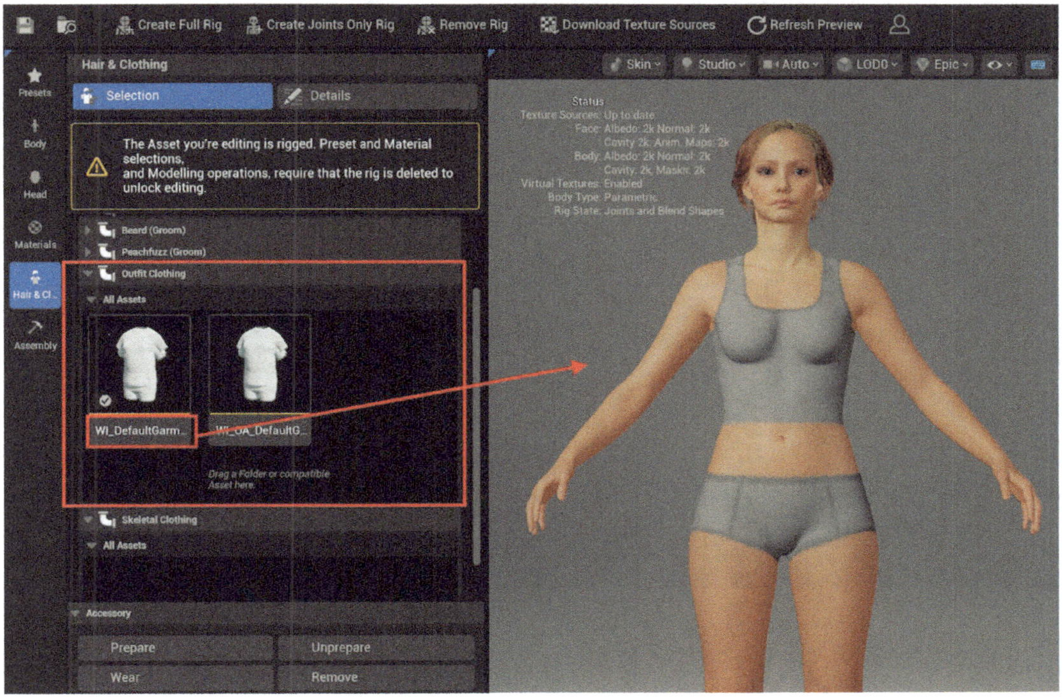

Figure 5.1: The Wardrobe section of MHC

The *wardrobe asset* is the product of a series of steps that allow the garment to be used in the MHC. In addition to being the only clothing asset allowed into the MHC, wardrobe assets are also very useful because you can still edit the body proportions of your character, and the selected wardrobe asset will autofit to the new proportion.

Let's see how we can acquire free wardrobe assets from Fab and apply them to our MetaHuman. Open the **Epic Games Launcher** and click on **Fab**.

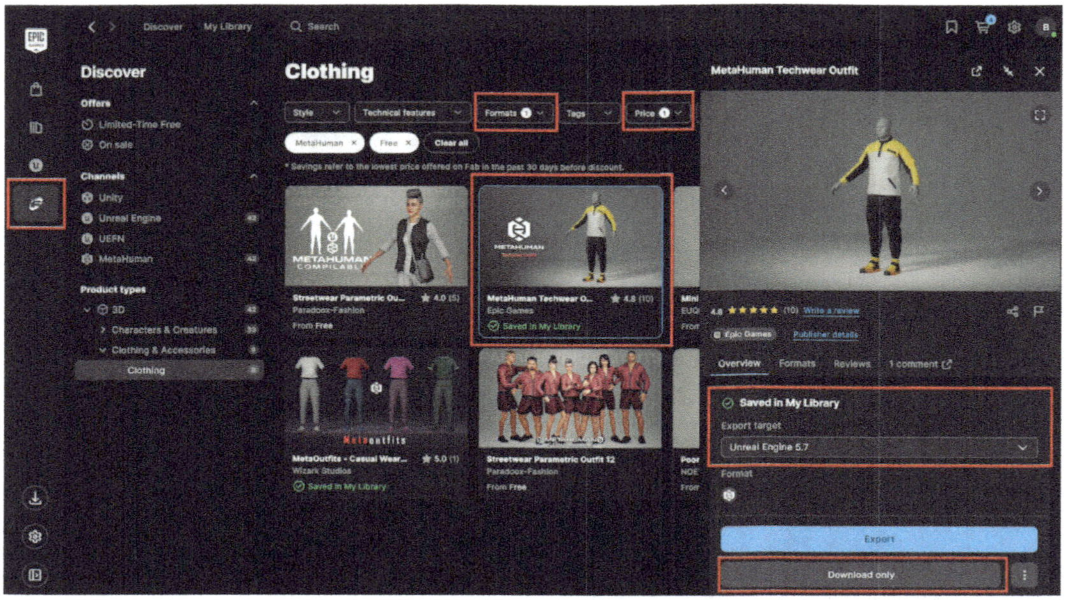

Figure 5.2: Choosing a free MetaHuman-compatible asset in Fab

In *Figure 5.2*, in the **Epic Games Launcher**, I've clicked on **Fab**, indicated in red on the far left and modified the search parameters so that I can only see free MetaHuman-compatible assets. You can see the MetaHuman logo on all of these asset thumbnails. This means that rather than just providing a simple mesh and textures for a garment, the author has gone through the arduous process of creating the cloth, outfit, and wardrobe assets for you.

If you remove the free search tag, you'll see there's a substantial amount of paid premade wardrobe assets to the sum of 1,500 at the time of writing.

To follow along, stick to the free items and choose the techwear outfit just like in *Figure 5.2*.

A pop-up will appear giving you the option of choosing the version of Unreal Engine you are running. I'm running UE version 5.7. You should do the same.

At this point, make sure your Unreal Engine project is still running so that when you hit Export it creates a Fab folder inside your project directory. You can either click Download Only and then export or choose Export directly. Be sure to select the correct Unreal Engine version.

Tip

Download Only stores assets in a temporary cache before they are exported into your project. Once you've confirmed the assets have been successfully exported, avoid relying on the temporary cache as a permanent storage location.

Jumping back into Unreal Engine, resize your **MetaHuman Creator** window so that you can see the MetaHuman Creator and the content folder of your project side by side. Navigate to the newly and automatically created `Fab` folder. You should see a `MetaHumans` folder, and in it will be the wardrobe asset for your new garment, the techwear wardrobe asset, as seen in *Figure 5.3*:

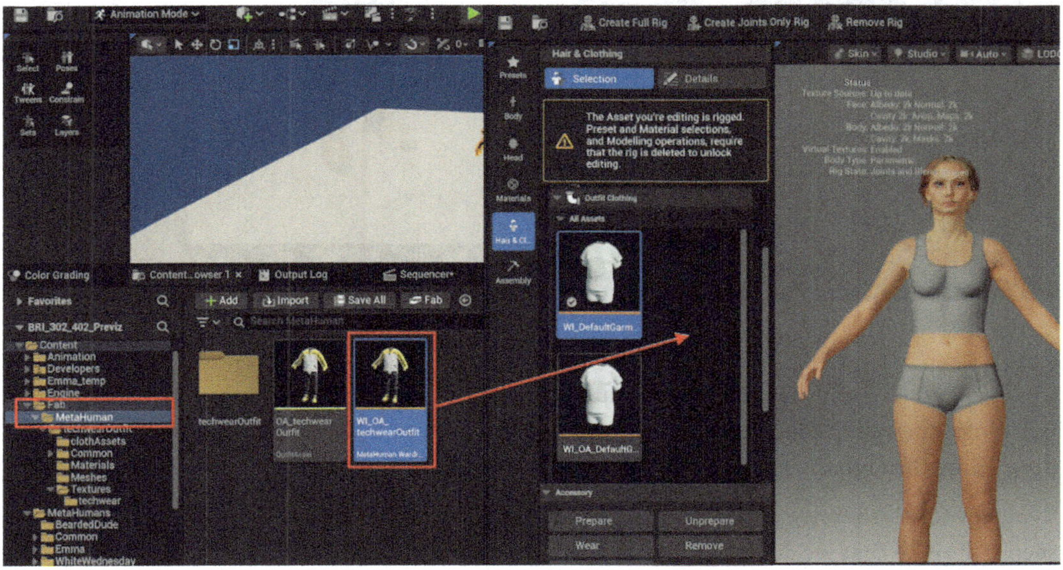

Figure 5.3: Drag and Drop the Wardrobe Asset

Drag and drop the **Wardrobe** item into the **Outfit Clothing** section of the MHC.

You should see a thumbnail of it appearing inside the **Outfit Clothing** section. You can either click on **Wear** or just double-click on the thumbnail to make your MetaHuman wear the techwear suit.

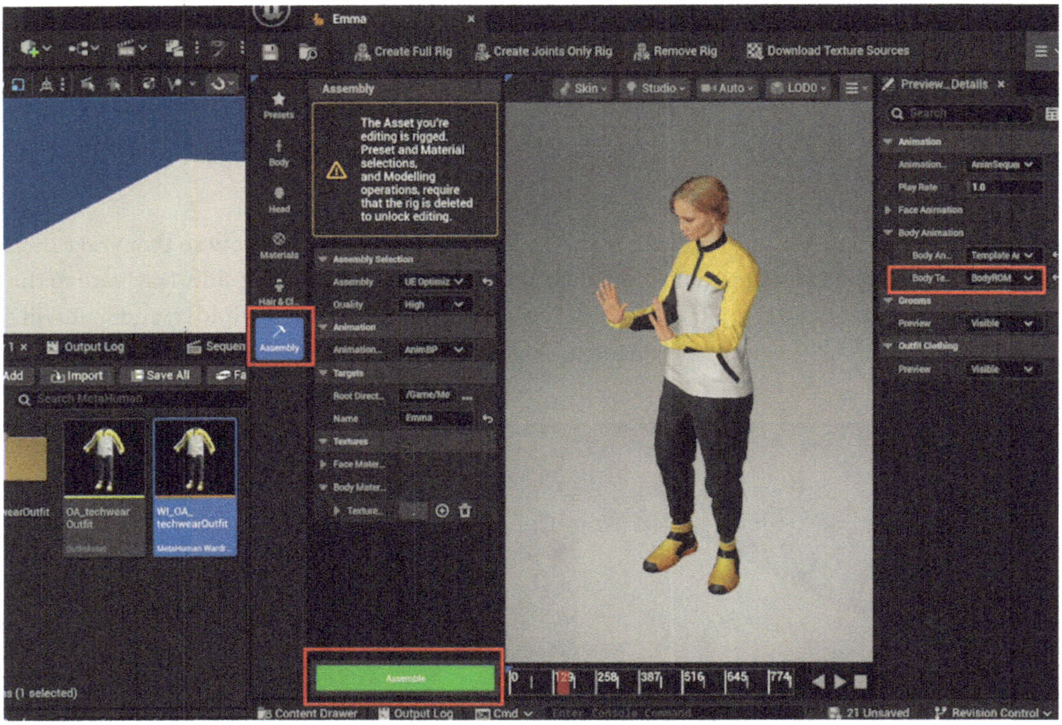

Figure 5.4: Testing animation and reassembling

Don't forget to remove the previous default garment by using the **Remove** button. Not doing so will almost certainly cause issues during animation, such as the shorts of the default garment protruding through the pants of the techwear garment.

Typically for clothes, we don't want anything in the character to be there if it is not going to be seen. This is so that we don't have strange things happening, like clothes sticking through other clothes, but there are also the performance ramifications of processing more geometry than we need.

In *Figure 5.4*, I've tested the animation. Because I'm in the **Assembly** mode, I can assemble or reassemble my MetaHuman, overwriting the original.

Because the wardrobe asset is parametric, you can test various garments long before you've finalized your character design.

While you are still in MHC, I recommend that you remove the rig and test out various body sizes using the **Model** function to see how the wardrobe asset responds to resizing. When you're happy with it, hit **Assemble**. You've now created your character Blueprint with clothing acquired from Fab.

Next, we're going to create a mesh asset based on our MetaHuman that another application can use in order to create our clothing.

Preparing your MetaHuman for third-party software

That heading might sound like this section is going to be complicated, but it's not. Inside the MHC, there's an option that allows us to export a body and head mesh with the underlying skeleton intact. This means that any 3D software can open up your MetaHuman, albeit a bald one. So, if you're a Maya, Houdini, Max, or Blender user, you can work with the highly detailed and very high-functioning MetaHuman in your favorite 3D app.

FBX workflow

For the purpose of this chapter, we're going to focus on exporting an FBX version of our MetaHuman from Unreal Engine into Marvelous Designer, fitting it with a garment, and then bringing that garment back into Unreal Engine to automatically place it on our MetaHuman Character Blueprint.

Although recent versions of Marvelous Designer also support direct DNA import, the FBX workflow remains widely supported, software agnostic, and useful when moving characters between multiple DCC applications such as Maya, Blender, Houdini, and Unreal Engine.

First, we need to jump back into Unreal Engine and open the MetaHuman Creator we used earlier. Alternatively, you can start from scratch as long as you're happy with your design.

Once you're back in MHC, you should see something like *Figure 5.5*:

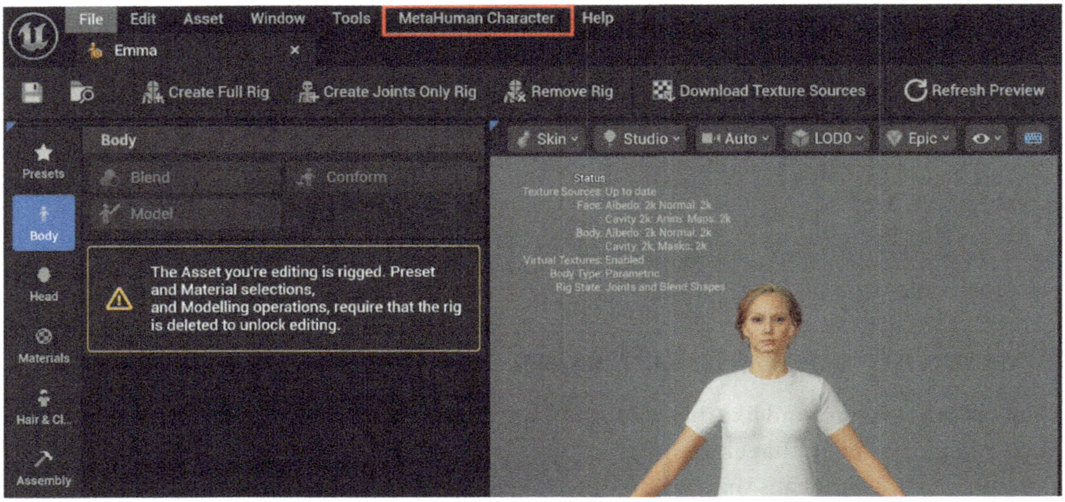

Figure 5.5: MetaHuman character export

We want to prepare a *combined* mesh of the body and the head from the MHC.

A combined mesh is necessary as we need the head because **Marvelous Designer** will expect a head for running cloth simulations and for the initial fit of clothing. If you try to export just the body, **Marvelous Designer** will assume the topmost part of the mesh is the head.

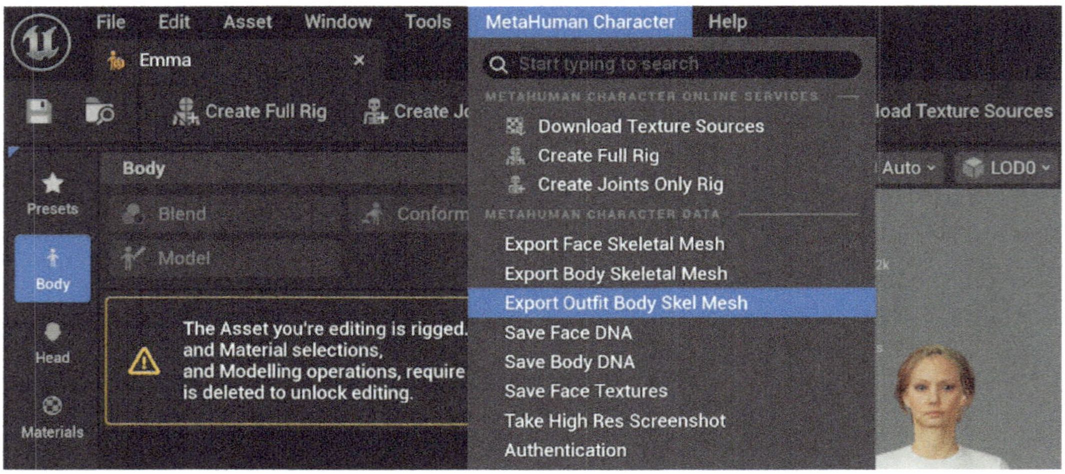

Figure 5.6: The Export Outfit Body Skel Mesh option

By choosing **Export Outfit Body Skel Mesh**, you can create a skeleton mesh asset inside your project folder. Be sure to remember where you save this skeleton mesh because you will need it in a moment. By default, the default suffix `CombinedSkelMesh` will be assigned:

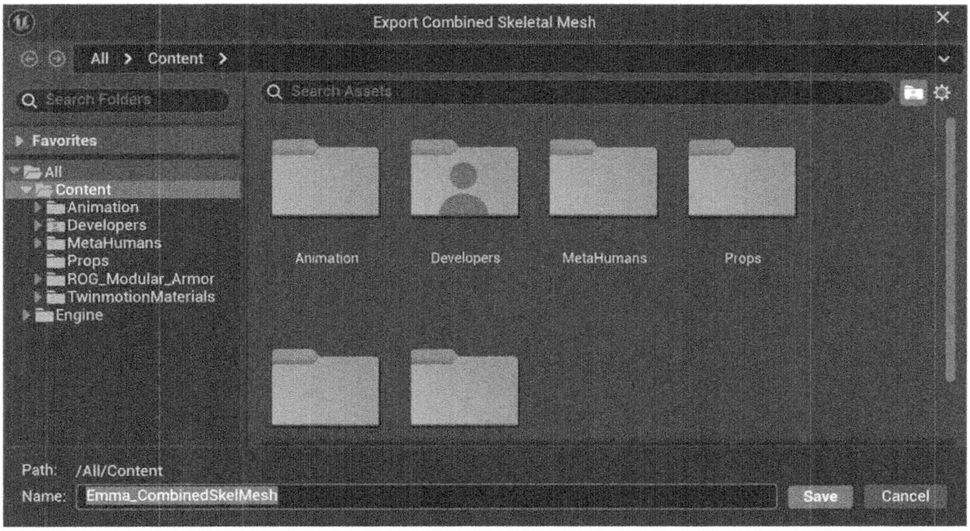

Figure 5.7: Saving the Combined Skeleton Mesh

Once saved, locate the combined skeleton mesh and *right-click* on it.

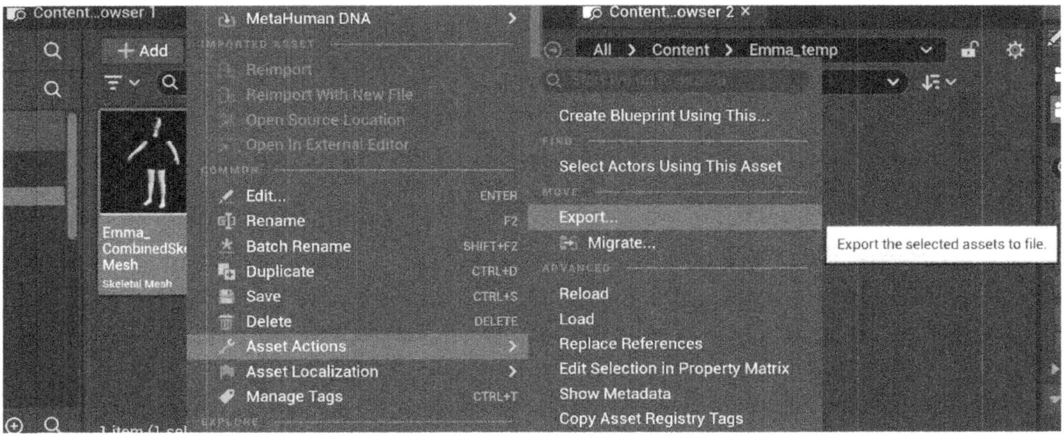

Figure 5.8: Exporting the Mesh for third-party software use

You need to export the skeleton mesh that is currently an Unreal Engine asset into something other applications can read. While there are a few options, FBX is the one we will use. It's also the most widely used format for Unreal Engine and third-party workflows. So, follow *Figure 5.8* by choosing **Asset Actions** and choose **Export...** from the dropdown:

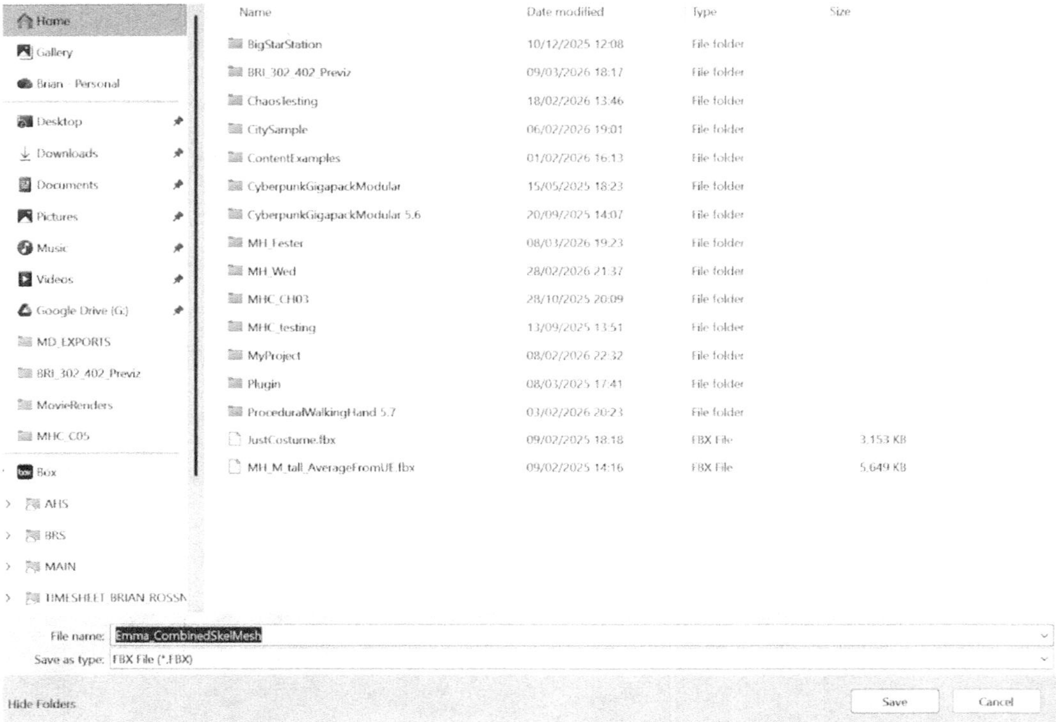

Figure 5.9: Finding a location outside your project folder to save the FBX

Be sure to take note of where you save your FBX file, as you're going to import it into **Marvelous Designer** in a moment.

FBX is the most widely used format in the 3D character animation world and, as a result, has a lot of functionality. When we export a combined skeleton mesh, we need to make sure it doesn't have **LOD (level of detail)** because if it does, many different meshes of varying complexity will be exported, which will prohibit **Marvelous Designer** from doing its job. So, make sure that the **Level of Detail** option is disabled, as seen in *Figure 5.10*.

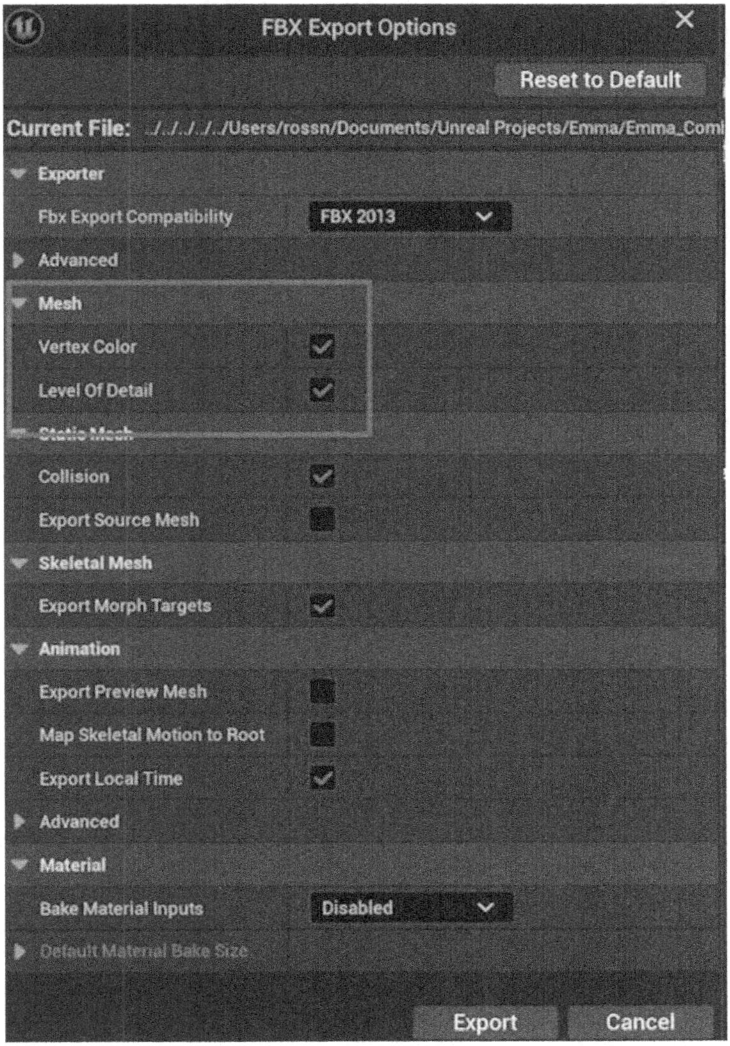

Figure 5.10: Disabling LOD

You can keep the rest of the default settings for this FBX export other than disabling LOD. Hit **Export** and take note of where you are exporting the file to.

In the next section, we will open up **Marvelous Designer**. If you haven't already downloaded **Marvelous Designer**, do it now: set up a **Clo** account, sign in, and hit **Download**, as seen in *Figure 5.11*:

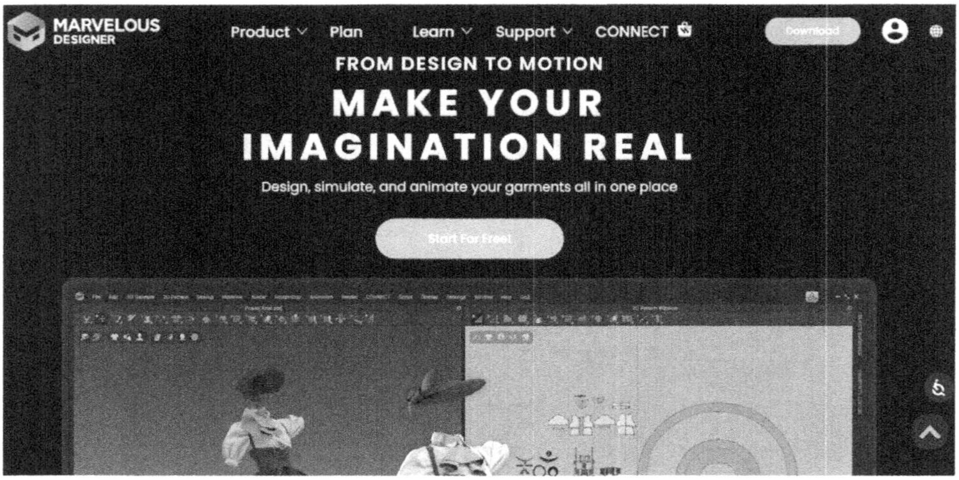

Figure 5.11: Marvelous Designer

Using Marvelous Designer

Marvelous Designer is a very powerful and relatively easy application to use. I've chosen it for two reasons in this book: first, it removes the need to manually model garments using Unreal Engine modeling tools, and second, it largely removes the need to think about skin weight painting. If you don't have access to Marvelous Designer, Blender provides capable cloth simulation tools and can achieve similar results, although the workflow is considerably more manual and requires additional setup. At this point, you'll have installed **Marvelous Designer** and will have made note of where you exported your FBX file of the combined skeleton mesh. Import the FBX file as seen in *Figure 5.12* using the **File** | **Import** | **FBX**.

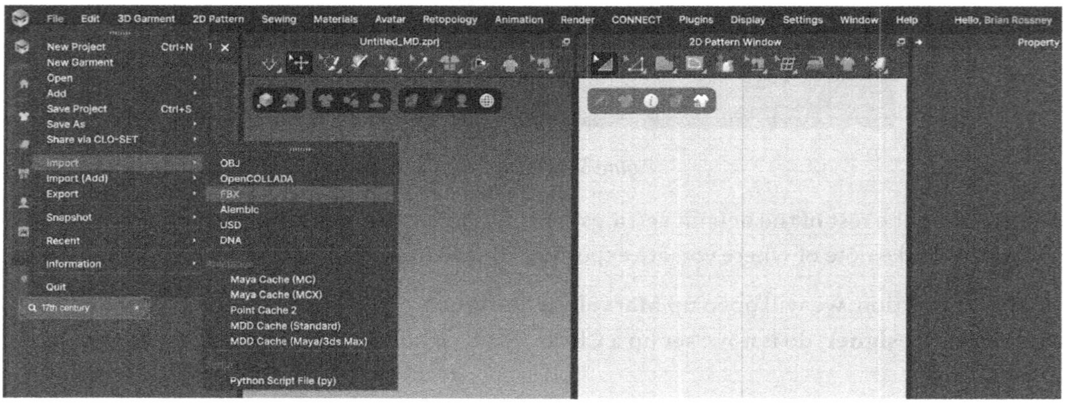

Figure 5.12: Importing the FBX combined mesh into MD

As soon as you select your FBX file to import, you'll be greeted with an **Import FBX** dialog box, as shown in *Figure 5.13*.

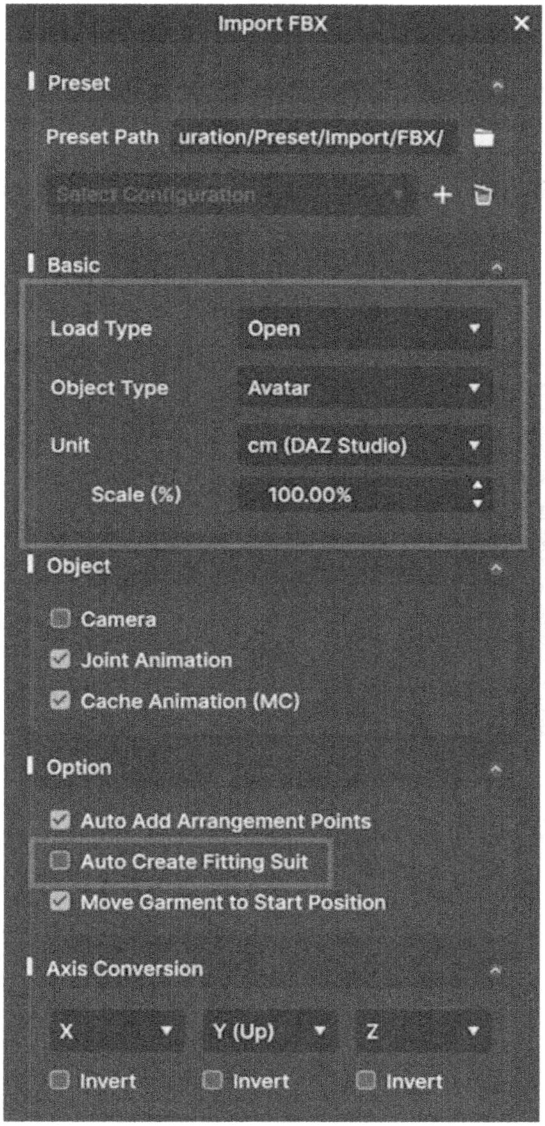

Figure 5.13: Import FBX settings

Our goal here is to bring in the combined body and mesh from earlier and use it as an avatar or dummy figure for garment fitting. Because we have an empty project, it is okay to use Open as the Load Type. We also want Marvelous Designer to recognize this mesh as an avatar, so choose Avatar as the Object Type. The cm (Daz Studio) unit preset corresponds closely to MetaHuman proportions, while the other presets can introduce scaling issues. As highlighted in red in *Figure 5.13*, we also disable Auto Create Fitting Suit. This FBX workflow uses a manually created fitting suit to establish reliable body regions for garment fitting and simulation. Readers using the newer DNA import workflow may find this step is generated automatically. Hit OK once you've made these changes.

You'll see your combined skeleton come in as a black character. What we want to do now is edit the avatar so that it has a fitting suit. Go to **Avatar | Avatar Editor**.

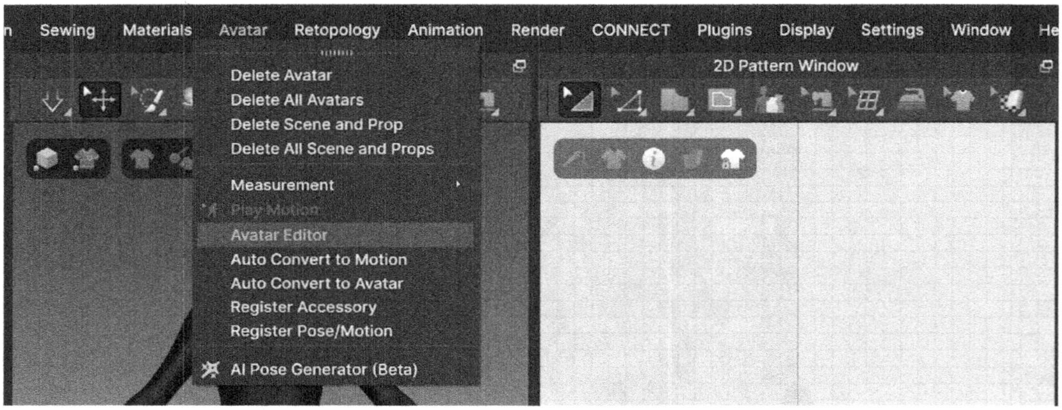

Figure 5.14: Avatar Editor

In the **Avatar Editor**, go over to the **Fitting Suit** tab and on the left-hand side viewport, you'll see a diagram outlining various sections for us to draw onto our avatar.

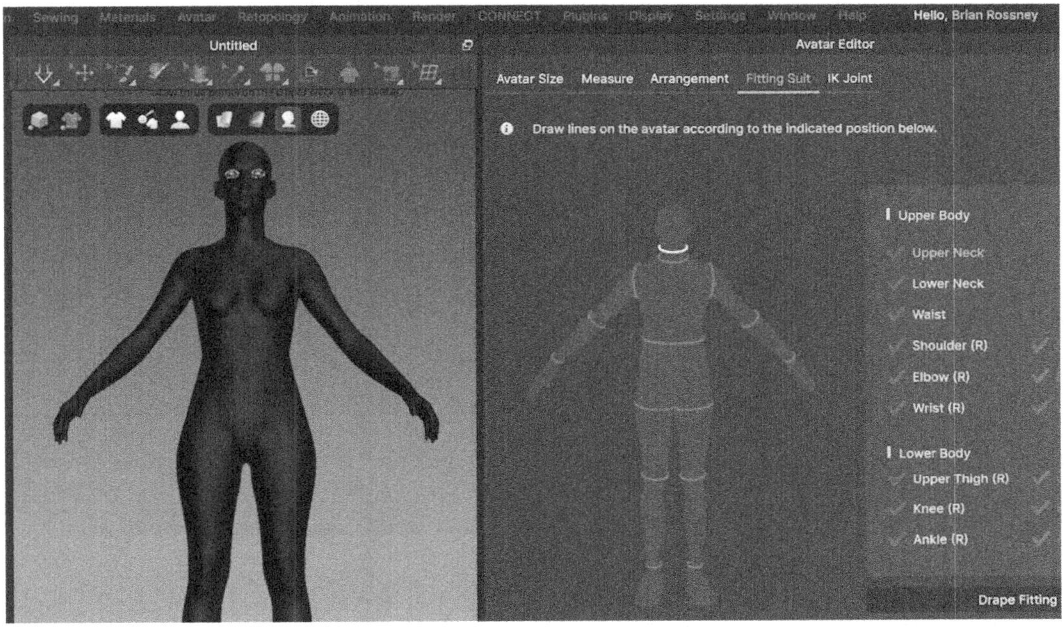

Figure 5.15: Fitting Suit tab

This gives us a **Pen** tool to draw. I recommend zooming and orbiting around various body parts, viewing from different angles other than just straight on.

You need to draw the key sections of the body as illustrated in *Figure 5.6*. You also need to draw them in order, starting with a line around the upper neck, tight under the jawbone. Effectively, you are creating a 3-point spline, and it will automatically give you an elliptical closed curve.

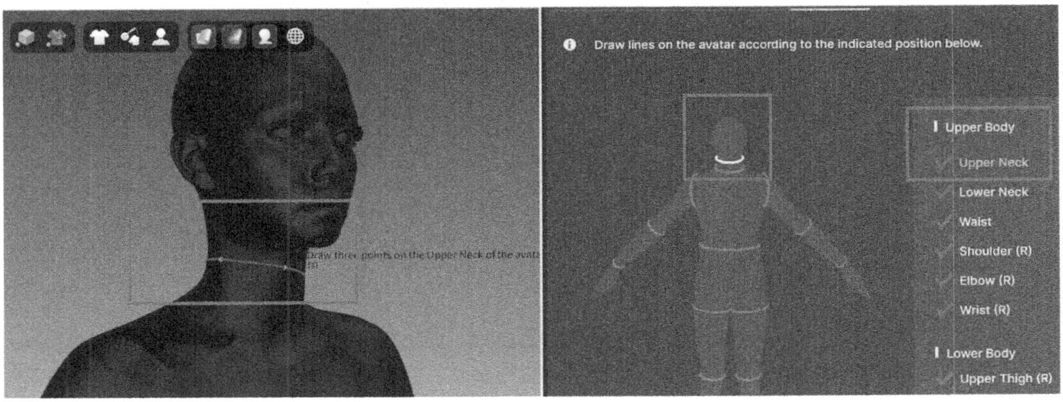

Figure 5.16: Avatar Editor drawing lines

I recommend drawing from the inside to outside. For example, from the inner thigh to the outer leg, from under the arm to the shoulder.

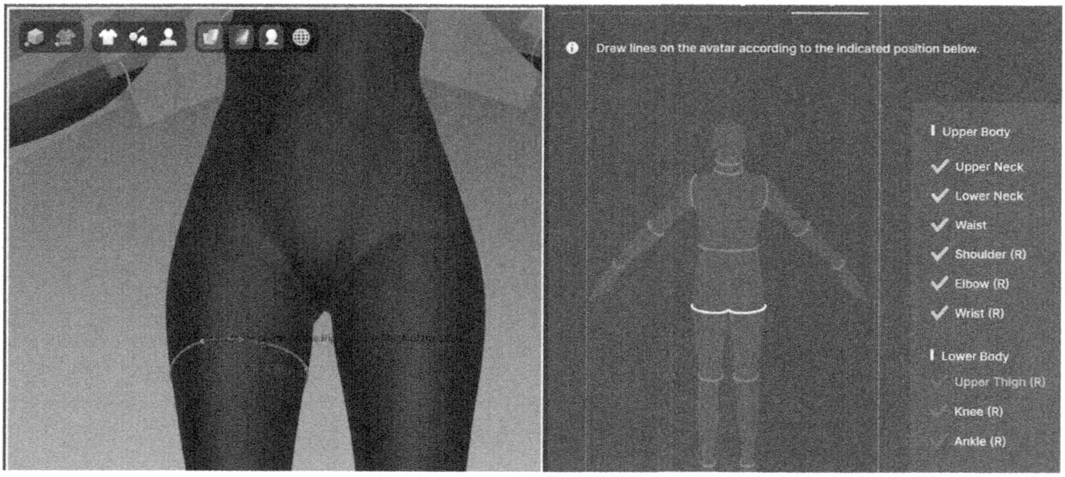

Figure 5.17: Plotting lines from inside to outside

As you get through each body part, the checklist will automatically update. Once you are happy with the placement, click on the **Drape Fitting Suit**, as highlighted in *Figure 5.18*:

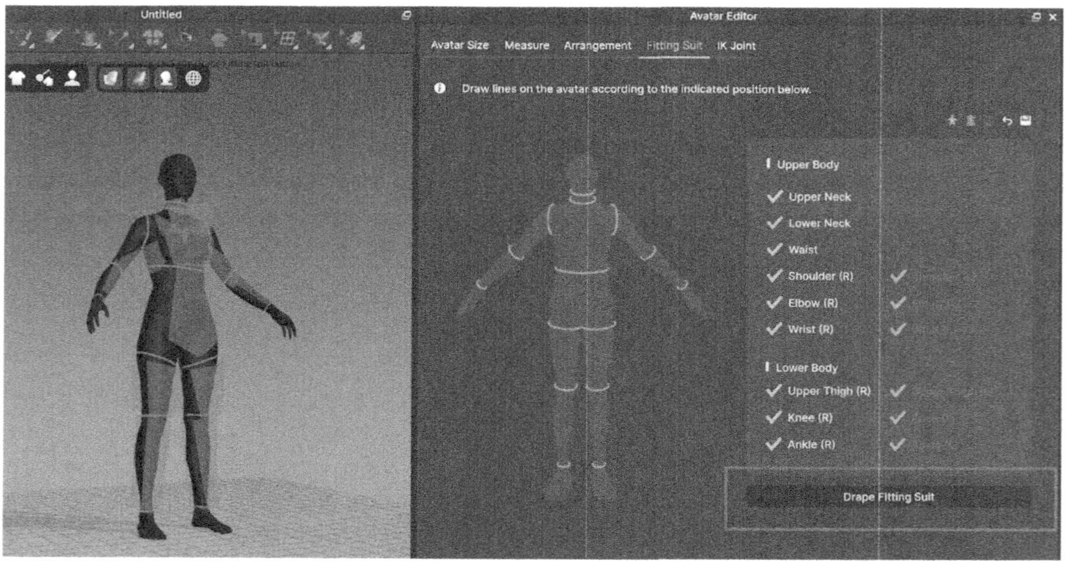

Figure 5.18: The Drape Fitting Suit option

You can check and even tweak the placement of the fitting suit as seen in *Figure 5.19*. For the most part, the placement of your splines as you go through the checklist will do most of the work and in most cases will get a perfectly good fitting suit every time.

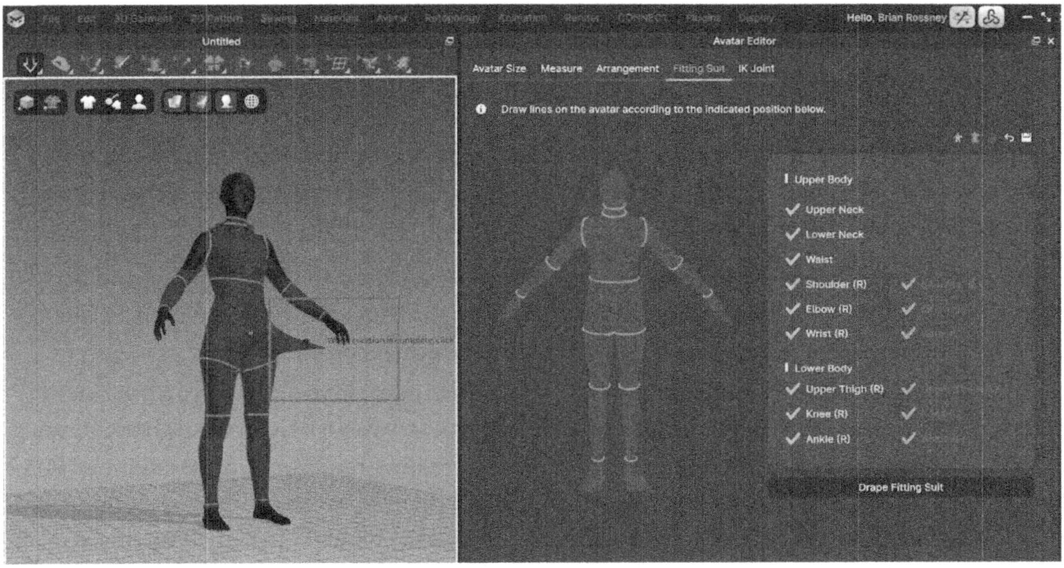

Figure 5.19: Making slight adjustments to the fitting suit

However, manually tugging in the suit can help a little, particularly around the wrists and removing any baggy areas such as around the crotch or lower back. If you look at the spline creation as doing the bulk of the work, then you can finesse it manually before committing it to be the new avatar for clothing.

As soon as you're happy with smoothing out all the crinkles, use the **Save** icon on the far right of the **Avatar Editor** dialog box. Save out your new avatar, making note of where it is going, as you're going to bring it back next.

Now, create a new **Marvelous Designer** project and this time, import an avatar by using **File | Open**. We are going to open your new avatar as a project.

Choose your avatar, assuming you've remembered where you saved it. Now you have a new project with your new avatar, ready to be fitted.

It is good practice in production to save the avatar if your character is going to have multiple costumes. **Marvelous Designer** has hundreds of garments that you can apply to your avatar that will fit perfectly and simulate like real cloth. This means that it will produce realistic cloth creases and respond to gravity. So loose baggy clothes will weigh down on the avatar. For the most part and particularly for most garments such as tight-fitting jackets, we can use **Marvelous Designer** to work out the initial fitting and the initial physics simulation. Then, we can export the avatar into Unreal Engine and use it with no additional cloth and physics simulation, and it will still hold up to scrutiny. However, there might be requirements for continual cloth physics such as a skirt or flowing dress, in which case, we have a choice from two of the following workflows.

1. **Minimal to no cloth simulations**: Import the garment into Unreal Engine and add **Chaos Cloth Physics** to the desired area of the garment, allowing Unreal to do the cloth physics. For games and animation, this is a reasonable approach.
2. **Baking out cloth simulation in Marvelous Designer**: Alternatively, you can run the cloth physics in **Marvelous Designer** which has very robust and realistic cloth physics. This would require you to export your character animation from Unreal engine as FBX or Alembic sequences, run the cloth physic and then export the animated clothing with the physics animation and add it over the animated character in Unreal Engine. As you can imagine, this can get messy as tweaking the character animation after a cloth simulation would require redoing the cloth simulation ever time.

For the purpose of spending most of our time in Unreal Engine, we will stick to workflow 1 and just use **Marvelous Designer** for the initial fit-out and initial simulation.

This brings us to the next step of finding a garment, fitting it, and running a quick simulation in just a few clicks.

Initial garment fitting

With your new avatar open, go to the **Marvelous Designer Library**. If you don't see it, press the *Y* key. It will appear on the left-hand side, and you'll see a search function.

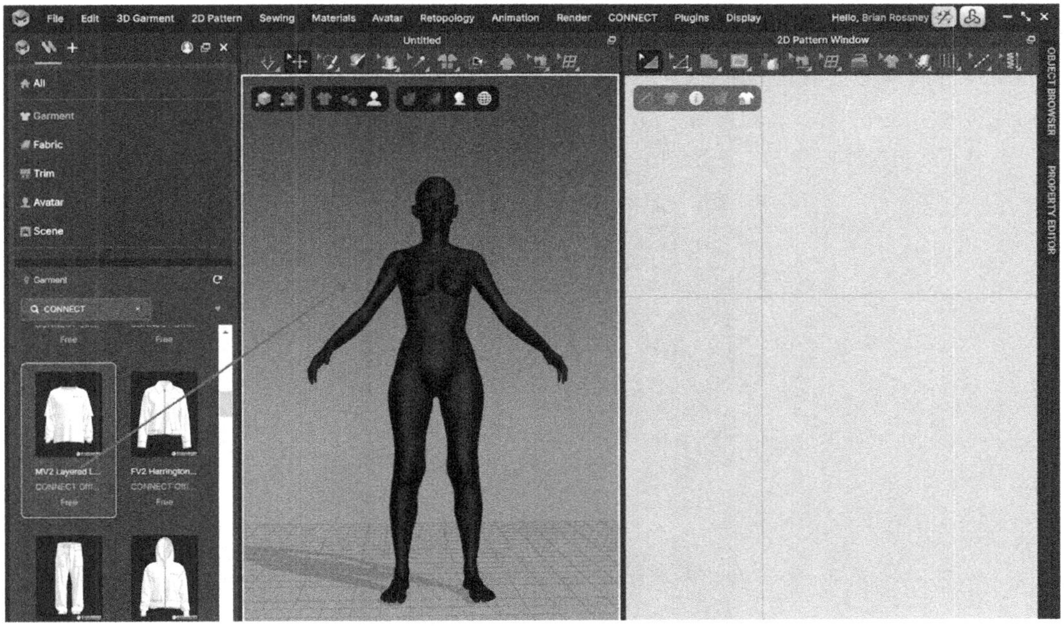

Figure 5.20: Searching for garments in the library

In my case, I'm going for a long sleeve top to dress my character with. In *Figure 5.20*, you may notice the white garment thumbnails. The one I have chosen has `CONNECT` in its title. **Connect** is part of the **Marvelous Designer** and **Clo Library**; Clo is a similar software application to **Marvelous Designer** but aimed more at the fashion industry, unlike **Marvelous Designer** which is aimed at animation and game projects.

The red arrow in *Figure 5.20* indicates the simple drag and drop of the garment onto the avatar, but a pop-up box will appear, as shown in *Figure 5.21*:

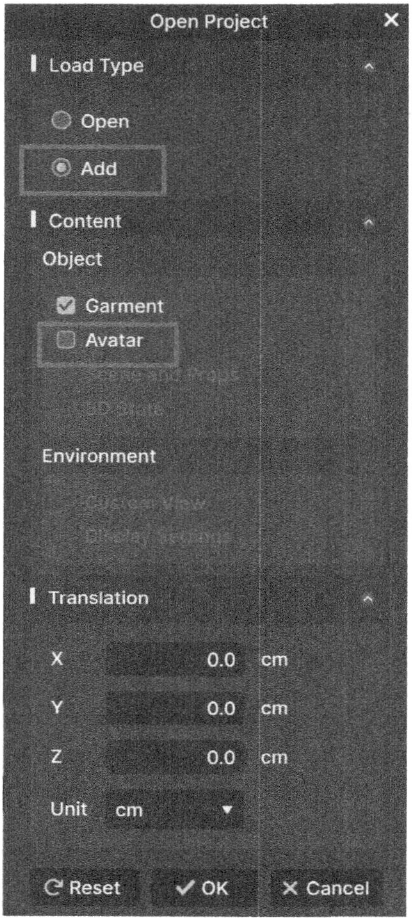

Figure 5.21: Unticking Avatar

The garment in question is a **Marvelous Designer** project in the cloud. We don't want to replace the project that has our brand-new avatar. Instead, we want to add it to our existing project. In addition, we are happy with our MetaHuman-based avatar, so we want to make sure we choose **Garment** as our object type. Click **OK** when you've made the same selections as per *Figure 5.21*.

As soon as you've done that, you'll see your garment haphazardly placed on our avatar or not even placed at all. That's normal. It's because we haven't fitted it yet. What we need to do is select all by using *Ctrl+A* or the **Select All** function in either the **3D Viewport** on the left or **Pattern Viewport** on the right.

Note the garment gaining a yellow outline. That means it's selected.

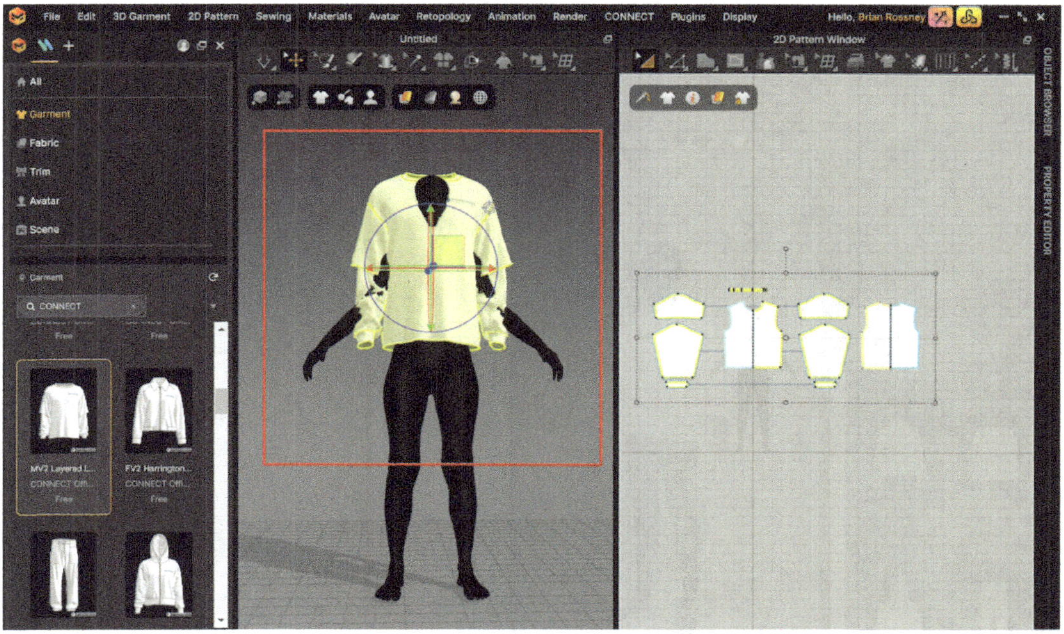

Figure 5.22: Assigned but unfitted garment

In the **Pattern Viewport** on the right, click on the **auto fitting** icon and select **OK**. See *Figure 5. 23*. The default parameters are fine, so we don't need to edit anything here.

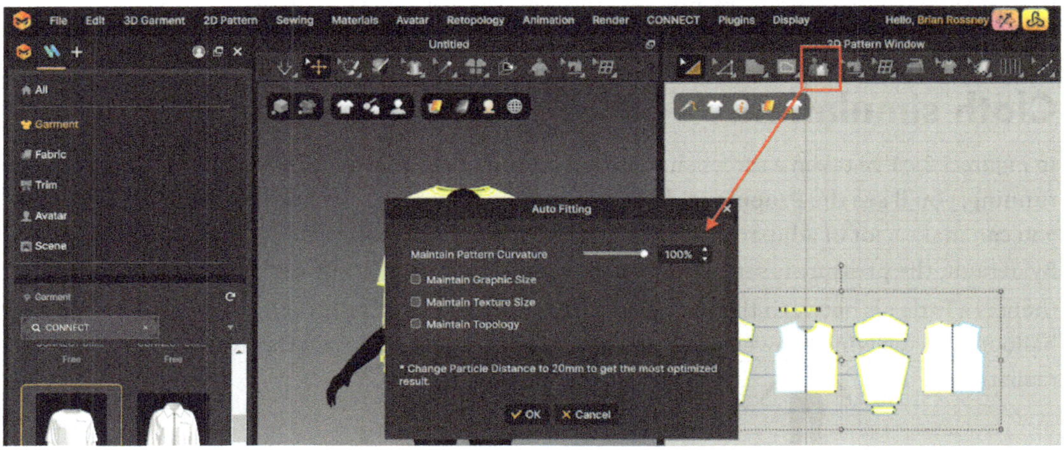

Figure 5.23: Auto fitting

Et voila! We have a perfect fitting garment. But it's a little starchy looking as though it is made of cardboard.

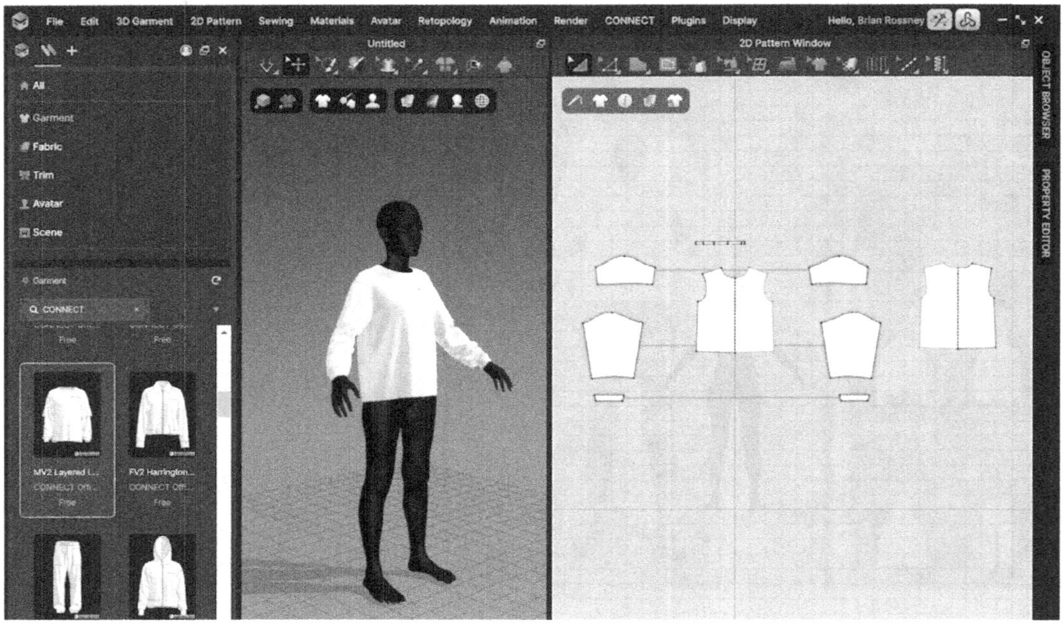

Figure 5.24: Initial fitting

The starchy look is exactly what you should expect from the initial fitting. The next step is running a simulation simply by pressing the *spacebar*. You can start and stop the simulation at any time and tug at the garment during a simulation to examine the feel of the cloth.

Cloth simulation

In *Figure 5.25*, I've taken a screenshot of my screen during a simulation. When the simulation is running, you'll see the **Property Editor** window appear on the right side of the screen. Here, you can make a lot of adjustments. I've highlighted pressure as it will get your results quickly. By default, the pressure is set to 1. It's a little high for default as it gives the impression that there is a little air between the garment and the avatar. Ramping it up further will give you a balloon effect. Giving a lower value will make it wrap tighter around the avatar more realistically.

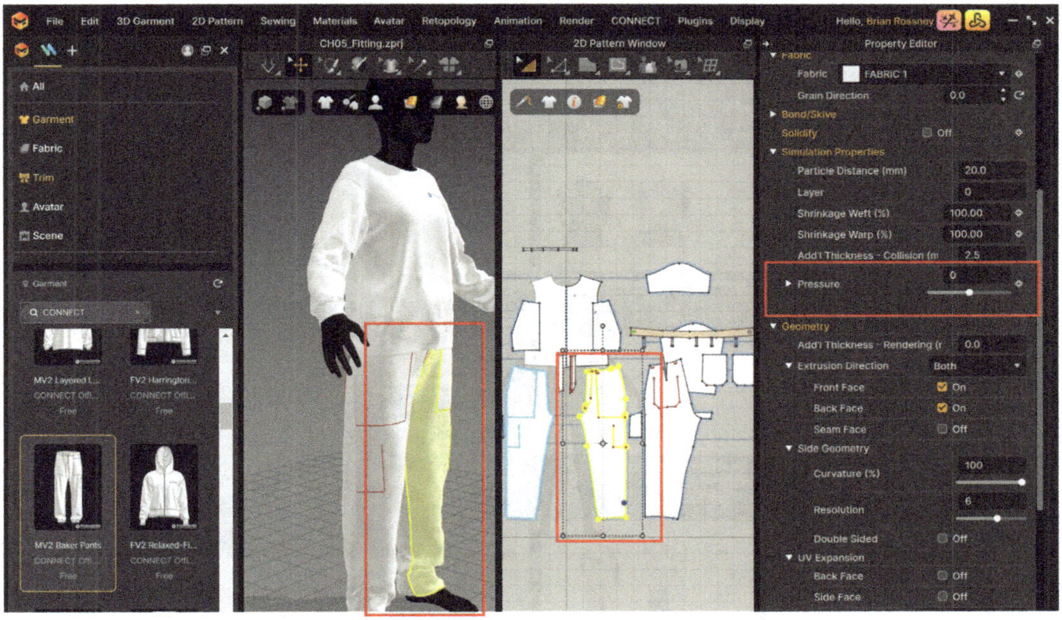

Figure 5.25: Running a simulation

I've reduced the pressure down to `0`. As you can see in *Figure 5.25*, the garment is sticking to the avatar a little more. I encourage you to play around with the settings.

Because we came here for a quick fitting and a basic simulation, it's time to import into Unreal.

If you're already familiar with importing FBX as garments, you can go to **File** | **Export FBX** and export the garment.

To make use of a more efficient workflow, we'll install the CLO Live Sync plugin, which allows us to transfer the selected garment directly from an open Marvelous Designer session into Unreal Engine. It provides a faster iterative workflow than repeatedly exporting FBX files.

Recent versions of Marvelous Designer also support USD-based workflows. However, Live Sync remains a practical and efficient option when rapidly testing garment changes during production.

To install this free plugin, open the Epic Games Launcher, go to the Fab tab, and search for `CLO`:

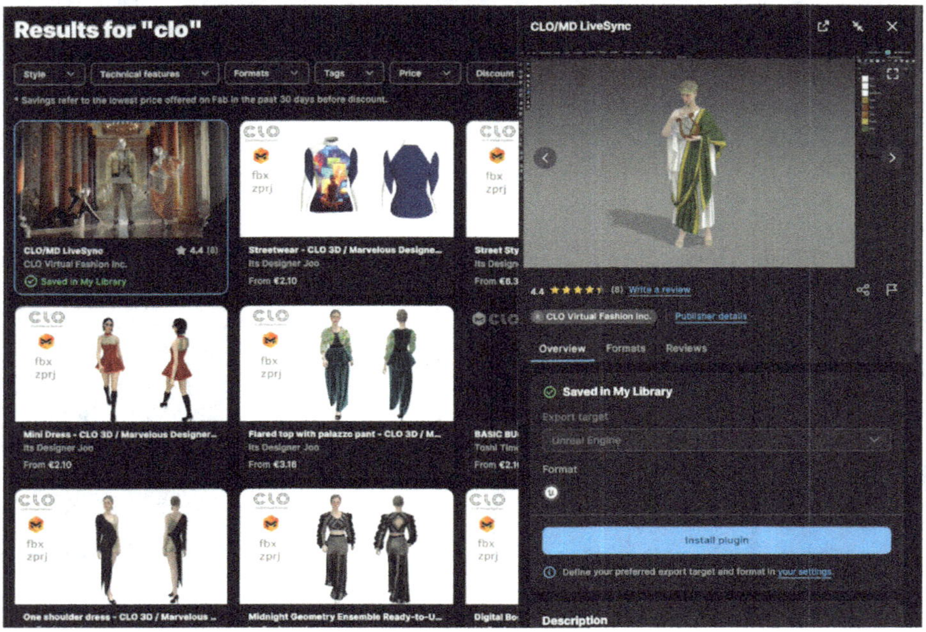

Figure 5.26: Installing the Clo/MD Live Sync plugin

Once installed, your copy of Unreal Engine will have a new section in the drop-down menu of Unreal's main toolbar.

Note that you will likely need a restart of the engine for this to become available. Once it's available, select it.

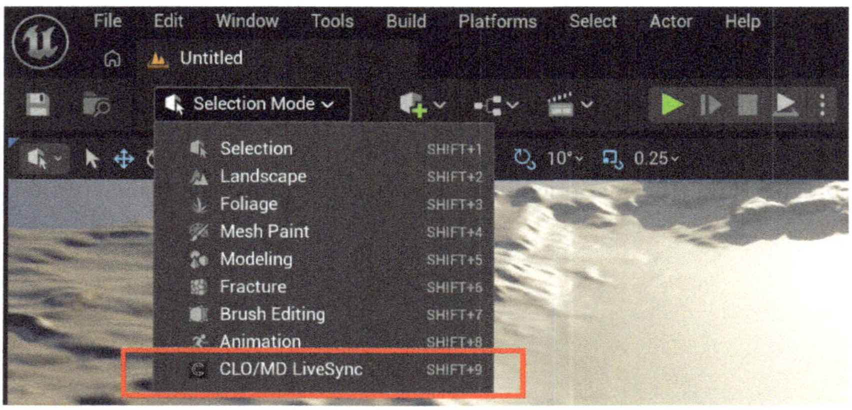

Figure 5.27: CLO MD LiveSync plugin

As soon as you select it, you will likely get the following message:

Please install the **Substance 3D for Unreal Engine** plugin to use **Substance** materials applied to CLO garments; otherwise, default materials will be applied to garments.

As we're not using any substance materials, we can ignore this and hit **OK**.

As soon as you select **OK**, you should see the following **CLO/Marvelous Designer** tool appear:

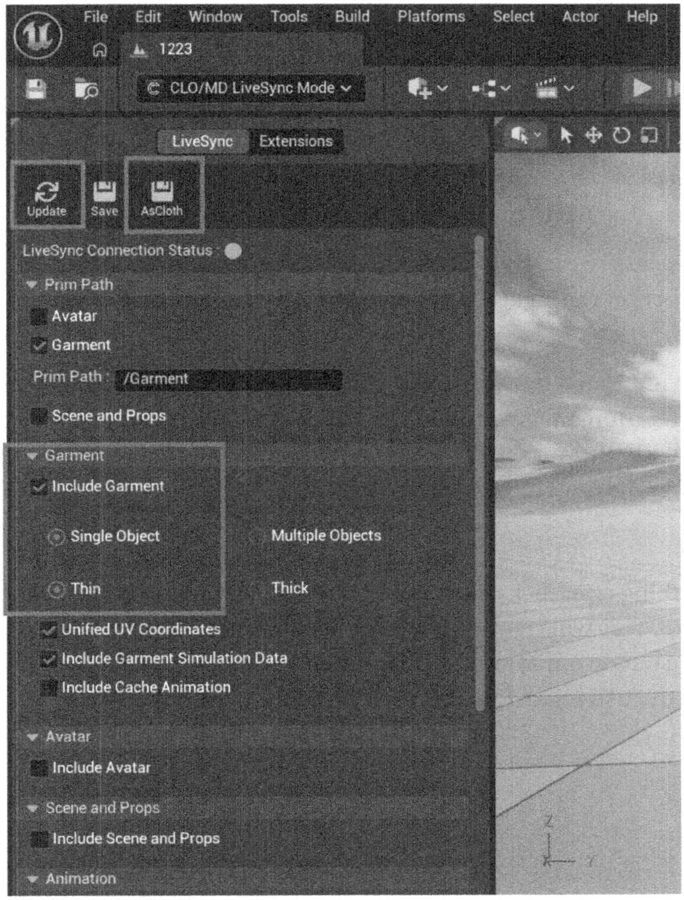

Figure 5.28: CLO MD LiveSync plugin settings

Now, let's pause for a moment. We're about to try to use this tool to pull in a garment. We can do this by using the **Update** button I highlighted in *Figure 5.28*. This will update Unreal by automatically pulling in the selected garment or garments in **Marvelous Designer**, provided it is still open.

However, we need to make sure we have our character Blueprint assembled, which you should have done earlier in this chapter. Before proceeding to the next section, locate your MetaHuman Blueprint, which should be in the `MetaHumans` folder inside the `Content` folder. Once located, drag and drop anywhere in your scene and ensure the Blueprint is selected.

Now it's time to go back to the **CLO MD LiveSync** plugin and change one setting before we update Unreal with the garment. We want the garment to come in as one mesh rather than a mesh for every piece of the garment, which would be messy. So, select **Single Object and Thin,** located under the **Garment** heading as shown in *Figure 5.28*.

We choose *thin* because we only want a single mesh for the surface rather than a mesh for the outside and another for the inside. But don't worry, we can use materials to make it look two-sided.

As soon as you've replicated those settings, click on **Update**. You should see the garments appear on your MetaHuman. If you had the techwear clothing on your character, they should now be replaced with the **Marvelous Designer** clothing. You should also see a new folder called `UsdAssets` in the browser. We'll come to that shortly.

Cloth asset

Before doing anything else, click the **As Cloth** button, which is highlighted in red at the top right of *Figure 5.28*. This will create a **Cloth Asset** to help us get the same functionality of the techwear clothing but on our **Marvelous Designer** garment. By default, that cloth asset should be created inside the UsdAssets folder.

Figure 5.29: C.O.W

Yes, that is a picture of a cow, or should I say **C.O.W.** When creating parametric clothing like the techwear example, it is helpful to know the order of the things we need to create and understand their relationship with each other.

COW is an abbreviation of the following assets: **Cloth**, **Outfit**, and **Wardrobe**.

We first need a **Cloth Asset**, then an **Outfit Asset** that will contain the **Cloth** asset and finally a **Wardrobe Asset** that will contain the **Outfit Asset**. This dependency chain is crucial and hopefully, I'll win the argument with my editor to keep the cow picture in the book...we'll see.

As you'll remember, we just used the **As Cloth** button, which was the first step of C.O.W.

Outfit asset

Next up we need an **Outfit** asset. So, next to your newly created **Cloth Asset**, which should have appeared in the `UsdAssets` folder, *right-click*, type **Outfit Asset**, and click on it to open it.

A pop-up window will appear. Choose **Resizeable Outfit**.

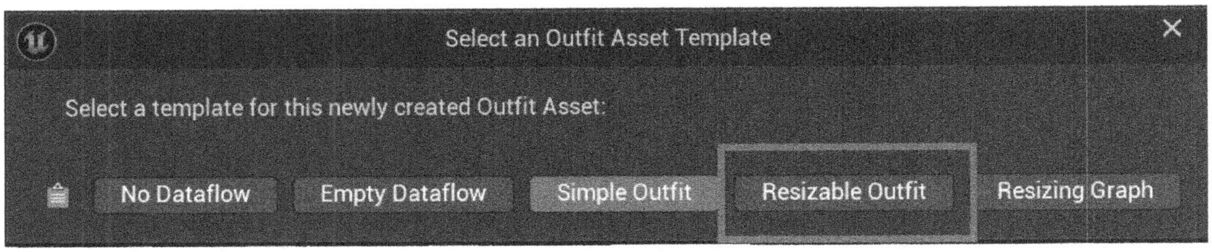

Figure 5.30: Outfit asset template

Inside the **Outfit Asset**, first, we need to tick **Sized Outfit Source**. Doing this will allow us to choose the **Cloth Asset** that we just created. Then we need to choose which skeleton we want to fit onto. In our case, this will be the combined skeleton mesh, the same one we used in **Marvelous Designer** to create our Avatar.

Figure 5.31: Editing outfit asset

Save the Outfit Asset and close it.

Wardrobe assets

Next, we need to create the **Wardrobe Asset** (the *W* of *C.O.W.*).

Again, inside the `UsdAssets` folder, *right-click*, type `Wardrobe Asset`, and *double-click* to open it.

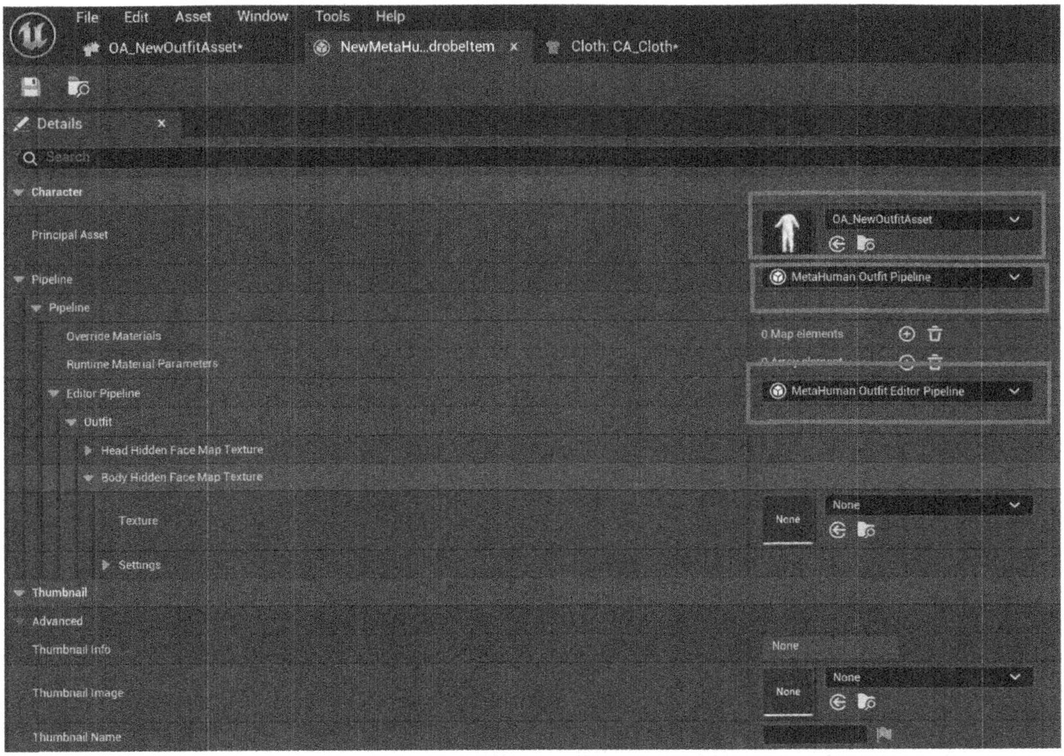

Figure 5.32: Wardrobe asset

When you open the **Wardrobe Asset**, you'll see straightaway that we need to apply the **Outfit Asset**. Remember C.O.W.

1. Under **Pipeline**, choose **MetaHuman Outfit Pipeline**
2. Under **Editor Pipeline**, choose **MetaHuman Outfit Editor Pipeline**
3. Save and close.

If you don't see the **Outfit Asset** in the drop-down menu, it usually means that something along the dependency chain is broken.

Usually, this issue is within the **Cloth Asset**.

Let's troubleshoot the **Cloth Asset,** that the CLO MD LiveSync plugin created for us. Locate the **Cloth Asset** in the USD folder and *double-click.*

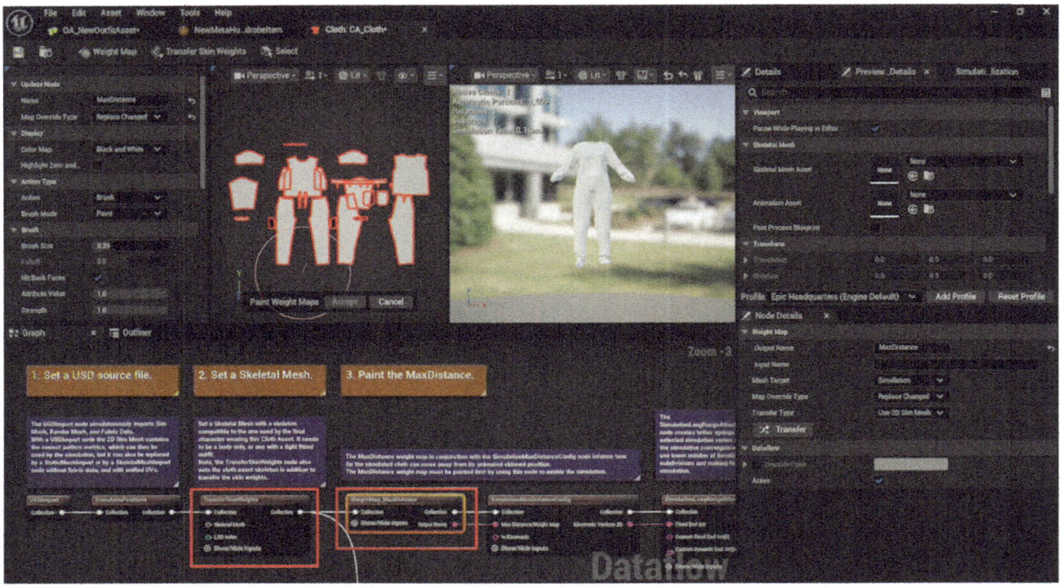

Figure 5.33: Why wardrobe or outfit assets don't work

In *Figure 5.33*, I've highlighted in red the usual reasons why we can't get the wardrobe asset or even the outfit asset working. If you didn't have the character Blueprint selected at the time when you ran an update with the **CLO MD LiveSync** plugin, it would have skipped choosing a skeleton or assigning Max distance painting. In other words, it wouldn't have known which skeleton to choose and what weight painting to apply to it.

By jumping into the **Cloth Asset**, we can do that manually. You can see from *Figure 5.32* that the nodes I've highlighted have descriptions above them. If you click on the first node, the **Details** panel on the top right will update, allowing you to add in the combined skeleton mesh (the one we used for creating the avatar in **Marvelous Designer**). Because it was missing when we used the **As Cloth** function in the **CLO MD LiveSync** plugin, we're going to have to manually paint them.

To begin with, a quick painting across all of the 2D patterns as seen in *Figure 5.32* will do. You might want to come back to it later. In general, you only need to add the cloth simulations to areas of clothing that actually move, such as sleeves, the hems of trousers, and lower parts of shirts or t-shirts. In other words, use it sparingly.

To see cloth simulation results, use the default settings, hit **Accept** in the painting viewport and save and quit from the cloth asset. You may need to go back to the **Outfit Asset** to choose the **Cloth Asset** again just to refresh. Likewise, you may then need to do the same refresh with the Wardrobe Asset.

> Note
>
> A brief observation. As you are progressing through the C.O.W. process, if at any point you don't see thumbnails for the proceeding step, such as not seeing a thumbnail for the **Outfit Asset** when you're editing the **Wardrobe Asset** or not seeing a **Cloth Asset** thumbnail when you are editing the **Outfit Asset**, then something is broken. It is a reliable visual debugging tip.

As soon as you've gone through the C.O.W. process, open up your character Blueprint to make it use the **Cloth Asset**. We're going to add a **Chaos Cloth Component**, which uses the **Cloth Asset**.

> Tip
>
> Unreal Engine automatically assigns assets to a component if you already have that asset selected. This saves you the time of manually searching for something when connecting dependencies.

As soon as you've opened up the character Blueprint, keep it open but select your **Cloth Asset**. Go back to your character Blueprint and create a **Chaos Cloth Component**. You should already see the component with the suffix of your selected `ClothAsset`.

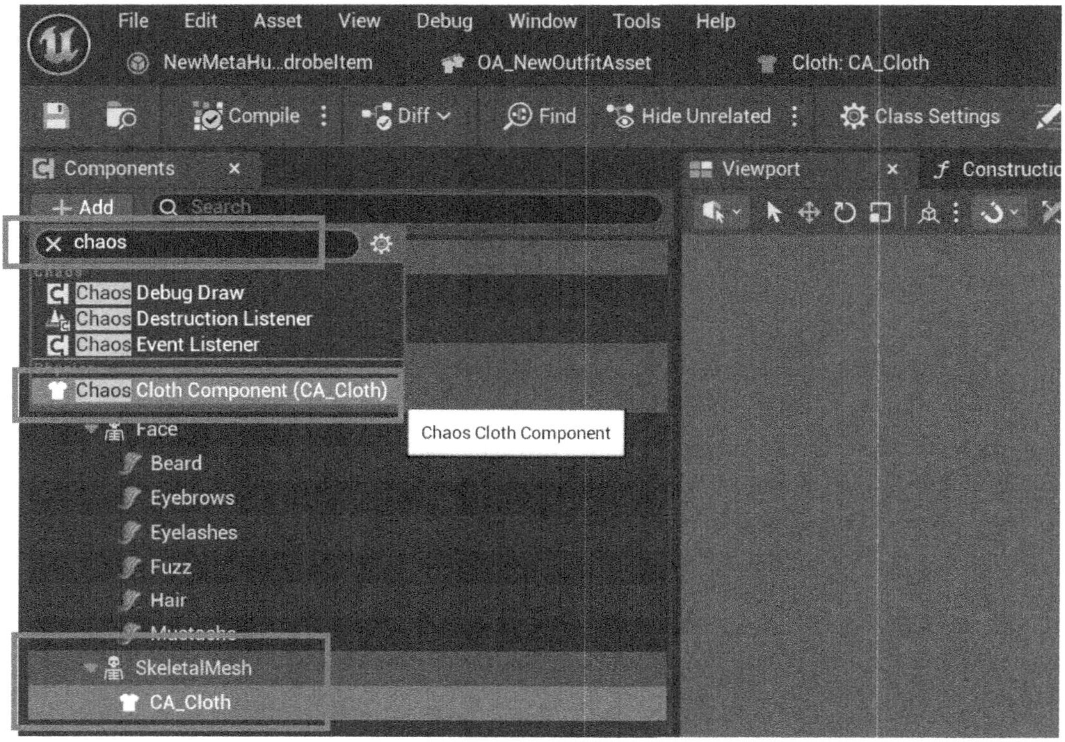

Figure 5.34: Adding a Chaos Cloth Component to the SkeletalMesh

Select the Cloth Asset Component and drag it under the `SkeletonMesh`, which contains your garment. Doing so parents the Cloth Asset to the garment so the **Chaos Cloth Component** can get to work. Incorrect parenting is a common mistake.

Compile the Blueprint and run a simulation by pressing *Alt+P*.

Because you dragged and dropped your Blueprint into the scene, you should see it wearing clothing and simulating cloth physics.

Figure 5.35: End result with lighting only

Note that cloth physics is a very complex concept and requires quite a lot of trial and error. For instance, you may find the cloth simulation to be far too intense and need to be dialed down, or so subtle it appears not to be working.

However, this approach simplifies the process of skin weight painting and cloth simulation, bundling both workflows into one procedure.

As soon as you have all three of the C.O.W. assets working with the cloth simulation being optional, you now have the option of treating this garment as a parametric just like the techwear. So, if you want to edit your character proportions or add the same garment to another character, you can do this in your **MetaHuman Creator** by using the drag and drop function with the **Wardrobe Asset**.

Summary

In this chapter, we covered cloth simulations and parametric clothing, a very practical and professional workflow that is highly efficient in an animation or game production environment.

In the next chapter, we're going to go over some old ground and look at animation retargeting using Mixamo, a free and very well catalogued resource with over 1500 motion capture files to choose from.

6

Retargeting Mixamo Animations

In *Chapter 5*, we completed the design aspect of the character by exploring clothing using a free and parametric clothing asset found on Fab. We also spent a lot of time exploring the industry standard in clothing creation with **Marvelous Designer** and how it integrates with Unreal Engine.

In *Chapter 4*, we briefly used free motion capture files to test our MetaHuman in motion. Now, in this chapter, we are going to go further afield and take animation from a third-party supplier, **Mixamo**, a very large online library full of motion capture files that you can preview on a web browser. You will learn how to use external resources such as Mixamo to give much more variety to your animations; this is important, as repurposing the same animations repeatedly makes for poor productions. We will also remain focused on working with body motion only in this chapter.

Compared to the first edition of this book, retargeting has become significantly streamlined and for the most part, you will already be familiar with the retargeting process from *Chapter 4* so you may feel like skipping the retargeting section.

So, in this chapter, we will cover the following topics:

- Introducing Mixamo
- Exploring animation in Mixamo
- Downloading the Mixamo animation
- Importing the Mixamo animation into Unreal
- Retargeting the Mixamo animation to your character

Technical requirements

To complete this chapter, you will need the technical requirements detailed in *Chapter 1* together with your assembled MetaHuman from *Chapter 3*. Unreal Engine should already be running, and your MetaHuman project should be open.

If you do not have the `CombinedSkelMesh` created in *Chapter 5*, don't worry. The assembled MetaHuman already includes a compatible body skeletal mesh (for example, `SKM_NewMetaHumanCharacter_BodyMesh`) that can also be used for the retargeting workflow in this chapter.

You will also need a stable internet connection, as we will be downloading FBX files directly from Mixamo into our project folder. We will effectively be repeating the retargeting workflow from *Chapter 4*, but this time using motion capture from a third-party source.

Introducing Mixamo

For a lot of artists planning on using MetaHumans in Unreal, Mixamo could easily be all they need in terms of body animation.

Mixamo is an online library containing thousands of motion capture (mocap) animations performed by real actors. Many of these animations include simple adjustment controls that allow you to refine the performance before downloading it.

As you already have experience using an online character creator such as MetaHuman Creator, you will find Mixamo straightforward to use and a very fast way of adding body animation to your MetaHumans.

The first thing you need to do is go over to `www.mixamo.com`. This is where you'll see the landing page for Mixamo as per *Figure 6.1*:

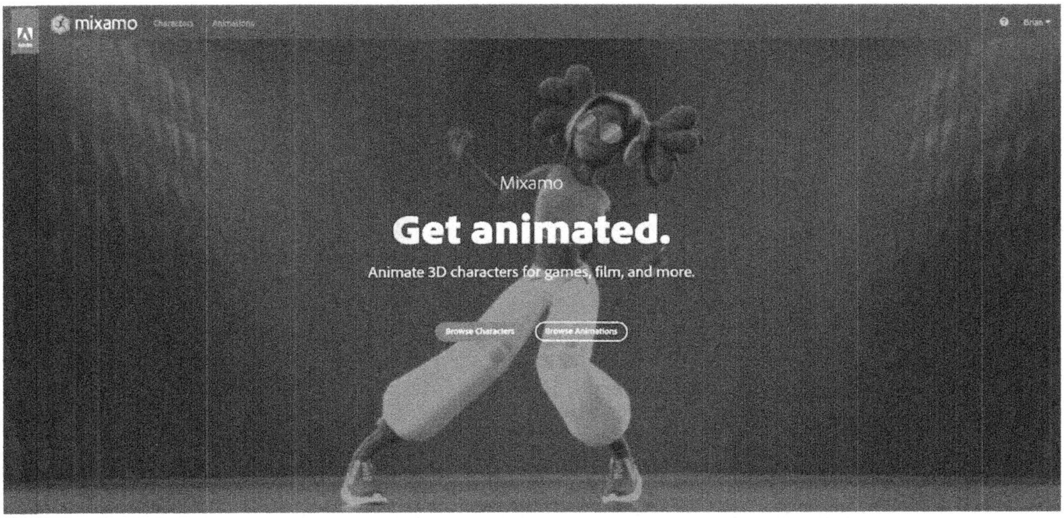

Figure 6.1: Mixamo home page

In the top-left corner, you will see an Adobe logo. Adobe, the maker of Photoshop and After Effects (to name but a few), acquired Mixamo but has kept it running, as it is a tremendous tool for character designers and animators.

You will also notice in the top-right corner that I have already signed in. Before you sign in, you need to create a Mixamo account. If you have an Adobe account, you can use that. If not, using an email and creating a password will suffice.

Once you've logged in, you'll be taken to the main Mixamo interface:

Figure 6.2: Mixamo Interface

In *Figure 6.2*, you'll see that the interface is made of two tabs: **Characters** and **Animations**. These two tabs will display thumbnails of the relative assets and a viewport for you to preview them. In this book, we are only concerned with animations and so you should select **Animations** (however, it is worth noting that regardless of which tab we are in, we can always upload our own characters).

Once the **Animations** tab is selected, we are greeted with an almost identical interface, with the exception that our thumbnails on the left now feature animation assets rather than character assets. In most cases, the thumbnail characters are in the Mixamo Mannequin style.

We've covered the basic interface and what Mixamo has to offer, and in the next section we'll explore Mixamo's extensive animation library and methods we can use to tailor these animations for our own purposes.

Exploring animation in Mixamo

In the Mixamo motion capture library, you'll see that all the animations are separated into different genres, just like in *Figure 6.3*:

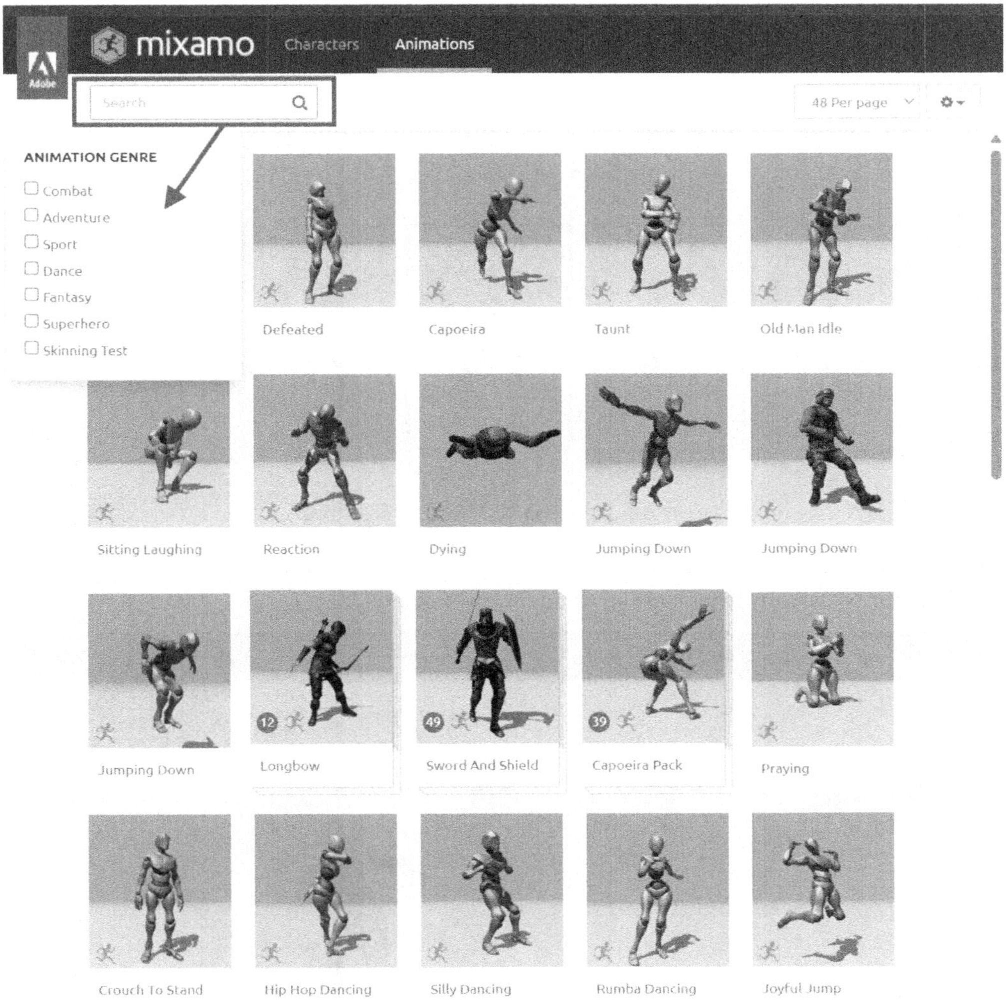

Figure 6.3: Mixamo Animation categories

This list of genres is quite helpful, but there's also a handy search function. Using either option, find the **Thriller Dance** animation (I am using this because it's a long animation and is great for testing how well the rig works with my character). Once you can see the thumbnail of your chosen animation, it just takes one *left-click* on the thumbnail to apply it to your MetaHuman mesh.

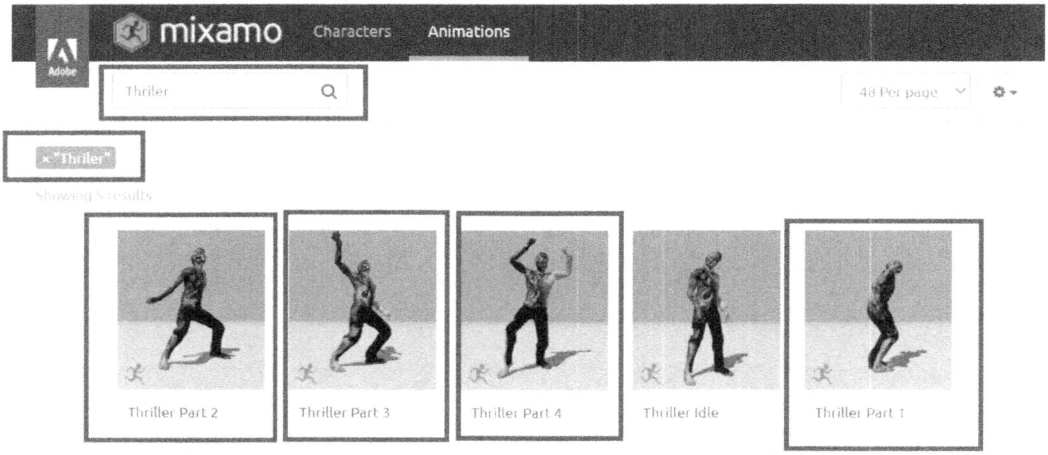

Figure 6.4: Searching for Thriller dance moves

In *Figure 6.4*, I ran a search for Thriller and found the dance in four parts. There's also an idle animation, but we're only interested in the dancing motion.

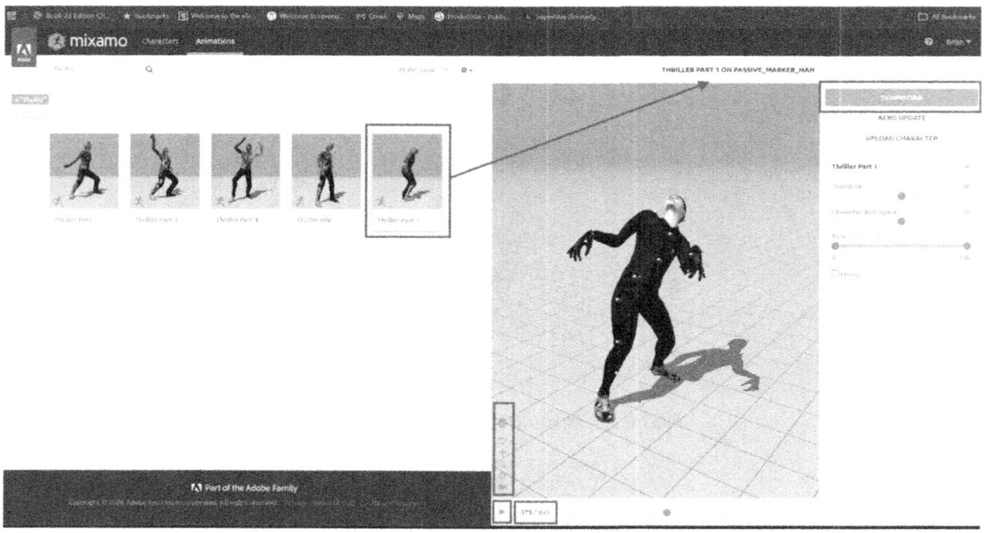

Figure 6.5: Applying Thriller part one to Mixamo Character

Take note of the sliders on the right-hand side, which you can manipulate to your liking. The parameters are not the same from one animation to the next.

Often, each motion capture file will have one or more bespoke parameters depending on the nature of the performance.

The three most useful parameters in all animations that you will find yourself editing are as follows:

- **Character Arm-Space**: This determines the distance between the character's arms and its torso. When reviewing how your mesh performs within the Mixamo viewport, you may see moments where the mesh intersects with itself, such as an arm going through a waist. Of course, you'll need to widen the arm space to accommodate that. For the Macarena dance, the mocap session may have been performed by a lean dancer rather than an overweight Glenda, so this intersection is likely to occur. With that said, there could be instances where the mocap performer and model are similar, but you still need to create a wider arm space to accommodate heavy clothing or armor, so it is worth being mindful of this when making these adjustments.
- Trim: This refers to how much of the animation clip we want to trim. You are simply editing out a portion of the original animation if you use the default setting. As a rule of thumb, it's better to have more frames of animation than not have enough.
- **Overdrive**: This will affect the speed. Overdrive simply means faster, so if you want to speed up, set the animation slider to a higher value in the **Overdrive** settings.

Go ahead and play with these settings until you're happy with how it looks. When you are done, click **Download**.

In the next section, we will explore some of the settings that you will see.

Downloading the Mixamo animation

Continuing from the last section, when you click **Download**, Mixamo will take you to the following dialog box illustrated in *Figure 6.6*:

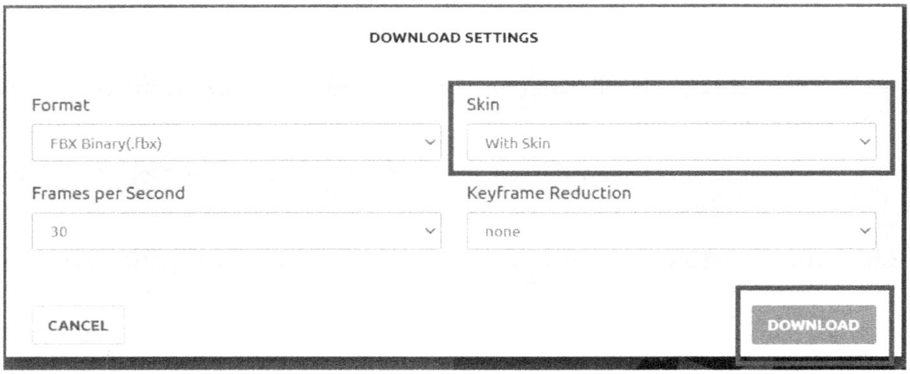

Figure 6.6: Use Skin and Download

Let's look at each of these options:

- **Format**: `FBX` is the same format you used when you exported from Unreal Engine; for the Unreal Mixamo pipeline, I strongly suggest you work with this preset. In the **Format** drop-down list, you will see other formats. Mostly, they consist of alternative and older versions of FBX. Another available format is `DAE`; however, it is not compatible with Unreal.
- **Skin**: The default setting is **With Skin**; this means that when you download the file, it will contain your original mesh along with the Mixamo Rig and the animation all within the FBX file format. If you have multiple animations for your character, you only need to include the skin on the first animation you download. Choosing **Without Skin** will contain the animation data only.

> **Note**
>
> The first time that you download your animation, keep all of the default settings. However, once you've downloaded the first animation with the skin intact, you don't need the skin for any subsequent animation downloads for the same character. However, there's no harm in just downloading with the default settings.

- **Frames per Second**: The options are **24**, **30**, and **60** fps. Higher frame rates are good if you wish to edit the timing of your animation within Unreal Engine, particularly if you want to slow it down. Most motion capture is captured at a higher frame rate, allowing for retiming of the motion. It is better to have that higher frame rate than to attempt to interpolate slow motion in Unreal synthetically in an advanced workflow. A lower frame rate would be good if you are taking in really long animations and running them on a substandard machine.

- **Keyframe Reduction**: This is best left alone. The data size of these files and Unreal's ability to read them don't require keyframe reduction or optimization. Without keyframe reduction, Mixamo bakes a keyframe for each joint rotation on every frame. With keyframe reduction, Mixamo adds a little math in order to reduce the data size, and this can reduce the quality of the animation. It's best for Unreal Engine to get that data to work. If there is any keyframe reduction required in Unreal, there are plenty of tools within Unreal to give you better and controllable results.

With all the download settings out of the way, it's time to bring the animation file into Unreal. In the next section, we'll cover how to do this.

Importing the Mixamo animation into Unreal

After clicking **Download**, Mixamo will ask you where you want to download your new FBX file; choose somewhere you will remember, ideally somewhere inside your project folder, as this will allow you to skip the following step.

In the interest of tidiness, create a folder called `Mixamo` inside your Unreal project. That will be the destination for the download.

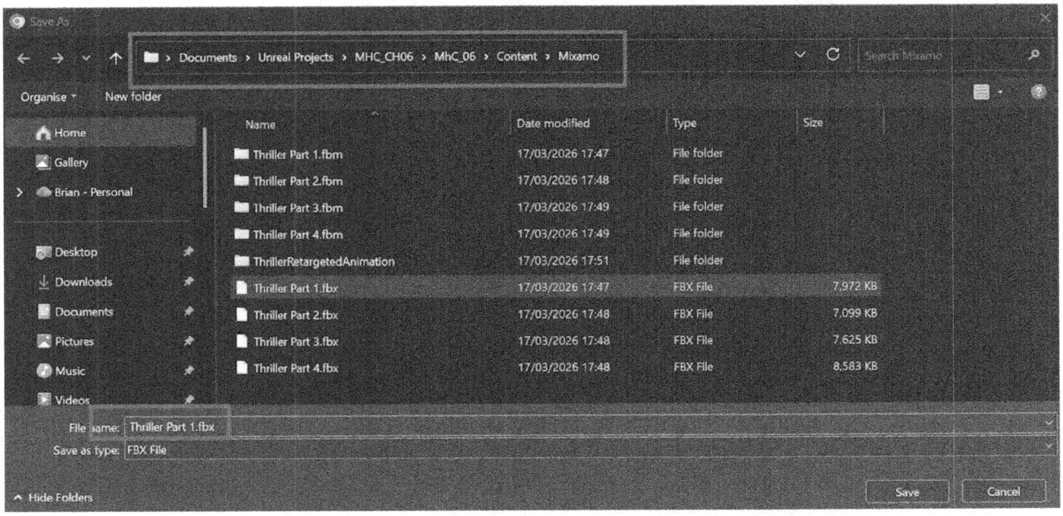

Figure 6.7: Saving the animation in the Mixamo folder of your project

In *Figure 6.7*, I've already created a `Mixamo` folder and have downloaded the `FBX` files.

Each time you download an FBX file into your project, back in Unreal you will get a pop-up window.

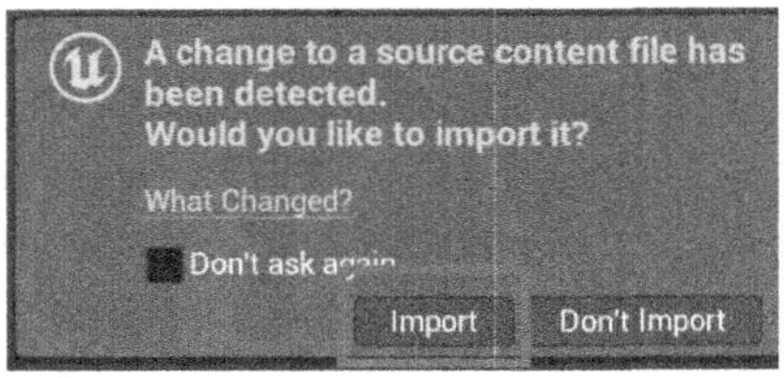

Figure 6.8: Import confirmation pop-up in UE

This pop-up box is important. Unreal detects that a new file is now in the project and is asking you what to do. Click on **Import**. As it imports, it will make a copy of the FBX file and convert it into an **animation sequence**, which is an Unreal Engine asset that only Unreal can understand. Skipping this will force you to manually import the FBX file, which is more time-consuming.

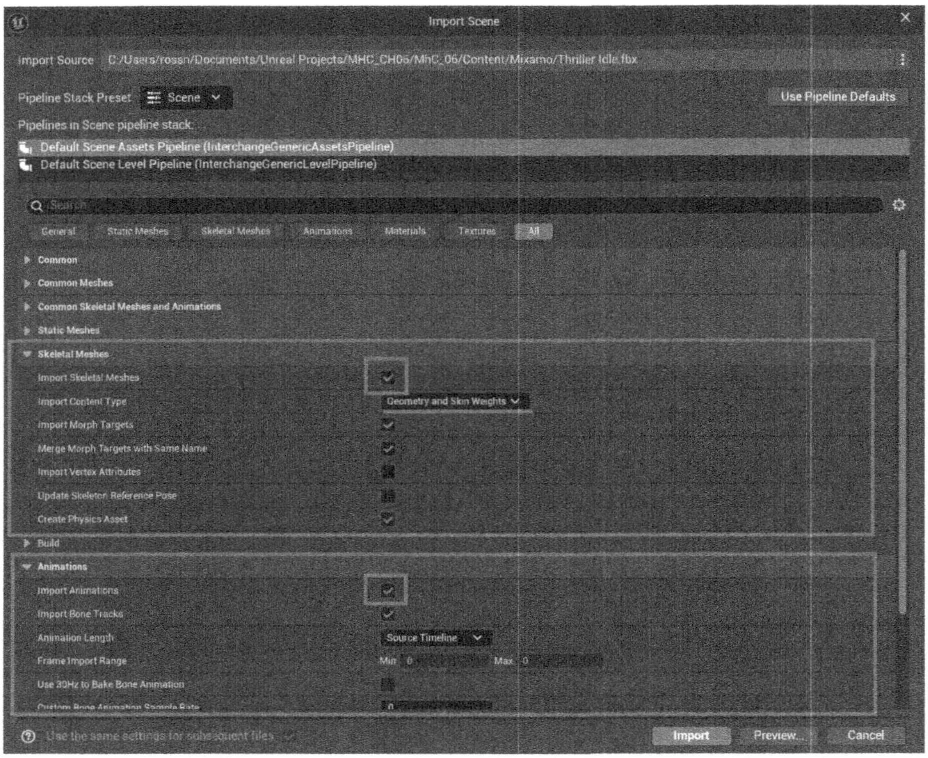

Figure 6.9: FBX Import Settings

In *Figure 6.9*, you can see the dialog box that appears after clicking **Import**. Because you exported a skinned FBX, Unreal detects both a skeletal mesh and an animation sequence. Make sure **Import Skeletal Mesh** is enabled; otherwise, Unreal will expect you to assign an existing mesh.

At the bottom of *Figure 6.9*, I've also highlighted the **Import Animations** option. To get through the four Thriller animations quickly, I recommend exporting each one **With Skin**, allowing you to reuse these same import settings.

> Note
>
> **Quick check**
>
> A successful import should produce a skeletal mesh together with one or more Animation Sequence assets inside your Mixamo folder. If you can double-click an Animation Sequence and see the Mixamo character animating inside Unreal, you're ready for the retargeting stage.

With the animation successfully imported, we now need to make it compatible with our MetaHuman.

Retargeting the Mixamo animation to your character

So now we have the animations inside our project, and they've been converted to the animation sequence format.

If, for whatever reason, you already have lots of different types of assets in the same folder, you can always use a filter to focus only on the **Animation Sequence** assets.

Figure 6.10: Filtering for animation sequences

In *Figure 6.10*, I have done just that by first clicking on the filter box, marked in red; then, under **All Filters**, I chose **Animation** and under **Animation,** I chose **Animation Sequence**. Now I can only see the animation sequences I just imported.

As you can see from *Figure 6.11*, the four parts of the thriller animation are now available.

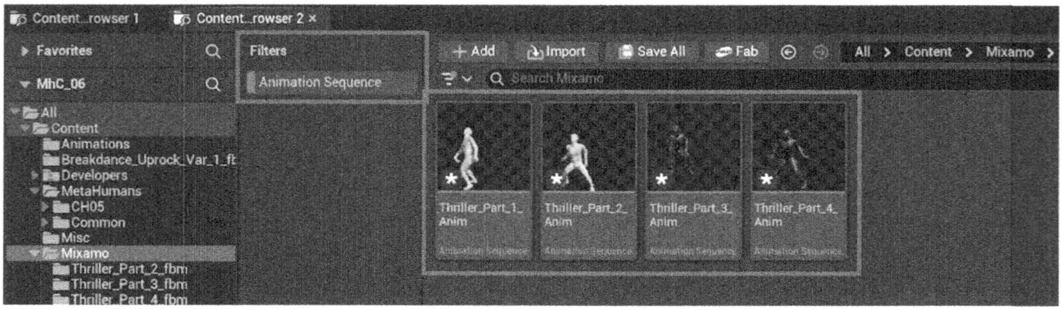

Figure 6.11: Filter Results for Animation Sequences

Now, remember, these animation files are associated with the mesh that came in from Mixamo, but they do contain animation. We want to retarget those animations so that they work on our MetaHuman. But, before we do that, let's take a look at what happens if we try to apply them to our MetaHuman without retargeting and how we can fix it quickly.

For animating most characters, we need a **Level Sequence**, which is basically a timeline where our animation tracks are contained. Make sure you have your character Blueprint somewhere in your scene. You may still have one from *Chapter 5*.

In the **Content Browser**, click the **+Add** button (marked in red in *Figure 6.12*), then click on **Level Sequence**, and double-click to open it.

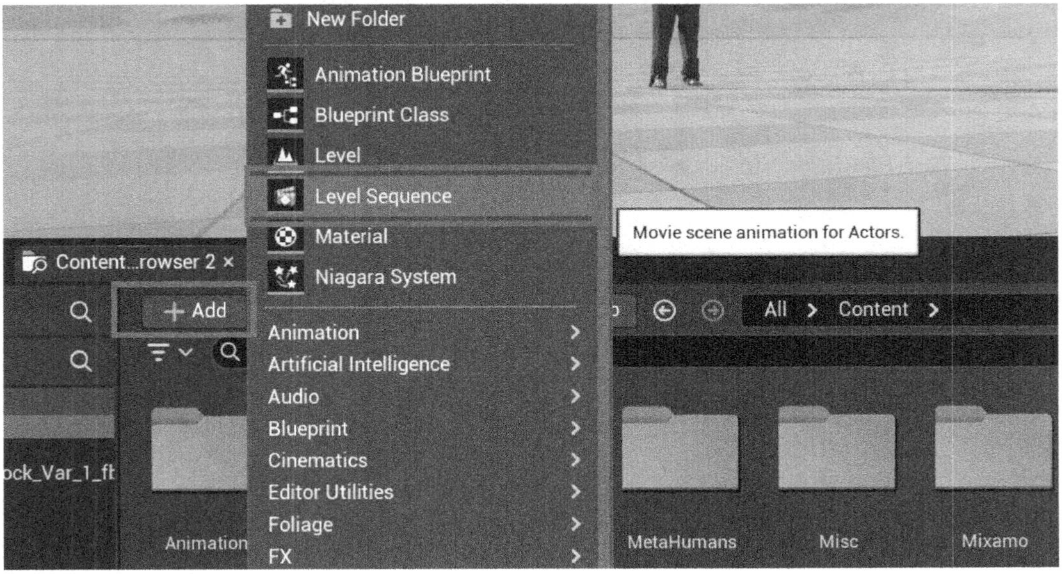

Figure 6.12: Creating a Level Sequence

With the **Character Blueprint** still selected, click **+Add** on the top right of your **Level Sequence** (Yes, the **+Add** button appears a lot in Unreal). Next, click on **Add Actor Track**, and you'll see that it automatically gives you your selected character to add, which saves you the trouble of looking for it.

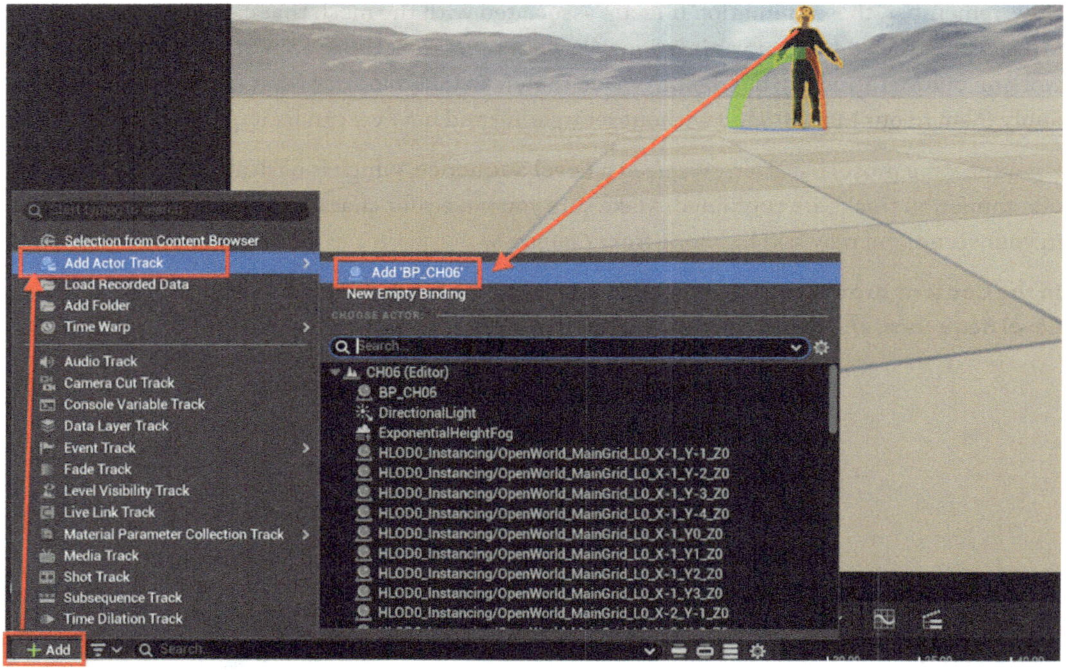

Figure 6.13: Adding the MetaHuman Blueprint to the Level Sequence

As soon as you click **Add** (in my case **Add 'BP_CH05'**), it will appear as a new track in the Level Sequence.

By default, the MetaHuman also includes two Control Rig tracks. We don't need them at this stage because they will override any body animation we apply from Mixamo. Delete both Control Rig tracks before continuing so that the imported animation can drive the character correctly.

Figure 6.14: Deleting both Control Rigs

With the control rigs deleted, we're going to add the recently imported animation to the body track; after all, they are body animations. Next to **Body**, you'll see a tiny + icon, which I've highlighted in red in *Figure 6.15*. This will open a dialog box where on the top you'll see **Animation**.

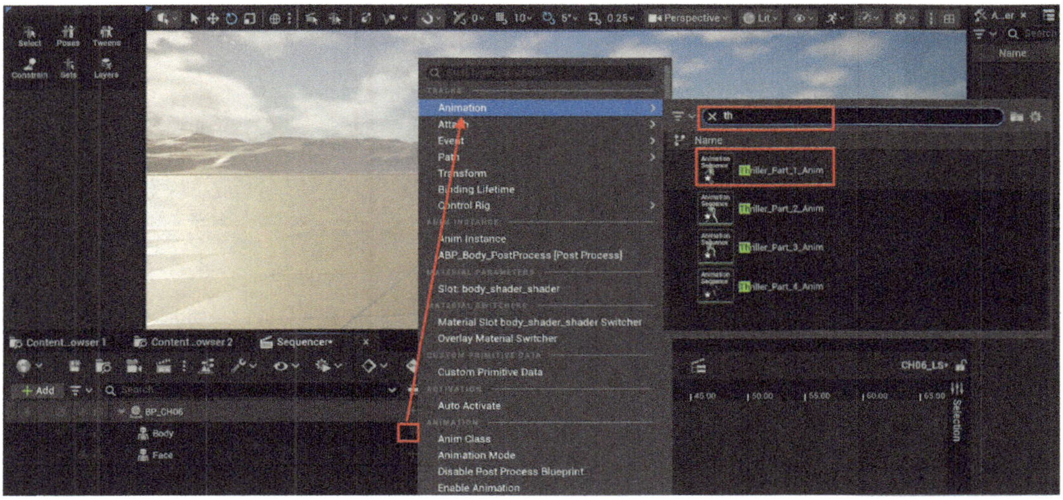

Figure 6.15: Adding Animation Sequence to the Body Animation Track

Simply type in `Thriller`, and you'll see the animation sequences you've recently imported. We can only add one at a time, so choose the first part, and it will populate the animation track.

We are going to add all four animations by repeating the same process, but this time, we will leave a small gap between each one.

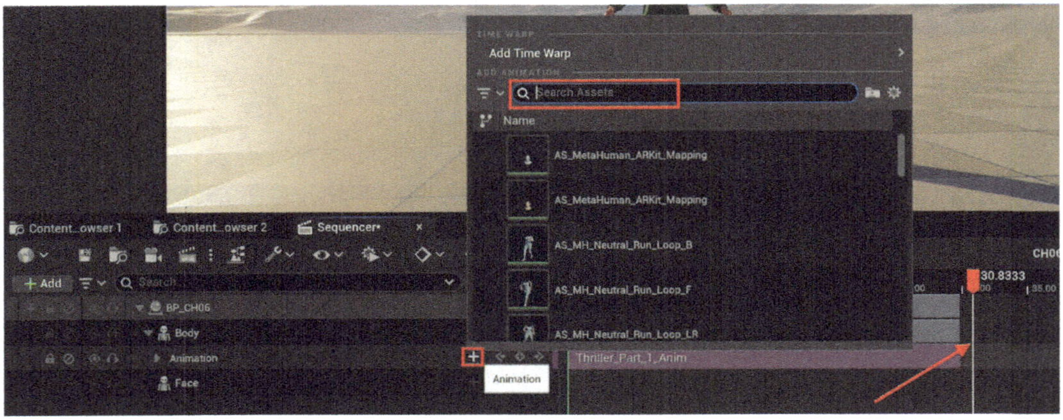

Figure 6.16: Adding the next Animation Sequence to the same Track with a gap

The reason is simple. If your cursor, as shown by the red arrow in *Figure 6.16*, is positioned over an existing track, the software will create a new animation track. We want all animations on a single track so they can be blended together later.

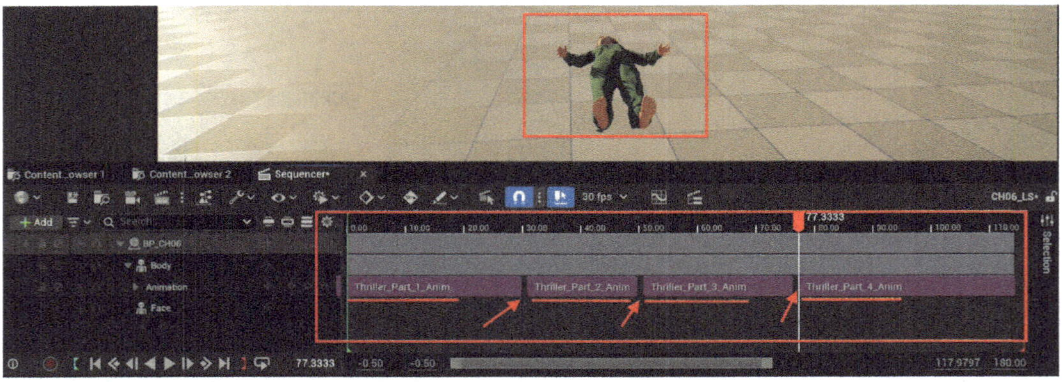

Figure 6.17: Adding all the sequences with gaps

In *Figure 6.17*, you can see that I've brought all four animations onto the same animation track, leaving a small gap between each clip exactly as intended.

Don't worry if your MetaHuman is still standing in an A-pose. This is completely normal.

At this stage, the animation is only affecting the root bone because it hasn't yet been retargeted to the MetaHuman skeleton. Feel free to scrub or play the timeline and you'll see the character moving in an unusual way.

We could have performed the retargeting earlier, but seeing this intermediate state helps illustrate exactly why retargeting is required.

Let's get these animations retargeted. But first, create another folder inside your Mixamo folder and call it something like `ThrillerRetargettedAnimations` if you want to be a little organized.

I tend to use filtering a lot as you can see in *Figure 6.18*, but if you have a clean folder with just the animation sequences, you don't have to. With just one animation sequence selected, *right-click* and choose **Retarget Animations**, as seen in *Figure 6.18*.

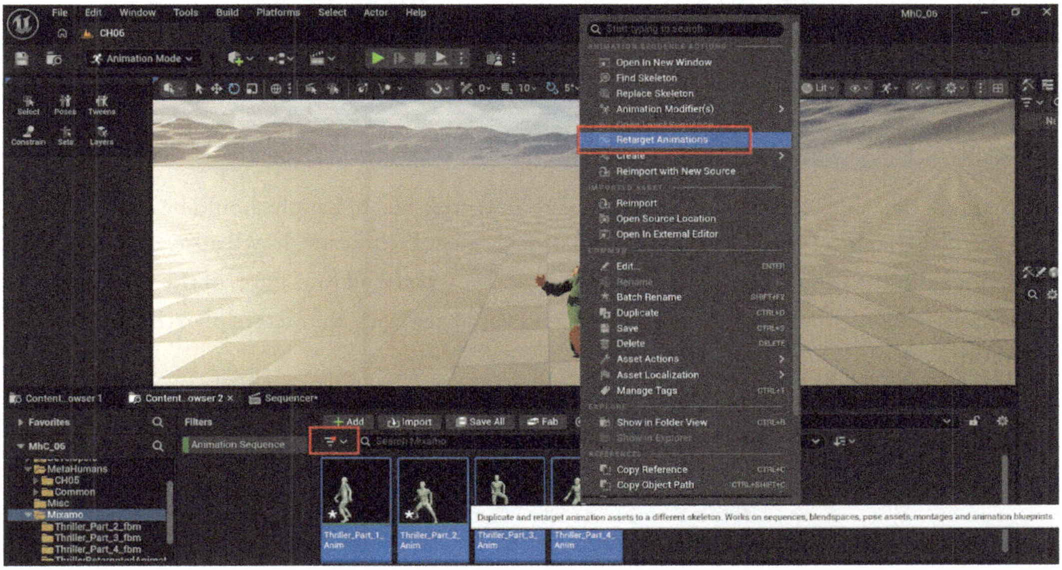

Figure 6.18: Retargeting the Mixamo animation sequences

As soon as you click on **Retarget Animations**, a dialog box will appear. At first, only the mesh belonging to the imported `FBX` will appear. That is your source mesh, where you want to retarget your animation from.

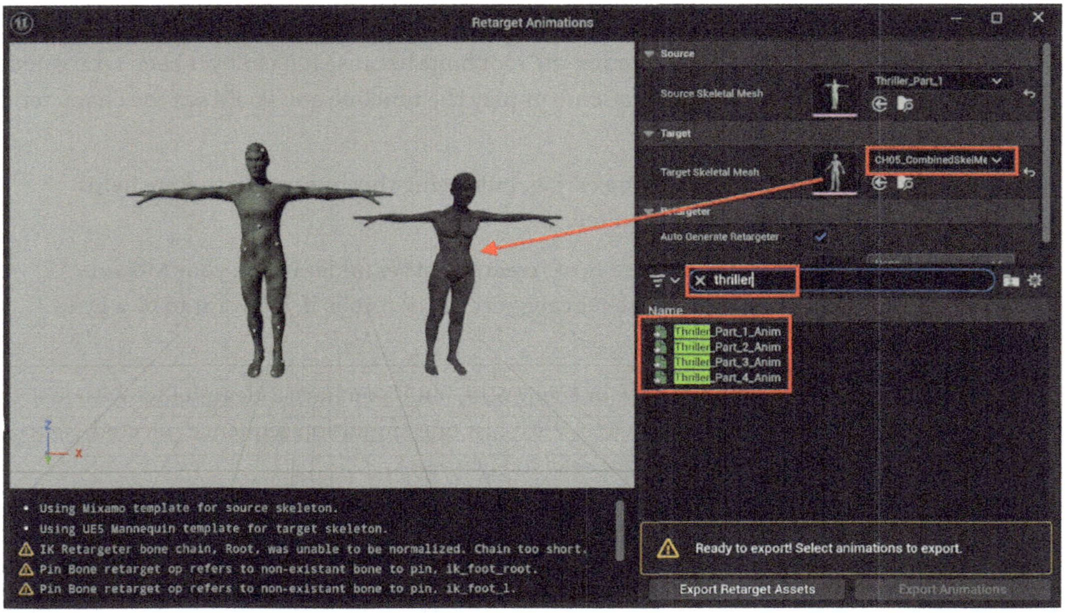

Figure 6.19: Batch retargeting all the Thriller animation sequences

In the target box, click on the scroll down box to find your mesh, which should be the `combinedSkelMesh` you used before. As soon as you select it, your mesh will appear on the right. Again, in the search bar, type in `Thriller` and you'll see all four parts of the thriller animation. Feel free to play any one of them, and you'll see both characters play the same animation.

Select all four of the animations and hit **Export Animations**. This will bring up another pop-up dialog box over the existing one.

Choose the Folder `ThrillerRetargettingAnimations` to place them in and use the Prefix `RT`.

> **Note**
>
> The prefix is more important than neatly creating folders, as you don't want to be in a position later where you are unsure which is the source animation, and which is the retargeted animation.

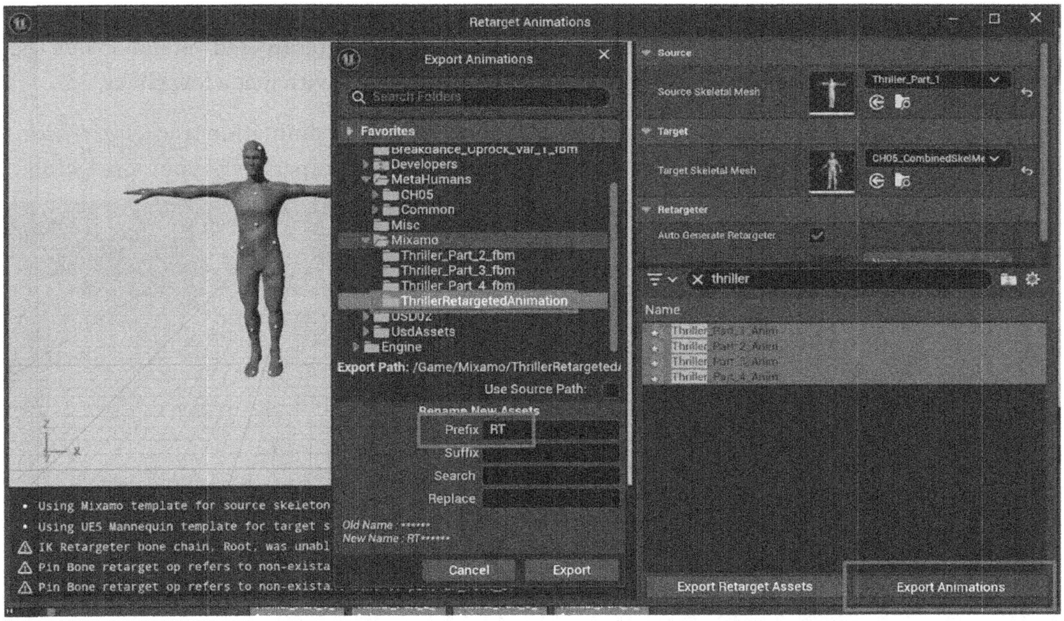

Figure 6.20: Choosing a new folder to save the Retargets to with a Prefix

Once you've chosen your target location and prefix, click **Export Animations**. A **Batch Export Options** dialog box will appear. Hit **Export**.

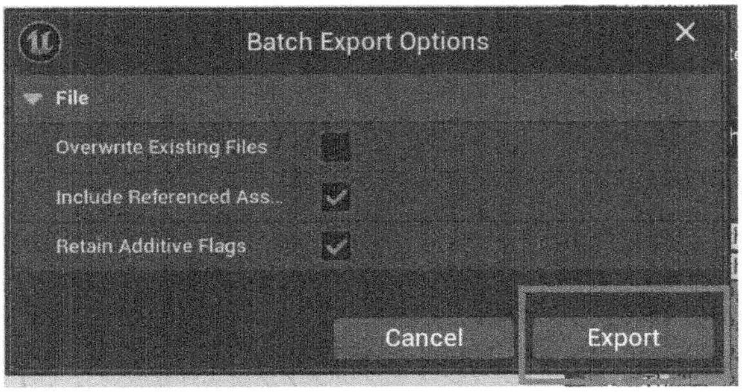

Figure 6.21: Hitting Export

This will batch transcode your Mixamo animation sequences into MetaHuman-compatible animation sequences.

So the hard part is over. You've successfully retargeted your animation. So now we need to update the animations from the original source animations to the retargeted version inside the level sequence, and we can do that directly in the level sequencer with just a few clicks.

Jump back in the **Level Sequence**. On the first clip inside the body animation track, *right-click* and you'll see a dialog box appear that will allow you to edit the properties of your animation.

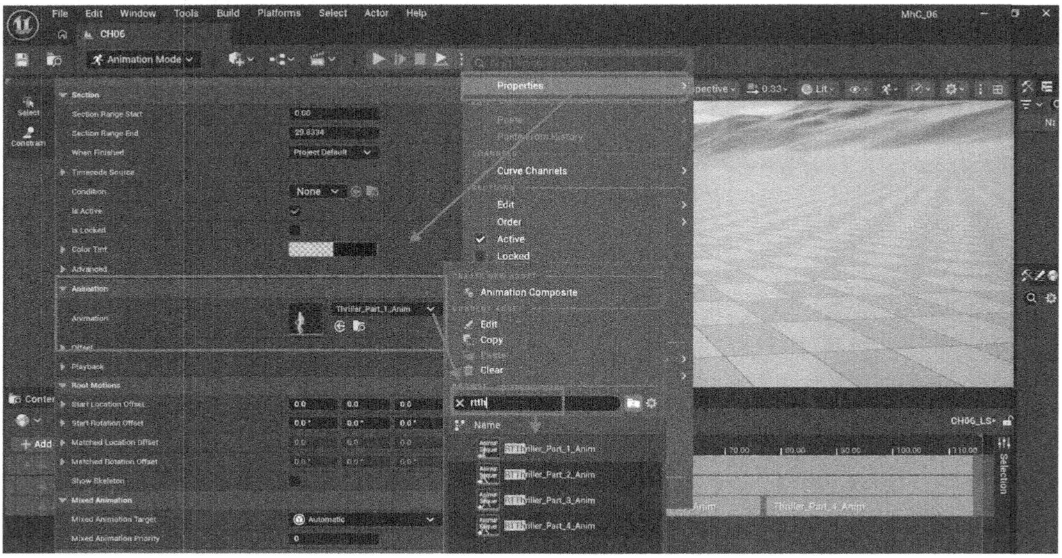

Figure 6.22: Right-clicking on an animation sequence in the Level Sequence

In *Figure 6.22*, I've highlighted the animation box which already contains the source animation we originally imported. Click on that to see the drop-down menu and type `RT` in the search bar. `RT` is the prefix to the filename you created earlier and now works as a filter to only show you the retargeted versions of your animation. Because we're looking at the properties of the first thriller clip, choose the first one, `Thriller_Part_1_anim`.

As soon as you click it, your animation will update to the retargeted version.

Figure 6.23: Retargeted Animation Sequence applied to the first clip on track

Notice that the name has also changed to `RTThriller_Part_1_Anim`. You can now play it on the **Level Sequence**, and it will work perfectly. Repeat this process for each of the four parts. As soon as you have all clips replaced with the retargeted versions, play or scrub through the **Level Sequence**. Disregard the gap between each clip for the moment and focus on the end position of one clip and the start of the next. Each clip starts at the same spot. What is happening here is that each clip is set to start at the origin but ends at the position where the performer stopped. As soon as the next clip begins, the character is transported back to the origin, which means there is no blending of the animations. Let's fix it.

To fix the above issue, we want to make sure that the bones of the second clip start at the same position where the bones of the first clip end. We don't have to figure this out for all the bones; just one will do.

Theoretically, any bone will do but generally, one of the foot bones works best. In short, any clip needs to match a bone position of the previous clip, and we need to do this one clip at a time. Let's match the second clip with the first clip.

In *Figure 6.24*, I've selected the second clip and right-clicked it. Instead of going to **Properties** like we did earlier, select **Match With this Bone in the Previous Clip**, then type `Foot` in the search bar, and choose either `foot_r` or `foot_l`.

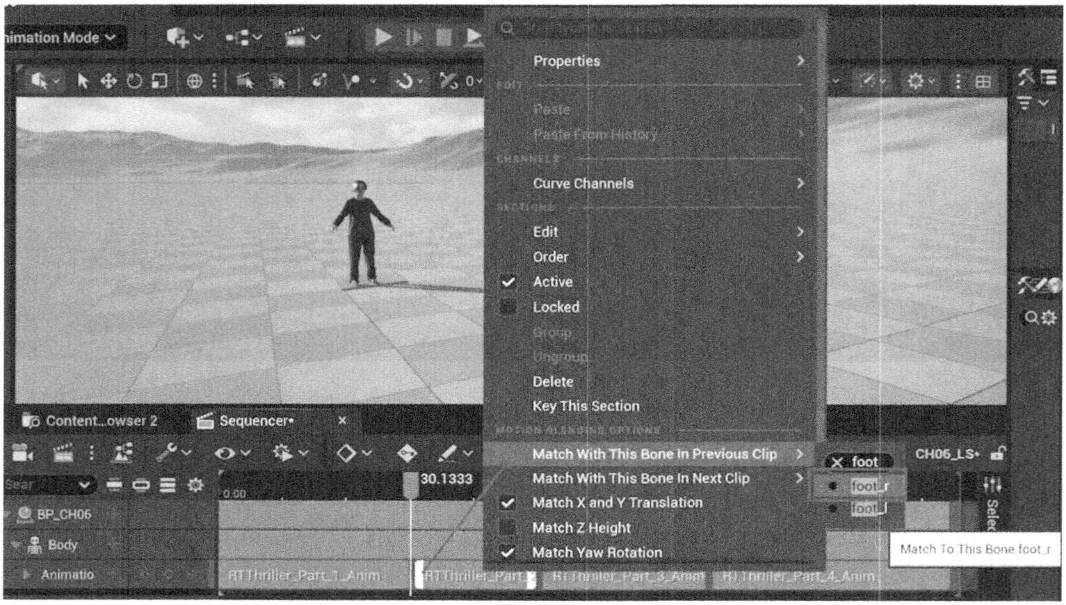

Figure 6.24: Preventing each clip from starting at the same position

This places the foot bone of the new clip in the same position as the foot bone at the end of the previous clip, which positions the character correctly for the transition between the two. You will then see the character shift so that the first frame of the new clip matches the final position of the previous clip. Repeat this process for each subsequent clip.

> **Note**
>
> You may need to alternate between left or right foot for best result.

To really get a sense that this is working, we finally need to remove that gap. Removing it is very easy. Simply drag each subsequent animation clip to the left so that they overlap by a frame or two.

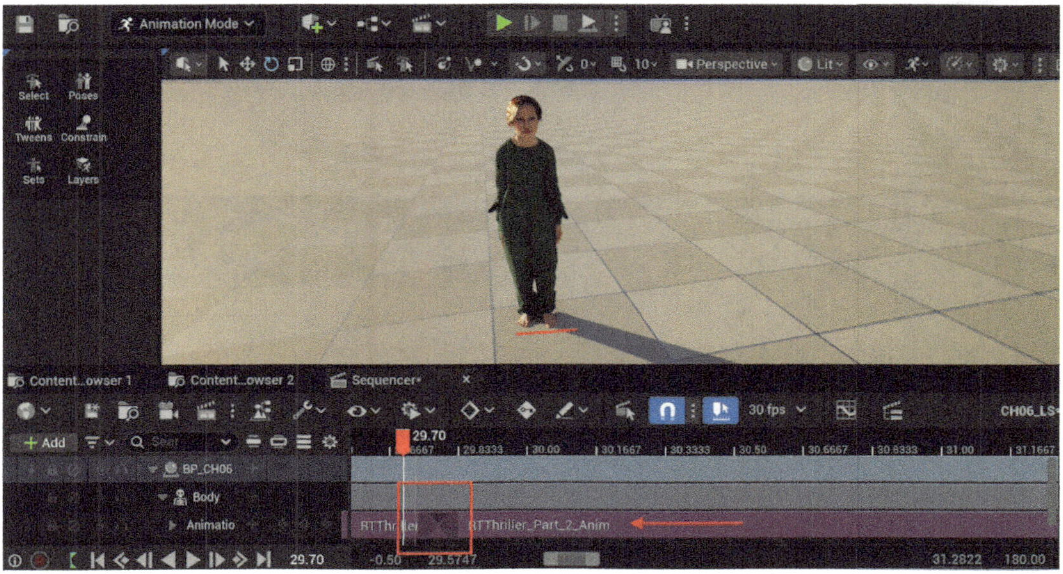

Figure 6.25: Moving the second clip backwards on the track to remove the gap

In *Figure 6.25*, I've highlighted the transitions that illustrate how Unreal adds an interpolation between overlapping frames. Depending on how precise the animations are, you may not need to have any overlap at all but generally the interpolation is so good that in most cases it helps.

Depending on the original motion capture performer or animation, we do tend to find errors where part of the character penetrates itself. In *Figure 6.26*, the hands are going through the legs for just a couple of frames. Considering that one clip is about 30 s long, it's not too bad and the solution is pretty simple.

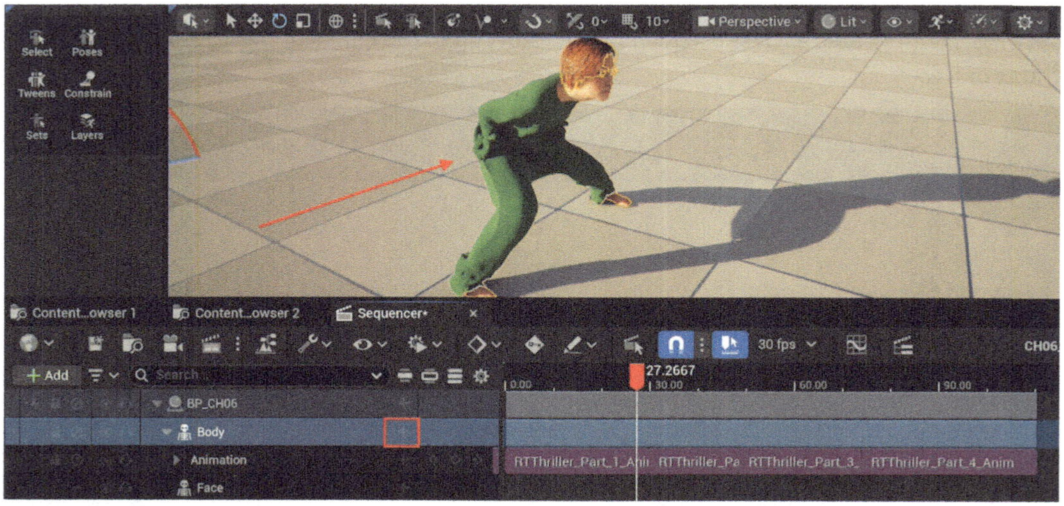

Figure 6.26: Hands penetrating through legs issue

We're going to add a MetaHuman control rig on top of the animation without overwriting the original animation. In *Figure 6.26*, it seems that the upper arms should have been rotated out a little more just for that section of the animation. In *Figure 6.27*, I've highlighted the + icon, which will allow us to add something to the body again.

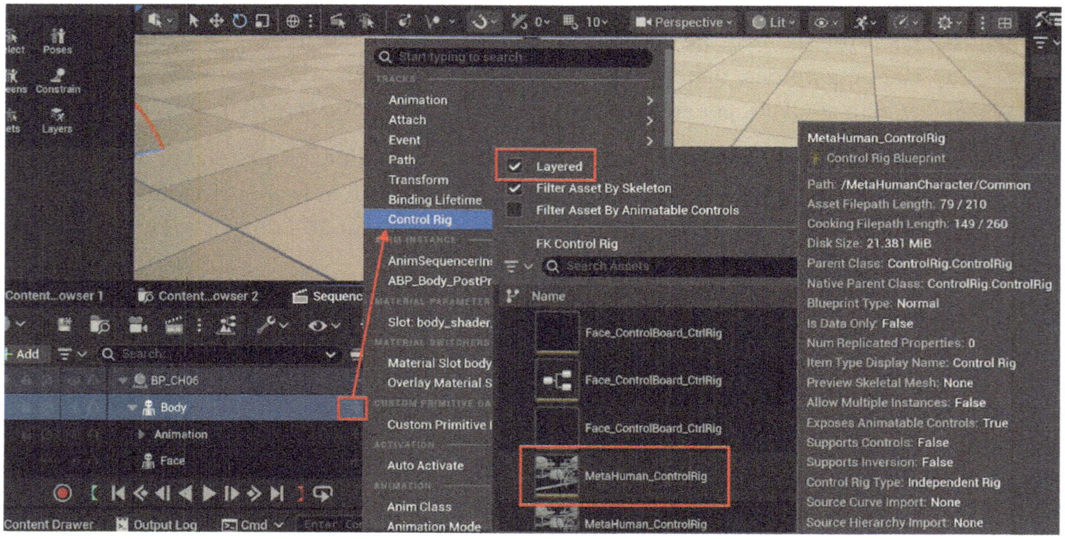

Figure 6.27: Adding MetaHuman Control Rig for refinement

By clicking on +, we get a few options (*Figure 6.27*). We're just interested in the **Control Rig**. Click on that, but make sure you choose layered, scroll down to **MetaHuman Control Rig**, and select it.

Isolate the problem area of the clip. As I mentioned earlier, I noticed that the upper arm seemed to be rotated in toward the body, so I need to rotate it out but only when it becomes a problem.

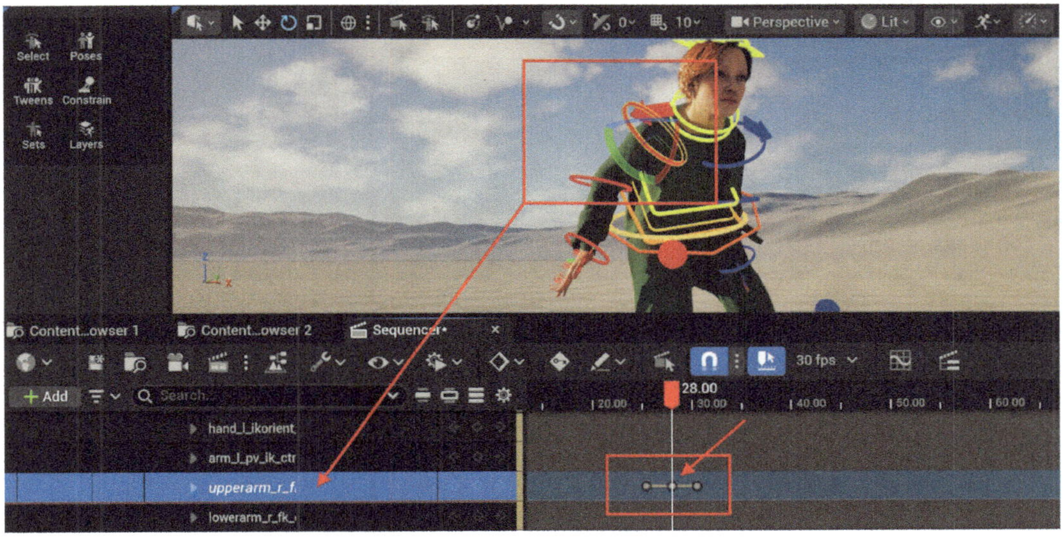

Figure 6.28: Adding keyframe to the problem area

As shown in *Figure 6.28*, first locate the moment before the upper arm was fine, then select the upper arm and place a keyframe. Then, go forward to when it was fine again and place another keyframe. Finally, go to the problem frame, rotate the arm outward, and place a keyframe to ensure the change was made. Playing it back, you will see that the problem was fixed without having any negative effects on the rest of the animation.

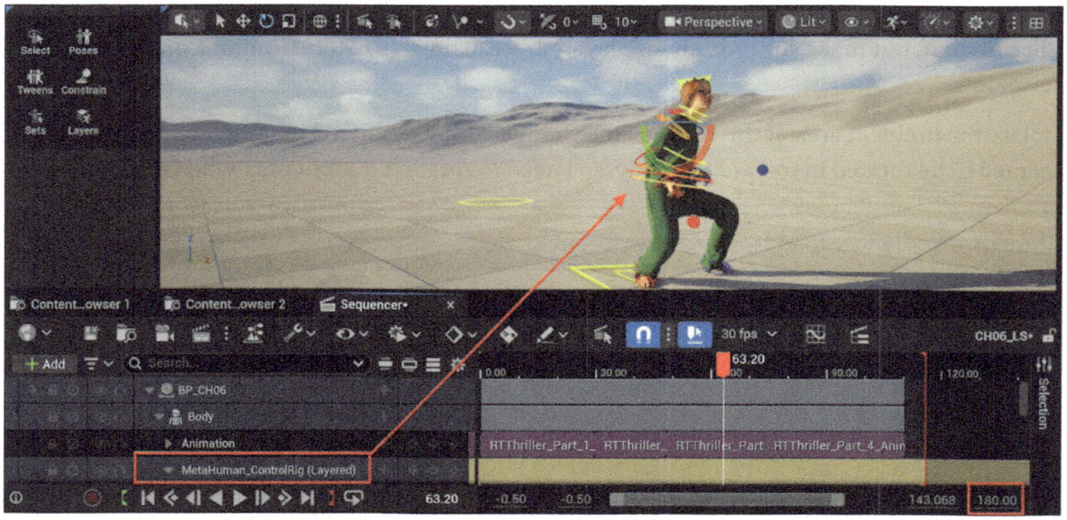

Figure 6.29: Using Control Rig for fixing and artistic refinement of mocap

The layered use of a Control Rig is useful not only for fixing issues such as hand or foot intersections but also for refining body posture, improving silhouettes, exaggerating performances, or making subtle artistic adjustments. In practice, the same workflow can be applied to almost any body animation that requires polish.

Summary

In this chapter, we explored Mixamo, which is an amazing free resource for motion capture files based on real actor performances, giving animation productions a huge lift in quality. We learned not only how to use it in Unreal but also how we can use new retargeting tools that have been drastically simplified since Unreal Engine 5.4.

We also covered the **Level Sequence**, which is the timeline for any animation and an absolute must-have for an Unreal Engine-based animation pipeline. We learned how to get our animations inside the **Level Sequence**, how to blend them together for a singular smooth animation, and how to fix problems easily with the very powerful control rig.

In the next chapter, we will continue with motion capture and explore how we can bring our own performance captures on video and convert them to FBX files using **DeepMotion**, a web-based motion capture tool.

7

Adding Motion Capture with DeepMotion

In *Chapter 6*, we were introduced to the motion capture library of Mixamo and how to make the Mixamo animations work inside Unreal. In this chapter, we are going to build on that knowledge and create our very own animation based on actor performance. We will be using another third-party online tool called **DeepMotion**, which includes a tool called **Animate 3D** that analyzes videos of human performances and, in return, creates a motion capture file. We will learn how to use a video camera effectively to record a performance, then use DeepMotion's Animate 3D feature to create your very own bespoke motion capture file. We will also look at a more advanced method of retargeting which helps to further explain the concept while offering solutions to potential problems.

As much as stock motion libraries such as Mixamo are great, you will need to have your own bespoke animation to give you creative freedom. Even if a solution such as DeepMotion's Animate 3D may not be as good as the results that you would get from expensive motion capture suits, it will be much better than the compromises you will make using library stock motion.

So, in this chapter, we will cover the following topics:

- Introducing DeepMotion
- Preparing our video footage
- Uploading our video clip to DeepMotion
- Exploring DeepMotion's animation settings
- Downloading the DeepMotion motion capture files
- Importing the DeepMotion motion animation into Unreal

- Retargeting the DeepMotion motion capture
- Fixing position misalignment issues

Technical requirements

In terms of computer power, you will need the technical requirements detailed in *Chapter 1*, and the MetaHuman character plus the Unreal Engine mannequin that we imported into UE5 in *Chapter 2*. Both of these will need to be saved in the same project in UE, and you will need to have UE running for this chapter.

You will also need a stable internet connection, as we will be uploading a MetaHuman preview mesh and a video file and downloading numerous animation assets. You will need a video camera: a webcam, smartphone, or a professional video or digital cine camera will all do, but note that there aren't benefits for video with greater resolution than HD.

Introducing DeepMotion

Until recently, bespoke motion capture solutions required expensive equipment and expensive software; think about movies like *Avatar*, *The Lord of the Rings*, or *Pirates of the Caribbean*, where performers have to wear motion capture suits with either reflective balls or checker markers with infrared sensors. This technology was only viable for large studios that could make such an investment, and as a result, independent studios and freelance artists had to make do with just motion capture libraries, such as Mixamo, as we have already discussed.

Recently, this has changed as more and more affordable markerless motion capture solutions have become available to artists. In researching this book, I tested several approaches, including browser-based AI services such as DeepMotion and QuickMagic, dedicated motion capture software such as Rokoko Studio, and open-source solutions such as FreeMoCap.

Each has its own strengths. Rokoko offers an excellent professional ecosystem that can grow into hardware-based capture, FreeMoCap provides a completely free open-source alternative for technically minded users, and QuickMagic is another capable browser-based AI motion capture solution.

For this book, I chose DeepMotion Animate 3D because it provides a straightforward browser workflow, requires nothing more than a video file to get started, integrates well with Unreal Engine, and is easy for beginners to reproduce regardless of their operating system or hardware.

> **Note**
>
> The DeepMotion Freemium plan is intentionally limited to 30 seconds of processed animation per month, making it best suited as a trial or learning tool. If you plan to create motion capture regularly or are working with longer performances, it is worth exploring the alternative solutions mentioned above to determine which best suit your workflow and budget.

DeepMotion's Animation 3D is an example of a **markerless mocap solution**. This involves a process where a video of human performance is captured with a video camera, with no special suit or markers required. The video file is analyzed by software that recognizes and tracks each body part. With machine learning aiding this process, the solution is able to utilize libraries or motion data to avoid errors. In addition, **inverse kinematics** is also utilized to further refine the process. This technology is constantly improving, and with machine learning being a key feature, the rate of progress is very fast indeed.

In the case of DeepMotion, the online tool allows us to upload a video of our performance and processes the motion capture for us to use in Unreal (or any other compatible platform). Though this process includes machine learning, fortunately for us, DeepMotion takes care of all that.

In the next section, we will dive into the nuts and bolts of how to record videos effectively.

Preparing our video footage

Before we go over to DeepMotion, there are some key factors we need to know with regard to recording our performances on video. Let's look at them now:

- **Camera quality and position**: DeepMotion is capable of working with low-end cameras such as webcams or old smartphones, all the way up to high-end cinema cameras, so long as the picture is sharp and steady and has a reasonably high frame rate. Many lower-end cameras have a minimum frame rate of 30 fps, but you will get a better result on fast-moving actors if you use a higher frame rate.
  Also, ideally, the camera should be stationary because the software works out the performer's motion based on a fixed floor position. The ideal position of the camera is about 2 meters from the performer.
- **High-contrast filming**: As this markerless mocap solution is tracking pixels rather than sensors, we need to make it as easy as possible for the software to differentiate the background from the performer. This is why we need to have a high contrast between

the two. If you plan to shoot against a dark background, such as a curtain, be sure to have your performer wear bright colors, and vice versa. Also, loose clothing can cause problems as, often, the clothing will be tracked; for example, if the performer is wearing very baggy sleeves, it's difficult for the tracker to tell the difference between an arm and a sleeve. The same applies to long garments that might flap around in front of a person's limbs.

- **Keep head to toes in shot at all times**: Although DeepMotion can do a good job at working out the motion of a character just from video of the waist up, as a rule of thumb, it is better to get more data than you need, so ensure that you capture head to toe shots of your performer as much as you can. Capturing the performer's whole body is also important as, even if your performer's feet or head go out of shot for a second, it can cause poor results throughout the rest of the motion-capturing process.
  With that said, if your intention is to capture the full body performance, then video capturing the full body is a must.
- **Calibration time**: Make sure that you have your performer in shot for a few seconds before and after the performance, preferably in a T-shaped pose and facing the camera. This gives DeepMotion time to align its skeleton to the performer's body before, rather than during, the performance.
- **Occlusion**: It is rare in video footage that we find performers not covering one part of their body with another. Typically, they have their arms in front of their body, but because DeepMotion can determine the skeleton's spine position, in such a scenario, that type of occlusion isn't a problem.
  However, when the body goes in front of a limb, there can be issues. Taking hands as an example, if and when they go behind the body or the head, DeepMotion has to guess where the hands should be because it has no pixels to tell it where the hands are. It will either try to guess or apply no animation at all to those problem areas.

  Also, occlusion can occur by objects that are between the performer and the camera, which can cause issues. For example, a tree branch or lamppost might momentarily get in the way but could inadvertently cause a lot more errors than expected.

  Therefore, shooting with anything in the foreground obscuring your performers is not recommended.
- **Performance speed**: DeepMotion isn't very good at detecting very fast motion in a clip. For example, for someone tap dancing or boxing, the software has a hard time keeping up with the rapid foot movement and, instead, gives a very poor result. A good rule of thumb is that if you see any motion blur in the video clip, it's not likely to give you a good result. Be sure to play the clip in slow motion to properly analyze it.

- **File size**: If you work with professional video file formats, there is no benefit other than the ability to shoot at higher frame rates. Compressed or lossy video file formats such as MP4 will do the job, and keeping the file size down to under 200 MB is best. Larger file sizes take longer to upload and longer to get analyzed. While MOV files are accepted, I recommend you use MP4 files instead.

In this section, we have covered all the major factors that need to be considered when it comes to recording a video of your performer. Given the nature of video and how every scenario will be different, there will be a certain amount of trial and error, so don't be disheartened if you don't get great results at first. You can always refer back to this section to troubleshoot any issues you may be having.

Alternatively, if you don't want to shoot anything yourself, you could go to a stock library and download a clip that matches the criteria mentioned earlier. For the purpose of this book, I have taken free clips from `motionarray.com`.

In the next section, we will upload your clip to DeepMotion, assuming that you have shot something.

Uploading our video to DeepMotion

In this section, we will head over to the DeepMotion site, register, and upload our footage.

The first thing you need to do is go over to `https://www.deepmotion.com/`. From the landing page, click on the **Sign Up** button as shown in *Figure 7.1*:

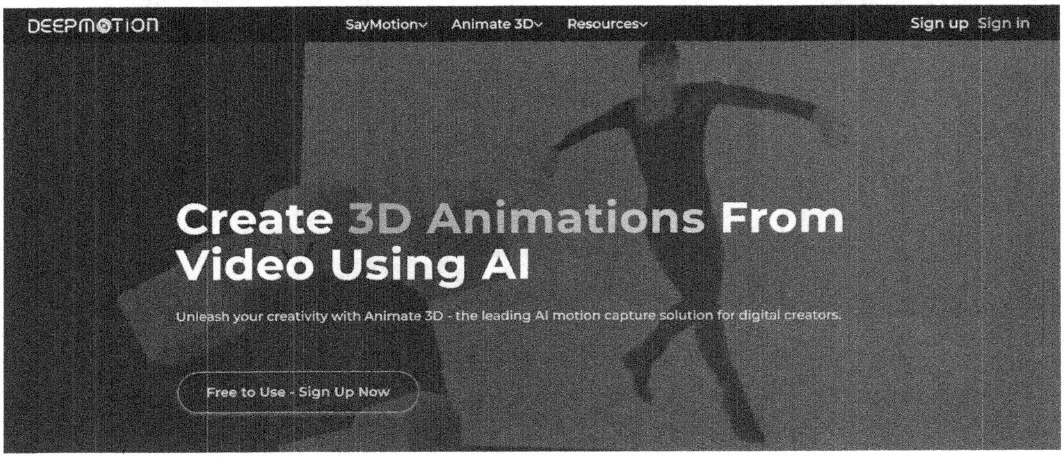

Figure 7.1: DeepMotion Greeting screen and signup button

Note

DeepMotion's Freemium account allows you to upload clips no longer than 20 seconds, with a maximum resolution of 1080p and a frame rate of up to 30 fps. The free plan includes a total allowance of 30 seconds of processed animation each month, so it is best viewed as a trial rather than a production workflow.

If you intend to create motion capture regularly, consider upgrading to a paid plan or evaluating alternative services that provide larger free usage allowances.

Now, you should see the form shown in *Figure 7.2*. Fill it out to create a Freemium account (and note the features on the right). You will also be asked to select the platform you want to sign up on: SayMotion or Animate 3D. We're only interested in Animate 3D, so be sure to click on that before creating your sign-in credentials.

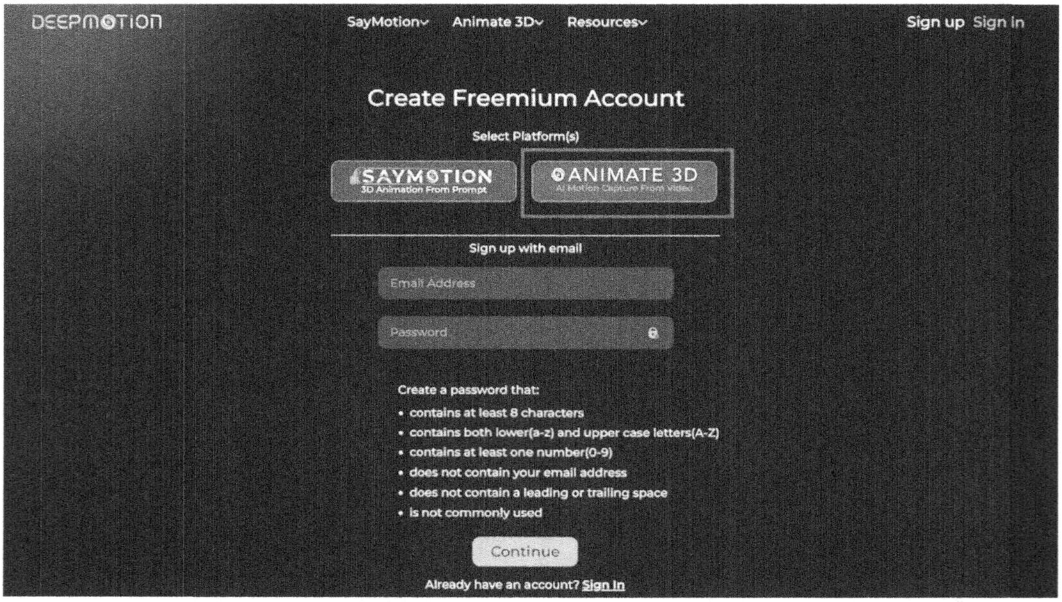

Figure 7.2: Choosing the Animate 3D platform before signing up

Once you have filled in your details, click the **Continue** button. You will either receive a link on your email address or be taken directly to the **DeepMotion Portal** page, as shown in *Figure 7.3*.

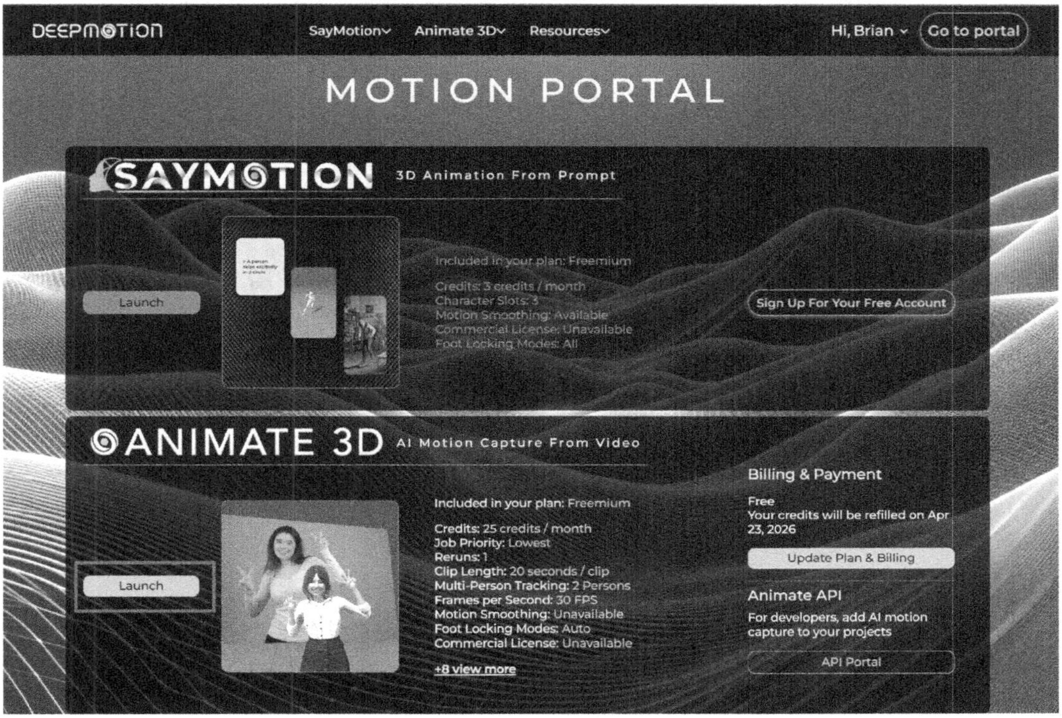

Figure 7.3: Launch Animate 3D

You can see that because we chose Animate 3D when signing up, we only have the ability to launch 3D, as we don't have an account with SayMotion, which is a text to animation AI tool.

With the Freemium account, the only feature available to us is the **Animate 3D** feature, and you can see some of the details of your account on the right-hand side of *Figure 7.3*. I recommend you stay with the freemium account until you really need to upgrade.

To get up and running, click on **Launch**. In the top center box, which I have highlighted in red, you'll see how many credits you have: 1 credit is equal to 1 second of animation.

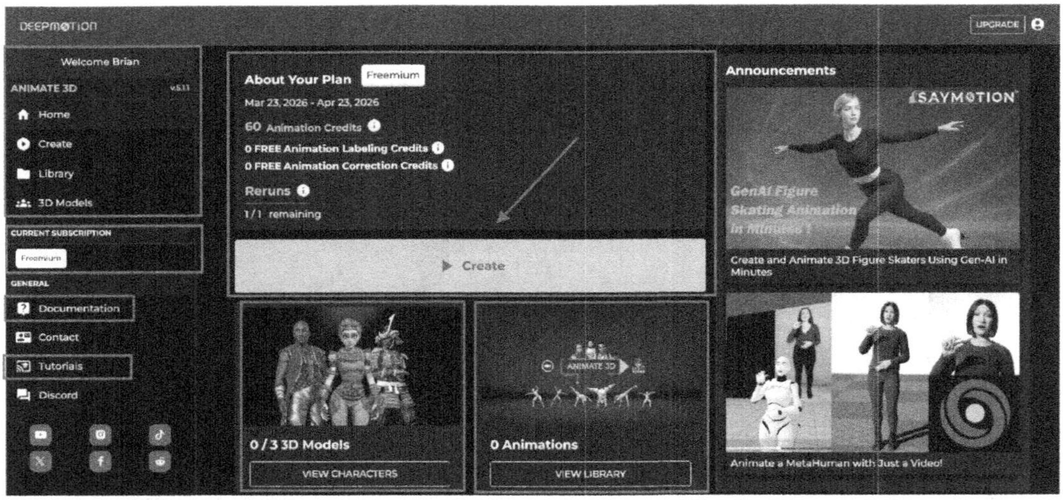

Figure 7.4: Portal Interface

The next option is **Reruns**, and this shows how many attempts you have to refine the capture process. Reruns allow you to make changes to your settings without using up any of your animation credits.

I've highlighted the top left section which for the most part does the same as the center sections. They both have a **Create** button and you can access the library of animations you've created. However, the box on the right has an additional section: **3D Models**. This would be for uploading your own 3D characters, and there's two reasons you may need to do this which are:

- You want DeepMotion to work out the skin weights of your character by determining the power of influence each bone has on sections of the body mesh
- You need to visualize your character to see how the performance looks before committing to a download

Because we already have a robust retargeting tool in Unreal Engine, we don't need to concern ourselves with the first point. In addition, in general a MetaHuman with the default clothing is well represented by the default DeepMotion mesh so we don't need to upload a MetaHuman body.

For this MetaHuman-centric book, we'll keep it simple.

In *Figure 7.4*, I've highlighted where we can see your current subscription (as you can see, I'm using a freemium subscription). I also recommend looking at the documents and tutorials for further explanations of some of the paid subscription benefits. You can view the help documentation here: `https://www.deepmotion.com/doc/animate-3d`

So, let's get started. Click **Create**. This will take you to the following screen shown in *Figure 7.5*:

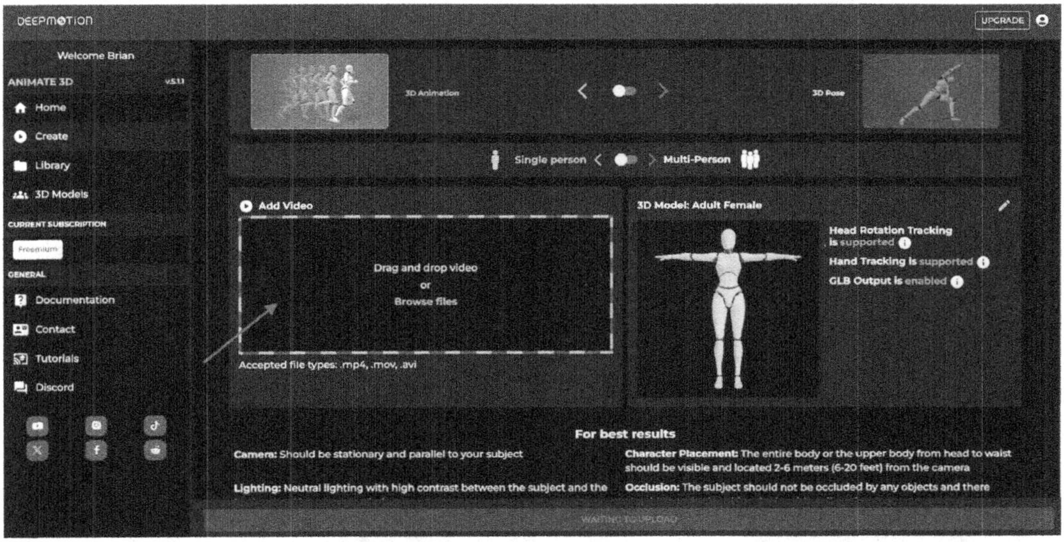

Figure 7.5: Create window

At the top of *Figure 7.4*, you can see two thumbnails: **3D Animation** and **3D Pose**. Make sure to switch to **3D Animation**.

Underneath, you have the option to either drag and drop your folder into DeepMotion or navigate through your folders to upload the file. They also provide a list of accepted file types: MP4, MOV, and AVI. If you have any other format, you will need to convert your files using an encoder such as Adobe Media Encoder, VLC Player, or QuickTime Pro.

> **Note**
>
> Unless there is any notable difference in quality between an original MOV file and an MP4 conversion, use MP4 as it will reduce the uploading and processing time.

Finally, at the bottom of the screen, you'll see a reminder of how to get the best results for your videos (which I expanded upon earlier in the chapter), and I advise you to take a look at that to make sure you get the most out of your limited credit.

Once you are ready, upload your video via whichever method you prefer; now, you will be able to view the video settings.

Exploring DeepMotion's animation settings

As soon as you have uploaded your video clip, you will be taken to the **Animate 3D** dashboard, as shown in *Figure 7.6*. If you want to use the same clip as me, I am using the clip of a dancing man, found here: `https://motionarray.com/stock-video/happy-man-dancing-vertical-814129/`.

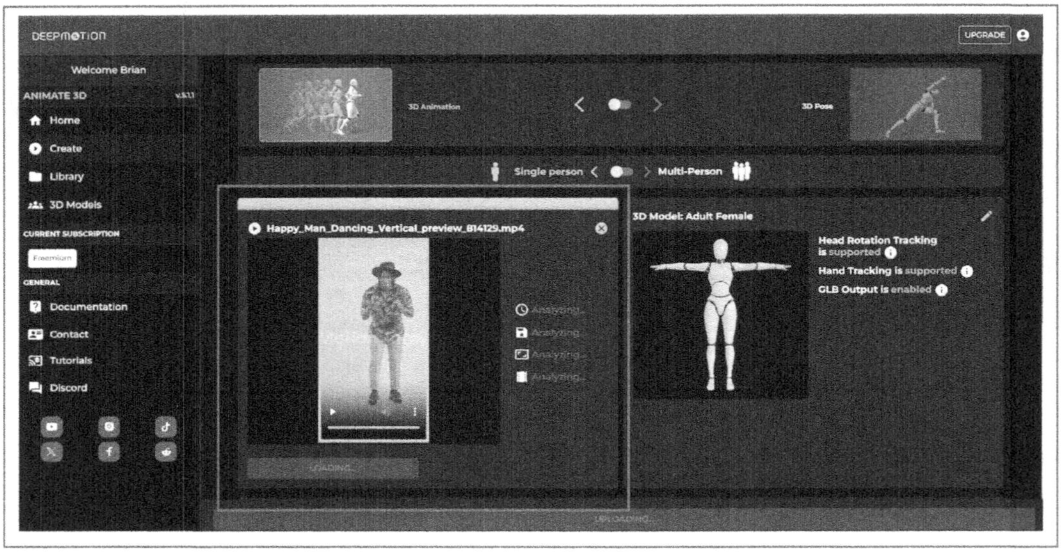

Figure 7.6: Uploading and analyzing a clip

In *Figure 7.6*, you can see a thumbnail of the video clip, along with the clip's filename, `Happy-man-dancing-vertical-814129_1.mp4`. The clip in question is longer than the freemium subscription allows. Because of that, the following pop-up will appear.

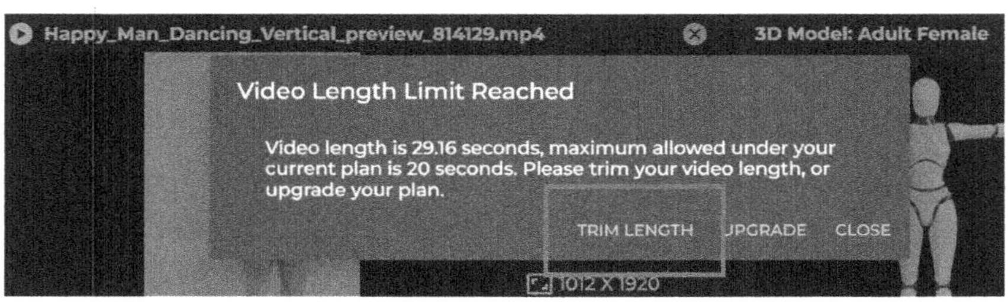

Figure 7.7: Trim length popup

Click on **Trim Length** to allow us to use this clip.

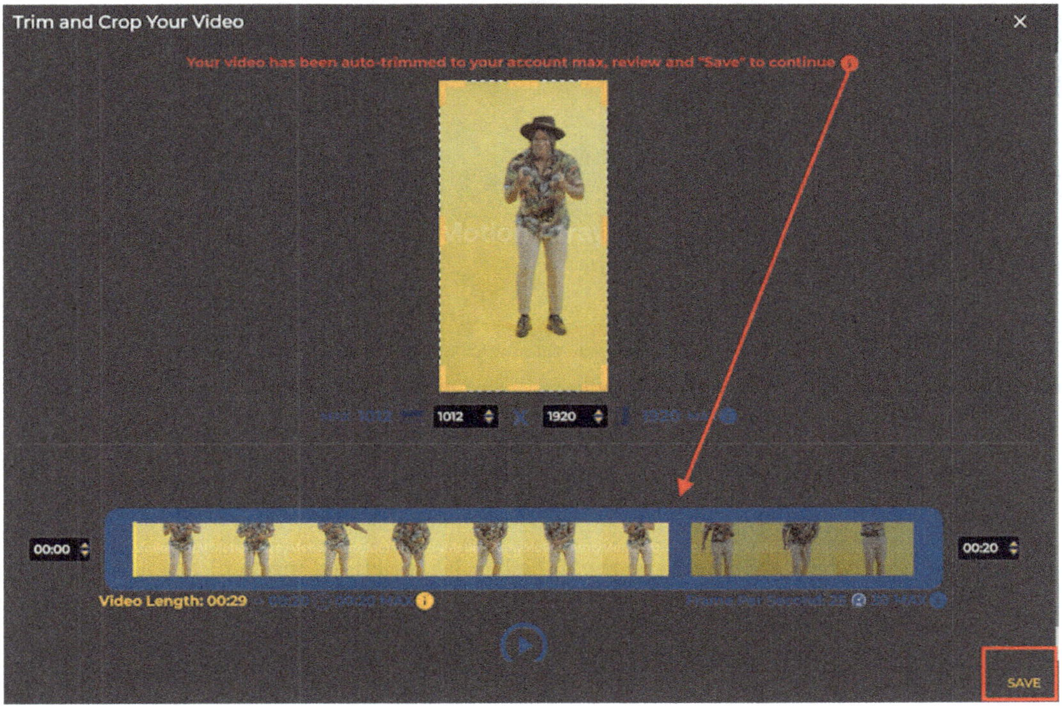

Figure 7.8: Auto trim based on account subscription

Once you click **TRIM LENGTH**, a basic video editor appears. A red message confirms that the clip has been automatically shortened to meet the maximum duration.

The trimmed section is shown in blue by DeepMotion. In *Figure 7.8*, I have added a red arrow to highlight where this edit occurs. By default, the system removes footage from the end of the clip. In most cases, whether you are working alone or within a studio, you will want to keep the middle portion. You can adjust this by dragging the blue handles to set new start and end points.

For this example, the default trimming will do. Hit **Save** when you're happy with your selection. When you hit **Save**, the clip attributes will update.

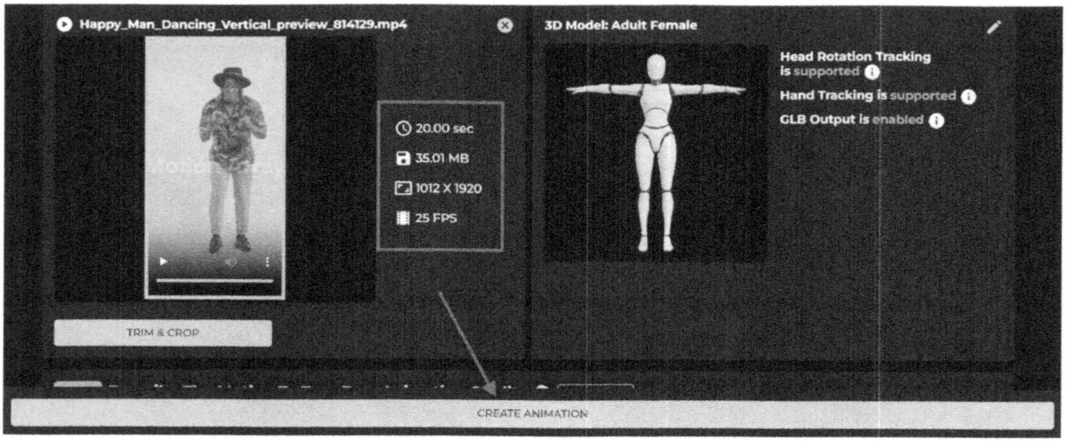

Figure 7.9: Create Animation

As you can see in *Figure 7.9*, the clip is now just 20 seconds long, so the auto trim has successfully cut out the 7 seconds from the end.

The attributes of the clip are present on the right-hand side of the thumbnail, as follows:

- **Duration**: This allows you to keep an eye on how long the clip is. A clip that is longer than is permitted based on your pricing plan will give you an error; in this case, you will need to upload a shorter clip.
- **File size**: If the file size is too big for your account setting, you will get an error. You will need to run the file through a compressor (such as Adobe Encoder) to reduce the file size and then reupload it. If you get an error during the upload process, it is likely that you have breached the limit of one or more of these attributes based on your account setting.
- **Resolution**: Each account setting has a maximum resolution. You will get an error if the resolution is too big, and you will need to reduce the resolution using a converter. For example, a clip that is 4,096 x 3,112 will be too large for the Freemium account, so you will need to scale it down to 1,920 x 1,080 (using Adobe Encoder or similar).

- **Frame rate**: If you have a Freemium account, using a higher frame rate, such as 200 fps, will produce an error. Typically, a webcam will produce a video with a frame rate of around 25 fps, so using a webcam can reduce the chance of this error.

With the video at the desired length, it's almost time to create the animation. But first, let's take a look at some additional and optional features. In *Figure 7.9*, you'll see a pen icon on the far right of the 3D model section. By default, the 3D model is the DeepMotion template, adult female. But, if you click on the pen icon, you can assign another template. The idea being that a template closely matching your character design will give you a better visualization. As shown in *Figure 7.10*, there are six templates to choose from:

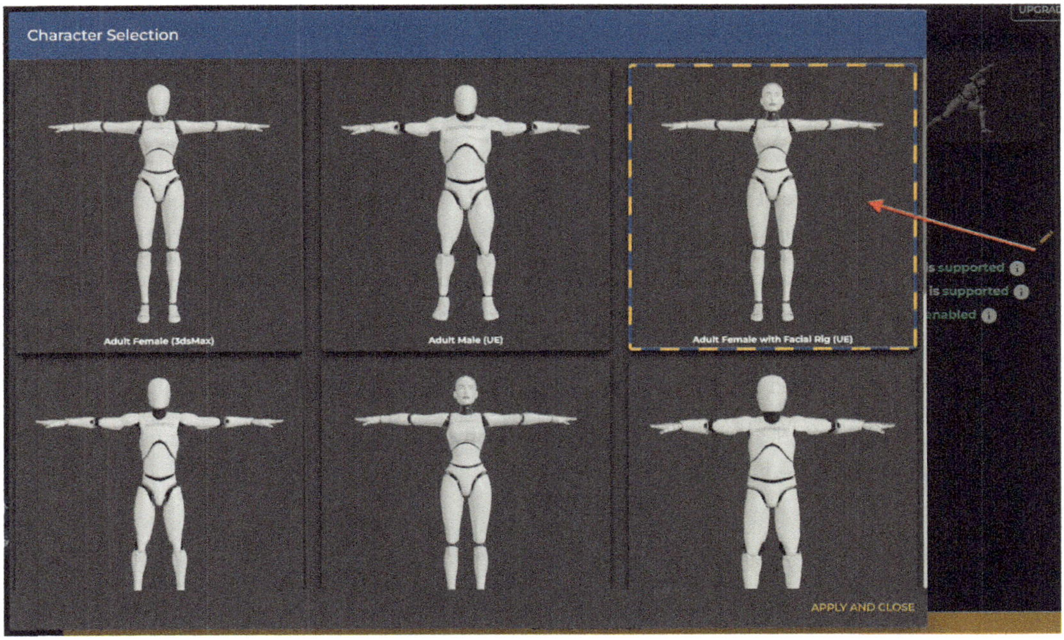

Figure 7.10: Character template selection

For the most part, the available templates will serve us, purely for visualization purposes. However, some of them have some basic facial capture functionality. You can choose this if you like, just to see how it looks, but we will cover far more adequate facial capture in *Chapter 9*.

> **Note**
>
> Choosing a template with the facial capture feature won't have any detrimental effects on the final animation. In fact, choosing any template won't have any detrimental effects on the final animation.

Okay, enough of these template shenanigans, so hit the **Create Animation** button.

In *Figure 7.11*, you can see the pop-up window that will appear as soon as you hit the **Create Animation** button. Here, you can see how a few features are disabled in the Freemium subscription.

- While the **Physics Filter** is shown as disabled, the Freemium account still applies a basic physics solution automatically, but without any user-adjustable controls.
- **Hand Tracking** and **Facial Tracking** are also limited in the Freemium plan compared with the Professional and Studio subscriptions.
  For the purposes of this chapter, the default Freemium settings are perfectly adequate, so there is no need to enable or purchase additional features simply to follow along.

  I will stress that that matches the quality of the dedicated MetaHuman facial workflows covered later in this book.

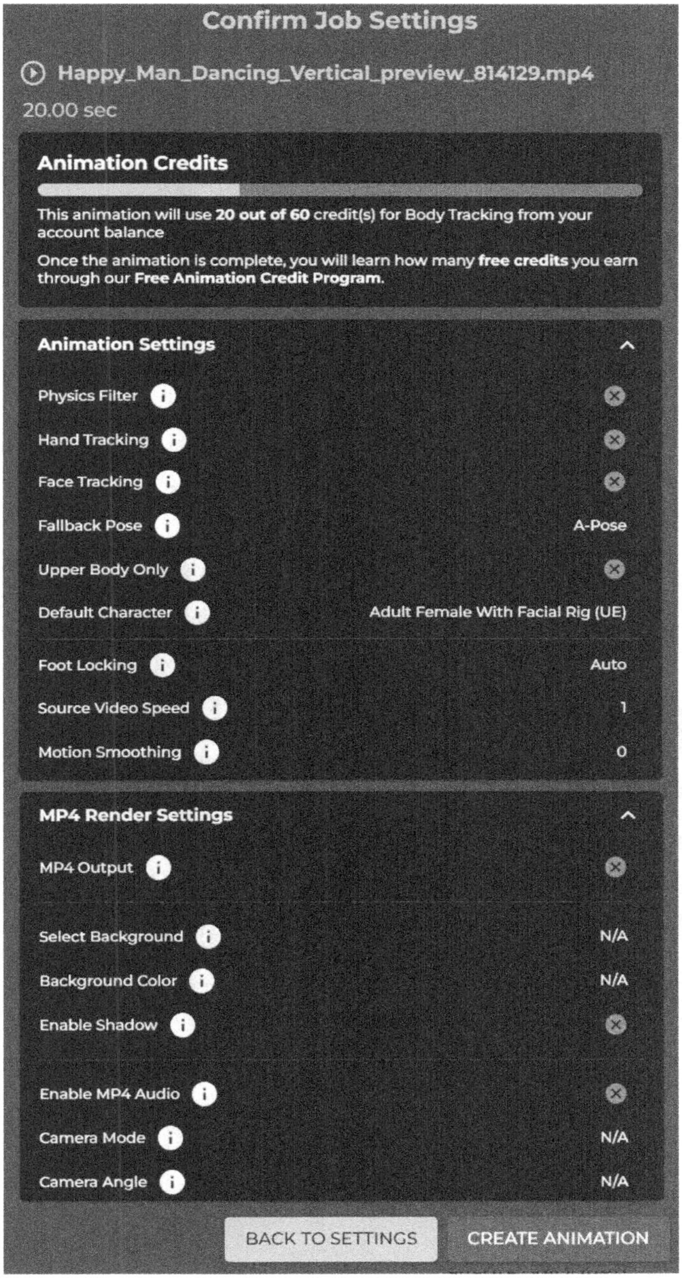

Figure 7.11: Confirm Job Settings

- The **Fallback Pose** is a handy option because when we go to exporting the animation, we are given two animation files, one with a calibration pose such as an A pose and one with no calibration pose at all. This is useful for cloth simulations.
- **Foot Locking** is also just basic, utilizing the auto option as the other options have advanced features for difficult shots but are only available in the professional and studio subscriptions.
- **Motion Smoothing** and **Eye Tracking** are also Professional and Studio subscription features.
- Regarding the **MP4 Render Settings**, they don't apply to us because we are only interested in getting animation data out of DeepMotion and into Unreal. We're not trying to use DeepMotion as a video creation tool.

As soon as you're ready, hit **Create Animation**. A progress bar will appear at the top. This could take a while, so now would be a good time for a cup of tea. As soon as it is completed, you'll see a **Preview** button appear, as shown in *Figure 7.12*.

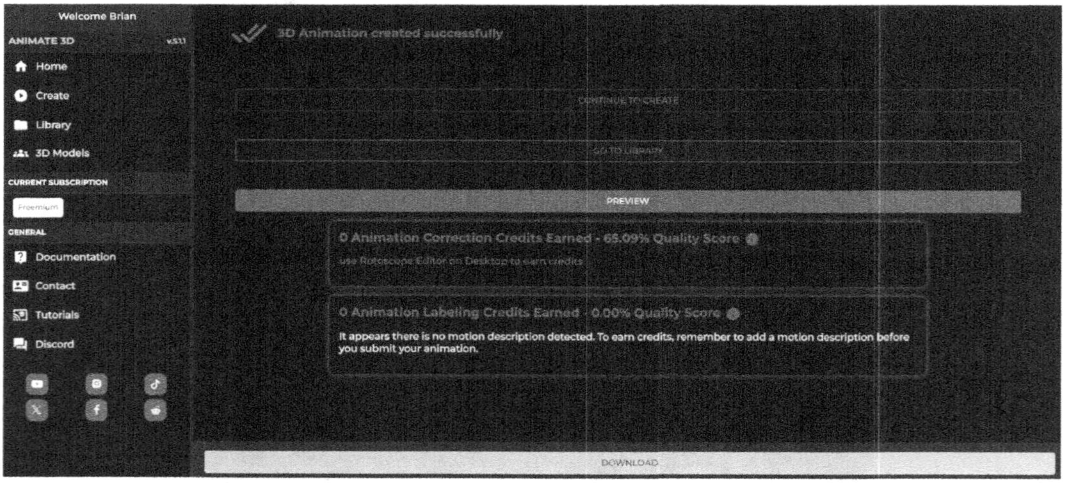

Figure 7.12: Processing finished preview

We're going to take a look at a preview and see if there's much we can do to improve the result with the few tools we have in the freemium subscription. In *Figure 7.13*, you can see the **Preview** tool where we can inspect the results.

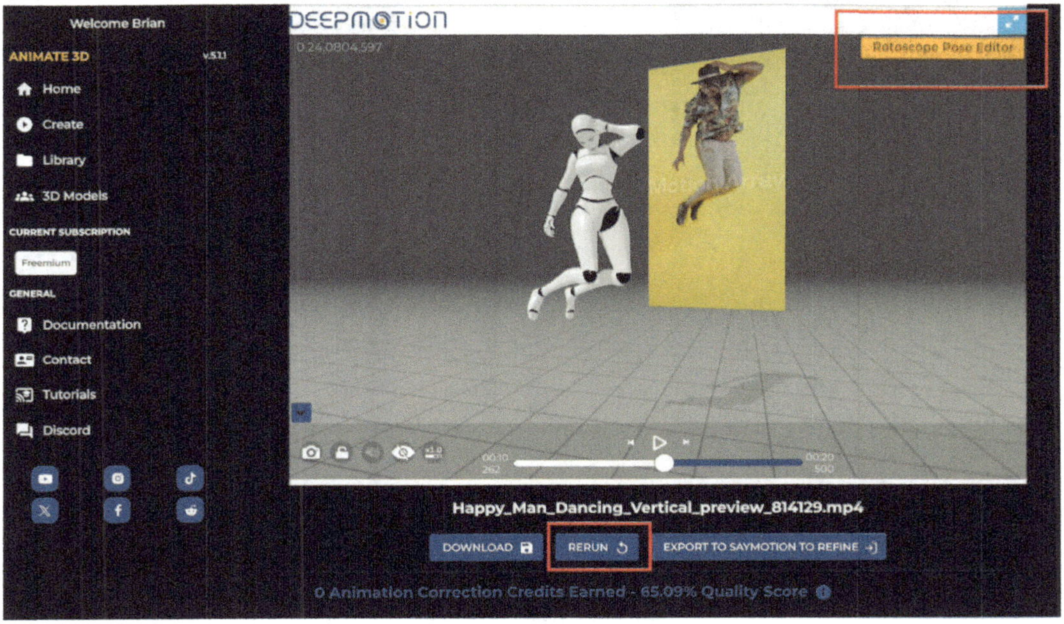

Figure 7.13: Preview and Rotoscope Pose Editor

It has a simple **Play** tool, and you may notice a frame count to the left of the player controls. You can also use the , or . keys to go backward or forward frame by frame. Generally, you'll see a reasonable result from the freemium subscriptions. In my example, nearly all the frames were well matched to the footage. However, there is a new refinement tool in DeepMotion called **Rotoscope Pose Editor**, where we can make per frame adjustments. Click on the yellow **Rotoscope Editor Tool**:

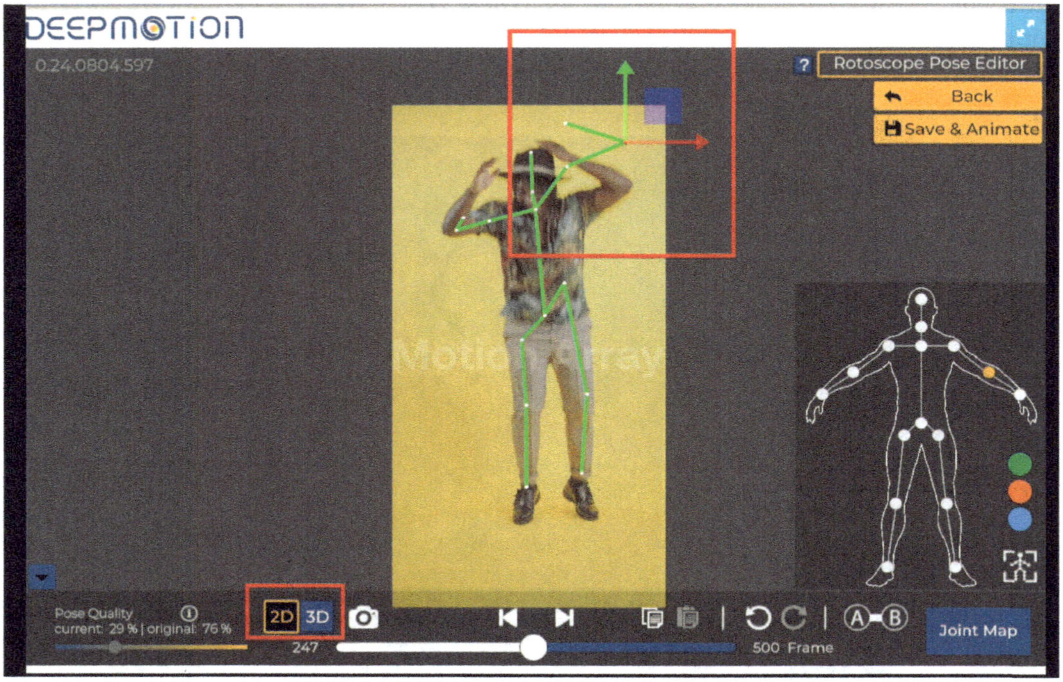

Figure 7.14: Refining Animation

You can see from *Figure 7.14* that I've identified a misalignment on frame 247. I've already got to work correcting one side. By clicking on a white point that represents a joint, you can see a gizmo. For full control of the x and y position of the joint, click on the blue square to quickly make adjustments rather than trying to adjust one axis at a time. You can use the joint map on the bottom right to easily make joint selections, because sometimes it's hard to see the joints in the main viewport. Look through all the frames, but as you do that, toggle between 2D and 3D for more accurate placement. As soon as you're happy with your adjustments, click the **Rerun** button. As soon as you hit **Rerun**, a dialog box as seen in *Figure 7.15* will appear.

Figure 7.15: Rerun processing

You'll already be familiar with the settings. However, this will reiterate what functions you can or cannot use depending on your subscription level. I have detailed below some functional considerations regarding a subscription level.

- **Physics Filter**: This enforces joint limits and attempts to remove collisions, such as hands drifting through the torso. If there are not any notable issues with the footage, I recommend you first attempt to process the animation with **Physics Filter** disabled, as it may produce a somewhat artificial result. Also, remember to take advantage of the **Rerun** option to experiment with **Physics Filter** if you don't get a good result the first time.
- **Foot Locking**: This addresses a common problem in motion capture, which is to do with when a foot leaves the ground and then is returned. For motion capture with suits, this is less of an issue, but with video motion capture, it can be difficult to ascertain when a foot is in contact with the ground or not. **Foot Locking** comes with four options:

    a. **Auto**: This is the most common mode to use as it will automatically switch between locking the foot position to the ground or letting it move. For a character that is walking or dancing, this is the most likely mode to use because the character will inevitably be lifting and resting their feet on the ground intermittently.

> **Note**
>
> Only the Auto setting is available on the Freemium account.

b. **Never**: In animations that involve swimming or continual falling, we know the character's feet will never connect with the ground, so we use this mode to avoid an error

c. **Always**: Best used for situations when the character's feet never leave the ground. It might seem a little obvious but when given the choice between **Auto** and **Always**, it is best to use **Always** when we know the character's feet don't leave the ground as the **Auto** mode could cause errors in this instance.

d. **Grounding**: Effectively, this keeps the feet at ground level but doesn't necessarily lock them to a fixed position. **Auto** works in a similar way but isn't as effective in fast movement; if your character is moving their feet in a sliding motion, **Grounding** mode is the best choice.

- **Default Pose**: This refers to a skeleton calibration pose when saving the animation file. Ideally, the calibration pose of the source animation should match the calibration pose of the target character. In this dropdown, we have four options:

  a. **A-Pose**: One of the most common calibrations poses used and the same pose in which MetaHumans appear in the UE5 engine. This pose sets the arms at a 45-degree angle.

  b. I-Pose: This is an unlikely pose to use but one where the arms are straight down

  c. **T-Pose**: Another standard pose and the default pose of an Unreal Engine Mannequin. The arms are straight out in this pose at a 90-degree angle from the body, thus providing a T shape.

  d. Sitting: Another unlikely pose, where the arms are similar to an A-Pose, but the character is sitting down

- **Motion Smoothing**: This option uses AI to determine how the character should move by looking at the trajectory of each joint and then removes any jitter or noise from the animation, which comes from constant recalibration. While useful to get rid of unwanted jitter, it can introduce some artificial-looking movement; you can dial up and down the intensity of the smoothing to get the results you want.

- **Root Joint at Origin**: This is a particularly useful feature for Unreal Engine artists as it creates a bone at the origin, which is on the ground between both feet. This bone is linked to the hip to correspond to the root position of a character. It is recommended that you turn this feature on for motion capture intended for use with UE, so we'll make sure to do that here.
- **Face Tracking**: At the time of writing, this tool is not a practical solution for the level of facial capture complexity that we will attain within the chapters of this book. Despite using ARKit technology, which is the underlying facial animation control technology for MetaHumans, the accuracy with DeepMotion is nowhere near as advanced as other solutions.
- **Hand Tracking**: This feature simply tracks hand movement but at a more advanced level, attempting to even track fingers. For Freemium users, it's worth considering the extra cost to use this feature; unless you are seeing significant errors in the hand movement, such as hands moving in strange ways or penetrating other body parts, I suggest you leave this to the default setting (which is off).
- **Speed Multiplier**: This is an advanced feature for Premium users and is a great way of adding more accuracy to the motion capture by using videos with higher frame rates (in other words, slow motion). **Speed Multiplier** allows for a range of multiplication of `0-8`. If your character moves at half speed (slow motion), adjusting the multiplier to `2.0` will give you the result of regular motion but with more accuracy. For the Professional and Studio plans, footage shot at up to 120 fps can be used. That footage would be very slow motion, which in turn captures a lot of very detailed and subtle motion. 120 fps is roughly 5 times slower than real-time, so you would use a **Speed Multiplier** of roughly 5 to get a real-time motion capture result and benefit from the increased accuracy.

I encourage you to experiment with these settings and complete a rerun.

A rerun will generally be a little faster than the original process. Once completed, click on **Download** and choose **FBX** from the dropdown menu. DeepMotion will prepare a zipped folder containing two versions of your animation: one regular animation and one with a T pose at the beginning.

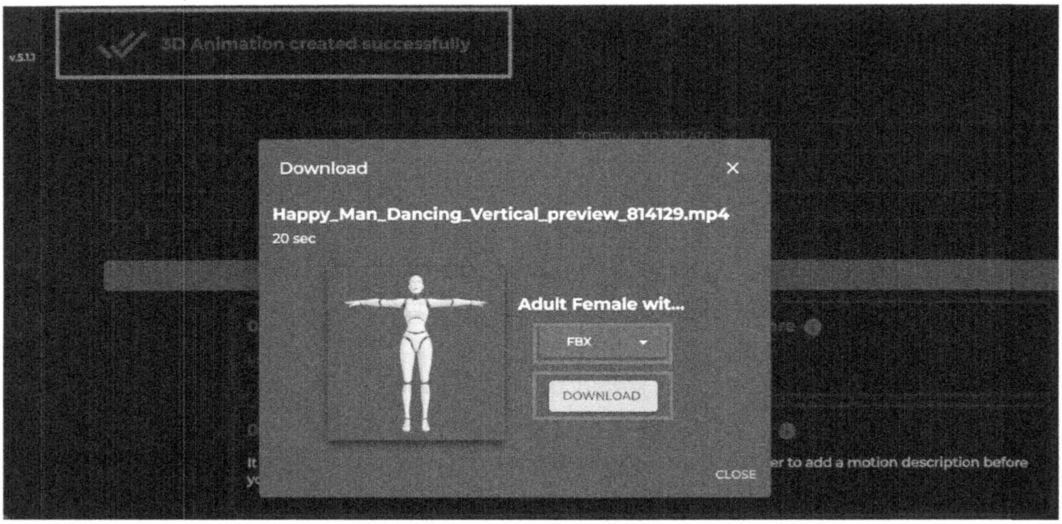

Figure 7.16: Downloading the FBX file

At this stage, choose where you want to save the animation ZIP file. You will still need to import it into Unreal Engine, so note the location. Make sure to unzip the file before importing, as Unreal Engine will not detect it while it remains compressed.

Downloading the DeepMotion motion capture files

The `FBX` file that has `TPose` at the end of the filename (`Adult_Male_Alt(includeTPose)` is given to the file that uses an actual T-pose at the beginning of the animation. The other file, `Adult_Male_Alt`, has no such T-pose at the beginning and, therefore, kicks in with the animation at the very first frame. Choosing one over the other isn't critical, as you can always remove the T-pose section from the animation, but the T-pose could become useful in instances where you need to align it for the purposes of retargeting. We will look at that at the end of this chapter.

Now that we have downloaded the relevant files, in this next section, we are going to import the DeepMotion motion capture file into Unreal so that we can retarget it to the MetaHuman IK Rig.

Importing the DeepMotion animation into Unreal

As mentioned at the very beginning of this chapter, we are building on what we have learned from the previous chapters, but don't worry, we'll use this section as a bit of a recap on how to import a character into Unreal.

The first thing you will need to do is to create a folder in your Unreal project called `Deepmotion`. Make sure that you are working in the project that you used in the previous chapter, where you have both a source and target IK Rig for your Mixamo character and your MetaHuman character.

Once you've created the `Deepmotion` folder, *right-click* anywhere within the **Content Browser** of your `Deepmotion` folder and look for your new DeepMotion `FBX` files. Choose the one that has the name `TPose` included. When you select it, you will then be greeted by the **FBX Import Options** dialog box, as shown in *Figure 7.17*:

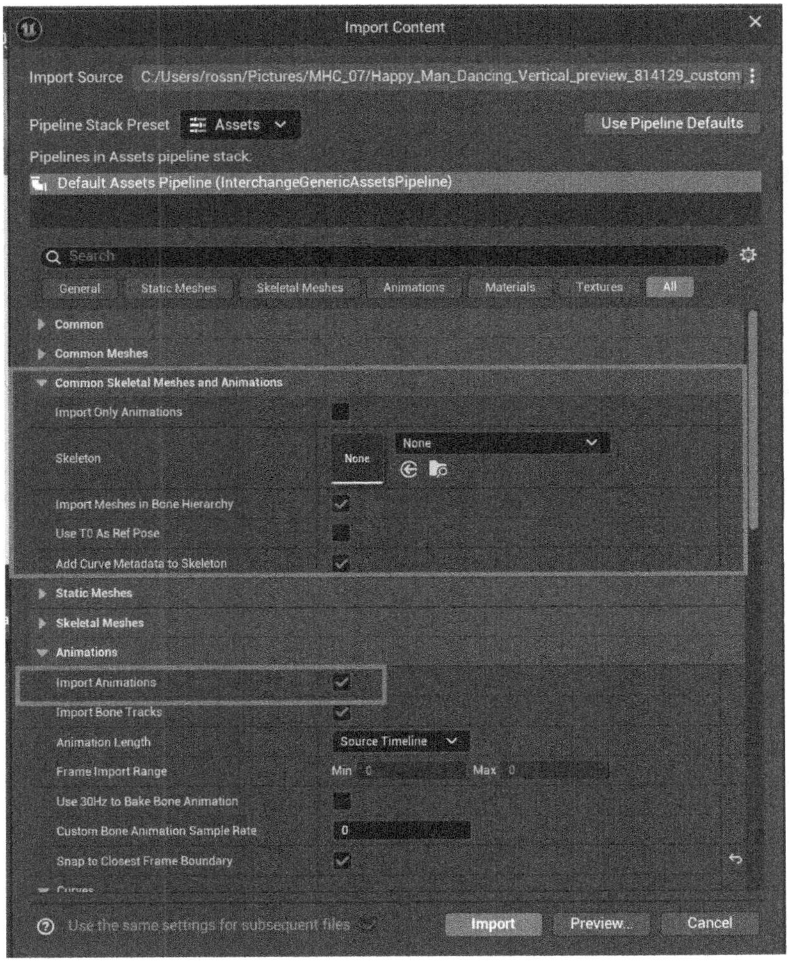

Figure 7.17: FBX Import Options

There are two things to consider here:

- First, we don't want to assign a skeleton to this import; we want to use one that is embedded in the file that we are about to import. So, under **Mesh**, leave **Skeleton** to its default position of **None**, and make sure the **Skeletal Mesh** option is selected so that it knows to choose the skeletal mesh from the file.
- Second, while it sounds obvious, make sure you tick the **Import Animations** option under **Animations**.

After those considerations, click on the blue **Import All** button. Don't be alarmed by the error that mentions smoothing that pops up; you can dismiss that.

Now, when you look at your `Deepmotion` folder in your **Content Browser**, you should see something similar to *Figure 7.18*:

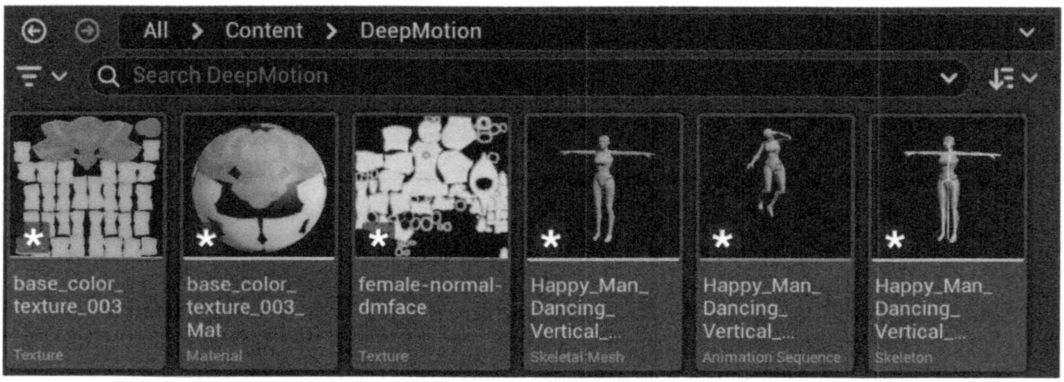

Figure 7.18: Imported DeepMotion assets

Much of what you see here should be familiar; from left to right, you will see the following:

- A material shader for the body
- A T-pose skeleton without animation
- The DeepMotion skeleton with animation
- The DeepMotion skeleton physics asset
- A T-pose skeleton without animation for editing
- A texture file used in the material shader for the body

In this section, we have successfully imported the DeepMotion file into Unreal Engine. In the next section, we will use the DeepMotion animation with our character.

Retargeting the DeepMotion motion capture

In *Chapter 6*, we used Unreal Engine's streamlined *right-click* | **Retarget Animation Assets** workflow. If that workflow produces good results for your project, you can continue using it and skip the remainder of this chapter.

Here, we'll take a more manual approach using IK Rigs and an IK Retargeter. While it involves a few extra steps, it gives us far greater control when solving difficult retargeting problems, correcting mismatched poses, or working with motion capture data from third-party sources.

The source and target skeletons will each be assigned an IK Rig before being connected through an IK Retargeter, allowing us to refine the transfer process in ways that the automatic workflow cannot.

First, you'll need to create an IK rig as the source. So, while in the `Deepmotion` folder, *right-click* anywhere, and choose **Animation**, followed by **IK Rig**, as shown in *Figure 7.19*:

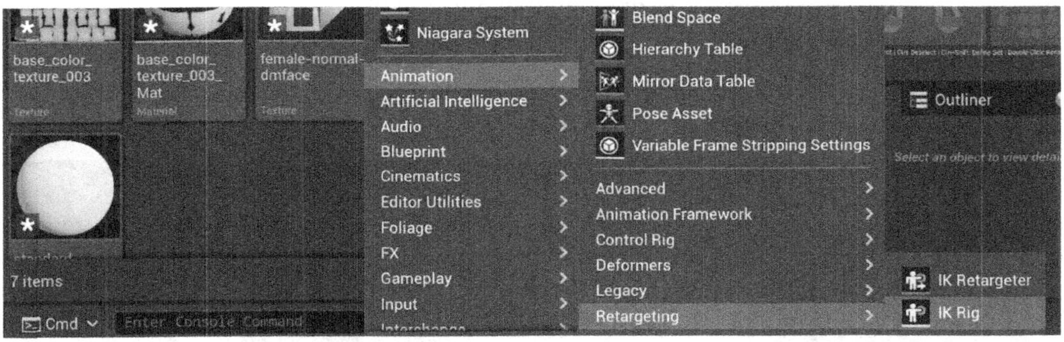

Figure 7.19: Creating an IK Rig Asset

To avoid confusion, call this IK rig `Source_DM_Happy` (this will help us later when we are looking for it).

The goal here is to tell Unreal exactly how the source and target are constructed by creating chains. A **chain** is a simple collection of bones that make up a limb, torso, etc.

We will need to create six separate IK chains corresponding to the following:

- The root to the hip
- The spine and head
- The left arm
- The right arm
- The left leg
- The right leg

The main variable when importing motion capture from different sources is the naming convention used by the skeleton.

Because we selected a **UE-compatible skeleton** in DeepMotion, the bone names closely match Unreal Engine's naming convention, allowing **Auto Create Retarget Chains** to work reliably.

If you're importing motion capture from another source and Auto Create Retarget Chains produces incomplete or incorrect results, you'll simply need to create or adjust the chains manually before continuing.

So, after creating an IK rig as a source, we need to import the source skeleton. *Double-click* the IK rig you just created to open it.

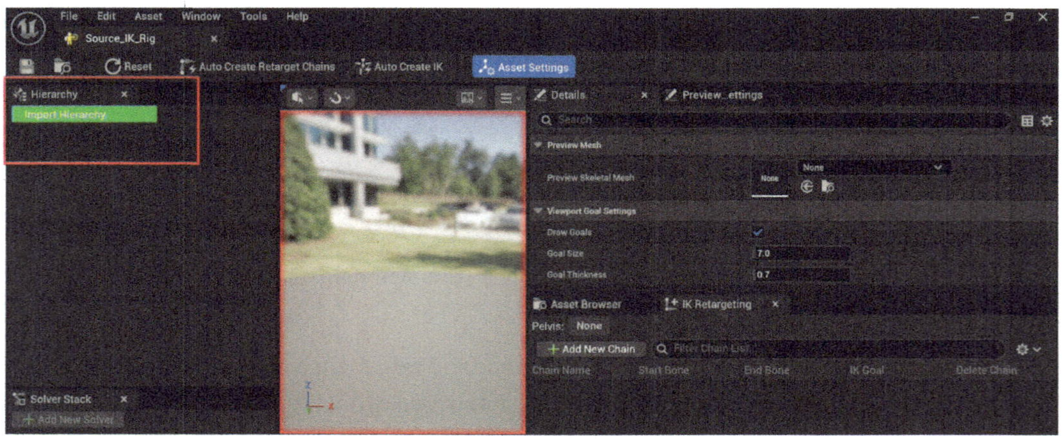

Figure 7.20: Inside the source IK Rig

We now need to click the green **Import Hierarchy** button to import the DeepMotion skeleton we imported earlier (*Figure 7.20*). This will give us the following pop-up window. Search for the skeleton.

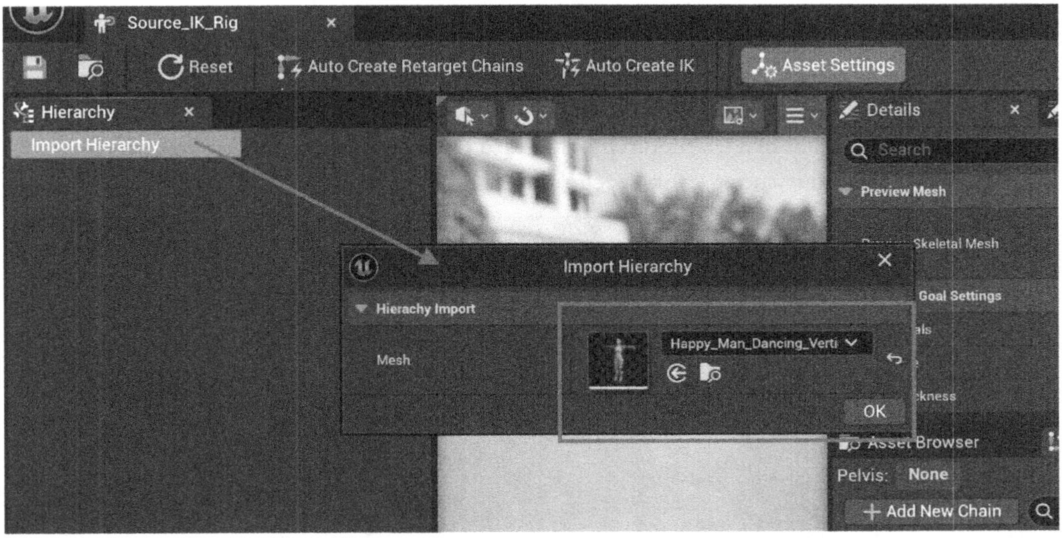

Figure 7.21: Importing the source skeleton hierarchy

Once you've selected your skeleton from the drop-down menu, hit **OK**.

Doing so will populate the IK rig with the entire hierarchy of the skeleton but with no chains. It is the use of chains that simplifies the targeting process.

In *Figure 7.22*, at the top, I've highlighted the **Auto Create Retarget Chains** option. We will use that. However, I've also selected part of the hierarchy to demonstrate what would typically form a chain.

Figure 7.22: Manually and automatically creating chains

The viewport confirms my selection. If we were to manually create a chain based on this selection, we would simply use the **Add New Chain** button on the right, also highlighted in *Figure 7.22*. We would need to do this for each separate selection of bones, for the other arm, both legs, and for the lower spine to the head—five chains in total. But because the naming convention matches that of a UE hierarchy, the **Auto Create Retarget Chains** button will do this automatically and without error. So, click on that button.

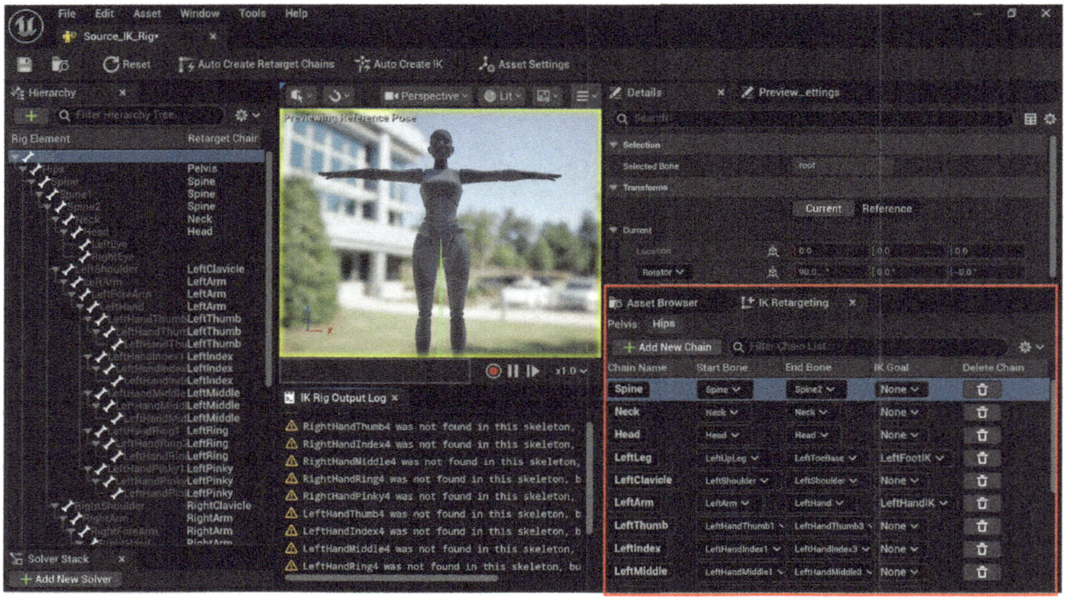

Figure 7.23: Result of Automatically Creating Chains

Save this IK rig and go to the `MetaHumans` folder, and inside the `Body` folder, create a new IK rig, called something like `Source_IK_Rig`. Repeat the exact same steps, except this time, you'll be importing the `SKM_NewMetaHumanCharacter_BodyMesh` hierarchy. In other words, you'll be using the target MetaHuman skeleton Mesh. With both your source and target IK rigs created, the next step is to create an **IK Retargeter**.

Note

Mocap fingers

Unless you're working with the professional subscription, you will be missing finger bones in the source IK rig, which are denoted by the message logs in *Figure 7.23*. Even with the professional subscription, finger tracking of markerless mocap solutions isn't at a production standard level. The highest standard is the use of mocap gloves, which are not perfect and frequently need fine tuning in animation.

Once you have created a new **IK Retargeter**, *double-click* on it to open it and you'll see a list of potential sources to choose from.

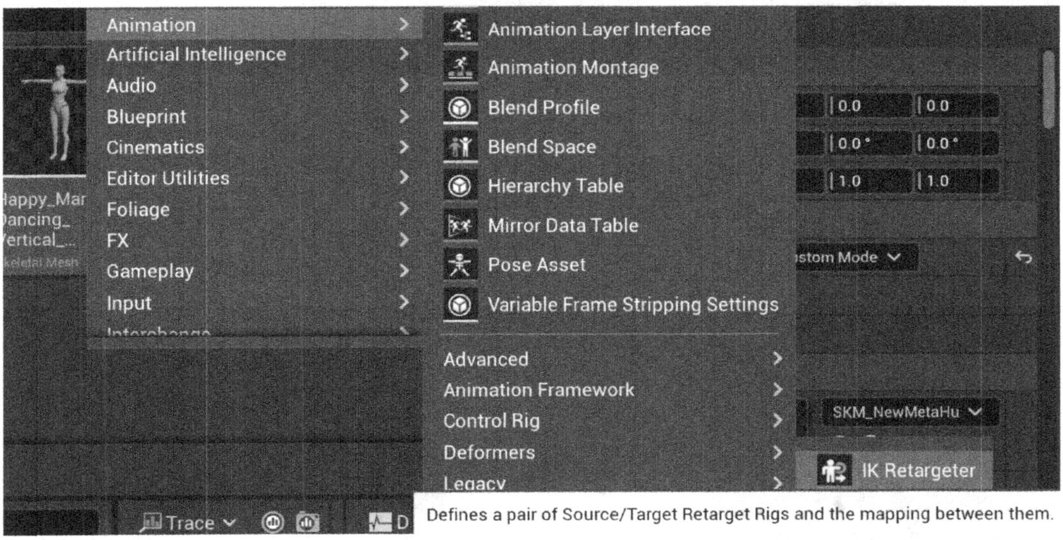

Figure 7.24: Creating the IK Retargeter

In *Figure 7.24*, you can see that I have a list of all the IK rigs that are saved in my project folder. In the source IK rig asset dropdown list, choose the source IK rig and hit **OK**. Follow the same step for the target dropdown menu. You'll see both skeletons overlap each other in the viewport. You should also see some issues as the DeepMotion skeleton has come in as a T-pose, and the MetaHuman one is an A-pose. Just to reiterate, the auto-retargeter tool featured in *Chapter 6* takes care of this issue.

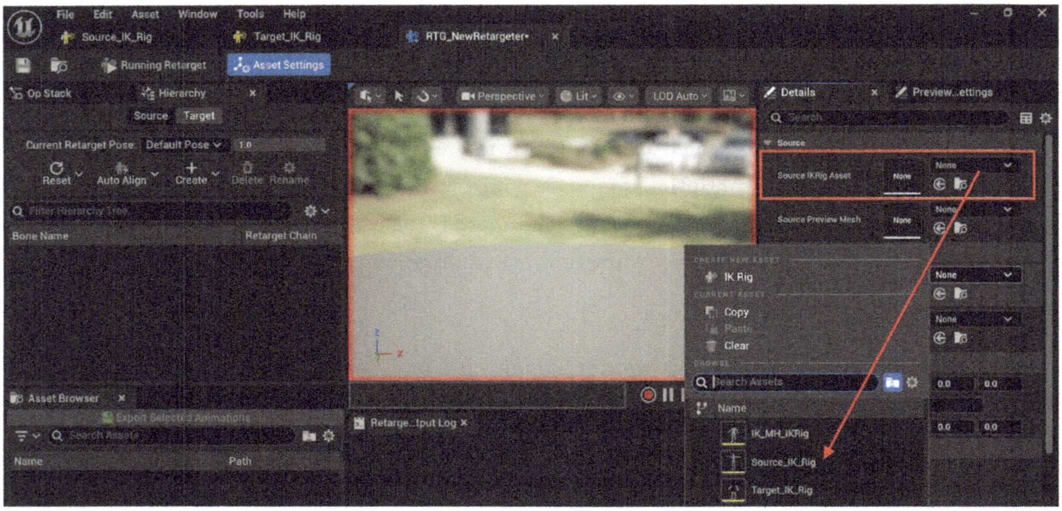

Figure 7.25: Choosing the source and target IK rigs

The T-pose and A-pose issue is the usual cause for issues and is generally the first thing to be looking at. The arms are in different rotational positions and, therefore, create significant issues in animation, usually causing the arms to penetrate directly through the torso. We don't want that, so the quick manual solution is to fix the source by making it an A-pose.

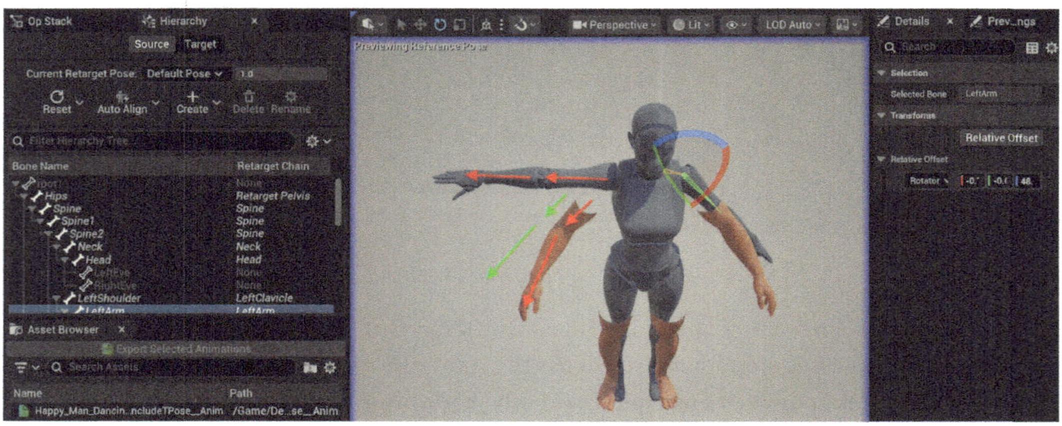

Figure 7.26: Rotating the arm and lower arm

In Figure 7.26, I'm viewing the skeletons from above so that the pose differences are easier to see. Rotate the source upper arms until they visually align with the MetaHuman A-pose, then introduce a slight bend into the lower arms to match the MetaHuman elbows. A small outward rotation of the upper legs will also improve the overall pose match.

Don't worry about achieving a mathematically perfect alignment. The goal is simply to create a close visual match between the source T-pose and the MetaHuman A-pose. Any remaining differences can be refined later using a MetaHuman control rig.

With the goal being to retarget the animation so that it works effectively on our MetaHuman, the last step in this process is to hit the **Export Selected Animation** button, shown in *Figure 7. 27*:

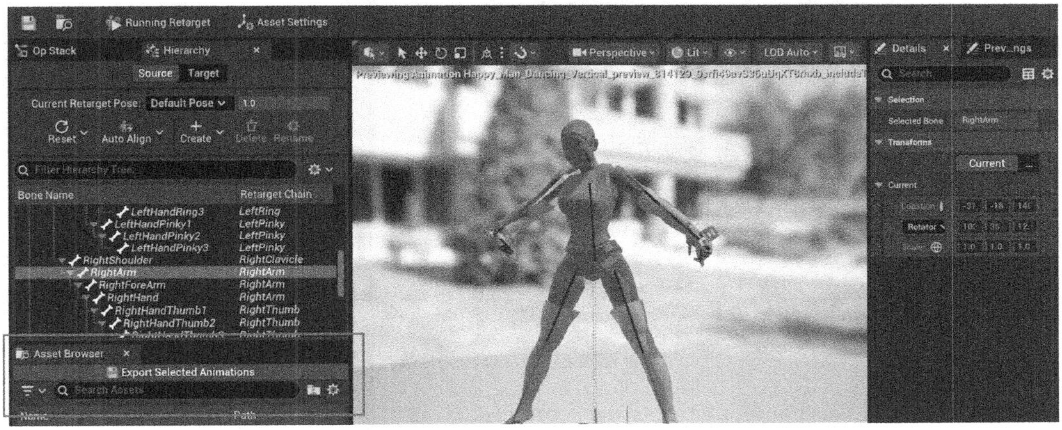

Figure 7.27: The Export Selected Animation button

Once you match the problematic limbs as much as possible, it's time to export the animation using the **Export Selected Animation** button. If there were a lot of animations, you could do them all in one batch by selecting them all. It's worth noting that any matching you can't get right here can easily be fixed using a MetaHuman Control Rig, which we will explore further in *Chapter 8*. The goal here was to get it as close as possible, which will minimize refining in the next step. Now, with the **Export Selected Animation** button pressed, the next dialog box will be familiar territory.

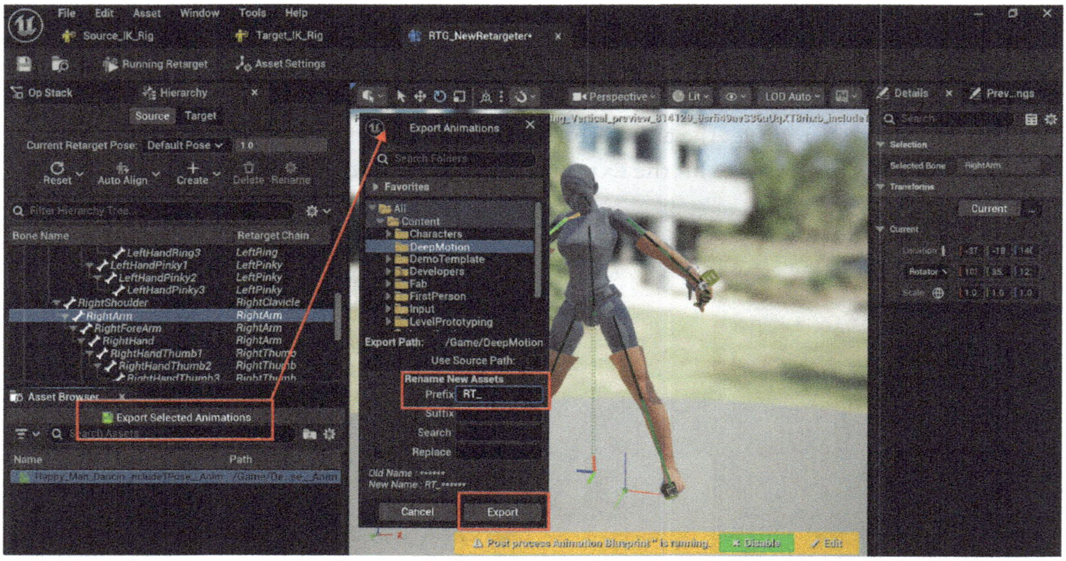

Figure 7.28: Exporting animation

As stressed before, it is good practice to use a prefix such as `RT_` to confirm that this is a retargeted asset and not an original. Once you've hit the **Export** button, you will now have a new animation that is compatible with a MetaHuman.

Summary

In this section, we covered how we can create our own animation with as little as a single video camera. First, we looked at some of the major considerations when it comes to filming, what to avoid, and what steps we can take to bring even more accuracy.

Then, we started using DeepMotion, exploring the various animation settings that it can offer us, including some artificial intelligence functionality. We explored the rotoscoping tool that allowed us to refine areas that weren't tracking correctly. We looked at some job settings in DeepMotion and the use of reruns before committing to the final animation.

Building on what we learned in the previous chapters, we once again retargeted our bespoke motion capture and applied it to our MetaHuman character, while looking a little more closely at A-poses versus T-poses. Finally, we covered an effective workaround for issues arising around those poses while also gaining a solid understanding of what is happening under the hood with the streamlined retargeter.

In the next chapter, we are going to look at the **Level Sequencer** and **Control Rig** and how to further refine custom motion capture in general.

8

Using the Level Sequencer

In *Chapter 7*, we learned how to bring our own motion capture data into Unreal and retarget it to a MetaHuman. However, there are times when we need to make adjustments that are required to fix issues or add an extra level of creativity to its performance.

One issue we came across in the previous chapter was caused by the discrepancies between using the A-pose and T-pose, and we were able to fix that by editing the A-pose of our MetaHuman inside the MetaHuman Blueprint.

In this chapter, we are going to look at another way to make changes to our character's pose to fix minor issues, such as an arm colliding with the torso of the MetaHuman, and we will also look at how we can refine the motion of the character. For this, we will use the **Level Sequencer**, which is the tool we use for animating anything in Unreal Engine, and in many ways works like a timeline in a video editing application. In addition, we will use the MetaHuman Control Rig, which is key to fine-tuning and fixing animation.

So, in this chapter, we will cover the following topics:

- Introducing the **Level Sequencer**
- Creating a **Level Sequencer** and importing our character Blueprint
- Adding the retargeted animation to the character Blueprint
- Adding and editing the Control Rig
- Adding a camera to the **Level Sequencer**
- Rendering a test animation from the **Level Sequencer**

Technical requirements

In terms of computer power, you will need the technical requirements detailed in *Chapter 1* and the MetaHuman plus the Unreal Engine Mannequin that we imported into UE5 in *Chapter 2*. Both of these will need to be saved in the same project in UE, and you will need to have UE running for this chapter.

For this chapter, you will also need to have access to the motion capture data that you retargeted in *Chapter 6* or *7*.

Introducing the Level Sequencer

Until now, you've been able to preview your animation either within the character Blueprint or within the viewport using the **Play** button.

You've also been introduced to the **Level Sequencer** when we blended the Mixamo *Thriller* dance clips together.

While a **Level Sequencer** can be used in gameplay, for the purpose of this book, we want to focus on using the **Level Sequencer** to make the most of our motion capture animation. A **Level Sequencer** is a timeline within our level where we can control our animations. There can be more than one **Level Sequencer**, and a **Level Sequencer** can contain another **Level Sequencer**. It is similar to any other timeline in an editing program, except that instead of adding video clips, we add elements to our scene and then apply animatable attributes.

When using Unreal Engine for animation, anything you want animated needs to be added to a **Level Sequencer**, including lights, cameras, actors, vehicles, and even video and audio.

The beauty of the **Level Sequencer** is that it allows you to only focus on the animated objects and also allows you to effectively tweak animation by adding independent keyframes without being overwhelmed by all the keyframes that come with the motion capture data. Using it, we can make changes to the motion capture animation without having to depend on getting absolutely perfect takes when working with a motion capture solution such as DeepMotion or motion capture library files such as Mixamo.

In the next section, we'll go through the process of getting a character into a **Level Sequencer**.

Creating a Level Sequencer and importing our character Blueprint

So, let's get started with creating a **Level Sequencer** (there isn't a lot to it).

First, you need to *right-click* anywhere within your `Content` folder; in my case, I did just that within my `MetaHumans` folder, which you can see in *Figure 8.1*. Then, go to **Animation** and then click on **Level Sequence**.

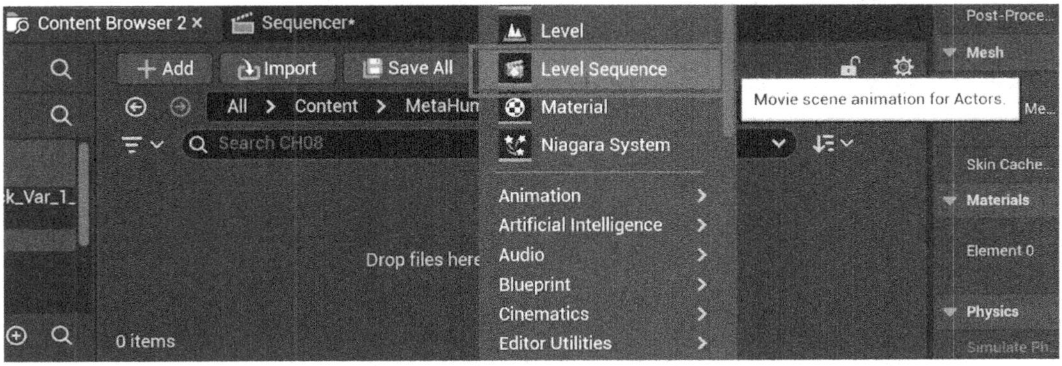

Figure 8.1: Creating a Level Sequencer

With the **Level Sequence** created, you'll see a **Level Sequencer** clapper icon in the `Content` folder. *Double-click* on the **Level Sequencer** icon to open it. You will see an empty **Sequencer**, as shown in *Figure 8.2*:

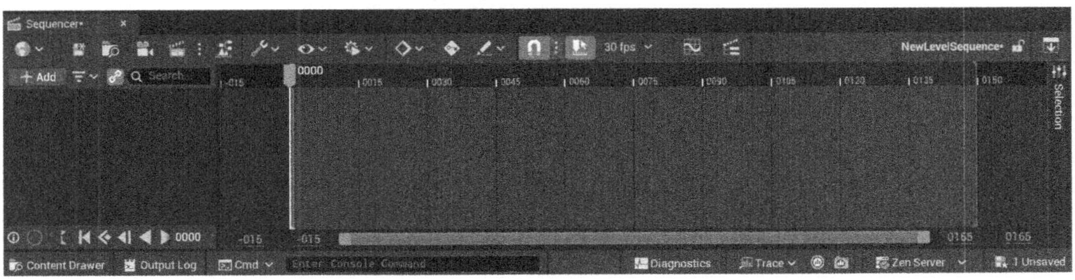

Figure 8.2: An empty Level Sequencer

In order to animate using the **Level Sequencer**, you need to add an **actor**. An actor can be pretty much anything that you want to animate. Once an actor is added to a **Sequencer**, an animation track is created.

Because we want to animate our MetaHuman character, we will need to add the MetaHuman Blueprint as our animation track. To do this, simply click on **+ Track** and then select **Actor To Sequencer**:

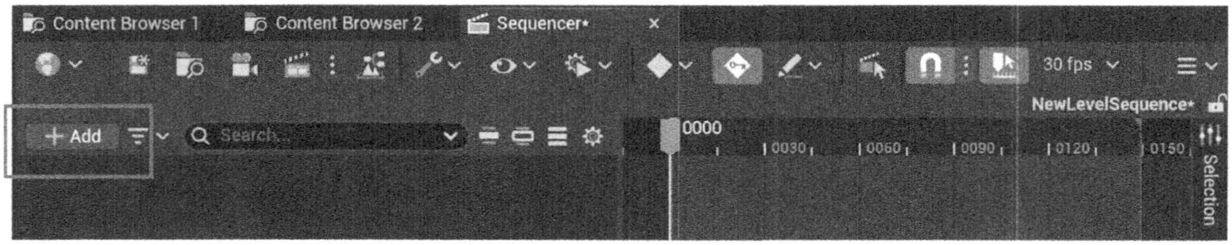

Figure 8.3: Adding an actor to a Level Sequencer

In *Figure 8.3*, you can see the **+ Add** button. Click on it and the following will appear.

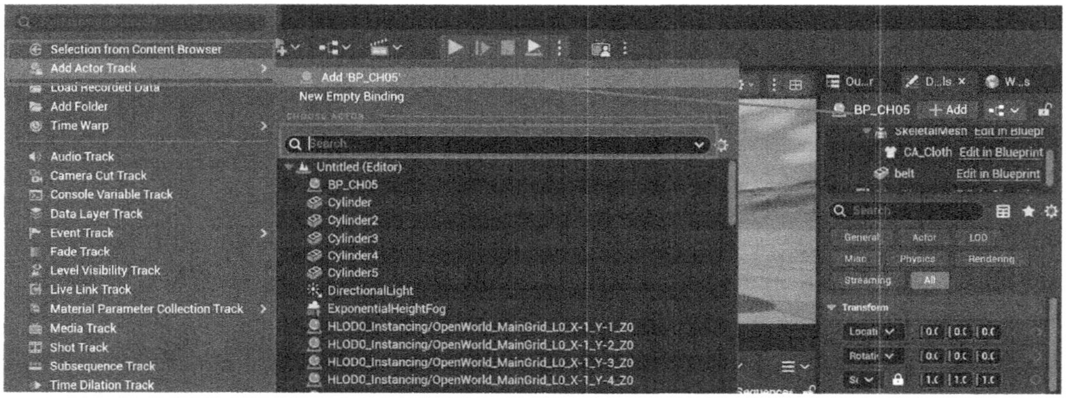

Figure 8.4: Ways to add actors to a Level Sequencer

Just like in *Chapter 6*, I had already selected my character Blueprint from the **Viewport**, the selection confirmed in the **Outliner** to the right of *Figure 8.4*. This speeds things up as it is the first suggestion, as indicated by my red arrow. This saves you having to type the actor in the search box to add it.

Once you add the character Blueprint to the **Sequencer**, you will get two tracks: one for the body and one for the face. This is because the **Level Sequencer** detects that there is a body and a face component in the Blueprint, designed to accept MetaHuman Control Rigs. As you can see from *Figure 8.5*, each of these tracks has a Control Rig. Initially, select the Face rig, which will reveal a yellow interface in the Viewport with controls for facial animation.

We won't be using these controls in this chapter because the next chapter is dedicated entirely to MetaHuman facial performance capture and animation, where we will make full use of the Face Control Rig.

Viewport with controls to animate the face (although we won't be looking at these).

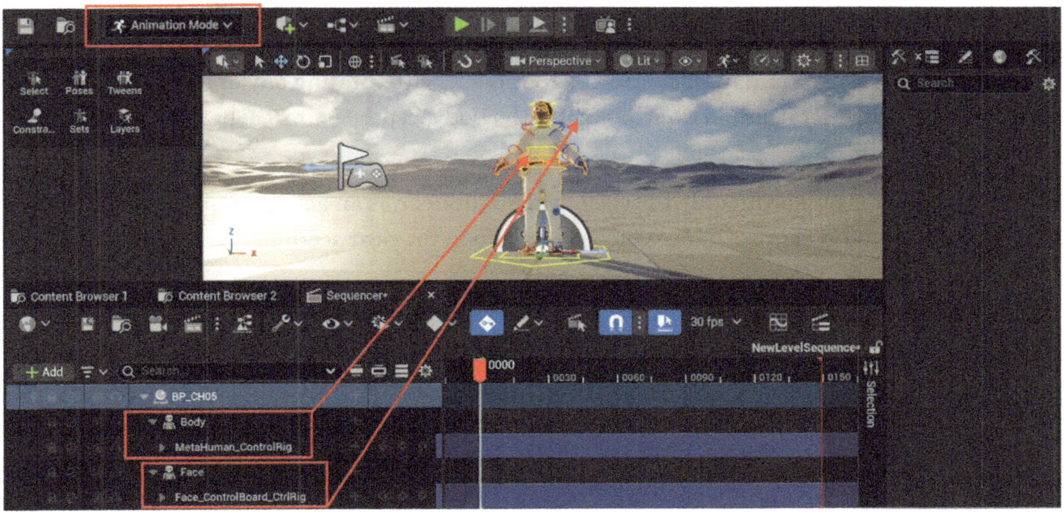

Figure 8.5: Automatic MetaHuman Control Rigs

The other rig available to us is the `Body` rig. If you select the `Body` track in the **Sequencer**, the rig will become visible in the **Viewport**, same as the `Face` Control Rig. You can always make sure you're in **Animation Mode** with *Shift+8*, which will show you both Control Rigs in the **Viewport**.

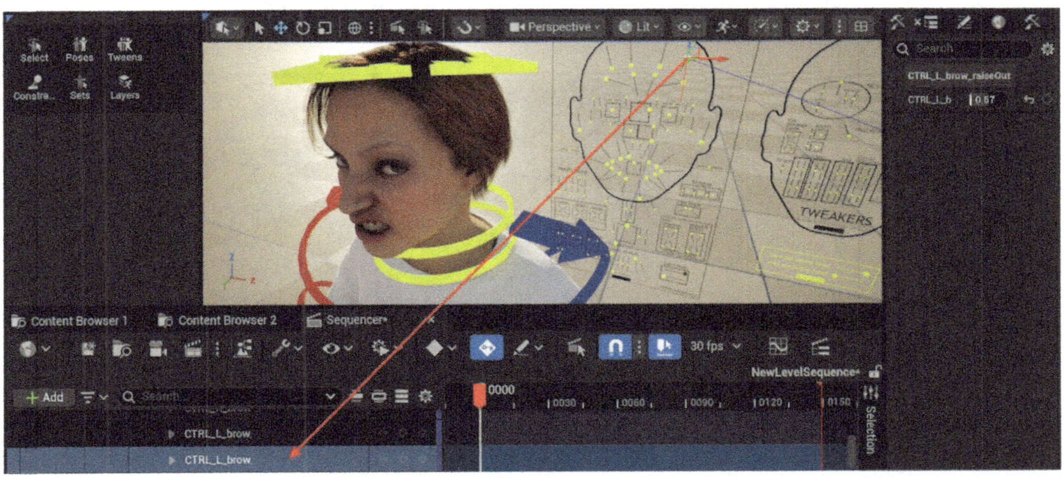

Figure 8.6: The MetaHuman Control Rig

You can immediately create expressions by using the control board or the Control Rig. Note the `Body` Control Rig is also available to pose the body.

At this point, you have just gained a vast amount of control over your MetaHuman Character in terms of animation. Whether you are a seasoned animator or a novice, I recommend you experiment with these animation controls. Experiment with rotating any of the colored components of the MetaHuman Control Rig for the body as per *Figure 8.5*, before you move on to the next section.

With the character Blueprint added to the **Level Sequencer** as an actor, we are now ready to bring in some motion capture data, which we will do in the next section.

Adding the retargeted animation to the character Blueprint

Before bringing the DeepMotion or Mixamo animation into the Unreal Engine Sequencer, we first need to remove the automatically created Body and Face Control Rigs.

This may seem counterintuitive, but those default Control Rigs are designed for creating animation from scratch and will override any imported motion capture animation.

Once they have been removed, we will reintroduce only the **Body Control Rig** as a **Layered Control Rig**, allowing us to preserve the original motion capture while adding corrective animation on top of it.

So, let's delete the two current Control Rigs. You can do this by simply clicking **on MetaHuman Control Rig** and `Face_ControlBoard_CtrlRig` in the **Sequencer** and pressing **Delete** on your keyboard.

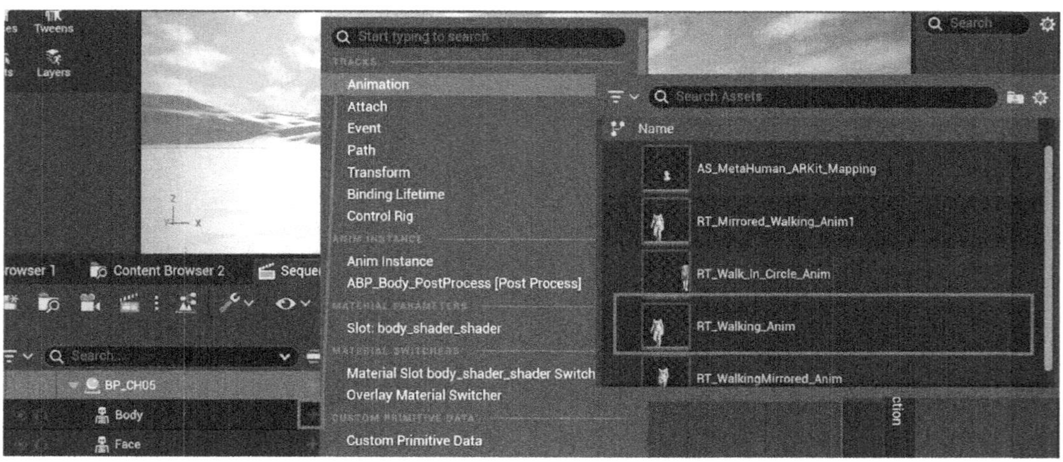

Figure 8.7: Choosing a Retargeted Animation

Now, with Body selected in the **Sequencer**, click on the + icon and, under **Animation**, search for any retargeted animation you have brought into the project, whether from DeepMotion or Mixamo. There are plenty of animations available on Fab, but remember to retarget them first.

Once you have selected the retargeted mocap, it will appear on the timeline within the **Sequencer**.

> **Note**
>
> The animation will start at wherever your **play head** is on the timeline. The play head is the position on the **Sequencer** timeline that it's currently paused at, and the frame the animation will start from. In *Figure 8.6*, my play head is at the frame numbered `0115` (indicated by the red arrow).

When you have imported the mocap animation as a track, you can reposition this track to start at any time by simply dragging the track left or right. The track itself includes the title of the animation displayed within it. In *Figure 8.7*, you can see the animation track under the horizontal blue line. Feel free to press **Play** to inspect the animation.

Figure 8.8: The Animation track and Playhead

In order to modify the animation, we need to add a Control Rig back again but unlike the default Rig, we need it to be layered to retain the original animation.

Adding and editing the Control Rig

In the previous edition of this book, we had the convoluted workflow of having to bake all the keyframes of the incoming animation onto a MetaHuman Control Rig and then add another MetaHuman Control Rig on top of that to add more animation. This entire setup is negated by the new **Layered** feature, so it is important that you choose that. As shown in *Figure 8.9*, click the + icon next to the body component, then click on **Control Rig**, tick **Layered**, and type `MetaHuman` to see the available control rigs we need to use.

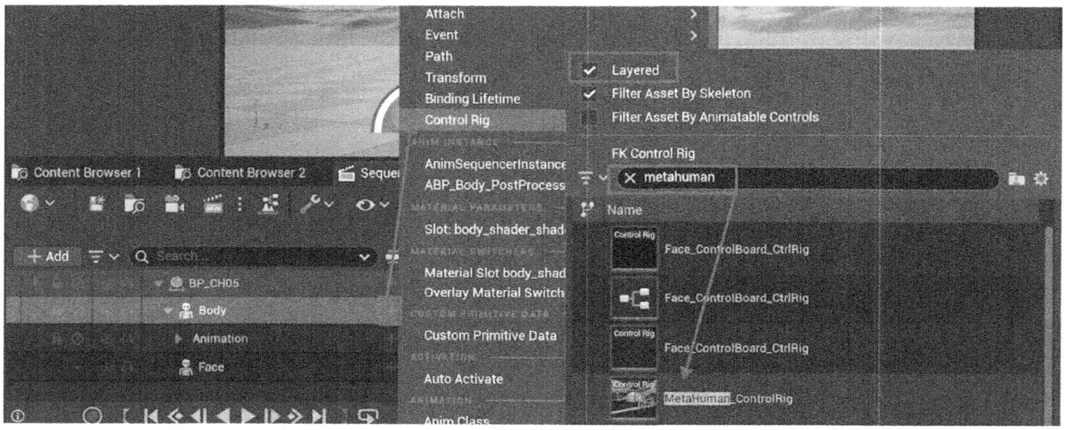

Figure 8.9: Applying a Layered MetaHuman Control Rig to the body component

Be sure to select `MetaHuman_ControlRig` as this is designed specifically for the body skeleton hierarchy. Once selected, a control rig is created around the body of your character, and you can see it still remains in the same pose as before you assigned the Rig. Press **Play** or scrub the timeline to see the animation is intact. You now have a Layered Control Rig to create additional animation while preserving the original motion capture data.

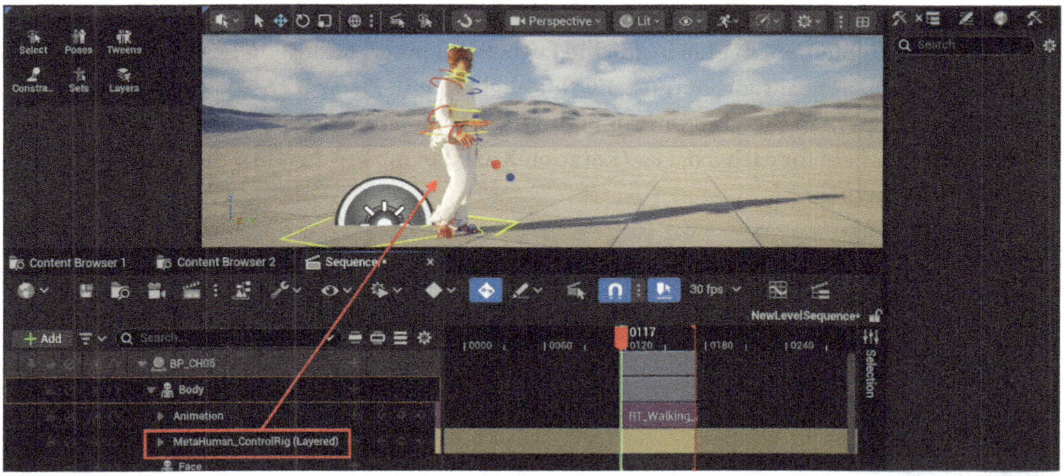

Figure 8.10: Layered Control Rig with original animation intact

Now it's time to make an adjustment. In professional production, the MetaHuman Control Rig is very powerful for quick technical and artist adjustments. Note that it can be used on any character with a similar hierarchy, so it is not limited to just MetaHumans. For this example, I'll just add a bit of a head turn with a slight body twist.

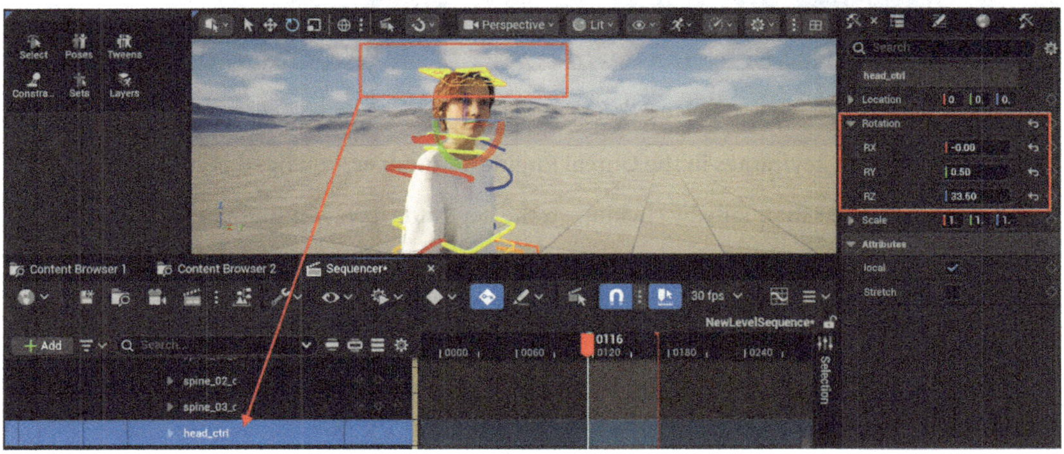

Figure 8.11: Rotating the head

By selecting the uppermost controller, a yellow cross-shaped icon, the `head_ctrl` track will display and be highlighted in blue inside the **Level Sequencer**. Additionally, the **Animations Details** panel will appear for that track. I've highlighted it in *Figure 8.12*. You can choose to make the adjustment in the **Viewport** or in the **Details** panel. Take note of the color scheme next to the entry field for each axis: Rx (Rotation X axis) being red, just like the rotational gizmo in the **Viewport**.

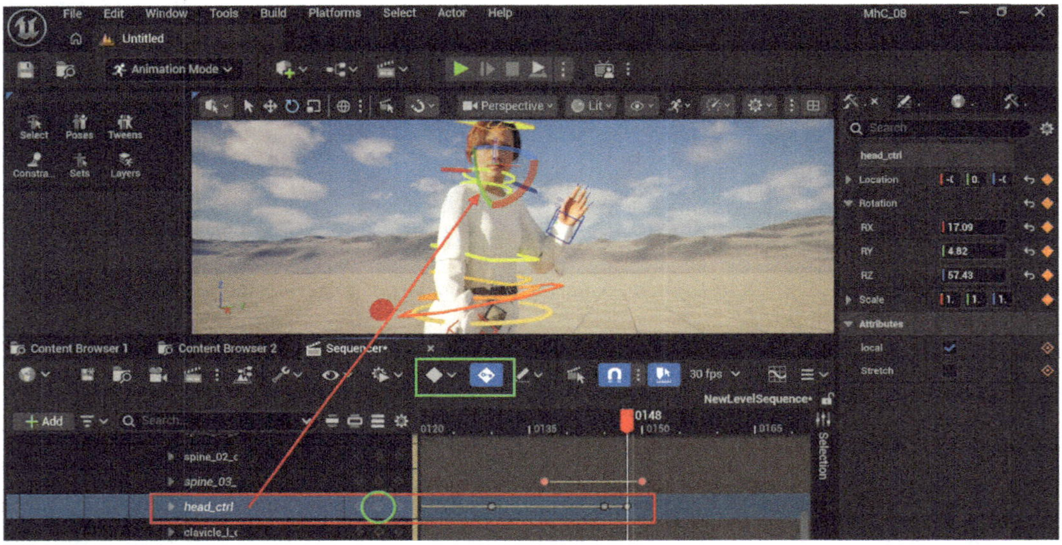

Figure 8.12: Keyframing rotational values

When working with keyframes in the Unreal Engine **Sequencer**, you have a few options.

You can set keyframes manually by clicking on the keyframe icon, highlighted by the green circle in *Figure 8.12*.

Alternatively, click the first icon on the left in the green highlighted box and choose **Key All**, shown as a gray diamond.

You can also enable automatic keyframing. Click the next icon so that it turns blue. Once active, any change you make will create a keyframe automatically.

As soon as you have multiple keyframes on any given track, you can reposition the keyframes simply by moving them with your cursor.

By default, all keyframes are cubic, which means motion speeds up after the keyframe and slows down before the next keyframe. This is the default mode of how the motion is interpolated between keyframes. If you *right-click*, you will see a list of available **Key Interpolation** types. For the most part, all the Cubic interpolations perform the same way, but it is the editing of them within a graph curve that is different. As you can see in *Figure 8.13*, we have four types of Cubic interpolation. A **Linear** interpolation has no speed up or slow down, the speed remains the same. **Constant** means that the value remains the same until the next keyframe, effectively not interpolating any value differences within the interval between keyframes.

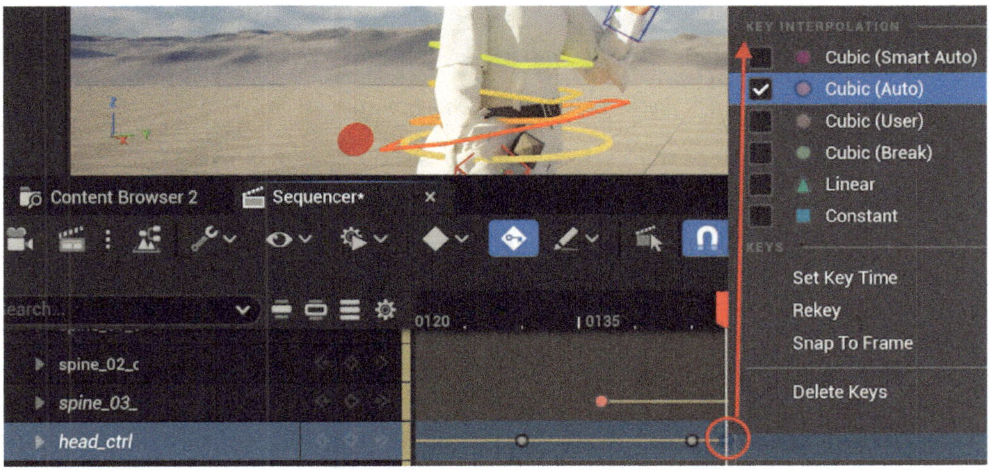

Figure 8.13: Keyframe for interpolation

I mentioned the **Graph Curve** when addressing Cubic interpolation. This is an essential editor for fine-tuning animation, although it can look quite daunting for people new to graph editing. For the **Level Sequencer**, when you click the curve icon, highlighted by the little red box in *Figure 8.14*, the **Sequencer** curve will open up.

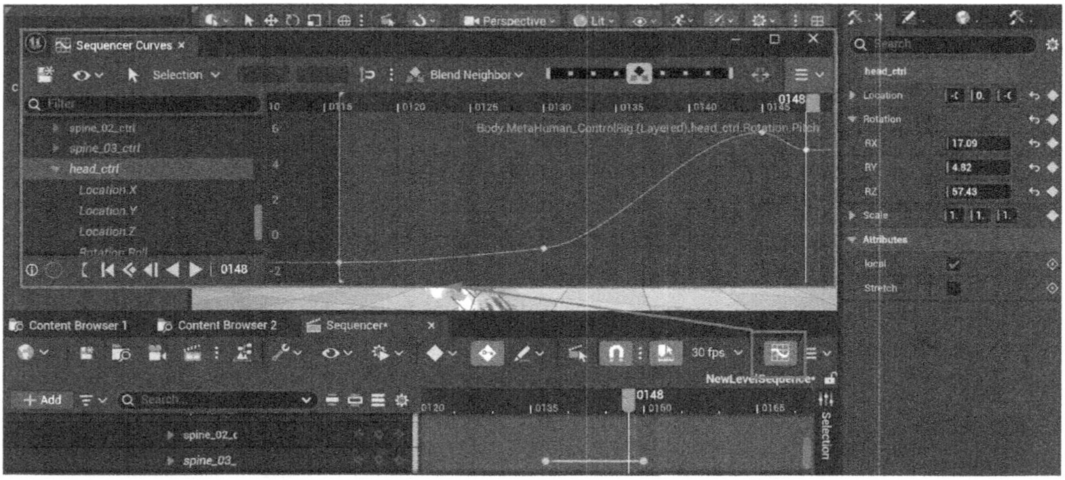

Figure 8.14: Opening Sequencer curves

Because I already had the head track selected, we can see that it is displaying the curve data for the `head_ctl`.

The green curve indicates that just one curve is displaying, the X axis curve, and you may be able to see the green text indicating what it is. Any curve lines or text in green are associated with the X axis.

In *Figure 8.15*, I've demonstrated that you can change the interpolation type directly in the curve editor.

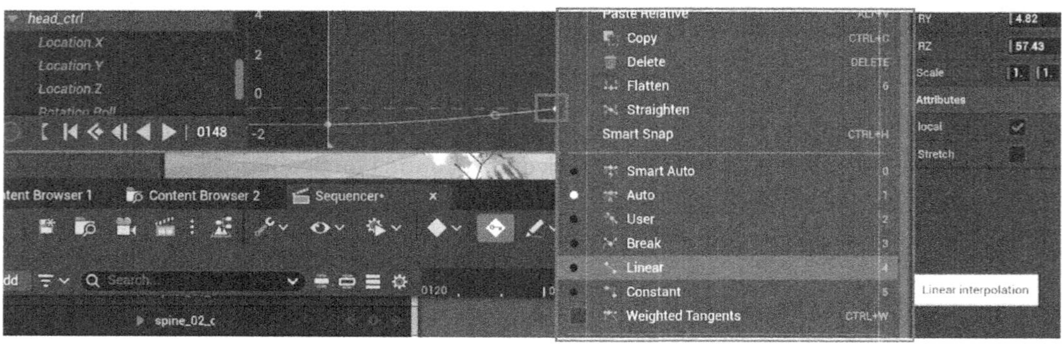

Figure 8.15: A keyframe inside the Sequencer curve editor

So, if you're like me and spend a lot of time working with curves, you can quickly make changes to the interpolation. A good all-rounder for interpolation when working with curves is weighted tangents, which gives you full control of the speed before and after a keyframe. Take note of the shortcut keys if you prefer working with curves versus sliding keyframes along an animation track.

Adding a camera to the Level Sequencer

The UE5 camera is a powerful tool, as it operates just like a real camera. I could write a whole book on the camera alone, but in the interest of completing this chapter, you'll just learn about some very basic camera tips that relate specifically to the **Level Sequencer**.

For simplicity, we are going to create a camera using the **Level Sequencer**. We also need a **Camera Cut**; this is like a master track, mainly designed for the use of multiple cameras, but we still need it for just one camera. The Camera Cut is only automatically generated when we create a camera from within the **Level Sequencer**.

Before we can do that, first we need to create a playback range. When you first create a **Level Sequencer** there is already a playback range indicated by the green and red line. If you don't see one, don't worry, as you can create one by right-clicking anywhere on the timeline within the **Level Sequencer**, choosing **Set Start Time**, and then clicking where you want to start the animation. Then, do the same with our **Set End Time**. The difference between these two times is the playback range. However, this range is also used for defining the render range for when you want to create video files.

Figure 8.16: Playback range

This ensures your playback range is the same length as the entirety of the animation. You can always extend your playback range by simply dragging the red line to the right-hand end of the timeline.

With the playback range created, now we can create a camera that will automatically create a **Camera Cut** to fill the playback range that we created. Very simply, click on the camera icon at the top of the **Sequencer**. I have highlighted this in *Figure 8.17*:

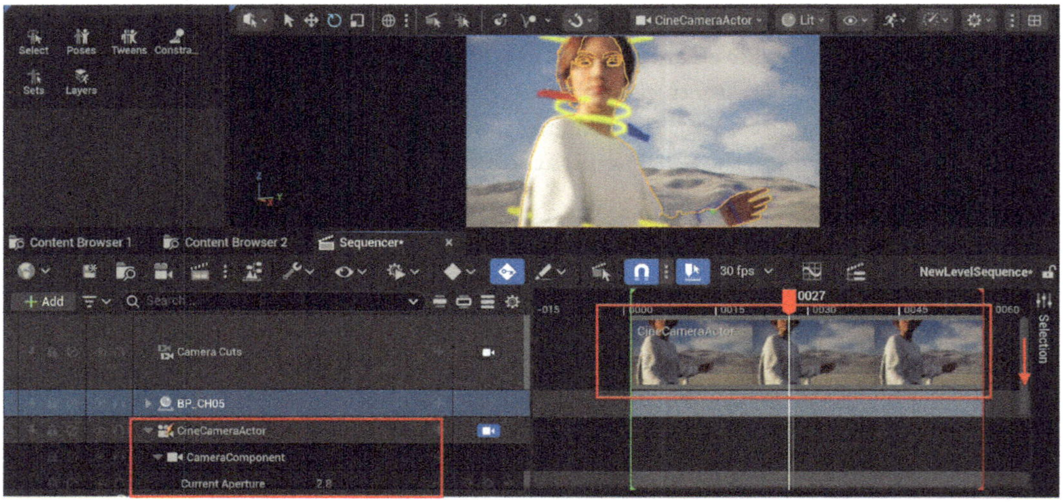

Figure 8.17: Camera and Camera Cut Created

As highlighted on the left of *Figure 8.17*, we have now obtained a **Cine Camera Actor** (which is a virtual version of a real camera). We have also created a **Camera Cuts Track** at the very top. With the camera, we also have a number of parameters, such as the following:

- **Aperture**: This is how wide the iris of the lens is. A lower number means that more of the picture will be out of focus, while a higher number provides a sharper image. This realistically mimics how cameras work in terms of depth of field, but not exposure.
- **Focal Length**: Just like with a real camera, the focal length is measured in millimeters. A lower number creates a wider-angle lens, and a higher number creates a telephoto or long lens.
- **Manual Focus Distance**: Again, just like a real camera, the focus area is set to a given distance from the camera. For example, you may only want to be focused on objects that are 5,000 mm away from the camera.

- **Spawned**: A feature aimed at game simulation. If checked, the game engine will spawn the camera when the game starts.
- **Transform**: An editable parameter for moving, rotating, and scaling the camera.

For the most part, you will only want to animate the following parameters: **Moving** and **Rotating** in **Transform**, along with **Focus Distance**.

Before you go about setting keyframes, a useful function is to pilot the camera to animate. In other words, you can see through the viewport to make sure you've got the best composition. In *Figure 8.18*, I have highlighted the camera icon on both the `CameraComponents` track and the `CineCameraActor` track. These need to be toggled until you get the **Eject** icon (the triangle), which I have also highlighted.

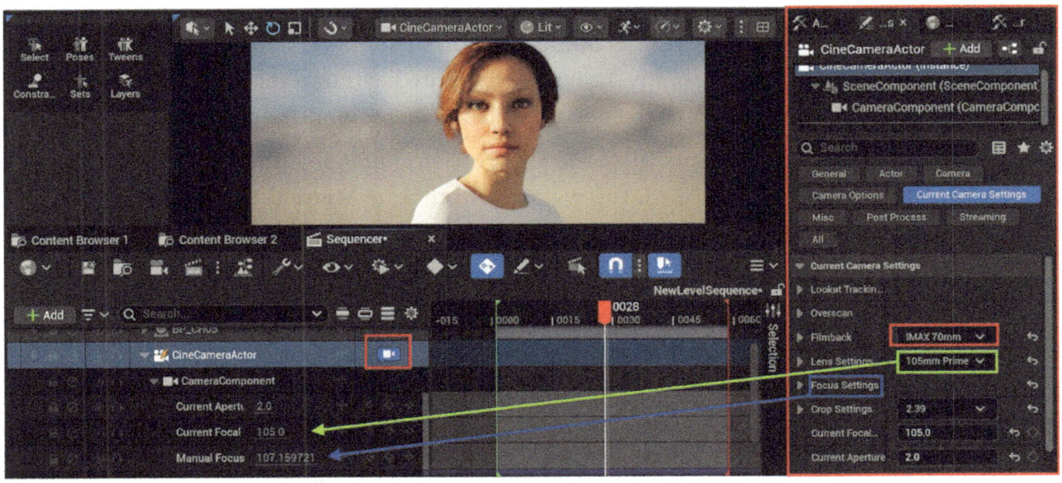

Figure 8.18: Camera Settings and Details panel

In *Figure 8.18*, I have clicked on the camera icon of the `CineCameraActor` track in order to pilot it. I've also highlighted the **Details** panel, which will replicate all the features of the drop-down menu but will also have significantly more. For example, I've changed the **Film Back**, also known as sensor, to be that of an Imax 70mm. I've also updated the focal length from a preset lens of 105mm in the **Details** panel, which automatically updates under the camera inside the **Level Sequencer**.

For every actor inside a **Level Sequencer**, including a camera, there is a corresponding **Details** panel that is much more powerful.

To navigate around the viewport while piloting the camera, use the following:

- *Alt + left-click* to orbit (move around)
- *Alt + middle-click* to track (move left to right and up and down)
- *Alt + right-click* to dolly (move forward and backward)

When you are familiar with navigating your scene with the camera, let's create your first animation of a camera:

1. Click on **Transform** under **CameraComponent** inside the **Sequencer**
2. Then, ensuring your play head is parked close to the beginning of **Play Range**, hit *Enter*. This will create a keyframe for all of the transform parameters, such as **Location**, **Rotation**, and **Scale**. Alternatively, if you have auto keyframe enabled, a keyframe will appear as soon as you tweak the position of the camera while piloting it.
3. Do the same with the **Focus Distance** attribute after first ensuring your MetaHuman is in focus just like in *Figure 8.18*. You will need to click on **Manual Focus Distance**, change the value, and click on the keyframe icon to set a keyframe.
4. When you're happy with both your composition and your focus, park your playhead at a different frame

You've now created your first animation of a camera while filming a MetaHuman. You may have to edit the **Focus Distance** attribute to make sure your MetaHuman remains in focus throughout the shot.

It takes a little while to plot camera moves, and you may find that you are creating keyframes only to have to delete them again and again. This is perfectly normal. Once you feel you've got a reasonable camera movement, it's time to render some animations.

Rendering a test animation from the Level Sequencer

To render out an animation, first, click on the **Movie Scene Capture** button (it's the clapper board icon) at the top of your **Sequencer**:

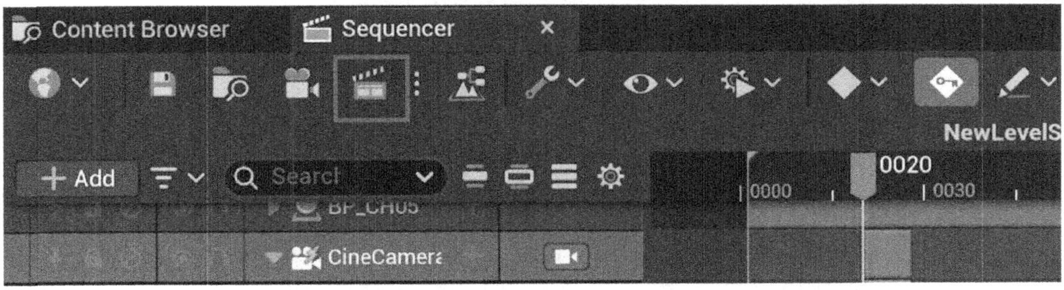

Figure 8.19: Render Movie settings

> **Note**
>
> If you have installed the **Movie Render Queue** plug-in, you will be given a choice of which renderer to use. If so, choose **Movie Scene Capture (Legacy)**.

For this chapter, we are going to use the Legacy renderer because it provides a quick and uncomplicated way to preview our animation.

Movie Render Queue, which we will explore in *Chapter 10*, offers significantly greater control over anti-aliasing, motion blur, sampling quality, image formats, and render passes, making it the preferred choice for final cinematic output rather than quick test renders.

You will then get the following **Render Movie Settings** dialog box:

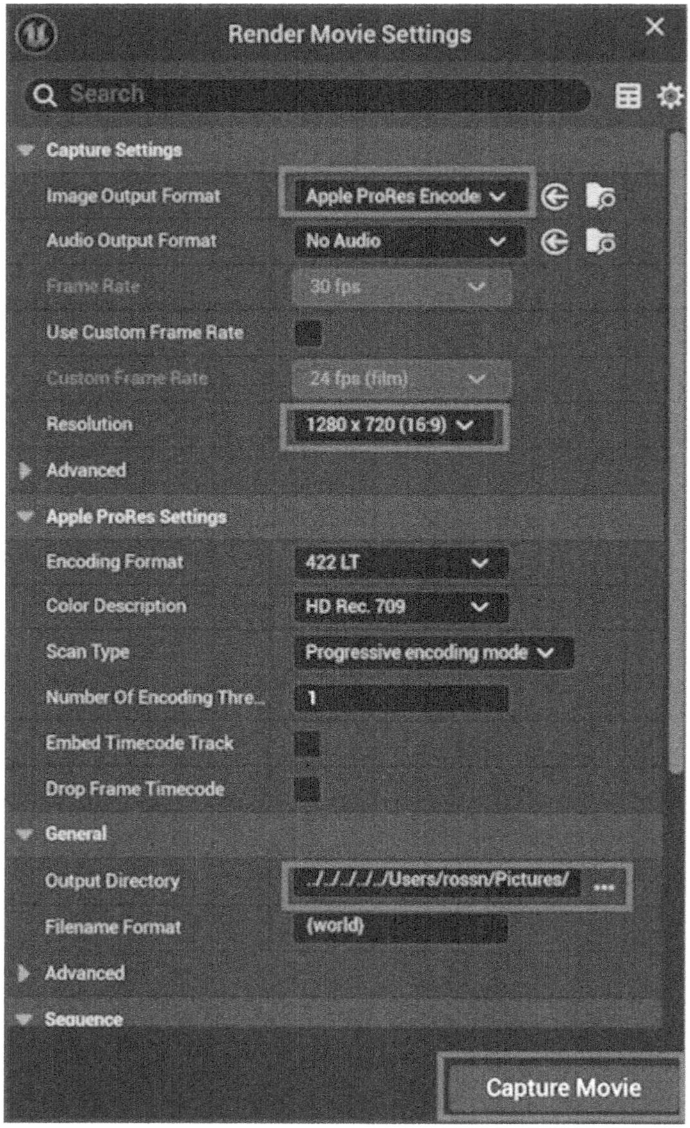

Figure 8.20: Capture Movie

In *Figure 8.20*, I have left all the settings with their default values. Three important settings to note are:

- **Image Output Format**: You need to render a movie in a format that your system can play. The default is **AVI** but you can change it to a **QuickTime Pro Res** file.

> **Note**
>
> To ensure that you can render **Apple Pro Res**, go to **Edit**, then **Plugins**, search for `prores`, and check the **Apple ProRes Media** checkbox. Then, you will need to restart Unreal.

- **Resolution**: The default resolution is **1280 x 720 (16.9)** pixels, but you can change it to a higher resolution if you like.
- **Output Directory**: By default, the **Render Movie** renderer will try to render the file to your project folder to use as the output directory. You can choose another directory if you prefer.

Once you are happy with your render settings, click on Capture Movie. On a typical mid-range workstation, rendering a 1280 × 720 preview can take anywhere from a few seconds per frame to several minutes for a short animation, depending on scene complexity and hardware.

While the render is in progress, you can monitor the preview window shown in *Figure 8.21*. You can also see that my file is being written to a bespoke directory created for this book. Notice that the preview window in the top right appears cropped. This is perfectly normal, as it displays the rendered pixels at 100% resolution rather than scaling them down to fit the small preview window.

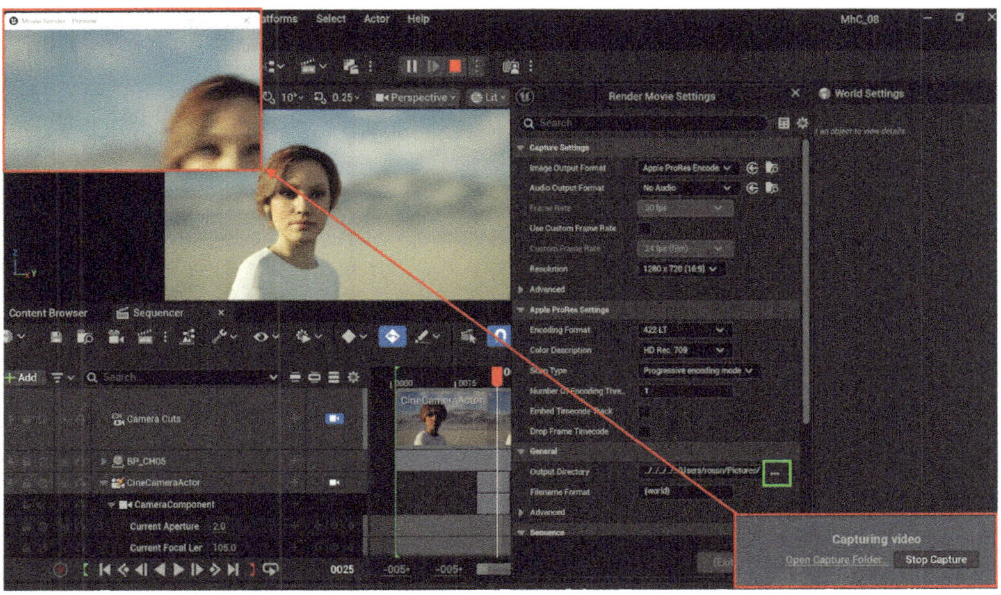

Figure 8.21: Viewing your rendering results

To view your finished video, go to the output directory on your PC and click on the **MOV** file created to play your animation. In *Figure 8.21*, I've highlighted in green the three dots. Clicking on that button will take you to the **Output Directory** to view your file.

> **Note**
>
> On slower systems, when your render looks like it has finished rendering, the render preview window will remain open. The renderer goes through a process of writing all the frames and then through another process of containing the frames within the QuickTime file. At higher resolutions, with bigger files, and on slower machines, this process can take almost as long as the initial render.

Summary

In this chapter, we learned how to create a **Level Sequencer** and add our character to it. We also learned how to create a MetaHuman Control Rig in addition to our mocap data to augment it.

Then, we briefly covered keyframing within the **Level Sequencer**, the more robust **Sequencer** curve graph editing tool, before moving on to creating a camera and animating it in the **Level Sequencer**. Finally, we learned how to export video files from UE5.

Please spend time importing and retargeting as many Mixamo animations as possible until you feel very confident with the process and have many MetaHuman-compatible body animations to choose from.

In the next chapter, we are going to work with facial motion capture using an iPhone.

Part 3

Facial Animation and Cinematic Rendering

In this third part of the book, you'll focus on creating believable facial performances and presenting your MetaHumans in a cinematic environment. You'll explore multiple facial motion capture workflows using both an iPhone and a standard webcam, learn how to combine facial and body animation, and use the Level Sequencer to manage complete performances.

You'll also discover techniques for lighting, camera work, and high-quality rendering to produce polished final results suitable for animation, cinematics, and virtual production.

By the end of this part of the book, you'll be able to create, animate, and render convincing MetaHuman performances from capture through to final output.

This part of the book includes the following chapters:

- *Chapter 9, Using an iPhone for Facial Motion Capture*
- *Chapter 10, Using a Webcam and Audio for Facial Motion Capture*
- *Chapter 11, Advanced Rendering with the Level Sequencer*

9

Using an iPhone for Facial Motion Capture

In *Chapter 8*, we took our body motion capture to the next level by learning how to adjust the animation and render video using the **Level Sequencer**. The **Level Sequencer** plays an integral part when it comes to managing animation, and we will use it again here as we explore facial motion capture.

In this chapter, we are specifically looking at facial motion capture for our MetaHuman, taking advantage of the iPhone depth camera and facial tracking features. MetaHumans come with dozens of intricate facial controls that respond to facial capture tools, giving you the power to create incredibly realistic facial performances including speech. This can capture your own performance or an actor's performance to such a degree that even very subtle nuances are reflected, thus making the overall result incredibly realistic.

So, in this chapter, we will cover the following topics:

- Installing Unreal Engine plugins: **Take Recorder** and **Live Link Hub**
- Installing the **Live Link Face** app
- Connecting and configuring the **Live Link Face** app to Unreal Engine
- Configuring and testing the MetaHuman Blueprint
- The **Take Recorder**
- The MetaHuman Identity
- Ingesting motion capture
- Processing facial motion capture

Technical requirements

In terms of computer power, you will need the technical requirements detailed in *Chapter 1* and the MetaHuman plus the Unreal Engine mannequin that we imported into UE5 in *Chapter 2*. However, you can create a new MetaHuman for this chapter if you like.

You will also need an iPhone and a stable Wi-Fi connection to install plugins.

Let's look at that iPhone requirement a little more. You will need an iPhone X or newer, or an iPad Pro (3rd generation) or newer. These devices include the TrueDepth camera required for MetaHuman depth capture.

> **Note**
>
> Epic also provides a Live Link Face application for selected Android devices equipped with Snapdragon 8 Gen 1 (or newer) processors. At the time of writing, however, the iPhone workflow remains the most widely tested and established option, so that is the workflow used throughout this chapter.

You will also need a long cable, approximately 2 meters, because it is best to have your iPhone on charge during motion capture sessions, as the process is quite battery consuming.

Installing Unreal Engine plugins: Take Recorder and Live Link Hub

Before we look at the iPhone, we need to make sure we have all the relevant Unreal Engine plugins that will allow us to receive data from the iPhone, capture it live and ingest prerecorded data. You need to ensure the following are installed:

- Live Link
- Live Link Control Rig
- Live Link Curve Debug UI
- Live Link Hub
- MetaHuman Animation Depth Processing (must be installed from Fab)
- MetaHuman Live Link
- Take Recorder

> **Note**
>
> MetaHuman Animation Depth Processing is installed separately from Fab rather than through the standard Unreal Engine Plugins window. Open the Fab window inside Unreal Engine, search for MetaHuman Animation Depth Processing, add it to your library, install it, and restart Unreal Engine.

You'll be instructed to restart Unreal for those plugins to be effective.

Note that these plug-ins take up a lot of data, so be sure you have enough space on your hard drive where your Unreal Engine has been installed.

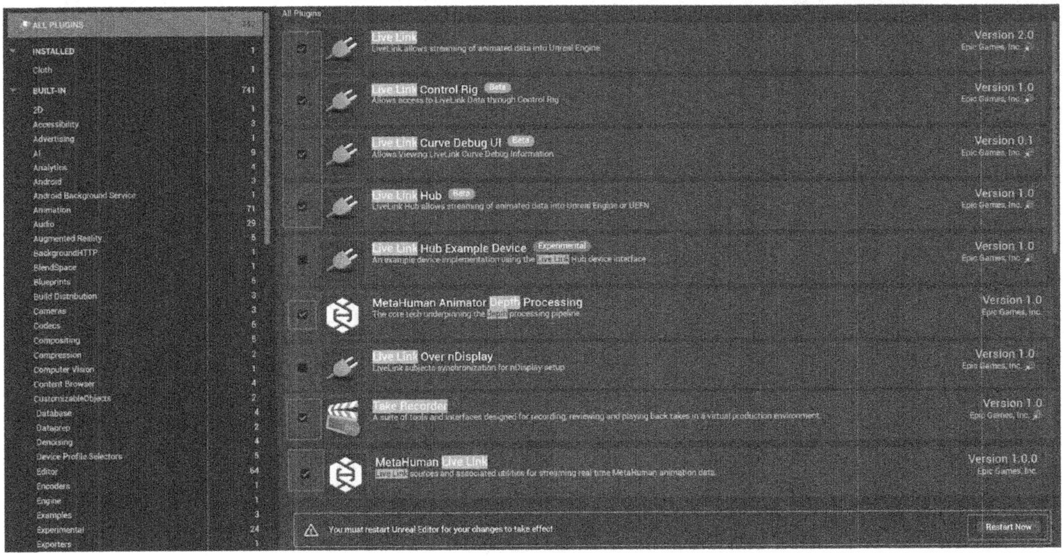

Figure 9.1: Install Plugins

There are two ways we can approach facial motion capture.

1. Stream the live facial capture onto our final character inside the Unreal Engine Project: This process is vital if we are broadcasting live. For instance, we may want a character moving and talking as part of a live event, such as a concert, a corporate broadcast or even a live television recording.
2. Record the facial motion capture to ingest and retarget into our final character: This is the usual process for professional high-end productions such as game cinematics, animated shows or visual effects elements for live action projects

We will explore both.

Installing the live link face app

The **Live Link Face** app is a free app that you can download onto your iPhone or iPad directly from the App Store. Its sole purpose is to utilize the iPhone's built-in depth camera, along with facial recognition and pixel tracking technology, to produce data that works within ARKit. In addition to collecting facial motion capture data in real time, it also transmits the data via **Internet Protocol** (**IP**) to your desktop computer using a Wi-Fi connection; this data is then picked up by the Live Link utility in Unreal Engine, which we shall delve into later.

Figure 9.2 shows the Live Link Face app in the Apple App Store:

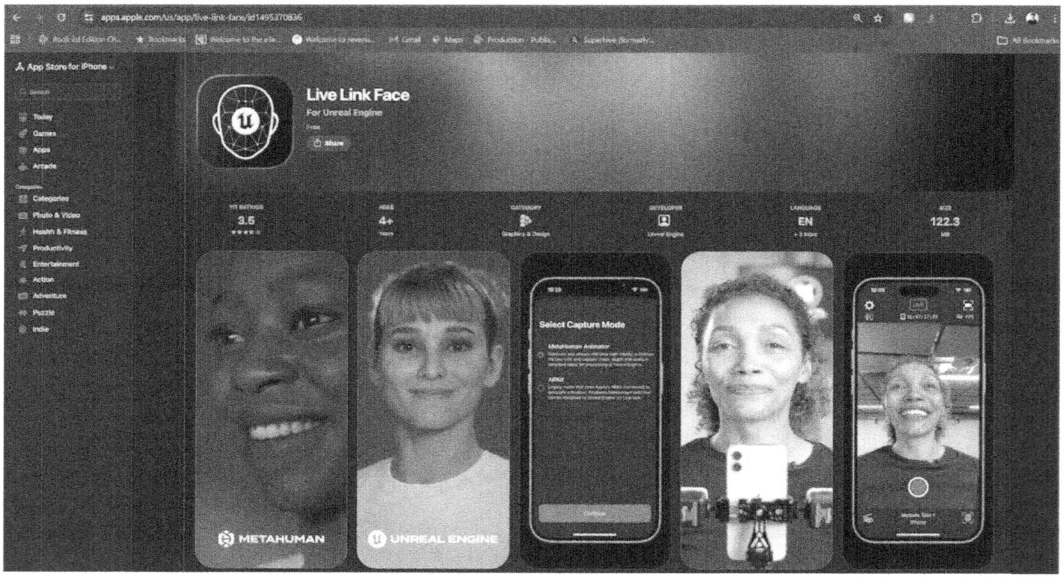

Figure 9.2: The Live Link Face app in the App Store

Once downloaded and installed, open the app to test that it is working. While looking at the display, you should immediately see your face. Before continuing, disable the iPhone's Auto-Lock (screensaver) feature for the duration of your capture session and make a note of the phone's Wi-Fi address from the Live Link settings page. Both will be needed shortly when connecting to Live Link Hub. By default, the mesh overlay is enabled as seen in *Figure 9.3*, and you'll see that the mesh very accurately tracks your face.

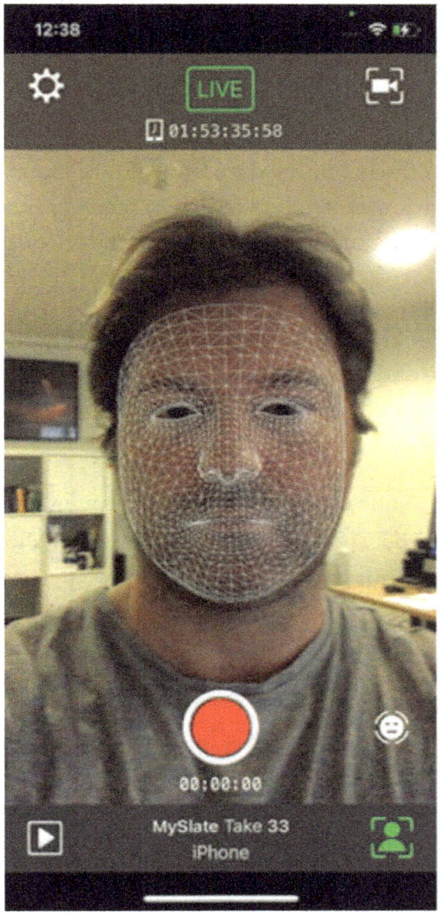

Figure 9.3: Opening up the Live Link Face app

As soon as our face is being tracked, we know the app is working. There is no need to do any more with the application for the time being. In the next section, we will enable a few more plugins.

Live Link Hub

Live Link Hub is the core plugin that allows third-party applications to stream animation data directly into Unreal Engine. Applications such as **MotionBuilder** and **Maya** permit users to make changes to these applications and see the results updated in the Unreal Engine viewport in real time. This functionality in the context of this book permits users to use other applications such as the Live Link iPhone app to stream data directly into Unreal Engine. Effectively, Live Link Hub is a separate application launched from Unreal Engine. By being a separate application, it can receive multiple face and body data streams from multiple performers and cameras, but it also serves as a motion capture data manager for users to ingest pre-recorded data.

Live Link Control Rig

Live Link Control Rig allows the incoming data from a third-party application to communicate with the animation controllers of a character. For instance, a MetaHuman has a control rig that allows users to manually animate it. Live Link Control Rig harnesses the same control rig protocol.

Live Link Curve Debug UI

For the purpose of debugging and viewing the connection from a third-party animation data source into Unreal Engine, we will use the Live Link Curve Debug UI plugin.

> **Note**
>
> Live Link Curve Debug UI, while not essential, is a convenient interface for troubleshooting issues when it comes to advanced refinement; however, discussing it in detail is beyond the scope of this book as it looks at every single control point of the face.

Take Recorder

We have one more plugin to enable, which is **Take Recorder**. Try to think of **Take Recorder** as a video camera. Effectively, it records the motion capture data received by Live Link and stores it for playback, which in turn is imported into the **Level Sequencer**. Just like a video camera, we can record multiple takes until we are happy that we have got the best one (or at the very least, as close as possible to the best!).

To enable **Take Recorder**, search for the plugin as shown in *Figure 9.1*.

> **Note**
>
> You may need to restart Unreal Engine if you have enabled any of these plugins for them to take effect.

With all the necessary plugins enabled, we can now move on to the next section, where we will configure the **Live Link Face** app so that it can send data into Unreal Engine.

Connecting and configuring the Live Link Face app to Unreal Engine

With the Live Link Face app installed on the iPhone and the Live Link plugin enabled in Unreal Engine, we now need to get them to talk to each other (figuratively speaking, of course). Our goal is to send motion capture data from the iPhone to the PC and/or the Live Link app to send this data into Unreal Engine. If you have been using the Live Link plugin in the past, you'll soon see that using the Live Link Hub is easier to set up. We just need to find out what our iPhone Wi-Fi address is. To do this, open the Live Link App and click on the settings cog icon.

Figure 9.4: Clicking on the settings icon

Pressing the cog will bring you to the **Settings** page as per *Figure 9.5*. When there, click on the Live Link option.

There are just two things we need to look at here in the settings.

- The iPhone's Wi-Fi address
- The Capture Mode

Unlike the predecessor of Live Link Hub, we don't use the PC IP address. Live Link Hub is designed to receive multiple sources simultaneously, as you'd expect in a professional production environment. So, instead we need to find the phone's Wi-Fi Address, which I've highlighted in red in *Figure 9.5*. Take note of that address as you'll need it for configuring and testing the Live Link Hub in the next section. You'll notice that the camera in use is the **Front TrueDepth Camera**. By default, it is set to capture Depth and record 60fps. Click on **Front TrueDepth Camera** to ensure those settings are correct.

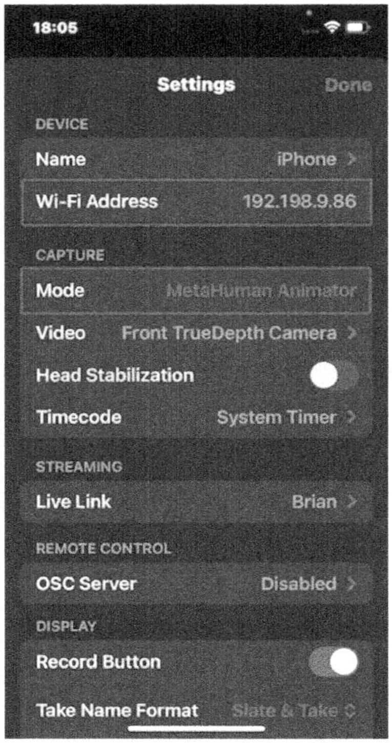

Figure 9.5: Clicking on Live Link iPhone

Under **Capture**, you need to make sure that the **Mode** is set to **MetaHuman Animator**, as this is what Live Link is expecting to receive.

> Note
>
> **MetaHuman animator**
>
> MetaHuman Animator is the newer and more advanced capture mode. It generates and streams real-time high-fidelity animation via live link and captures video, depth and audio in recorded and live takes for processing in Unreal.

Once you have taken note of your iPhone's Wi-Fi address, you need to switch over to Unreal Engine again to see whether you are receiving a signal.

In Unreal Engine, go to **Tools**, then **Live Link Hub** to launch the **Live Link Hub** application. It will take a minute to boot up.

Figure 9.6: Live Link Hub Application Startup

In *Figure 9.7*, you can see on the top left in red that I have switched to **Live Data**. This is essential as we need the Hub to be in Live Data in order to receive a signal from the iPhone. I've also highlighted in red the **Add Source** button. You need to click on that and add the **Live Link Face** option. This option is specifically referring to the Live Link Face app that you have installed on your iPhone.

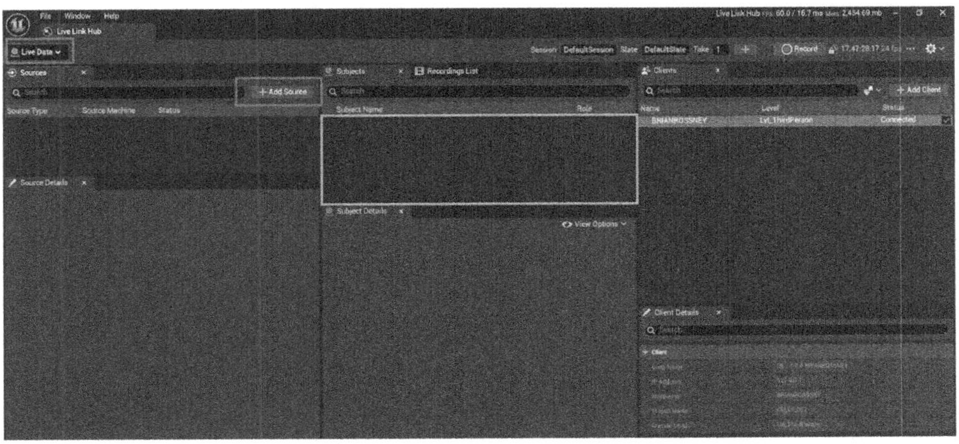

Figure 9.7: The Live Link Hub interface

I've also highlighted in red in *Figure 9.8* that the mode it is expecting is the **MetaHuman Animation** mode.

Note

ARKit mode

ARKit mode will not work with the MetaHuman Live Link workflow described in this chapter. If you accidentally select ARKit mode, simply return to the Capture Mode settings in the Live Link Face app and switch the mode back to MetaHuman Animator before reconnecting to Live Link Hub.

The **ARkit** mode will not work with Live Link Hub.

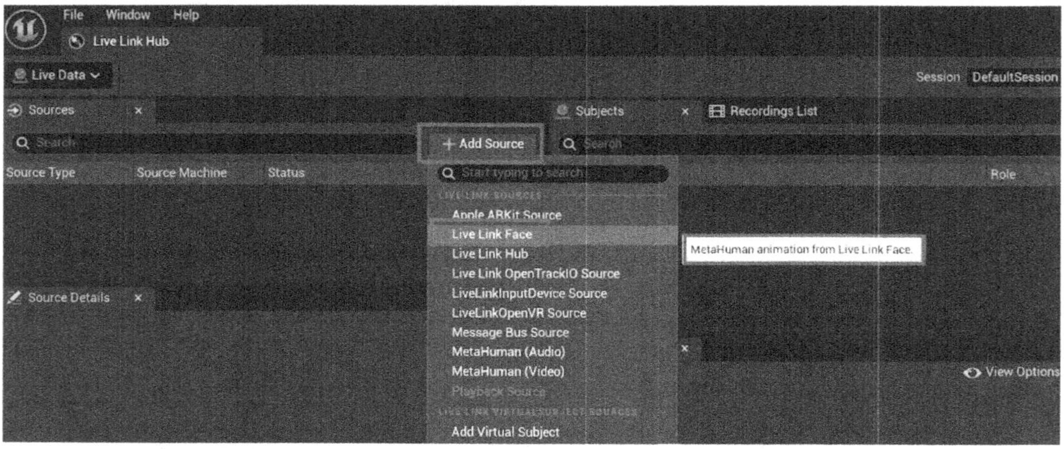

Figure 9.8: Live Link Face as Source for MetaHuman Animation Data

On *Figure 9.8*, I've highlighted in red that the Live Link Hub has a source preset exclusively to receive MetaHuman data via the Live Link app on the iPhone.

Once you've clicked on that, you'll see that the status is set to **Disconnected** and the IP address field is empty.

You need to type in the Wi-Fi address of your iPhone that you took note of earlier.

Note

Recommendation

I recommend putting the Wi-Fi address somewhere you can easily copy and paste from as you will need it every time you need to renew your connection.

Once you have typed in the Wi-Fi address of your phone, in the **Subject** field, type in the name of your phone or any name you would like to remember, perhaps the name of the performer or the character they are playing.

Click on the **Connect** button. You may see a green circle appear with a tick. That tells you your connection is solid and data is flowing.

You will most likely not see this initially, and that is because you need to be transferring animation data. So, with the connection still running but no green icon, go back to your iPhone and make sure the Live Link app is running and there is a face in front of it being tracked.

Sometimes the iPhone screensaver will kick in, so you'll need to disable it entirely when using the Live Link App, as it will halt the connection.

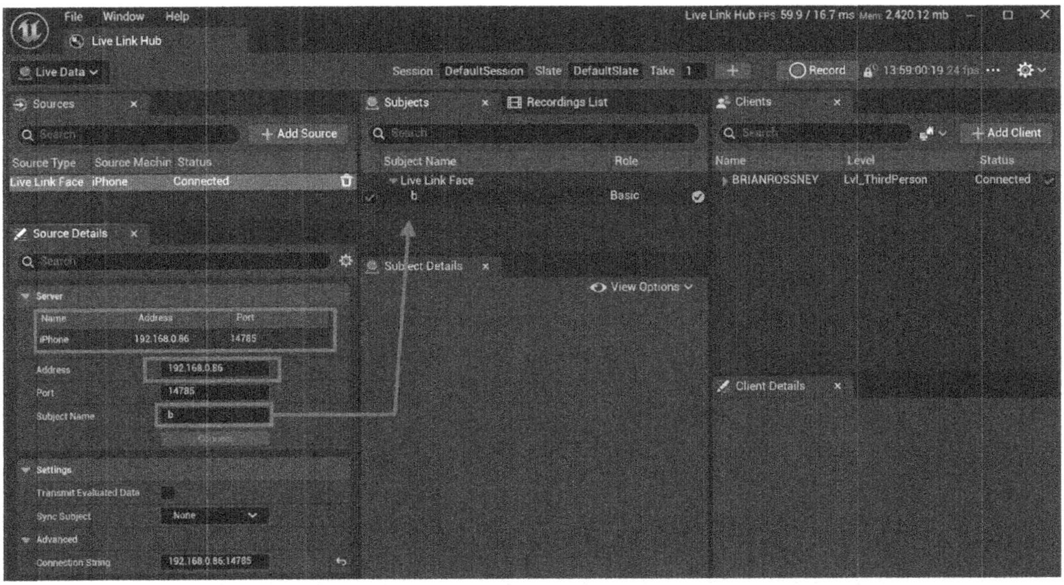

Figure 9.9; Live Link Hub with working signal

Also in *Figure 9.9*, next to where it says **iPhone**, you'll see that under **Role** it says **Basic** and to the right of that is a yellow dot. This dot indicates the status of the signal, which can be interpreted as follows:

- If the dot is red, it means there is no data coming in, which could be caused by improper configurations such as the Live Link Face app being closed or the phone being off

- The yellow dot indicates that both applications are pinging each other, but no active data exists, which usually indicates there's no person in front of the iPhone
- A green dot indicates that there is data coming into Unreal Engine from the Live Link Face app

Knowing that both apps are effectively speaking to each other means that we can go on to the next step and configure our MetaHuman character to receive data.

Configuring and testing the MetaHuman Blueprint

We must now tell the MetaHuman Blueprint to receive data from Live Link. As it happens, this is very simple:

1. Place a MetaHuman into the scene
2. Create a level sequencer and add the MetaHuman to the **Level Sequencer**
3. Delete the MetaHuman Control Rigs
4. Select the MetaHuman Blueprint in the Level Sequencer. Ensure you haven't selected either the Body or Face Components.

With MetaHuman Blueprint selected in the **Level Sequencer**, go to the **Details** panels.

Ensure that the subject matches the subject in Live Link Hub and that you have ticked **Use Live Link**. With that, your character should come to life, provided you are using the Live Link App.

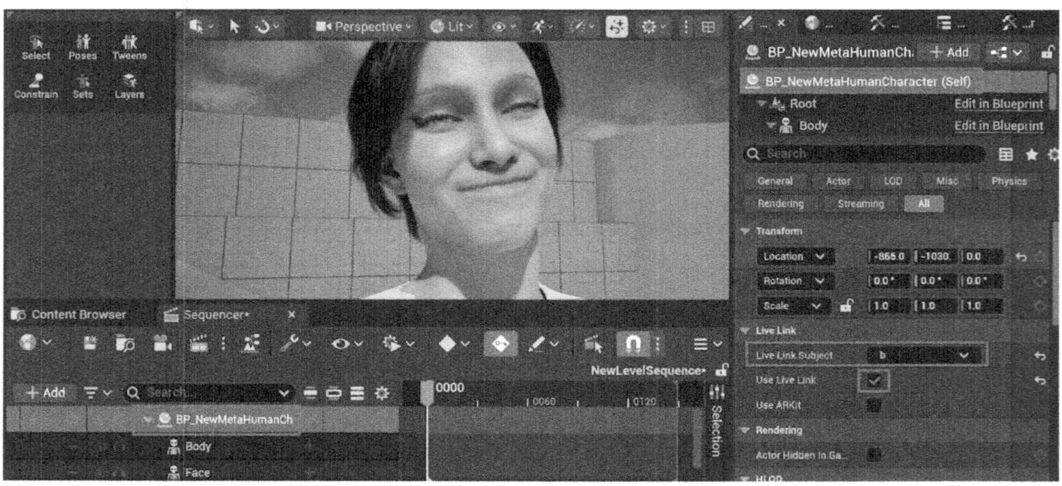

Figure 9.10: Editing the MetaHuman Blueprint settings

With the live data flowing in and animating the MetaHuman, you should get a good idea of what live facial motion capture looks like. I suggest you play around with it for a while before we get to the next step. You'll notice that the head moves, and there's also a bit of neck and upper body movement. This is great for live work, and many artists produce videos of just the upper bodies for live broadcasts. If this suits your needs but you prefer not to work fully live, you can still achieve a near-live result. Use the Take Recorder to quickly capture a performance.

However, live streaming of data has its drawbacks. It's not as accurate as pre-recorded data, which can be calibrated and processed for accuracy. It's also driving a MetaHumans motion, and if the rendering quality is set to maximum and the Take Recorder is recording, the poor responsiveness resulting from high rendering settings will be recorded too. This is why we need to reduce the viewport scalability down to **Low**. If you don't see a noticeable improvement, try displaying wireframe in the viewport by typing *Alt + 2*. In addition, you may not be hitting the target 60fps over Wi-Fi.

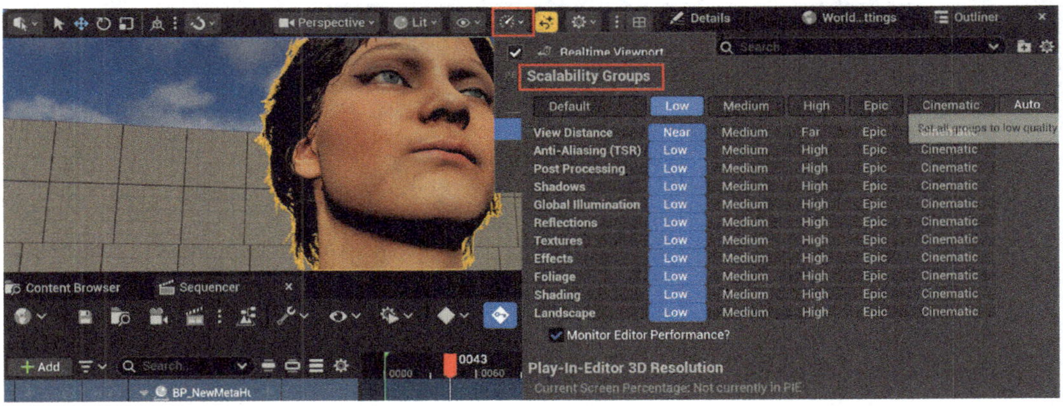

Figure 9.11: Viewport scalability

To get set up quickly with facial motion capture, I used a new MetaHuman with all default settings unchanged. If you are working with an older character that has already been tested and adjusted, you may run into a common issue where no animation appears, even though the data seems to be coming through.

In this case, everything may be configured correctly on the phone and in Live Link Hub, yet the viewport remains static. A frequent cause is that the animation mode has not been set to use a Blueprint.

As shown in *Figure 9.12*, select the face, go to the **Animation** section, and check the **Animation Mode** setting. It should be set to **Use Animation Blueprint**. This is required for the character to receive and apply live data.

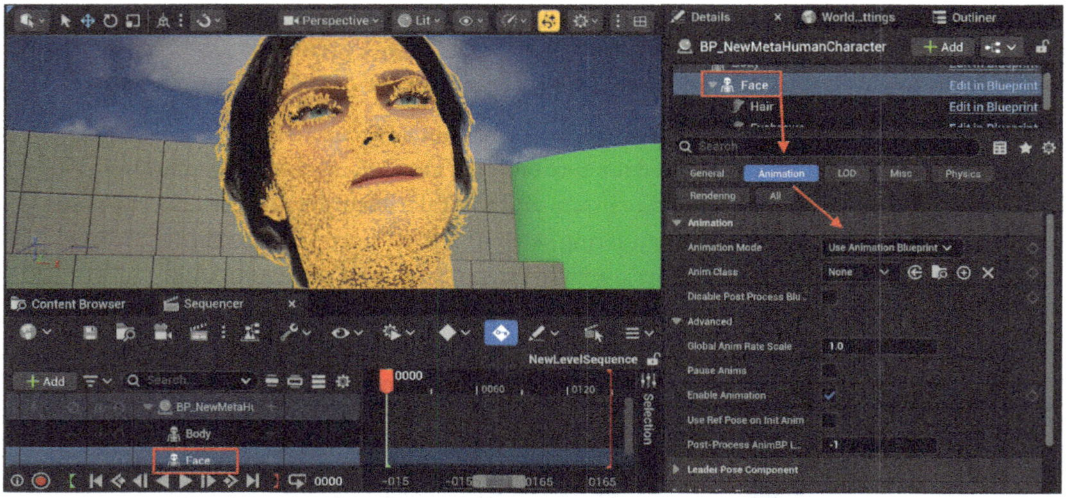

Figure 9.12: Animation Mode set to Use Animation Blueprint

Inversely, if you are not doing live capture but choosing to animate your MetaHuman through pre-recorded data, then the **Animation Mode** must be set to **Use Animation Asset**. While this seems like an obvious one, it is the single most overlooked feature where users simply forget to switch between the two.

Just like in the Live Link Hub where a live signal was indicated by a green icon with a tick, think of the **Animation Blueprint** as live and the animation asset as pre-recorded.

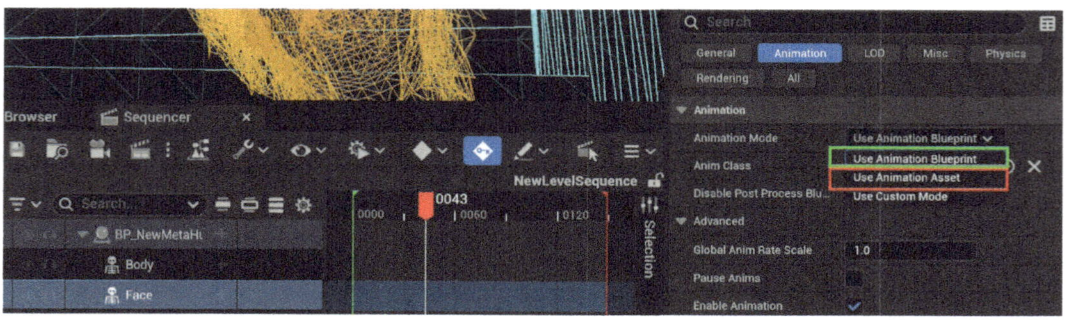

Figure 9.13: Switching Animation Modes

Note

Editing the Animation Mode in the Blueprint

If, in the **Details** panel, the **Animation Mode** keeps reverting to either **Use Animation Blueprint** or **Use Animation Asset**, you will need to edit the actual Blueprint. In *Figure 9.12*, where I have highlighted the face in red, you can see next to it that the words **Edit in Blueprint** appear, which is a link to make those changes inside the Blueprint. If the settings are constantly reverting to their original state, it is because those settings are being overridden inside the Blueprint. It is an easy fix to just click on **Edit in Blueprint** to access the **Details** panel there.

In the next section, we will record a facial mocap take using the **Take Recorder**. To do this, go to **Windows | Cinematics | Take Recorder**. Do the same for **Take Browser**. By default, they arrange themselves next to each other in tabs.

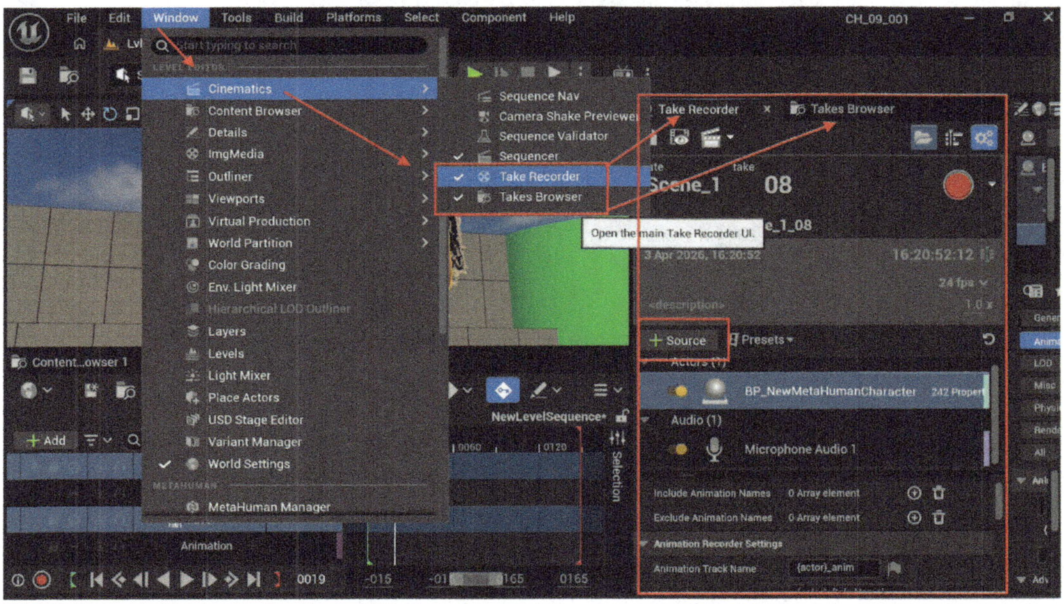

Figure 9.14: Opening the Take Recorder

With both **Take Recorder** and **Take Browser** opened, go to the **Take Recorder** and add a source using the **+ Source** button as indicated in *Figure 9.14* in red. If you still have the MetaHuman Blueprint already selected in the **Level Sequencer**, **Take Recorder** will automatically suggest you choose that as a source.

Alternatively, you can use the search field. You can see from *Figure 9.14* that I've already added the `BP_NewMetaHumanCharacter` to my **Take Recorder**. I've also added a microphone audio, which will be the same as your system audio input. So, if you have a webcam and it works, then most likely that will be the audio input.

The next step is to hit the big red record button. As soon as you do that, the recording will count down, usually for three seconds, and then start recording. You'll see a track being recorded onto the **Level Sequencer**, but this is only temporary. What is really happening is the **Take Recorder** is recording both the live facial motion capture data and the audio. The data capture is being converted into an animation sequence and is being stored inside the **Take Browser**.

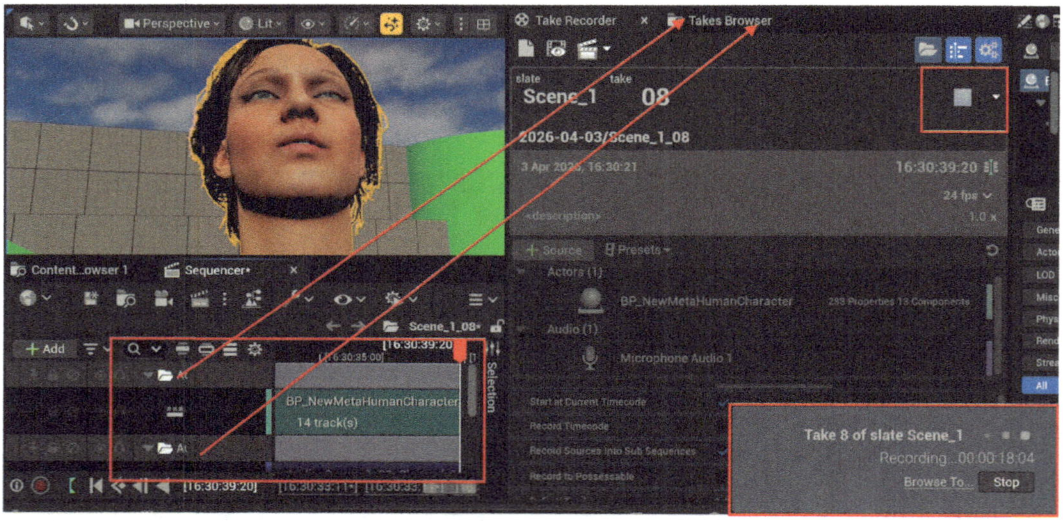

Figure 9.15: Take Recording in Progress

In *Figure 9.15*, you can see the live data being recorded as tracks. However, you'll see folder icons indicating that they are being written to folders and not being written to the **Level Sequencer**. Unreal is just using the **Level Sequencer** as a visualizer for the data.

To assign the data to the **Level Sequencer**, you'll need to find it in the **Take Browser**. Unreal conveniently creates a dated folder for you. On the left of *Figure 9.16*, you can see that I first clicked the + icon of the face **Component**. This gave me the option to choose **Animation**.

This just gives me a drop-down menu with a list of all the available animations. It's not ideal for us to be typing in the name of the animation. So instead, with the **Take Browser**, it's easier for us to find the folder with today's date and locate the most recent **Animation Sequence**.

Take Recorder will automatically create a folder structure on its first recording in a project with the following hierarchy: **MetaHuman | Cinematics | Takes | (Recording Date)**.

You can see from *Figure 9.16* the folder structure in the **Take Recorder**. Inside the dated folder, there is `Scene_1_07_Subscenes`, which corresponds to how many takes I recorded.

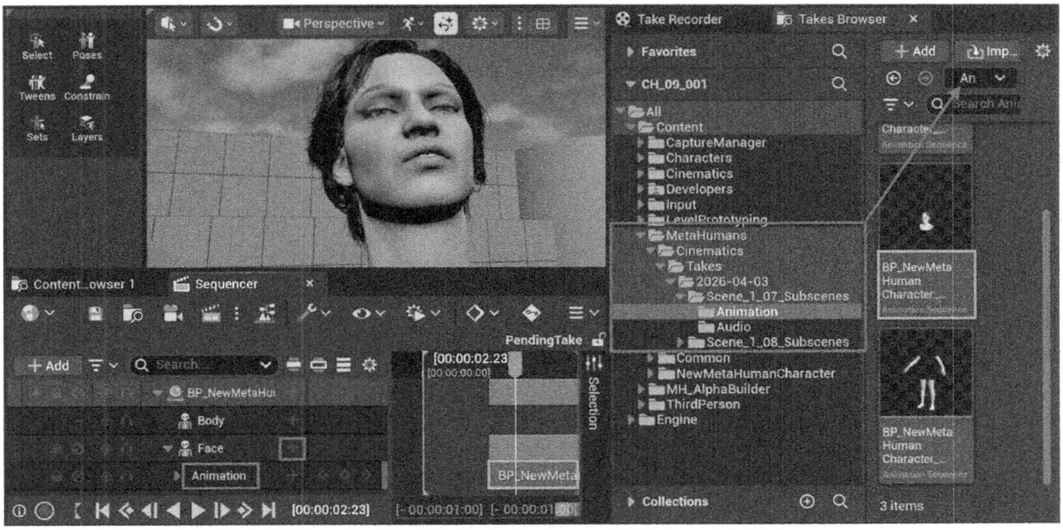

Figure 9.16: Locating your Recorded Take

When working with a lot of animations, it's not feasible to be typing their names into a search field in order to apply them. There is a drag and drop feature as illustrated in *Figure 9.17*. It does come with the caveat of having to create an animation track first by using any animation asset (provided it is a face **Animation Sequence**). While you can't preview the facial animations as thumbnails like in Mixamo, you can double-click them to open up the **Animation Sequences** to inspect them.

The drag and drop functions allow you to drop the animations at any point on the timeline which you can later mix and trim.

Figure 9.17: Dragging and dropping Take Recorder Assets

That sums up the basics of live facial motion capture. You can see there are limitations, which I already identified regarding the responsivity based on rendering settings. But there are also the overall system specifications, such as CPU and GPU speeds, memory and of course the Wi-Fi connection.

Next, we are going to look at a far more robust way to get prerecorded data with much more accuracy. We'll be utilizing the MetaHuman Identity, a new feature in Unreal Engine since version 5.6.

We will be using the iPhone as the recording device and Live Link Hub to process the data cleanly.

MetaHuman identity

The idea behind the MetaHuman Identity is to create a version of the performer, a skeleton mesh that resembles the performer as much as possible. This will allow their motion capture to be far more accurate. Having this saved as a DNA asset for each performer negates the need for calibration.

The way it works is by creating a mesh based on four poses of the performer:

1. Looking left (not fully profile)
2. Looking right (not fully profile)

3. Looking straight ahead
4. Looking straight ahead and showing teeth

You will need the iPhone and the **Live Face App** to capture these poses, and you will need to do it as one single take.

The goal behind the MetaHuman identity is to create a DNA with as much information about the performer as possible. When we go to process the motion capture data, we use that DNA to calibrate the data during processing.

For this, we need to:

1. Capture the calibration footage on the iPhone
2. Ingest the Footage using the Live Link Hub Content Manager
3. Create a MetaHuman Identity
4. Create the DNA by processing the poses

Capturing the calibration footage on the iPhone

With the Live Link App open, record a short 10-second video demonstrating the following poses. You don't need a perfect or plain background, but do make sure you or your performer are well lit.

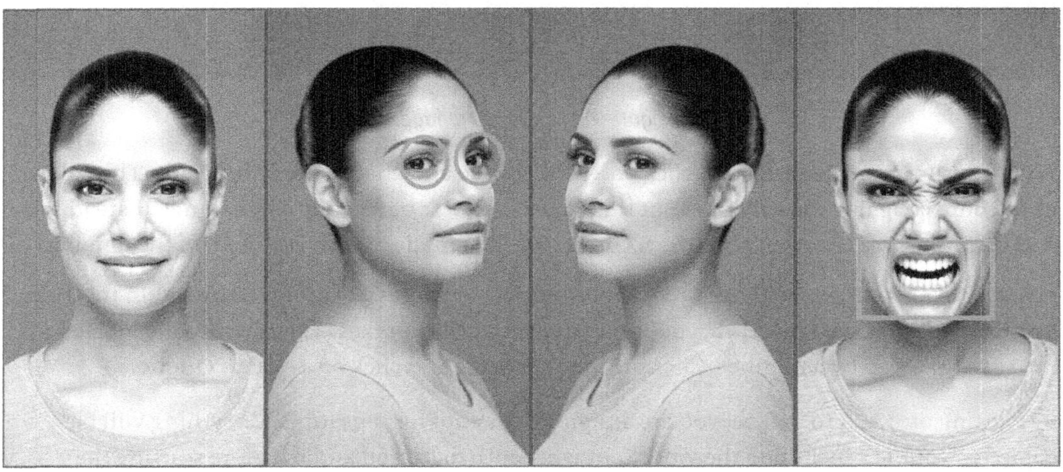

Figure 9.18: Four Calibration poses

Aim for a neutral pose for the first three poses. For the second and third picture, ensure that both eyes are visible in each angle. This needs to be an angle somewhere between front-on and profile. Expect that part of the eye in both the second and third pose will be occluded by the nose.

The final pose is showing all teeth. A smile won't do but a snarl will generally show more teeth. Be sure to hit record when doing all these poses and play it back to ensure all of the face is in frame at all times and that there is no motion blur during the main poses. It helps to hold each pose for a second or two.

The next step is to bring that recording into Unreal Engine.

Ingesting the footage using the Live Link Hub content manager

Open up **Live Link Hub** by going to **Tools** and choosing **Live Link Hub** and on the top left corner, switch from **Live Data** to **Capture Manager**.

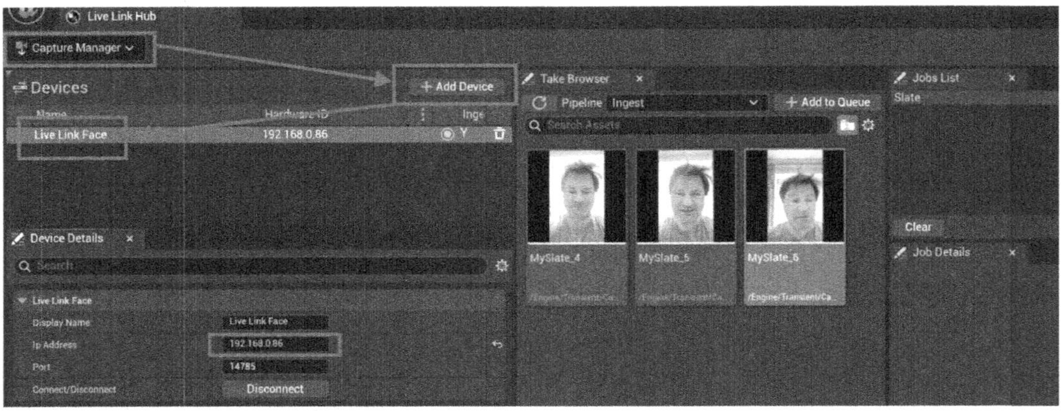

Figure 9.19: Capture Manager

With Capture Manager selected, click on **+Add Device** and choose **Live Link Face**. This allows us to connect again to the iPhone. But this time, we won't be seeking a live signal. Instead, we will get a direct connection with the recording we just made, which is stored on the iPhone.

It is very likely that you will need to re-enter the Wi-Fi address. Click on **Connect**. In the **Take Browser** within **Live Link Hub**, you'll see your most recent takes. They are usually labeled as `MySlate` followed by a number. Click on your best take and click on **+Add to Queue**.

By clicking on +Add to Queue, you are assigning the shot for ingesting. Everything will be copied to your PC, including the video footage, depth data, and audio. Before starting the ingestion process, make sure you have several gigabytes of free disk space available.

During ingestion Unreal creates image sequences, depth data, and Capture Assets, all of which can consume considerably more storage than the original recordings.

During the ingesting process, your video, which would have been recorded as an MOV file by default, will be converted to the jpg or png image sequence format. In addition, the ingestion process is creating an asset called a **Capture Asset**, which connects all of the ingested material together for processing.

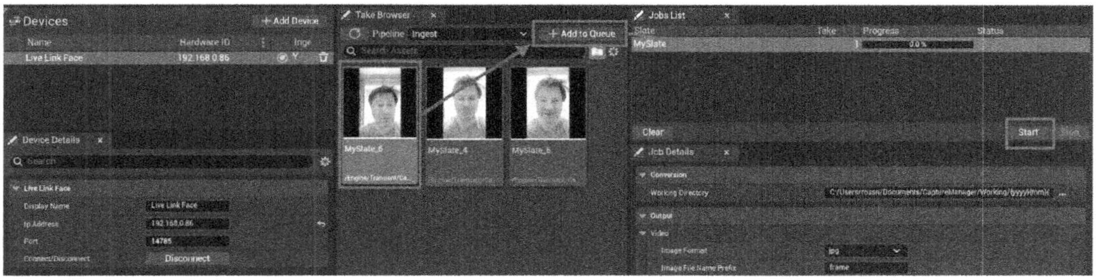

Figure 9.20: Ingesting the Best Take

In *Figure 9.20*, I have selected just one take. In a production, a performer would have their designated iPhone and all of their takes for that day would be selected, rather than just the one. They would all be added to the queue for batch ingesting all in one go. For this example, I have just selected one that gets highlighted in blue. When you click **+ Add to Queue**, you can see a progress bar indicating a zero percentage as it is waiting for the **Start** button to be pressed. Click on the **Start** button and watch the progress. It may take a minute to ingest the calibration clip.

Generally, when the progress bar gets to about 65% it means the ingestion process has finished and the remaining 35% involves writing the data to disk. This will fail if there isn't enough disk space. The default destination for ingestion is a Capture Manager in the following location:

```
Documents/CaptureManager/Working/{yyyy}{mm}{dd}/{device}
```

You can change that to inside your project folder. If you choose the `Content` folder as your destination within your project, you will be asked if you wish to import. If you choose yes, Unreal Engine will import every frame and give notifications for each. This is a minor annoyance but doesn't affect the final result.

Creating a MetaHuman identity

Once the ingestion process is finished, we can head back to Unreal Engine.

This is where we will create our MetaHuman Identity to use what we just ingested.

Inside your `MetaHumans` character folder in the **Content Browser**, *right-click* and go to **MetaHuman** and then **MetaHuman Identity**. This will create the **MetaHuman Identity**, which you can rename to your liking. *Double-click* to open it.

Figure 9.21: MetaHuman Identity main toolbar

In the main toolbar of **MetaHuman Identity**, you can see that the steps are nicely laid out horizontally. We can only progress to the next step once we've completed the first. We have:

- Create Components
- Promote Frame
- Tracker Markers (Active Frame)
- MetaHuman Identity Solve
- AutoRig (MetaHuman Identity)
- Fix Teeth
- Prepare for Performance

Create components

To get started, we need to add a footage component for the clip we ingested earlier. Go to **Create Components** | **From Footage**, and from the drop-down list, you'll see a list of available **Footage Capture Data Assets**. If this is your first time, you'll just see the **Capture Data Asset** you made during the **Ingestion** process. Remember, this contains everything that was captured using **Live Link Face App**, including, video, audio, depth, and other data. Choose the asset that corresponds to your clip. In my case it's `MySlate_9`.

Figure 9.22: Creating a footage component

The footage will appear in the main viewer in the middle with a timeline you can scrub through at the bottom. In *Figure 9.23*, I've highlighted the **Promote Frame** button and the + icon as they do the same thing. You can use the – icon to remove a frame.

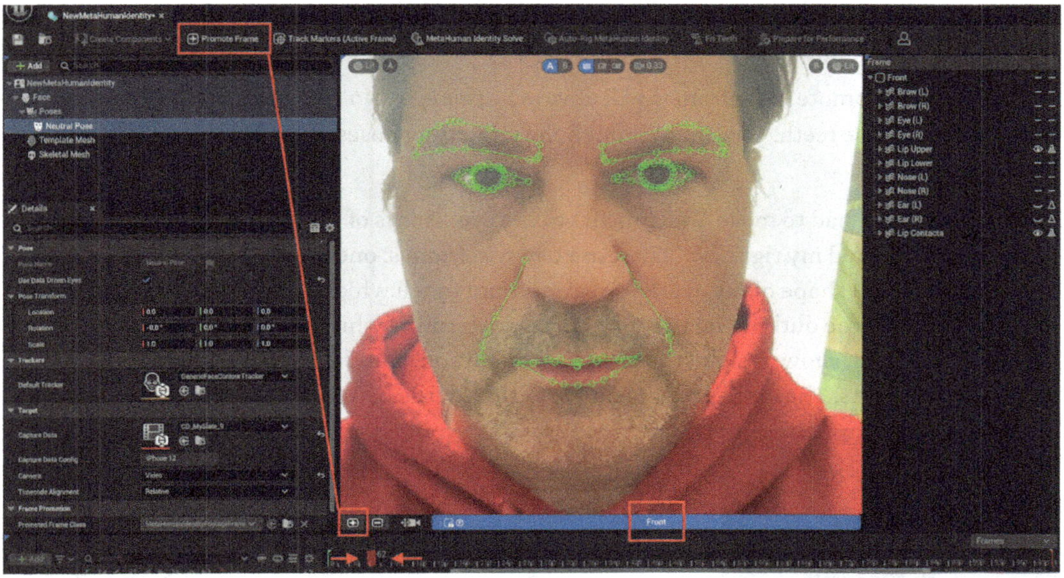

Figure 9.23: Promoting a frame

Take note of the camera icon next to it. You'll need to press that in order to proceed to your next frame. You can also rename the promoted frame if you like. I've named mine `Front`.

Promote frame

We need to help Unreal understand what the facial features are of each pose. For the most part, it gets it right by using a built-in facial tracking system, but there are convenient tools to allow us to assist. First, we need to tell Unreal what the best frames of our footage are to promote as a solid reference.

You'll see a **Promote Frame** button as per *Figure 9.23*. You need to promote a frame for each of the poses in *Figure 9.18*. Leave the teeth pose for later. You can put your cursor in the timeline and use the left and right arrows on your keyboard to fine-tune the position. You may see the **Promote Frame** button flicker, and that is because not all frames are promotable. As soon as you find a frame like my references, click the promote frame. You'll see a green overlay as Unreal detects the facial features as best as it can. Using the middle mouse button, you can zoom into each feature to inspect how aligned the overlay is to the facial feature and make the necessary adjustment.

Unreal Engine does a pretty good job at detecting the facial features, so editing is usually very minimal, if at all. When you're happy with any tweaking and want to move onto the next **Promote Frame**, click on the **Free Roaming** camera mode indicated by the transform and camera icon as seen at the bottom of *Figure 9.23*. This will allow you to advance to the next appropriate frame on the timeline for promotion.

The options to promote more frames will always be there, but in general, you only need four poses including the teeth. Continue through the remaining poses and adjust the green overlay lines if needed.

In *Figure 9.24*, I've had to make adjustments to the eye. This is of my left side, where my nose has partially covered my right eye. There are two wireframes: one for my pupil and one for my eyelids, the overall shape of my eye. Because it is hard to tell which is which on account of the overlap, I've used the outliner on the right to help determine which is which. The information icon, when clicked, shows an illustration of the pupil. You can edit the shape with both the lines and the points. The more precise you are with this, the better the result will be.

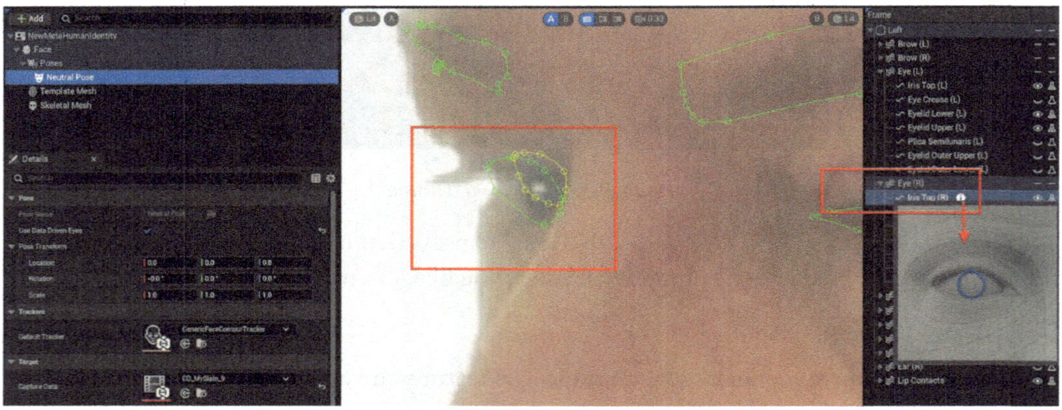

Figure 9.24: Making adjustments

As soon as you have just one promoted frame, you'll notice the **MetaHuman Solve** button will become active.

MetaHuman identity solver

Click on the **MetaHuman Solve** button. It will take a minute or two to work. Once completed, you will get a message saying that your MetaHuman DNA has been created.

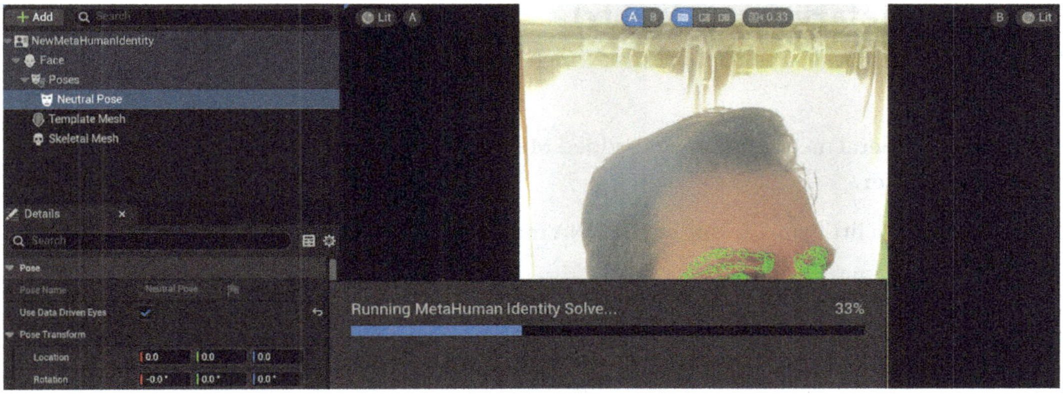

Figure 9.25: Running the Solve

Create a `Teeth` component and then promote a frame with the teeth showing. At the top left click the **+Add** button and choose **Add Pose**, followed by **Add Teeth**. Back in the timeline, promote a frame for the teeth. Ensure you have enough promoted frames and have done the necessary tweaking.

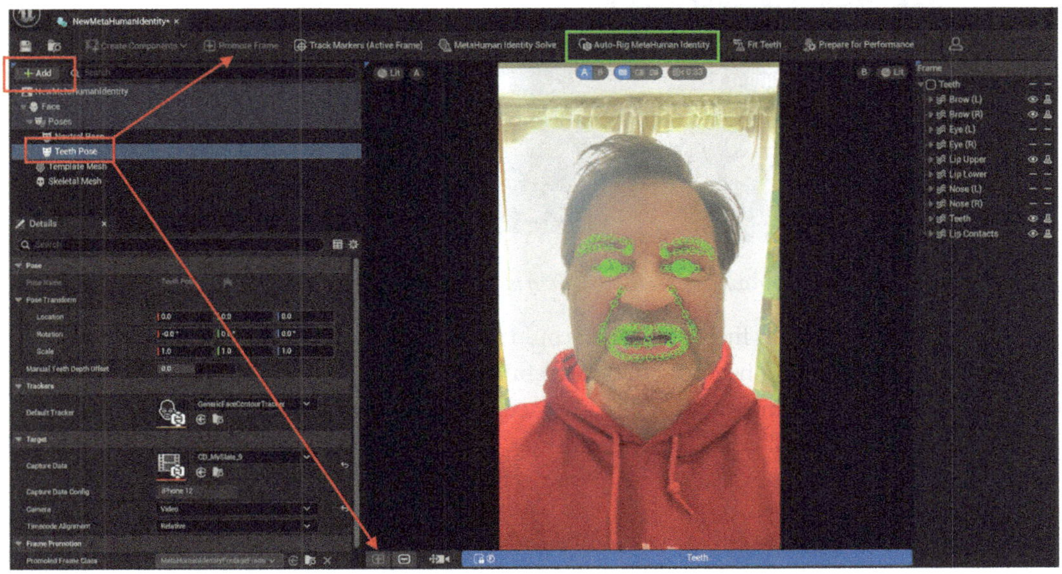

Figure 9.26: Adding teeth pose and promoting teeth frame

AutoRig (MetaHuman identity)

We're nearly there. Go on to the next task which is **AutoRig MetaHuman Identity** and click the button.

You'll see. A skeletal mesh with an embedded MetaHuman DNA is now available in your **Content Browser**.

This message is a little misleading as the DNA may be available but it's not usable. Hit **OK**.

Because we already added teeth pose and promoted a frame, when we hit **OK**, it will finalize the Fix teeth task.

Prepare for Performance

This is the final step. Click on the **Prepare for Performance** button. This could take a while and is usually the longest step to get processed. Without this step, we won't be able to add our MetaHuman DNA when processing any new facial capture.

You should see a dialog box on screen letting you know that the **MetaHuman Identity** is being trained for performance processing.

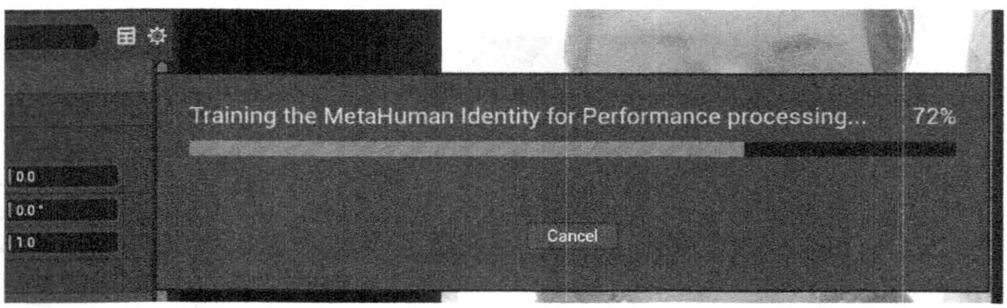

Figure 9.27: Training the MetaHuman Identity for Performance Processing

As soon as the processing is finished, which could take a few minutes, save the **MetaHuman Identity** and close it. You'll be left with two useful assets that will significantly help with the processing of your performance. They are the MetaHuman identity you just saved and the skeletal mesh that has a likeness to the performer. To see that, go back to the **Content Browser** to where your MetaHuman Identity is, and you should see a skeletal mesh next to it sharing the same name. *Double-click* it to inspect it.

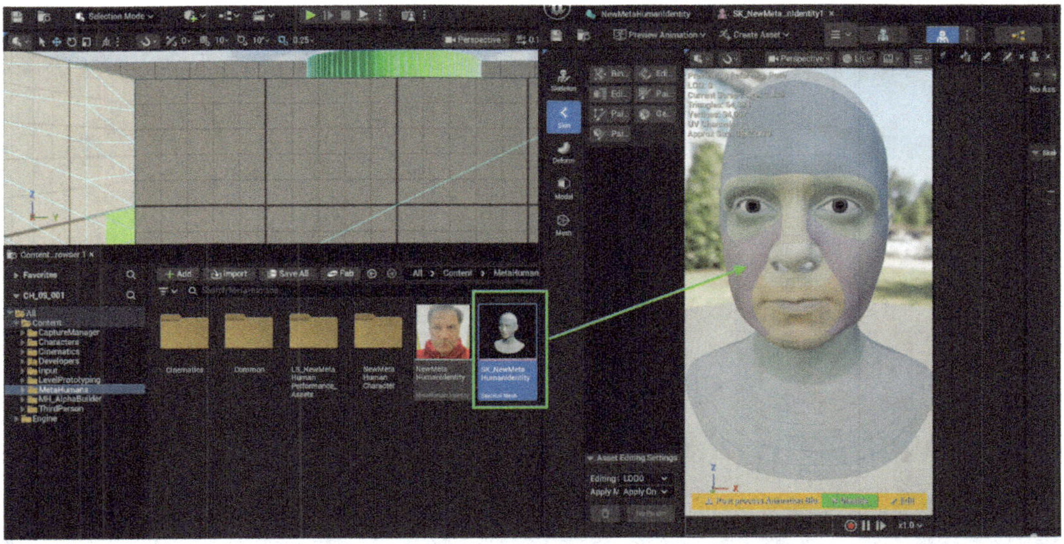

Figure 9.28: The Skeletal Mesh

In *Figure 9.28*, despite having no texture, you can see that the skeletal mesh has a significant likeness to me. It shares the same proportions. Not only do we get a great deal of extra detail in the animation, but we can repurpose this mesh to create a MetaHuman to resemble the performer if that is the goal. If you want to find out how to do that, jump ahead to *Chapter 11*. As we come to the end of this chapter, let's test out a motion capture by using the **MetaHuman Performance Asset**.

Processing facial motion capture

Our final step in this chapter is to process facial capture using our MetaHuman identity and the likeness of our performer to visualize the accuracy of the performance capture.

In the same folder as your **MetaHuman Identity**, *right-click*, go to **MetaHuman** and choose **MetaHuman Performance**. This will create a new **MetaHuman Performance Asset**. *Double-click* to open.

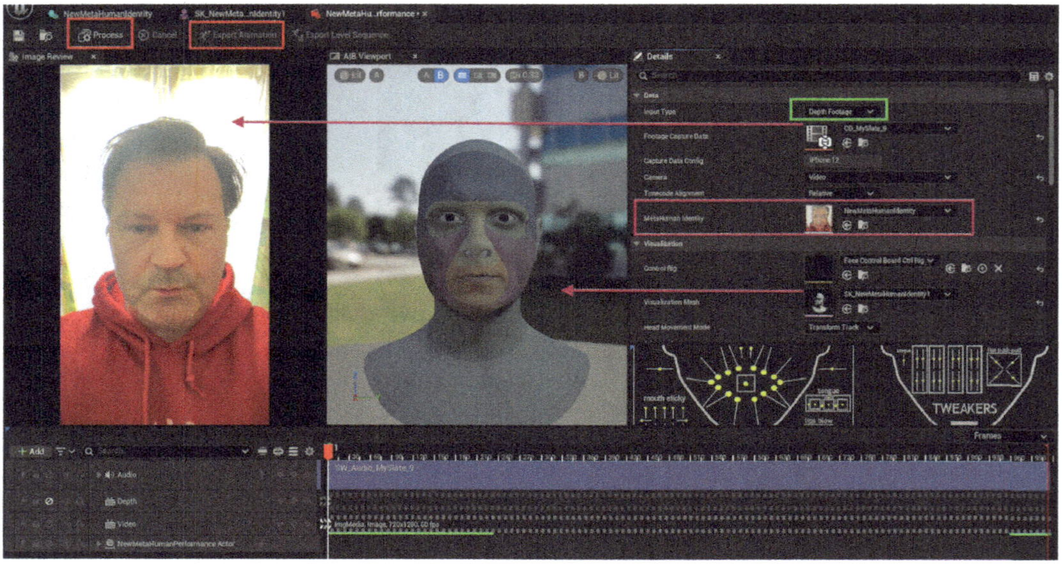

Figure 9.29: Exploring the MetaHuman Performance Asset

Take a look at *Figure 9.29* of the **MetaHuman Performance Asset**. This is the tool we use to process all of our facial animation.

Starting at the top, I've highlighted the **Process** button, which we will use shortly.

Next to it I've highlighted the **Export Animation**, which is the most practical way of getting the processed animation out of this tool.

- On the right-hand side panel at the top, I've highlighted in green that I've chosen **Depth Footage** as the input type to make the most of the iPhone's capabilities.
- In the **Footage Capture Data** slot, I've repurposed the calibration footage. As soon as it is selected, the viewport to the far left updates.
- I've chosen the very recently saved MetaHuman identity that holds all the data for calibration.
- Below that, in the **Visualization Mesh** slot, I've chosen the newly created skeleton Mesh. This automatically updates the viewport on the right.

Now I've got the video capture of me with a digital representation of me side by side. With just those four settings, we are ready to hit the **Process** button on the top.

> **Note**
>
> **Head movement node**
>
> The head movement node is left as **Transform Track**, which is the default. If a headcam and body motion are being captured, this would be set to disabled.

Processing can take some time and with **Depth** footage as the input type, it will require two processing passes, one for each track.

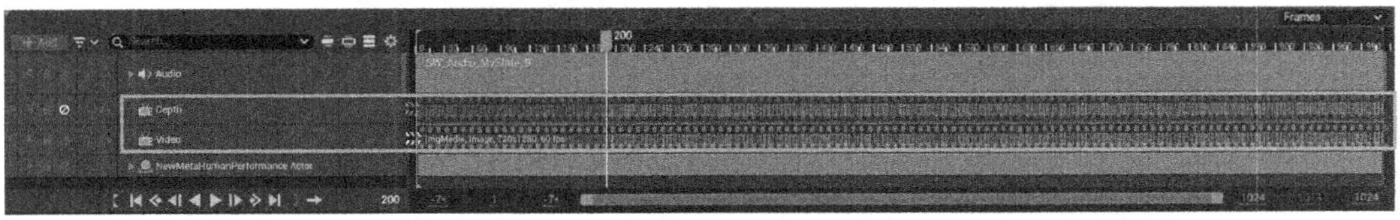

Figure 9.30: Processing both the Depth and Video Tracks Separately

As the tracks are being processed, you'll see the visualization mesh move in sync with the footage. Generally, the processing takes around the same time as ingesting. If you see any strange glitching occurring, you may have to go back to tweaking the MetaHuman identity like I did in 9.24. Once you're happy with the result, click on **Export Animation**. You'll be asked where to save your animation, which will be an **Animation Sequence Asset** just like you've used before earlier in the chapter when using the **Take Recorder**.

Once you've chosen the destination for your new Animation Sequence, you'll be asked what skeleton to target to as per *Figure 9.31*. I've chosen to target the skeleton that was created of me. However, if you plan to use a different character that you haven't even designed yet, you can always choose the **FaceArchetype Skeleton**, which is available in the drop-down list. Take note that you get a second opportunity to disable the head movement. Hit **Create**. We are now finished processing facial motion capture with the iPhone and **Live link Hub**.

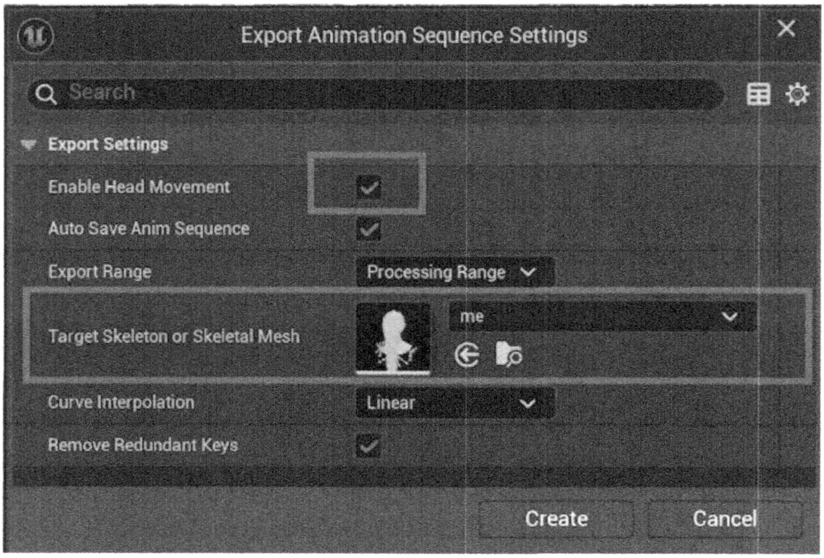

Figure 9.31: Target Skeleton

Note

It is advised that you capture the body and face simultaneously because most performers lead with their heads and the head leads the body. Getting both the body and head in sync can only really be done properly when both elements are captured at the same time.

The iPhone solution can work simultaneously with DeepMotion Animate 3D. To do this, you need a facial capture rig to ensure that the iPhone's depth camera is facing you at all times and that your hands are free. Ideally, the camera needs to be at a consistent distance at all times. Any movement of the camera separate from the head will be interpreted as a head movement.

Companies such as MOCAP Design specialize in creating helmets that work with iPhones. You can see some of their iPhone and GoPro camera solutions at `https://www.mocapdesign.com/m2-headcam`.

Summary

In this chapter, we have explored the iPhone's facial motion capture solution for MetaHumans in Unreal Engine. We listed all the plugins we need to enable for the process. We used the **Live Link App** on the iPhone, along with **Live Link Hub** to manage both live and pre-recorded motion capture. Additionally, we used the **Take Recorder** plugin in conjunction with the **Level Sequencer** as a way to record and manage our mocap.

We then shifted into a more professional workflow utilizing the **MetaHuman Identity** for calibration and creating a likeness of our performer and the **MetaHuman Performance Asset** for final processing of our depth and video motion capture.

In the next chapter, we will continue our facial motion capture but use just a webcam. We will also make use of the built-in audio to face animation tool.

10

Using a Webcam and Audio for Facial Motion Capture

In *Chapter 9*, we focused on facial motion capture using the iPhone. We explored two types of capture.

Live facial capture, recording the live takes within Unreal using the **Take Recorder**.

For a more accurate motion capture, we also used the iPhone for the recording, ingested it with Live Link Hub Capture Manager and processed the capture with MetaHuman performance with help from a MetaHuman Identity.

It was a long chapter, and we covered a lot of ground.

In this chapter, we will be covering much less and dividing the information into much smaller chunks. You'll already be familiar with some of the tools.

We will cover the following topics:

- Camera setup
- Editing the MetaHuman Use Animation Blueprint mode
- Setting Live Link Hub to receive a webcam signal
- Editing the MetaHuman to receive the new webcam signal
- Recording the performance and microphone with Take Recorder
- Locating the audio file to repurpose for audio to animation
- MetaHuman performance using audio
- Processing just the mouth animation
- Copying curves from the mouth animation

- Pasting curves into the facial mocap for better lip sync
- Applying filters

You'll be pleased to know that this chapter is not only shorter, but it is aimed at readers who don't have access to an iPhone.

Technical requirements

In terms of computer power, you will need the technical requirements detailed in *Chapter 1* and the MetaHuman plus the Unreal Engine mannequin that we imported into UE5 in *Chapter 2*. However, you can create a new MetaHuman for this chapter if you like.

You will need a webcam with audio or a webcam with a separate audio input.

If you want a true live video signal from a camera that isn't a standard webcam, the simplest solution is to route it through a virtual webcam. Connect your camera to your PC (via HDMI capture card or similar), bring the feed into OBS Studio as a video source, and then enable OBS's Virtual Camera output. This turns any connected camera into a webcam-style device that Unreal Engine can detect and use as a live input. Inside Unreal, you just select **OBS Virtual Camera** as your video source, and you get a real-time feed with far more flexibility than a typical webcam setup.

Camera setup

Unlike the iPhone, we don't have depth processing to fall back on, so video image quality is important to get right. The subject needs to be well lit and the subject's face needs to fill the frame as much as possible.

A good rule of thumb is that the subject's head takes up a minimum of 25% of the entire frame.

Most laptop webcams offer a recording dimension of 1920 x 1080 with a frame rate of 30 fps.

If you are choosing a webcam for this, aim for a higher frame rate rather than trying to exceed the 1920 x 1080 dimension. A 3840 x 2160 pixel dimension isn't going to offer an advantage compared to a higher frame rate.

Overall, a webcam will do a great job at tracking if the subject's face is close enough.

In the next section, we need to make sure our MetaHuman is all set to receive a Live Link feed.

Editing the MetaHuman with the Use Animation Blueprint mode

Ensure you have a MetaHuman in your scene.

You can check the outliner for this or drag the MetaHuman from your content folder into your scene.

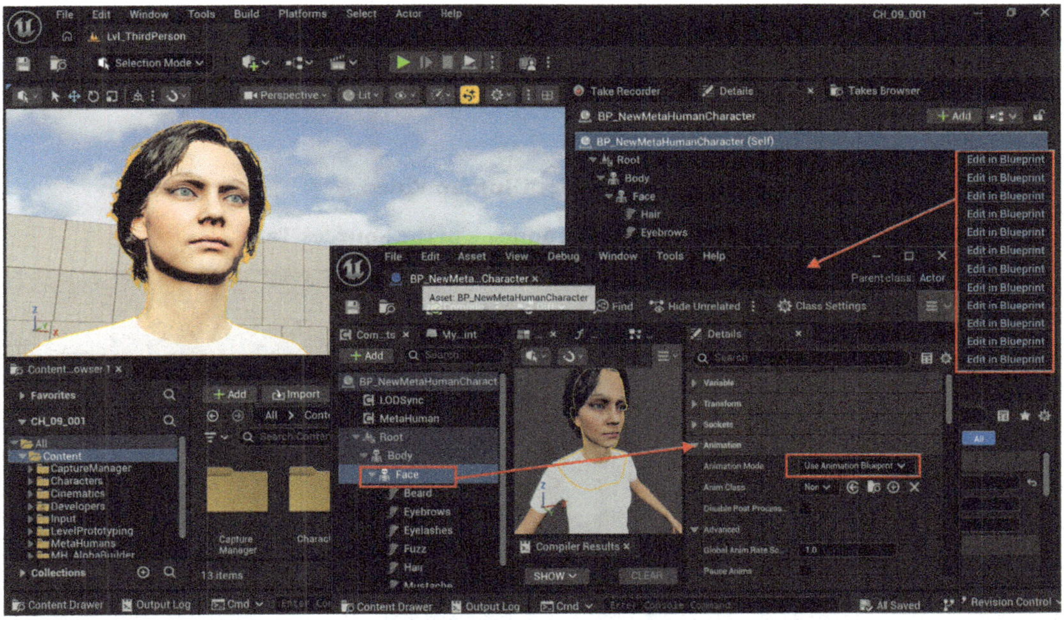

Figure 10.1: Animation Mode

The next step is the same as in the previous chapter. We need to change the animation mode to **Use Animation Blueprint**. When the MetaHuman Blueprint is in the scene and selected, you will see you've got access to the **Details** panel, where you can change the animation mode.

Just like in the last chapter, if your animation mode keeps reverting to **Use Animation Asset**, find your MetaHuman Blueprint in the outliner and use the **Edit Blueprint** link to edit the **Details** panel from within the Blueprint. The **Animation Mode** needs to be set to **Use Animation Blueprint**. You'll need to hit **Compile** once you've changed the **Animation Mode** to **Use Animation Blueprint** as shown in *Figure 10.1*.

If you can't find the **Animation Mode**, click on the **Face Component** of your MetaHuman within the **Outliner**. With the **Animation Tab** selected, **Animation Mode** will be at the top of the list.

Note

To quickly find anything specific in the detail panel, use the search field.

Setting Live Link Hub to receive a webcam signal

As soon as you've edited the **Animation Mode**, boot up **Live Link Hub** by going to **Tools** | **Live Link Hub**. It will take a moment to boot up. While that's booting up, make sure your webcam is working.

As soon as **Live Link Hub** is running, ensure **Live Data** is selected from the drop-down list on the top left.

Click the **+ Add Source** button and choose **MetaHuman Video**.

Click on the **MetaHuman Video** text when it appears in the **Sources Tab**.

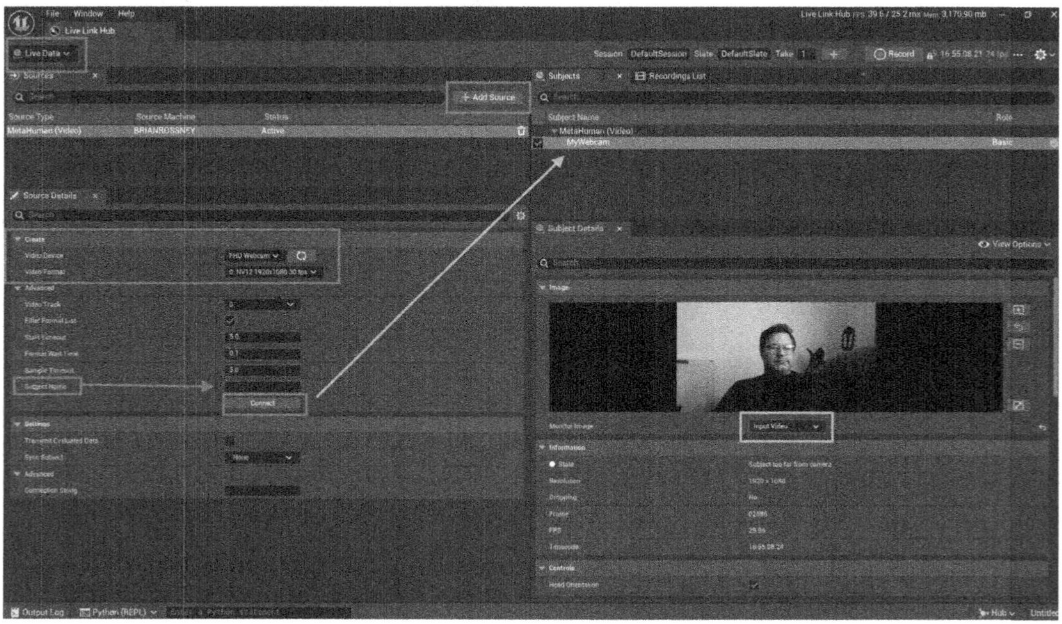

Figure 10.2: Setting Live Link Hub to receive a webcam signal

The **Source Details** tab will populate with information.

In the **Video Device** field, choose your webcam. You may need to click on the **Update** button to see its name.

Video Format will detect the available settings of your chosen device.

In my case, I just have two settings available:

- 1920 x 1080 30fps
- 1280 x 720 30fps

I'll pick the first one as it offers a slight advantage.

In the **Subject Name** field, type something you'll recognize when back in Unreal Engine, such as **MyWebcam**.

Click on Connect.

You should see the subject name appear in the **Subjects** tab on the right, along with **Basic** as the role and, if everything is configured correctly, a **green circle with a tick**, as shown beside **My Webcam** in *Figure 10.2*.

> Note
>
> **Checkpoint**
>
> Do not continue until you see the green tick.
>
> A green tick confirms that Live Link Hub is receiving a valid webcam signal. If the indicator is yellow or red, revisit your webcam selection and calibration settings before proceeding.

In the **Subject Details** panel, the first setting is **Image**. Choose **0** as the image you want to monitor.

In **Information**, you can see the resolution and frame rate.

You'll also see **State**, which indicates the quality of the input video. If you move the subject backward, away from the webcam, it will turn yellow. This means the subject is too far from the webcam, so the facial features may not be recognized and tracked.

Under **Controls**, we are going to leave everything in the default settings. However, we have three calibration buttons to click on.

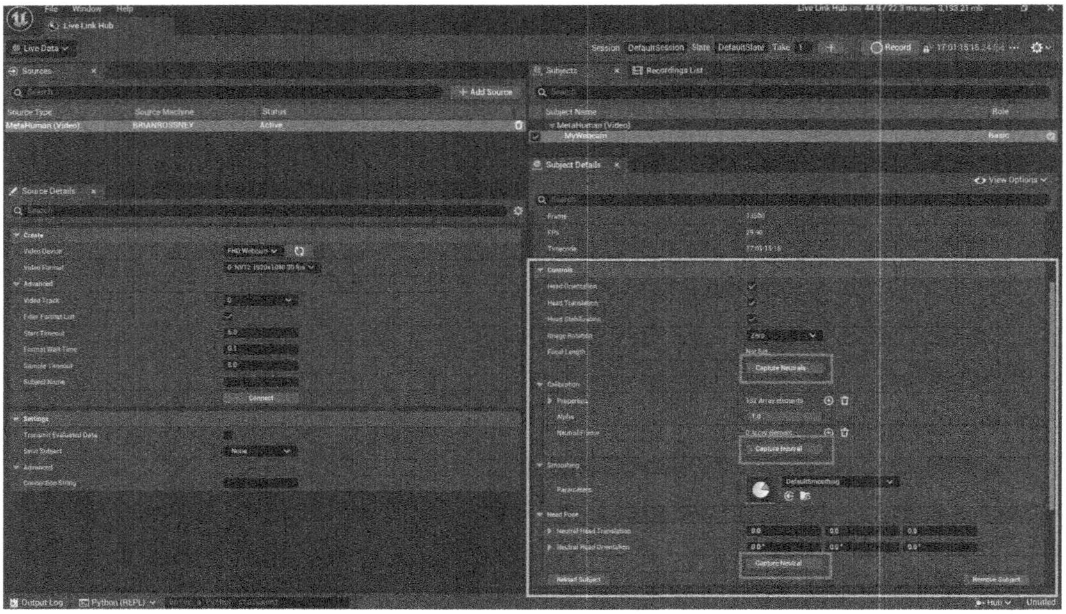

Figure 10.3: Calibration Controls

Each Capture Neutral button performs a different calibration task:

Focal Length estimates the camera lens characteristics and improves overall facial tracking, particularly when the background is busy.

Calibration records a neutral facial expression that Unreal uses as a baseline for detecting expressions. Keep your face relaxed and look directly into the webcam.

Head Pose establishes the default head orientation so that future head movements can be measured accurately.

For all three captures, ensure the subject fills the frame, remains well-lit, and maintains a neutral expression while looking directly into the webcam.

With the calibration process over, it's time to go back to Unreal Engine.

Editing the MetaHuman to receive the new webcam signal

You need to make sure you have clicked on the **MetaHuman Blueprint** in the **Outliner**. Now, go to **Details** panel, and under **Live Link Subject**, choose the **Webcam**. This should be the name you gave it earlier in the **Live Link Hub** in the **Subject** field.

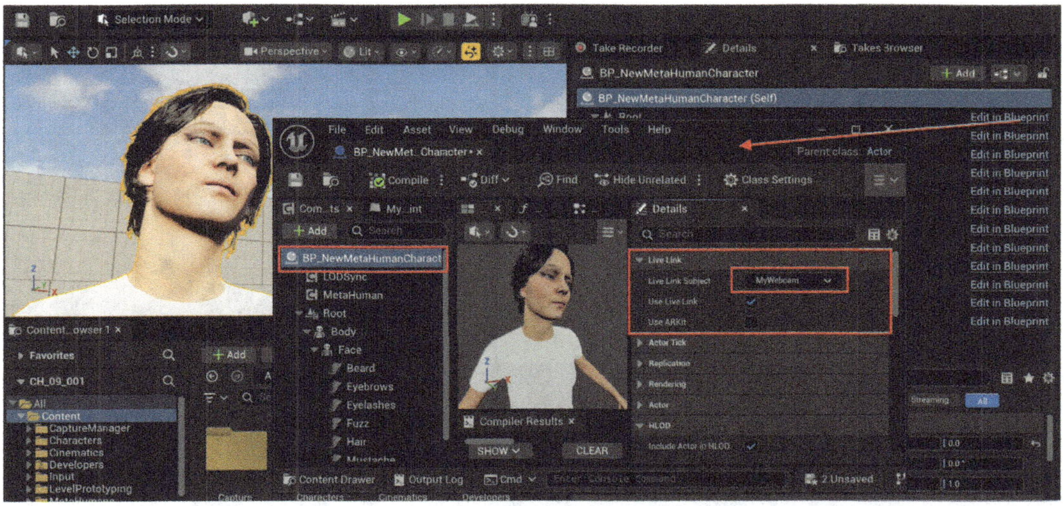

Figure 10.4: Enabling Webcam and Live Link in MetaHuman Blueprint

If your MetaHuman hasn't come to life, tick the Live Link box.

You should now see a live performance driving your MetaHuman.

If you're working on a lower-spec machine, you may notice reduced responsiveness while simultaneously running Live Link, the Level Sequencer, and Take Recorder. This is normal and can usually be improved by lowering the viewport scalability settings or temporarily switching the viewport to Wireframe mode during recording.

Take some time to gauge the best distance from the webcam. Moving away from the camera shows an immediate loss in motion capture quality.

Recording the performance and microphone with Take Recorder

If you want to record a session, you can do so by opening **Take Recorder**, adding the MetaHuman Blueprint along with an audio device like we did in *Chapter 9*. It's always faster to select the **Blueprint** in the scene, so that when you select **From Actor**, it will appear at the very top of the list. Adding **Microphone Audio** will add whatever default audio device your system is using.

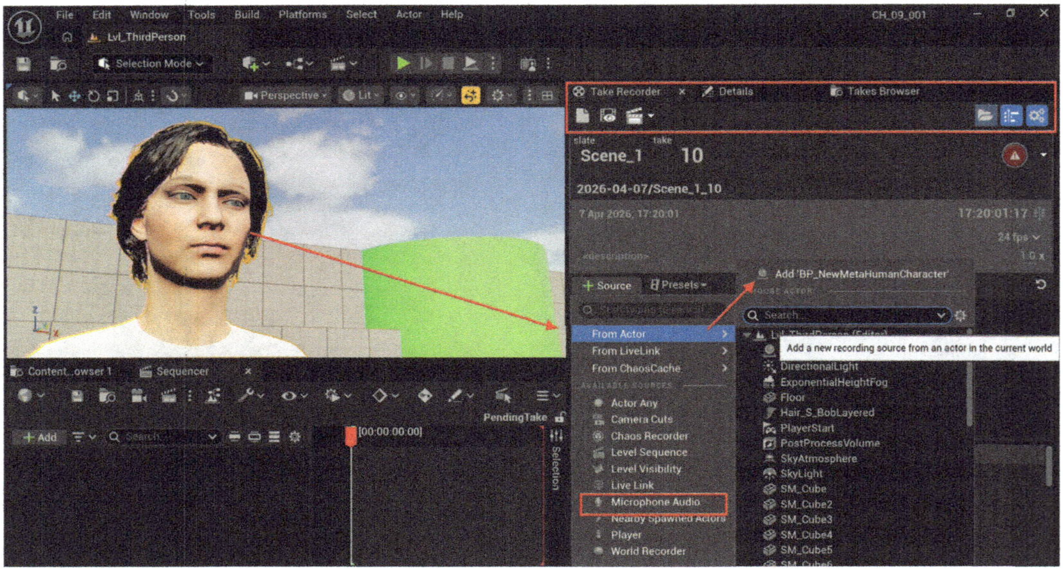

Figure 10.5: Adding Sources to Take Recorder

Let's assume you have used the **Take Recorder**, recorded mocap data along with audio of a performer reciting a poem. Once the recording is done, you can observe the **Animation Sequence** via the **Take Browser**. *Double-click* on it and play from the timeline. Without sound, it may be hard to judge the lip sync.

Locating the audio file to repurpose for Audio-to-Animation

To get a better idea on the quality of the mocap, add the **MetaHuman Blueprint** to a **Level Sequencer** like you've done in *Chapter 9*. Delete the control rigs and add the new **Animation Sequence** to the face component.

Then add an audio track to the **Level Sequence** and choose the audio that was just created in the **Take Browser**.

The most recent takes will be placed in a folder `Scene_XXX_Subscenes`. It will contain an `Animation` and an `Audio` folder, both relating to the same take. The `Audio` folder will only be created if you added an audio input as a source. In *Figure 10.6*, I've highlighted how Unreal automatically creates a folder structure depending on the **Take Recorder**'s input configuration at the time of recording.

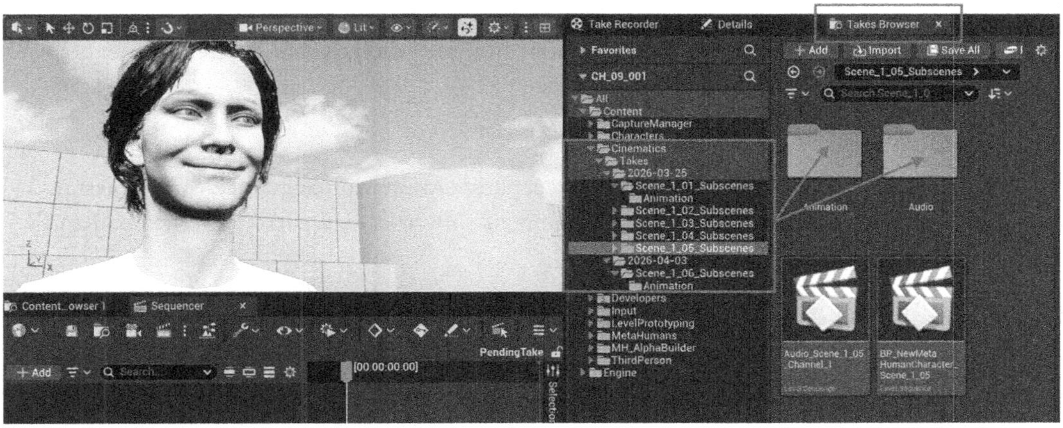

Figure 10.6: Take Browser

To save time, click on each of these assets, starting with the animation and hit *F2*, then *Ctrl + C* to copy the name. Go to the Face component of your character Blueprint in your **Level Sequencer**. Add an animation and in the **Search** field, hit *Ctrl + V* to paste the name of the animation and select it. This will add the asset into the track. Do the same for the audio in the audio track of your **Leve Sequencer**. You can see from *Figure 10.7* that I've pasted the name from the selected asset into the **Search** field so that only that asset is available to select.

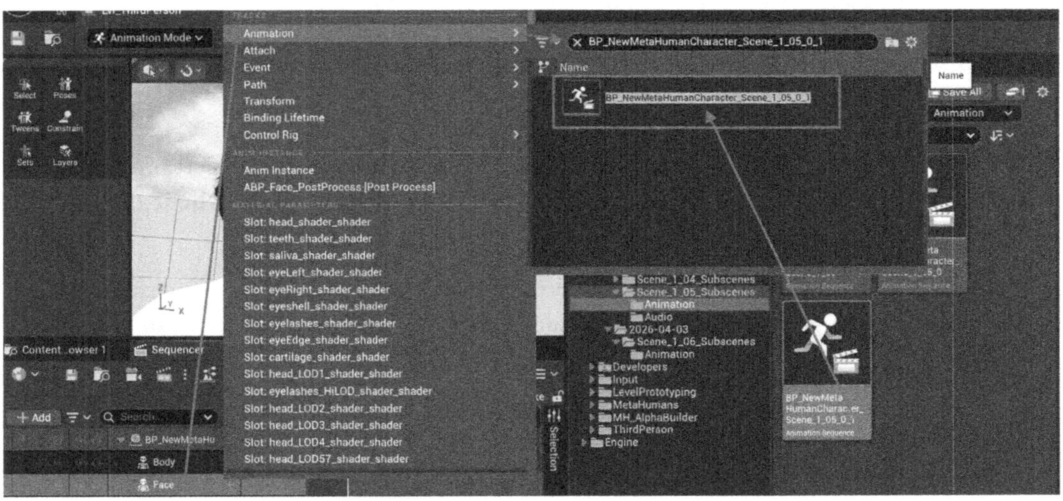

Figure 10.7: Copying asset title to repurpose in Search field

Make sure both the animation and audio are set to begin at the exact same time, preferably at the very beginning of the **Level Sequencer**.

Now play the Level Sequencer to see and hear the result.

At this point, you'll notice that the face and head animate correctly, but the head appears to move away from the body.

Don't worry. This is completely expected.

The Take Recorder stores head movement as a separate Animation Sequence. Simply assign that Animation Sequence to the `Body` component, as shown in *Figure 10.8*, and the head and body will move together correctly.

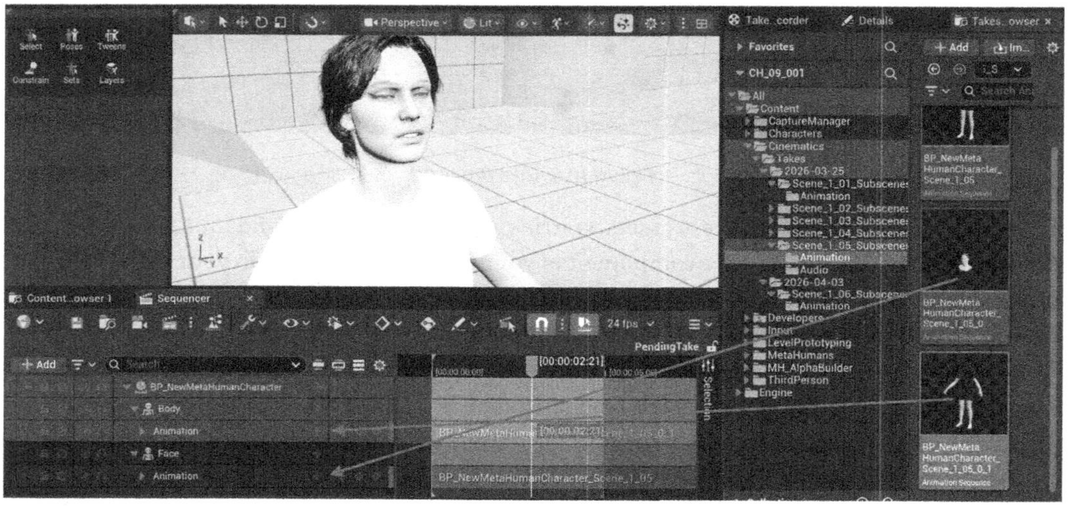

Figure 10.8: Assigning animation to Body and Face

You may have noticed that the result is pretty good for just a webcam and is certainly on par with the results we got with the iPhone when doing a live capture with the iPhone... if not better.

As impressive as this is, the mouth movement can sometimes appear weak, with minimal motion in certain areas, often caused by the subject moving too far away or shifting side to side.

Even when a subject delivers an otherwise perfect take with strong expressions and audio, the lip movement may still fall short—something you might only notice after the opportunity to re-record is gone.

This scenario isn't a complete disaster because we can repurpose the audio to drive the mouth movement when the facial capture fails or is weak.

MetaHuman performance using audio

The Audio to Face feature was originally introduced as a separate plugin but, in Unreal Engine 5.7, it is integrated directly into the MetaHuman Performance workflow and does not require any additional plugin installation.

It generates detailed mouth animation directly from an audio recording while also supporting emotional presets such as Happy or Angry and automatic blinking. By default, the emotion preset is set to Auto Detect, allowing Unreal to analyze the audio and generate appropriate facial expressions automatically.

For this chapter, we are only going to focus on the mouth to complement the webcam facial capture for more realism. For this, we need to create a **MetaHuman Performance Asset**.

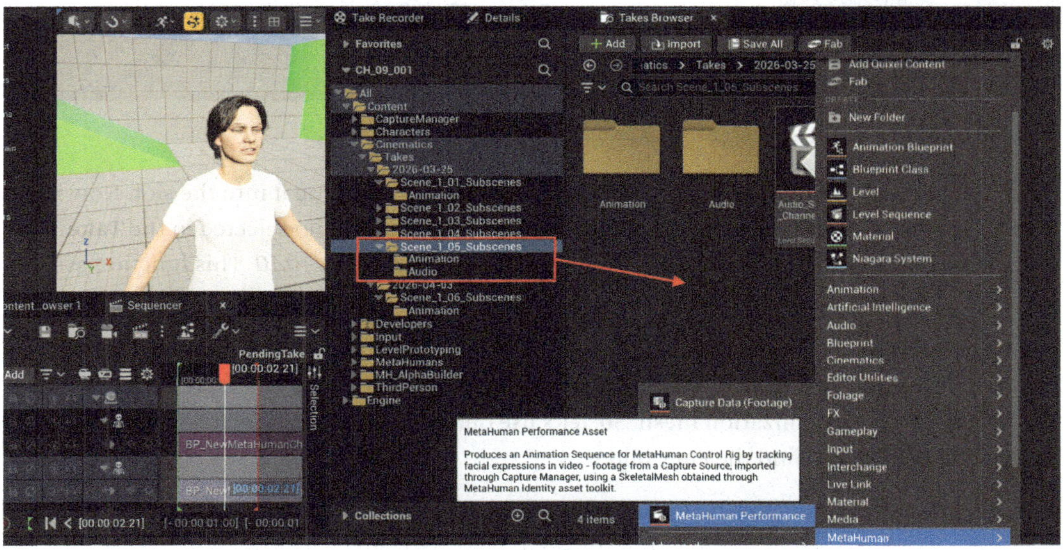

Figure 10.9: Creating a MetaHuman Performance Asset

Go to your audio asset and copy the name. In your `Take` folder, go to **MetaHuman** and **MetaHuman Performance Asset** and open it.

Go to **Data** | **Input Type** and choose **Audio**.

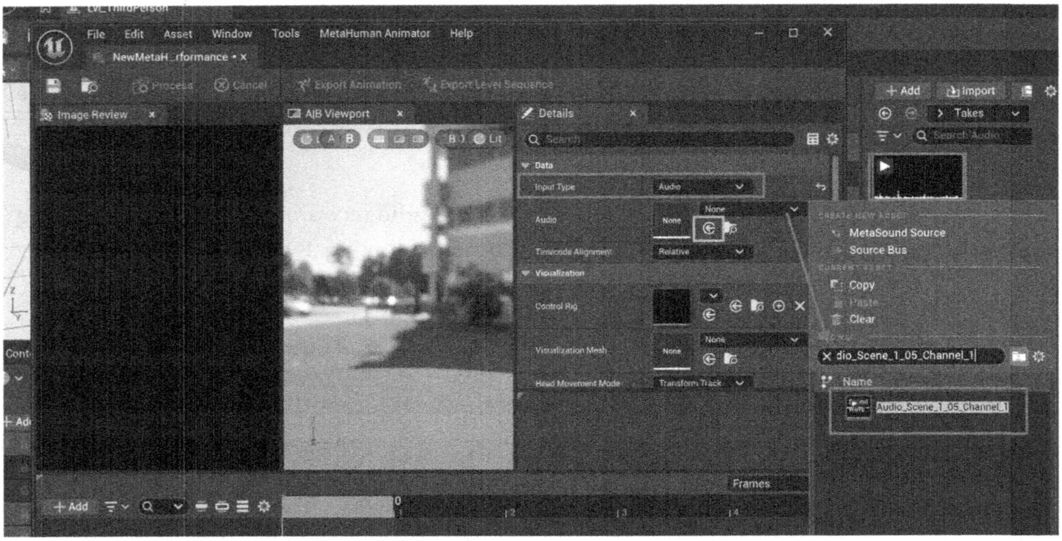

Figure 10.10: Assigning the Audio Take from the Mocap Session

Type the name of the audio asset in the **Search** field or drag and drop it into the slot. Now it's time to process the audio into motion data. If you still have the audio selected in the **Take Browser**, you can also use the arrow, as highlighted green in *Figure 10.10*. This function assigns whatever asset has been selected.

Once the audio has been assigned, you'll see a waveform track of the audio appear in the timeline at the bottom of the screen. However, the **Viewport** remains blank because we haven't assigned a visualization mesh. So, let's use our MetaHuman's face. Navigate to your `MetaHumans` folder and find the `Face` folder.

You should see a skeleton mesh of your character's head. It usually starts with a prefix of `SKM`. Select the skeletal mesh and assign it to the **Visualization** slot by either dragging it into the slot or using the arrow feature to select it from the **Browser**.

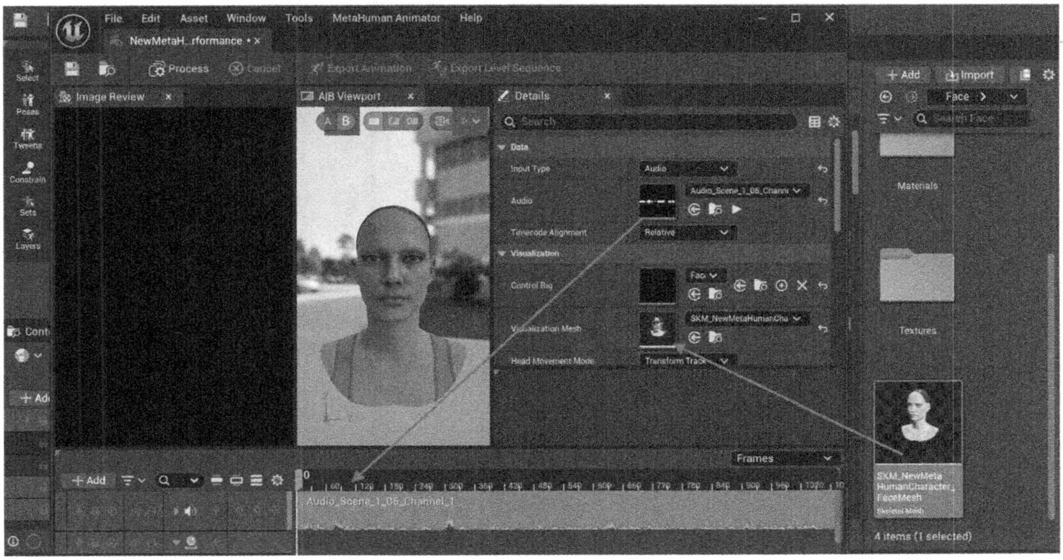

Figure 10.11: Audio waveform and visualization mesh

Processing just the mouth animation

With the visualization mesh in place, go down to **Processing Parameters** and then to **Process Mask**.

You have a choice here. You can leave the process mask to be the whole face, which will use the audio to drive the mouth and will apply generic animation to the rest of the face based on an AI algorithm that detects tone from the audio, or you can select the mask to just create movement for the mouth. Either way, it works because we are going to only use the mouth animation later on.

Select either and click on **Process**. It will take a little while to process (less if you just process the mouth area). When finished, click on **Export Animation** and choose the same **Take Recorder** location as your audio so we can find it later.

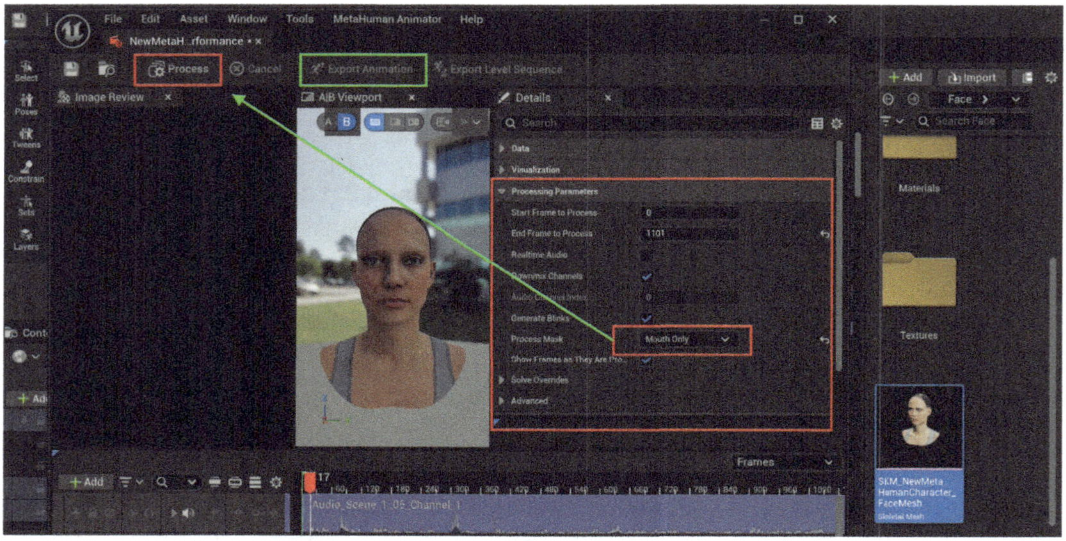

Figure 10.12: Assigning the Mouth Only processing mask

A dialog box will appear. Make sure you select the same skeletal face for the head that is being used for your MetaHuman's face.

Once you've exported the animation, you now have an **Animation Sequence** of the mouth movement based solely on the audio, created by AI.

We want to copy all that more precise mouth movement and paste it onto our motion captured performance. To do that, *double-click* on the AI-generated animation sequence that we just created.

Copying curves from the mouth animation

In the tab in the middle under the **Viewport**, you'll see many tracks with curves. We want to use the filter and type in the word `Mouth`. We're only interested in the mouth data.

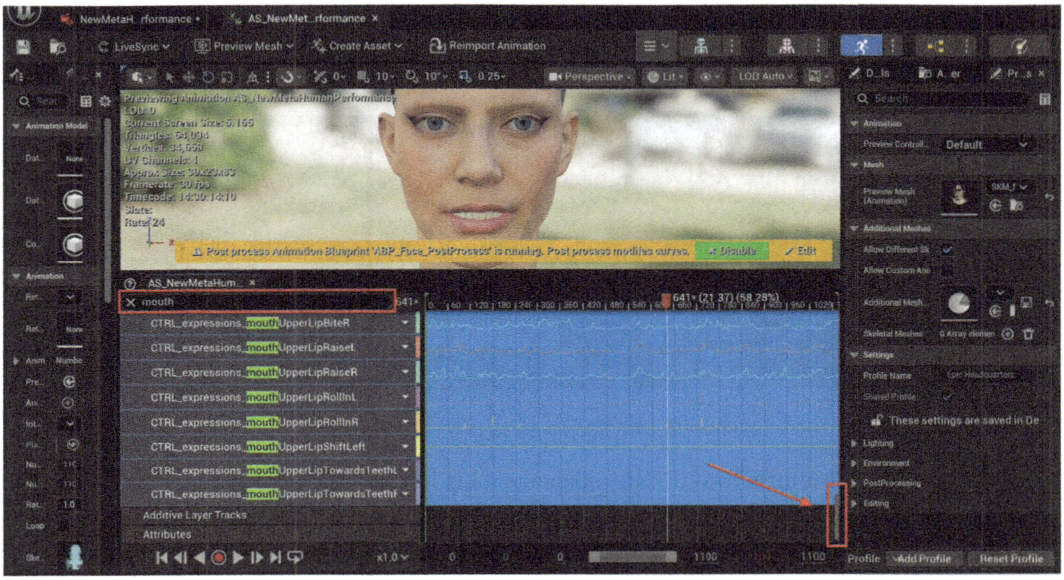

Figure 10.13: Copying all of the Mouth Curves

Below the filter search area, you'll see a drop down under **Curves**. Now you can see just the **Mouth** curve tracks. Click on the top curve, scroll down using the middle mouse wheel or the scroll bar highlighted in red in *Figure 10.13* to the bottom curve, then press *Shift* + *click* to select all tracks, and hit *Ctrl* + *C* to copy them.

Pasting curves into the facial mocap for better lip-sync

Next, we want to paste the selected mouth curve tracks over the mouth curve tracks of our motion capture animation sequence. So, back in the `Takes` folder, *double-click* the animation sequence we captured and run the same **Mouth** filter. Select all the mouth curves as before, and this time hit *Ctrl* + *V* to paste all of those AI-driven mouth curve tracks. Save the animation sequence and go back to the **Level Sequencer** to review.

You'll see that the mouth movement is now a lot more detailed, with every sound from the audio being represented by a mouth movement.

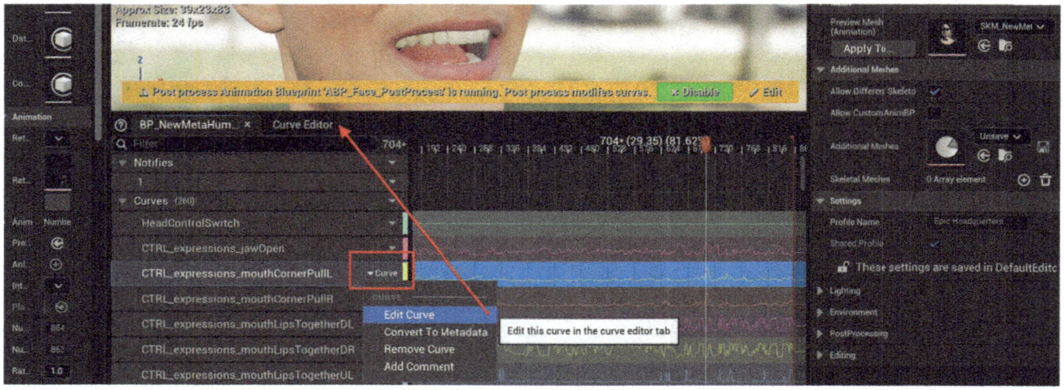

Figure 10.14: Adding a curve to the Curve Editor

If you feel it might be a little too strong, you can usually identify the problem by scrolling through all the mouth curves that you pasted in and looking for a track that is very busy looking, particularly a curve with a lot of peaks. There could be a few, and the process to fix this is the same.

Go to a problem curve. The issue is usually that the curve is going too high up in response to high amplitude in the audio.

On the left-hand side of each track, there is a drop-down menu. Select it and choose **Edit Curve**. This will assign it to the **Curve Editor** tab.

Applying filters

Sometimes, it's a question of just applying a filter to smooth out the curve to make it look less jerky or intense. This is usually the best route rather than manually trying to move points on a curve.

If it is a temporal issue where there is just too much movement, it's usually because there are too many keys or points in the curve. We already chose to edit curves so you can see all the curve shapes and their associated keys. Select the area you want to fix, *right-click*, and choose **Filter**.

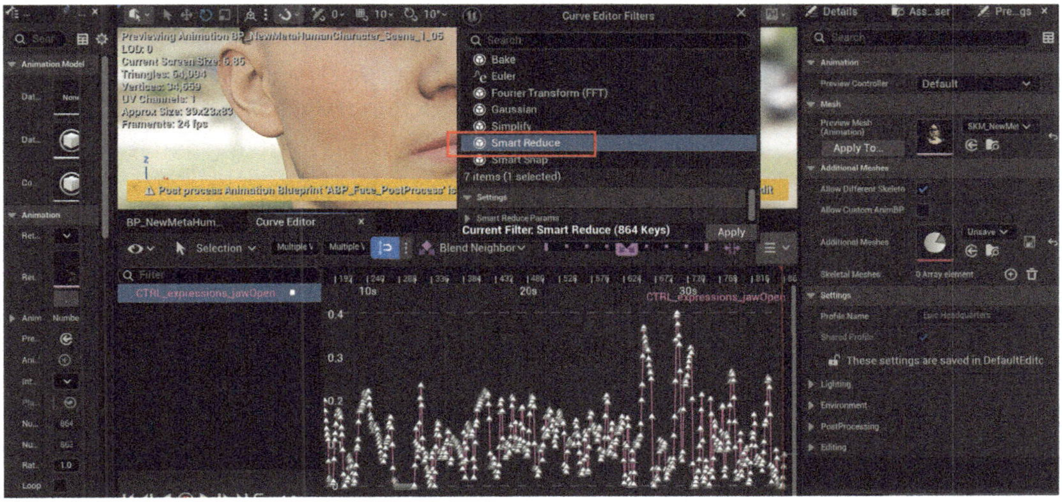

Figure 10.15: Smart Reduce Curve Editor Filter

We want to add a filter to fix this issue. In this case, there are too many keys and there's a filter called **Smart Reduce**. So, apply that filter by clicking **Apply**.

You may want to increase or decrease the values depending on your desired result. If filtering doesn't work, manually deleting the more obvious areas where there are clearly too many keys may be a faster option.

If it is a spatial issue where the movement has gone too far, for instance a lip movement for the pronunciation of an R sound is looking more like a snarl shape, then the issue is that curve has moved too far.

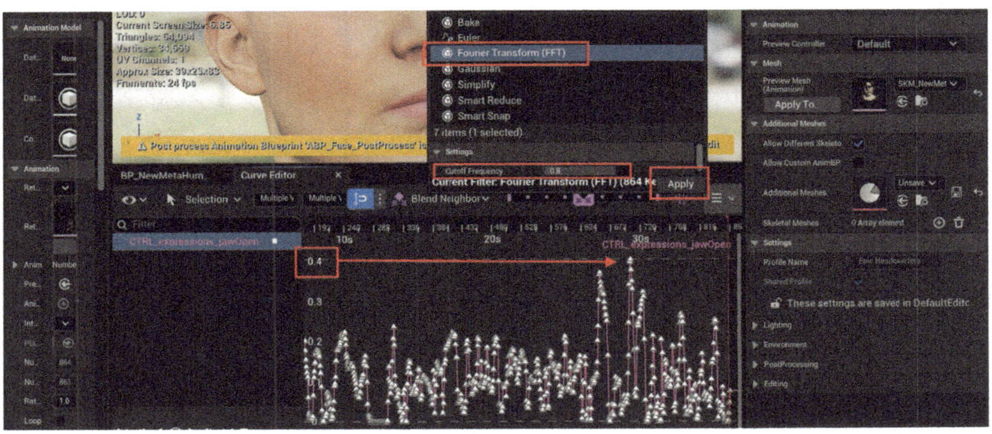

Figure 10.16: Applying Fourier Transform to Reduce Peaks

The best filter for this is the **Fourier Transform** filter, which will dampen down the highest point of the curve and bring up the lower points, effectively compressing the curve. In *Figure 10.16*, I've highlighted the **Cut-Off Frequency**, which is set to 0.8. I would need it to be below 0.4 to have any effect on the peak that I've pointed to with the arrow.

> **Note**
>
> In the example, I've selected all the keys on that track which show white. Applying filters on the entire track takes a while to process. It is best practice to apply filters to just the problem keys by making small selections.

These filters will take effect straight away in the animation sequence as soon as you select **Apply**.

Once happy, hit **Save** and inspect the changes in the **Level Sequencer** with sound.

You have successfully used the built-in **Audio to Animation** feature to enhance your lip sync for your web camera-based motion capture.

Note that you can use the exact same process of editing curves for problem areas of your facial capture. For instance, you might find one eyelid flickering occasionally. In that case, you swap the word `Mouth` with `Eyelid` or `Blink`, depending on the exact issue.

You can also add multiple tracks to edit simultaneously. So if you want to manually add extra blinks for both eyes, type in `BlinkL`, followed by `BlinkR`, and both blink tracks will be added. For manual placement of keyframes, you can use the middle mouse button to place your keyframes.

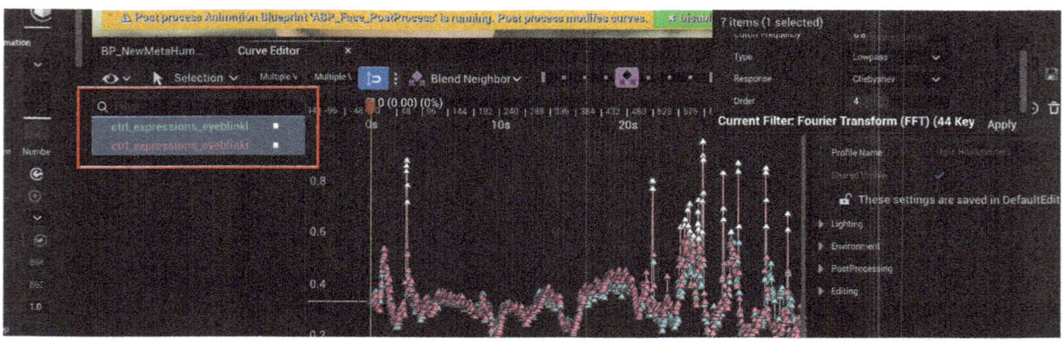

Figure 10.17: Editing multiple Curves

Using curve editing and filtering in this way is a good way to remove any shortcomings of the webcam mocap. For the most part, the **Curve Editor** is the go-to tool for cleaning up jitter from motion capture rather than a creative tool to enhance animation.

As I mentioned earlier in the chapter, the higher the frame rate and the clearer the video, the better the motion capture and the less clean-up will be required.

Summary

In this chapter, we covered how to get reasonably good facial performance capture with just a webcam while also doing a little bit of revision from the previous chapter. Additionally, we learned how to use the **Audio to Face** feature to complement the webcam capturing.

We also looked deeper into some of the professional tools used to clean up motion capture by opening the animation sequence and using the **Curve Editor** while exploring filters and manual adjustments.

In the next chapter, we are going to spend more time on the **Level Sequencer** to cover the best practices when creating animation for the purpose of rendering. We will look at camera settings, lighting, and rendering techniques to elevate the final look of your animation. Additionally, we will learn industry-level concepts when it comes to rendering, color theory, and compositing.

11

Advanced Rendering with the Level Sequencer

In the previous chapters, you've been equipped with a choice of facial motion capture methods, be it using an iPhone or a webcam. A common thread in all of this is the **Level Sequencer**.

Some of this chapter will feel like revision as we return to the **Level Sequencer** and apply body and face animation to our MetaHuman. However, we will be using different techniques to handle a different type of animation, such as **Animation in Place**.

However, for the bulk of this chapter, we will be discussing lights, camera, and rendering. In other words, how to make your MetaHuman look good!

We will cover the following topics:

- Adding the MetaHuman Blueprint and body mocap data to the **Level Sequencer**
- Exploring advanced rendering features

Technical requirements

In terms of computer power, you will need the technical requirements detailed in *Chapter 1* and the MetaHuman plus the Unreal Engine mannequin that we imported into UE5 in *Chapter 2*.

If you have followed along with all of the chapters, you will also have Mixamo and DeepMotion data from *Chapter 5* and *Chapter 6*. At this stage, I expect you to be familiar enough with Mixamo, and either of the iPhone and Webcam facial capture processes to add animation to a **Level Sequencer**, but we will revise the subject in the next section. I also expect you to have many different mocap assets in your project for both `Body` and `Face` from *Chapter 6* on Mixamo and *Chapter 7* on DeepMotion.

Adding the MetaHuman Blueprint and body mocap data to the Level Sequencer

In this section, we will once again add our MetaHuman to the **Level Sequencer** so that we can apply both body and facial capture data to it.

Adding the MetaHuman Blueprint

To start, first, create a new **Level Sequencer** by right-clicking anywhere within your **Content Browser** and clicking **Level Sequencer**.

Once your new **Level Sequencer** is created, locate your MetaHuman Blueprint and drag and drop it into the **Viewport**. *Double-click* your new **Level Sequencer** to open it and add a track by clicking **+ Track** at the top and then click on **Actor To Sequence**. As usual, above the search field, you'll see the selected actor: your MetaHuman Blueprint.

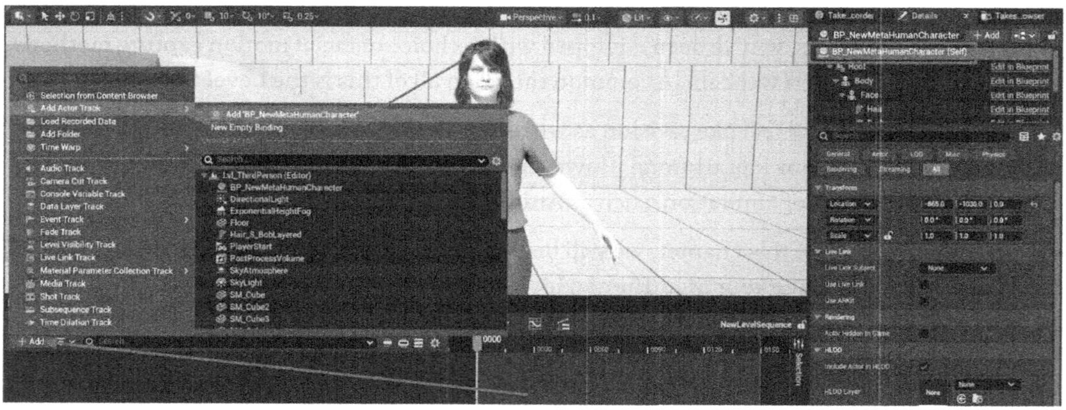

Figure 11.1: Adding the Blueprint to the Level Sequencer

As soon as you have your MetaHuman Blueprint in your **Sequence**, delete the MetaHuman control rigs for both the `Face` and `Body`. Remember, we're going to add some mocap for both.

Figure 11.2: Deleting the Control Rigs

For the moment, we don't need the control rigs because we're just learning how to manage our animation data, which we will add in the very next section. So, delete both rigs highlighted in the **Level Sequencer** in *Figure 11.2*.

With the **Level Sequencer** still open, we are now ready to add our body mocap data.

Adding previously retargeted body mocap data

If you have followed along with all of the chapters, you will have created body motion capture files with Mixamo and DeepMotion.

To add body animation, just click on **+Track**, then go to **Animation**, as shown in *Figure 11.3*. Provided you've used the `RT_` Prefix, you should find your retargeted assets quickly.

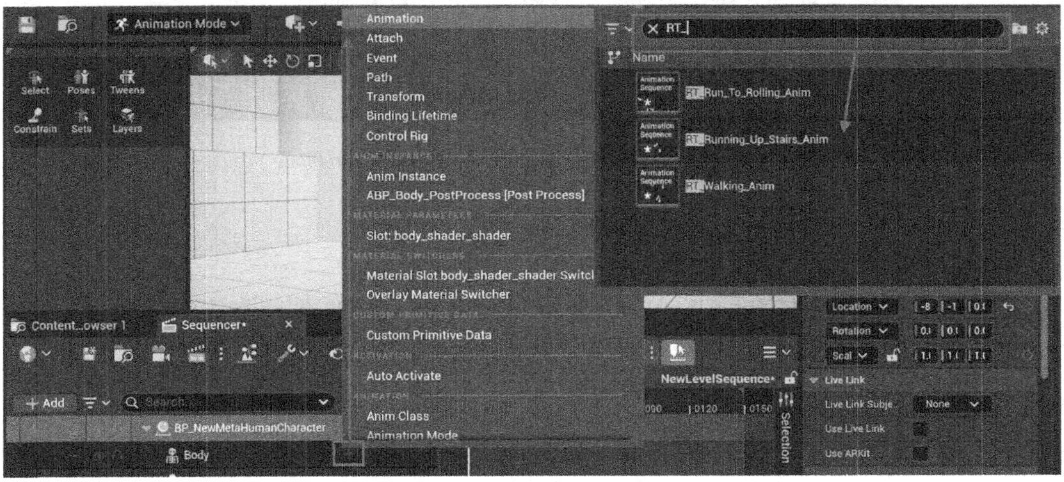

Figure 11.3: Locating a Retargeted Mixamo Animation

In *Figure 11.4*, you can see that I've added a track. You can even see that it has the track title, which can confirm at a glance that you are using the correct animation sequence. I've intentionally brought in an animation that has a common problem. While it is just a simple walk cycle, the issue with the file I downloaded from Mixamo is that it *animates in place*, a term used to describe an animation that remains in the same position. It may be a problem, but it isn't a mistake. For instance, characters in first-person games are animated in place, but the player moves the character in different directions.

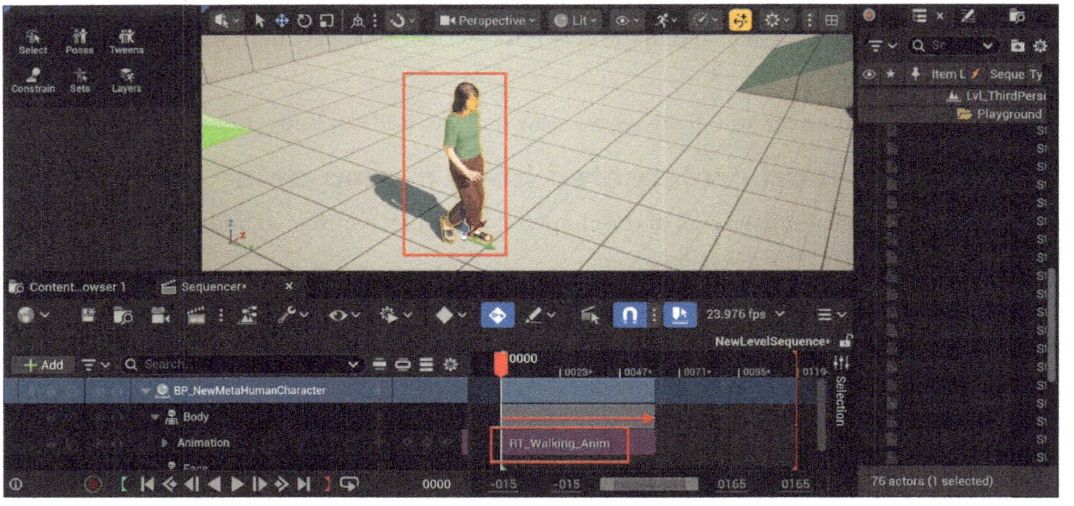

Figure 11.4: An added track that has Animation in Place

> **Note**
>
> **Animation in Place and Mixamo**
>
> Mixamo animations come with **Animation in Place**. It is not the default setting and needs to be enabled in the animation controls in Mixamo by ticking the **Animation in Place** box.

Animation in place can give an animator a little more control when blocking out a scene. For instance, they want their character to go from A to B over X amount of time. No prerecorded animation is going to give them exactly what they want, so the animator can just place the character in A position, then over X amount of time place them in B position and give keyframes for both. Then it is just a matter of changing the walk cycle speed. I'm going to show you how to do that now.

To animate the position of the character, we need a transform component. The **Transform** component needs to be on the root or the body. Either will work.

The animation I used is a loopable walk cycle. Most of the walk cycles are loopable, meaning the pose of the first frame is identical to the pose of the last frame. My animation is only 62 frames long, but it's enough.

In *Figure 11.5*, I added a **Transform** component by clicking the + icon on the same track as the body and selecting **Transform**. This component contains **Location**, **Rotation**, and **Scale** values.

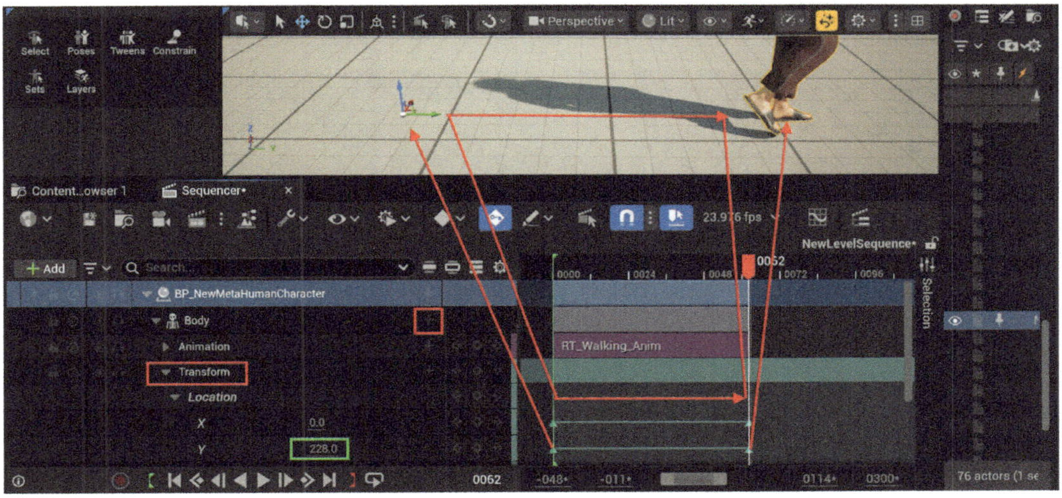

Figure 11.5: A and B position using a Transform Component

For this example, we are only interested in the value that controls the direction in which the character is moving. I've highlighted the Y-axis Location value in green on *Figure 11.5*. This matches the **Viewport** convention, where the Y-axis is also represented in green.

In the **Viewport**, you'll notice a gizmo (indicated by a red arrow) that includes a green arrow showing the Y-axis direction. This helps confirm that the Y-axis is the correct axis to work with for this movement.

The red arrow on the left, pointing from a keyframe to the gizmo, represents the *starting position* (*position A*). Looking back at the **Transform** values, you'll see that the **Y** value is at `228.0`, which corresponds to the character's position (*position B*) at that specific moment in time.

By moving the playhead to *frame 62*, the end of the animation, and setting a keyframe on the **Transform** component, we can see that the character travels *228 units along the Y axis* from *frame 0* to *frame 62*. This movement is illustrated by the red arrow spanning from the start frame to the end frame.

Using the default keyframe type (**Cubic Auto**) for the start and end keyframes would be problematic. Loopable animations such as a walk cycle are designed for constant speed. So, the keyframes need to be changed to linear by right-clicking and choosing **Linear**. You can select all the keyframes, which will highlight blue, and then apply the change to all of them simultaneously.

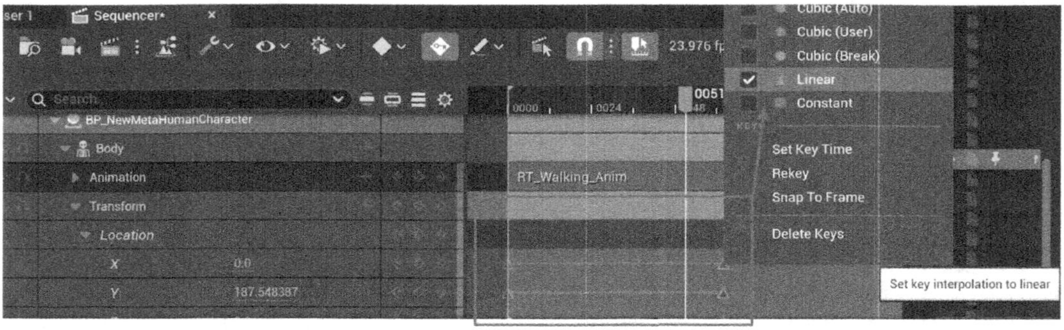

Figure 11.6: Setting Keyframes to Linear for Consistent Speed

As soon as you've changed the keyframes from cubic to linear, you'll find that getting a more realistic walk from A to B is entirely possible. Ultimately, you want each foot when stepping on the ground to remain in the same position until it is raised from the ground again. If the animation is of high quality or acquired from motion capture, you'll achieve solid results quickly.

To extend the animation further, some simple math is involved.

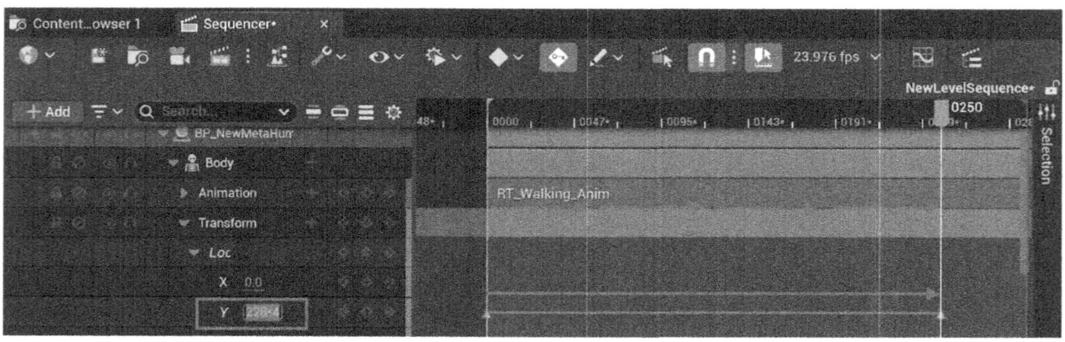

Figure 11.7: Multiplying loop count by Y-axis units

For instance, my animation lasts 62 frames. At *frame 0* the Y value is 0. At *frame 62* the Y value is 228. If I want to double the duration of the walk cycle and make it 124 frames, then I have to double the Y value to 456 units. In short, multiply the loops by the axis units. A faster way of doing this is noting the Y axis unit count for one loop. Then, extend the track by the amount of loops you want. I've extended it by four loops and set a keyframe at that position which is frame 250. In the Y axis value field, I simply added the sum 228*4, and it calculates the value for me for that new keyframe.

That's enough of the body animation. It's time to get some quick facial animation working on our character.

Adding face animation

Create a new MetaHuman performance asset or reuse the one from chapter 10.

For this, we're just going to use the demo audio that comes with MetaHuman but you can use your own recording.

In *Figure 11.8*, I've opened up a **MetaHuman Performance Asset**. At the very top you can see the input is set to **Audio**. For those who may not have access to a microphone, you'll be pleased that Epic Games have provided demo audio titled `I_Am_MetaHuman`.

I've used the MetaHuman Identity I created from *Chapter 9*.

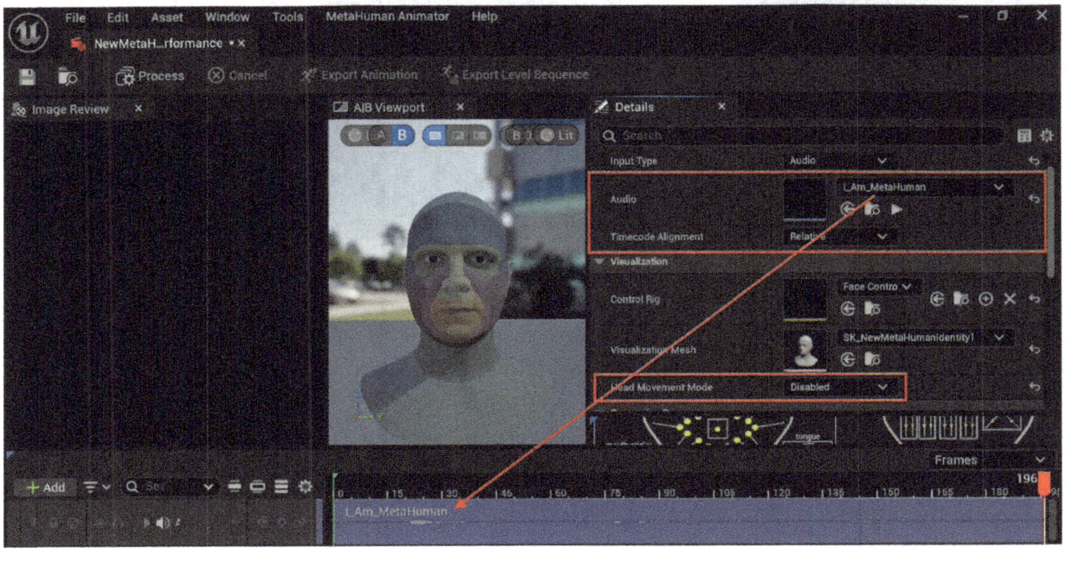

Figure 11.8: Adding Audio for Audio2Face Animation

As you can see, I've disabled the **Head Movement Mode** because I have enough head movement in the Mixamo animation.

In chapter 10, I only processed the mouth because I wanted to repurpose mouth keyframes to augment the webcam facial motion capture. For this example, I'm happy to use the audio to completely drive the facial animation. Along with using the **Animate in Place**, using audio to drive facial animation makes a lot of sense when roughing out or previsualizing a scene.

In *Figure 11.9*, you can see the **Process Mask** is set to **Default (Full Face)**. I've also changed the **Mood** from **Auto-Detect** to **Excited**. You can see my avatar being uncharacteristically excited after I've hit **Process**. You can always reprocess from the list of **Moods** until you get the desired result. You may want to reduce the **Mood Intensity**, but for the most part, the default settings work well.

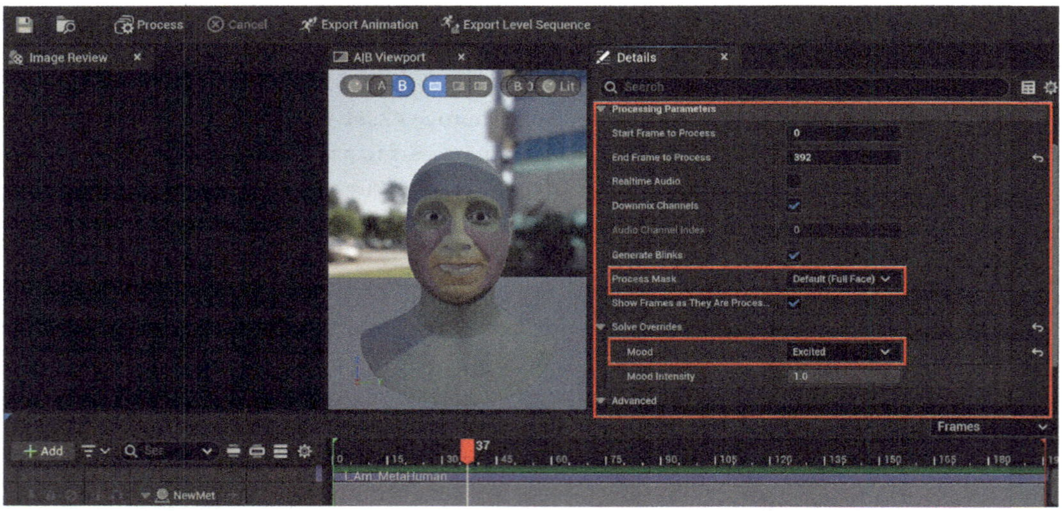

Figure 11.9: Processing Parameters

As you are exporting the animation, make sure to disable head movement. We only want the facial animations, lip movement, expressions, and eye direction.

Figure 11.10: Disable Head Movement

We don't want the head rotations as we're keeping those from the body mocap. Also, make sure you choose the correct target skeleton, which will be the face skeleton of your MetaHuman. It's not the end of the world if you use the wrong one, as you can always go back to the MetaHuman performance asset and export again. Of course, saving everything helps.

Just like in *Chapter 10*, click on **Export Animation** and assign it to the `Face` in your **Level Sequencer**.

In *Figure 11.11*, I've applied the facial animation. It's somewhat shorter than the body motion capture but that's fine. We have more than enough body motion to last through the facial motion.

Figure 11.11: Face Animation Applied

What we're left with is a basic walk and talk shot.

In the next section and throughout most of the remaining chapter, we're going to focus (no pun intended) on all things camera, lights, and rendering related.

Now that we've done our little refresher from the previous chapter, it's time to explore how we can compose and light our character.

Exploring advanced rendering features

I've said this before and I'll say it again: Unreal Engine is a very powerful tool, and when it comes to rendering, it doesn't disappoint. Unreal can deliver outstanding results that are comparable to traditional path-tracing renderers such as Mental Ray, Arnold, V-Ray, and RenderMan. Unreal now supports path tracing, which is the foundation of how these other renderers work.

In the context of filmmaking, Unreal has real-time rendering capabilities that should be explored to unlock its full potential. The camera and lights have features that we find in 3D programs such as Maya, Houdini, and Blender that use path tracing renderers. It's possible to export whole scenes from any of these applications with the camera and lighting settings intact and compatible with Unreal.

So, without further ado, let's look at some of these great rendering features.

Adding and animating a camera

The reason why we create cameras from within the **Level Sequencer** is because there are a few benefits that speed things up. Firstly, you can work out the approximate position you want your camera to face and, by selecting the camera icon, the camera will match the same perspective. In addition, it also creates a cut track automatically. A cut track is what the renderer will refer to when rendering. No cut means you get nothing but black in your render. A cut track acts as a vision mixer, allowing you to view the output of multiple cameras, cutting from one camera to another through the timeline. It works like a video editor, allowing the user to reposition the cut points to reduce or increase the length of a shot or swap the shot with another camera output. It also gives you a preview of what the output is. You can see in *Figure 11.12* that the first thumbnail image of the cut track is what we see in the **Viewport** at frame 0.

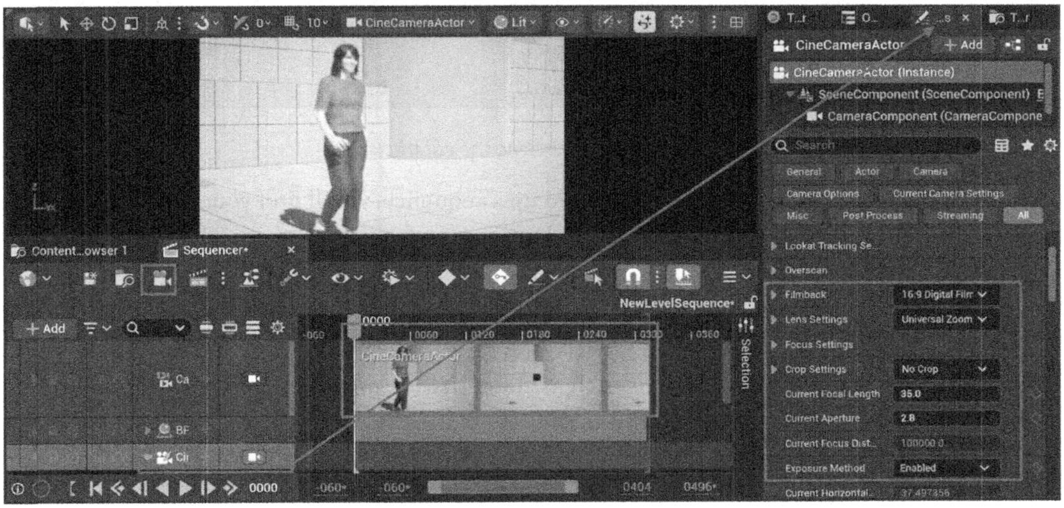

Figure 11.12: Creating a Camera from within the Level Sequencer

The next thumbnail shows a frame later on in the timeline where the character has left the frame. The frequency of thumbnails changes depending on how far we have zoomed in to the cut track. If zoomed in 100%, the cut track resembles a film strip with a thumbnail for every frame.

In *Figure 11.13*, I have locked the cut track by clicking the camera icon on the cut track. This means we are now looking at the output of the camera or cameras assigned to the cut track. If I had selected the camera icon of a camera track, my view would be locked to the output of the selected camera.

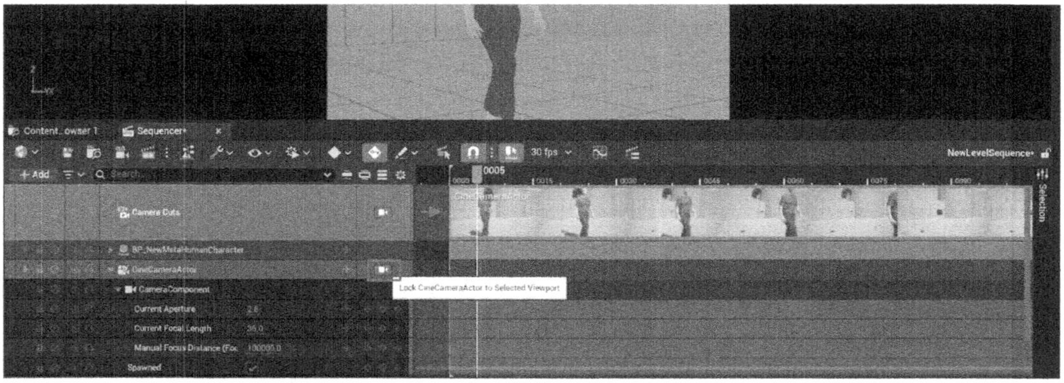

Figure 11.13: Locking the cut track

When working with multiple cameras to build up a sequence, you'll find yourself toggling between the output of individual cameras and the cut track quite a lot.

I've placed a red arrow indicating that the Cut track starts at frame 0 by default.

You can also extend the cut track backward so that it starts a few seconds before frame 0.

This is primarily useful for simulations such as cloth, hair, or particles, giving them time to settle naturally before the first visible frame is rendered.

If your scene does not contain simulations, you can safely ignore this step.

We have a camera in the scene, but I need to add the audio that I used to create the facial capture. Because I want the voice and the facial mocap to start later, I can just drag both of them along the timeline. For instance, I could start the sequence with the first camera really high with a wide-angle lens such as a 24mm, perhaps moving downward simulating a camera shot. Then, we could cut to a second camera with a tighter lens, like a 50mm at eye level and dollying backward, keeping the subject in shot as she begins to talk.

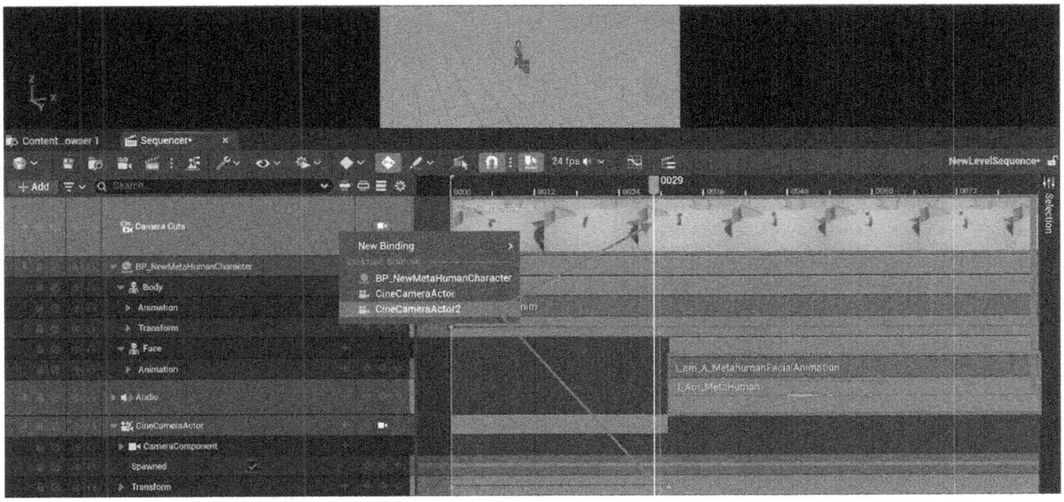

Figure 11.14: Delaying face + audio track and adding a second camera

In *Figure 11.14*, I've added an audio track, but I have also dragged that audio track down so that it sits right under the `BP_NewMetaHumanCharacter` track. This way, I can easily select both and reposition them together, so they remain in sync.

By going up to the camera cut track and clicking on the **+** icon, I can now choose to add the second camera I created. By selecting `CineCameraActor2`, the second camera will appear in the cut track at the exact playhead position as indicated by the top red arrow. The bottom arrow illustrates that I have ensured that we cut to the second camera before the camera's last key frame. I do this because I want to cut to the second camera before the first camera stops moving.

I've used the auto-key function by pressing the auto-key icon in blue at the very top of *Figure 11.14* and I converted both keyframes to linear so the camera animation is at a constant speed rather than speeding up and slowing down.

In addition to just animating the camera position, you can also animate what the camera is focusing on. A very convenient tool for focus is the **Debug Focus** tool, illustrated in *Figure 11.15*. This tool gives us a clear visual indication of what is in focus. With the camera selected, tick the **Draw Debug Focus Plane** option; you'll see a pink plane appear. Anything on that pink plane is going to be perfectly in focus:

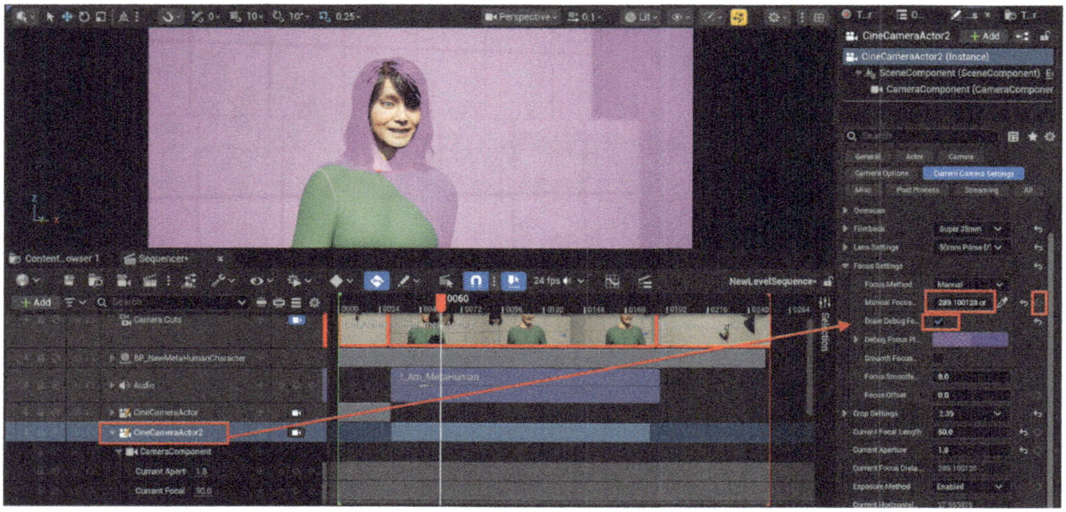

Figure 11.15: Camera Settings in the Details panel

You can control the focus and animate focus distance within the **Level Sequencer**, but use the debug plane for precision focusing. For my shot, I didn't need to lay down any keyframes because my camera is moving and keeping a consistent distance from the subject. Note that there are many different settings available. In *Figure 11.16*, I've highlighted most of the go-to settings in red.

Figure 11.16: Advanced camera settings

From left to right, you can see:

- **Filmback**: If you know your cameras, you'll want to know what filmback or sensor you're working with. For example, you might want to emulate an old 16mm film camera so the starting point would be to match the film back because focal lengths, and aperture settings are different for each filmback.

- **Focal length presets**: In **Lens Setting**, we have a drop-down menu for focal length presets. Its effectively just a list of lenses, but depending on the filmback, the result will be different. For example, a **Micro Four Third Sensor** with a 50mm lens will look more like a **Super 35mm** with a 100mm lens.
- **Crop settings**: Next, we move onto crop settings. There aren't a lot of presets to choose from here and that's because most things you see in the cinema will be either a 1:2.39 aspect ratio (width vs height) or a 1:1.85 aspect ratio. Most television is presented in a 1:1.77 aspect ratio, most commonly called 16:9.
- **Aperture**: By default, aperture will only affect just how blurry the out of focus areas of the frame will be.
- **Exposure**: Changing exposure to manual and applying **Physical Camera Exposure** will make the aperture behave like a real camera. So, reducing the aperture value will increase the amount of light but make the out of focus areas blurrier. You can use the **Compensation** tool above to get around any exposure issues. On the far right of *Figure 11.16*, the **Exposure Compensation** setting is enabled. The default value is 1.0, which means no change to the exposure. In situations where a low aperture is used, such as f-stop of 1.2 to increase bokeh blur, the image may become overexposed when **Physical Camera Exposure** is enabled. Reducing the **Exposure Compensation** value lowers the overall brightness and brings the image back to a correct level without affecting the desired blur. This is often more practical than adjusting ISO for exposure control.

Adding and animating lights

Most of the template levels in Unreal Engine have lighting setup. Usually, all your lights will be available in a `Lighting` folder in the **Outliner**. To start from scratch in terms of lighting, delete all of the lights in the **Outliner**.

Go to **Windows** and search for `Environment Light Mixer` or `Env. Light Mixer`. This will call up all the available light elements.

You can see from *Figure 11.17* that I have a black viewport from deleting all my lights. I also deleted everything in the outliner that is highlighted in red in the **Env. Light Mixer**, just to show you what it looks like when you have an empty scene. Choose **Normal + Advanced** to show all of the options. Now, click on all the buttons shown to populate the scene.

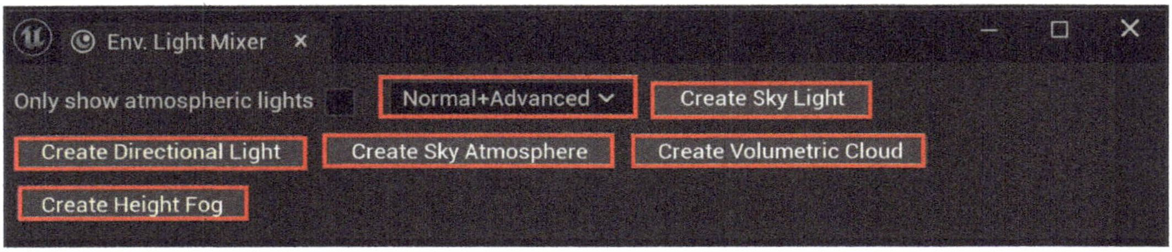

Figure 11.17: The Env. Light Mixer

Once you've done that, your scene should be lit. To change the direction of the light, which is now a directional light, choose **Directional Light** from the **Outliner**. *Right-click* somewhere in the **Viewport** and hold down *Ctrl + L* while moving your cursor around in the **Viewport**. You should see the light angle change.

If changing the light angle this way just isn't your vibe, you can always make changes to it in the **Transform Controls** in the **Details** panel.

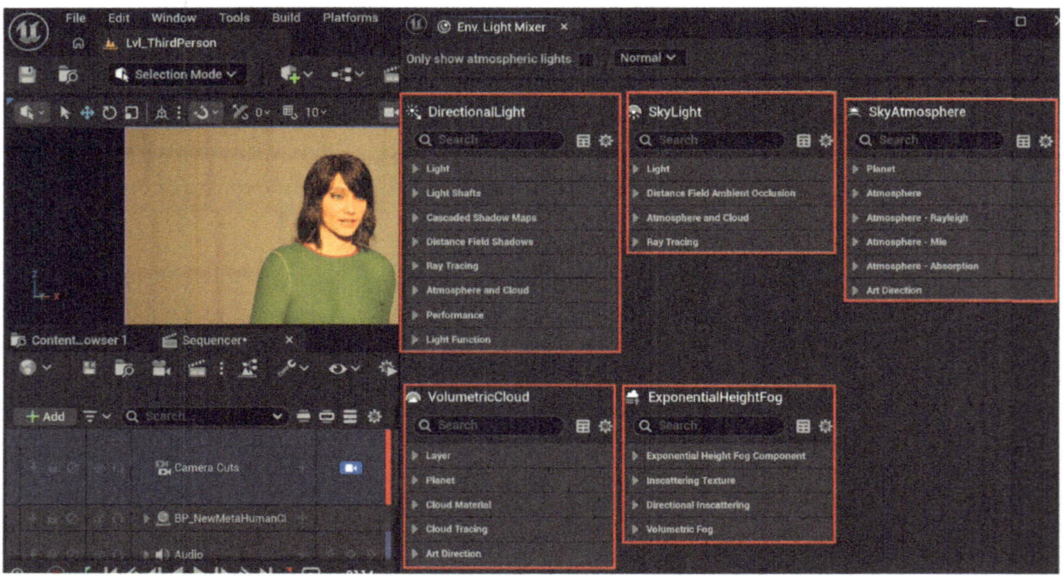

Figure 11.18: The Env. Light Mixer for editing

You can do most of your lighting with the **Light** mixer, and it is very suitable for outdoor lighting as the focus is on one central directional light that emulates the sun. Spend as much time as you can playing with the various settings.

Actors are added to the **Level Sequencer** with only some attributes animatable by default. Additional attributes can be animated, but they must be manually added to the **Sequencer**.

Lights are also actors and can be added to the **Level Sequencer** just like a camera. By default, only light intensity is animatable, but many more attributes can be enabled.

In *Figure 11.19*, clicking **+ Track** next to the camera component in the **Level Sequencer** gives access to nearly all attributes from the **Details** panel. Selecting any of these makes them animatable within the **Sequencer**.

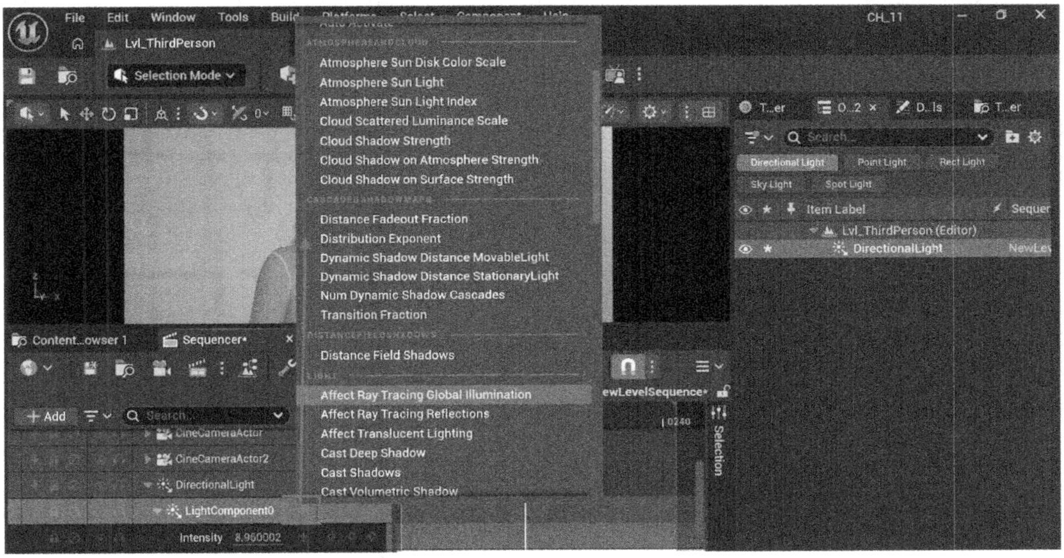

Figure 11.19: Adding Light attributes for animation

Generally speaking, animating lights is rare, much the same as moving lights in a live-action shoot is rare, but not unusual. Perhaps you want a flashing light from a police car or a lighthouse lamp spinning around, or you want to tweak a light's intensity for when a character walks under it. I could spend a whole chapter on lighting in Unreal, if not a whole book on the subject, but we must move on to a very important feature, **Post Process Volumes**.

Using post process volumes

Post Process Volume is an interesting tool as it gives us massive control of the final picture. Typically, **Post Process Volume** would surround your entire scene and is a volume in the sense that it is an area within your scene that is affected by input from an artist.

In essence, **Post Process Volume** is an effect and grading tool with much of the toolset aimed at the camera. For instance, we can control flares, blooms, and chromatic aberrations, which are all very specific lens characteristics, along with film grain, change exposure, white balancing, and so on. If you look at any settings inside a modern video camera or digital cinema camera, **Post Process Volume** pretty much has a matching feature. Epic Games has done incredible work giving artists real-world tools when it comes to their scene for real-time rendering.

In *Figure 11.20*, I have utilized some of these features:

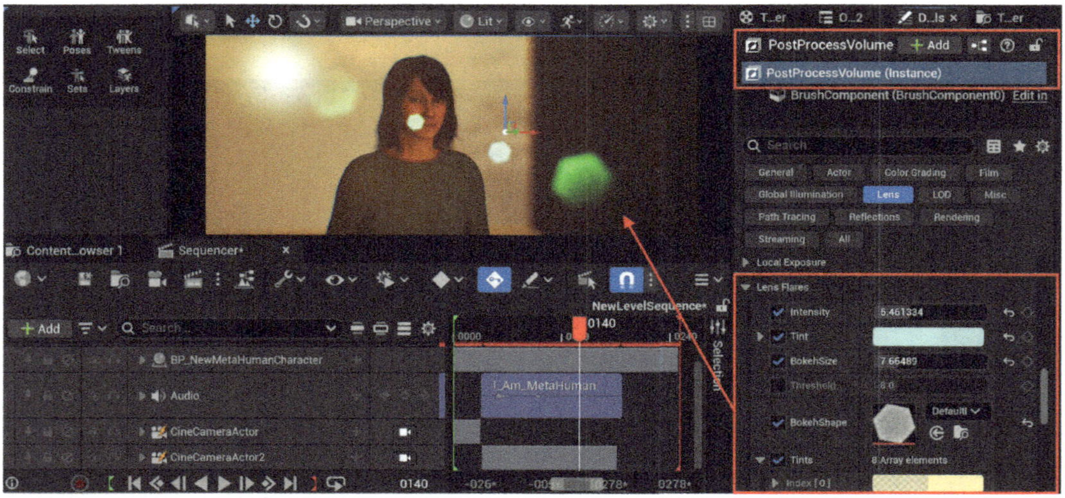

Figure 11.20: Post Process Volume

Let's look at some of the features that I used:

- **Lens Flare** is obvious to see. If you're not familiar with lens flares, they're the light spots in the picture that cross over Glenda's face—they react with the light source, which is a directional light behind Glenda. I've added a pink tint to the lens flare and increased the Bokeh size, which effectively increases the size of the lens flare.
- I have also added a **Bloom** effect, which gives us a realistic light glow from her hair. A bloom effect simulates filters used on real-world lenses, such as pro mist filters, which soften highlights in the image.
- In addition, I've added **Film Grain**, **Chromatic Aberration**, and a **Vignette**, which are far too subtle to see here but are commonly used to enhance realism:
- **Film Grain** is used to simulate film stock or digital noise that is present in film or digital cameras.
- **Chromatic Aberration** is a natural phenomenon found in photographic lenses where a very subtle rainbow effect appears, particularly from highlights in the image.
- **Vignettes** are a common artifact of photographic lenses where the edges of the image are darker than the middle of the image.

As the name suggests, **Post Process Volume** is a *post-production* tool. In terms of Unreal Engine, most of the difficult things such as lighting direction, shadow, skin shading, reflections, and so on are already set, but **Post Process Volume** adds an extra layer of effects over that. In a way, the **Level Sequencer** is like the camera and **Post Process Volume** is like Photoshop.

As a rule of thumb: it is best to get all of your lighting and camera work as close to the final look as possible and rely on **Post Process Volume** for things you couldn't achieve otherwise.

There are quite a lot of settings in **Post Process Volume** and, unfortunately, too many to cover in a book about MetaHumans. However, they will make your MetaHumans look amazing when it comes to rendering.

> **Note**
>
> If you would like to learn more about advanced lighting and rendering techniques, I recommend you take a look at the following video tutorial, which you can purchase from the Gnomon Workshop: `https://www.thegnomonworkshop.com/tutorials/cinematic-lighting-in-unreal-engine-5`.

This brings us to the next section, where we will take a close look at rendering out files from the **Movie Render Queue** for compositing and color grading.

Using the Movie Render Queue

When we are setting our renders from the **Level Sequencer**, we are given a choice of which render queue to use. To see what render queues are available to you, click on the three dots next to the clapper icon, as per *Figure 11.21*:

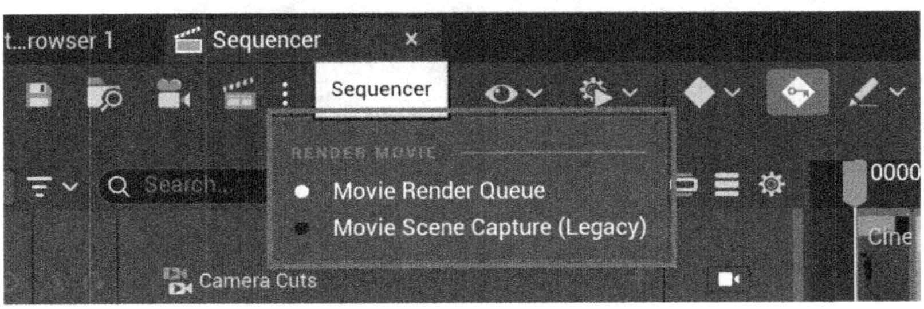

Figure 11.21: Movie Render Queue

It is quite likely that you will only see **Movie Scene Capture (Legacy)**, which provides only a basic rendering workflow.

The recommended alternative is **Movie Render Queue (MRQ)**, which offers significantly greater control over quality, anti-aliasing, motion blur, output formats, and render passes.

Unreal Engine also includes **Movie Render Graph (MRG)**, a newer node-based rendering workflow aimed at more advanced productions. However, because the concepts explored in this book focus on cinematic rendering rather than pipeline automation, we will continue using Movie Render Queue throughout this chapter.

To enable Movie Render Queue, head over to the Plugins section and search for **Renderer**. In *Figure 11.22*, you can see that I have already enabled both plugins, which you should do too.

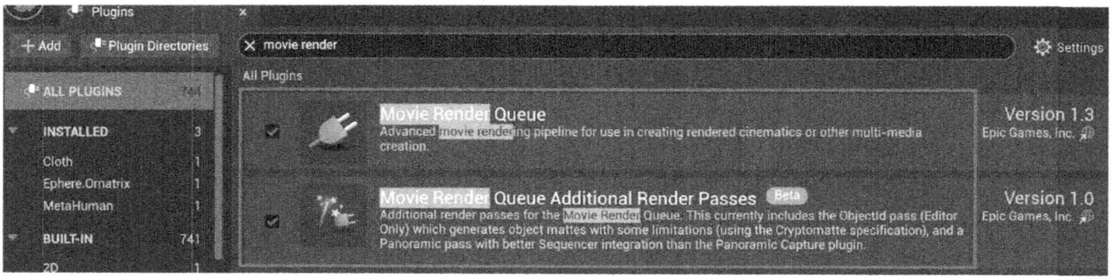

Figure 11.22: Enabling Render Queue Plugins

Now, when you click **Movie Render Queue**, as per *Figure 11.23*, you'll see the following screen:

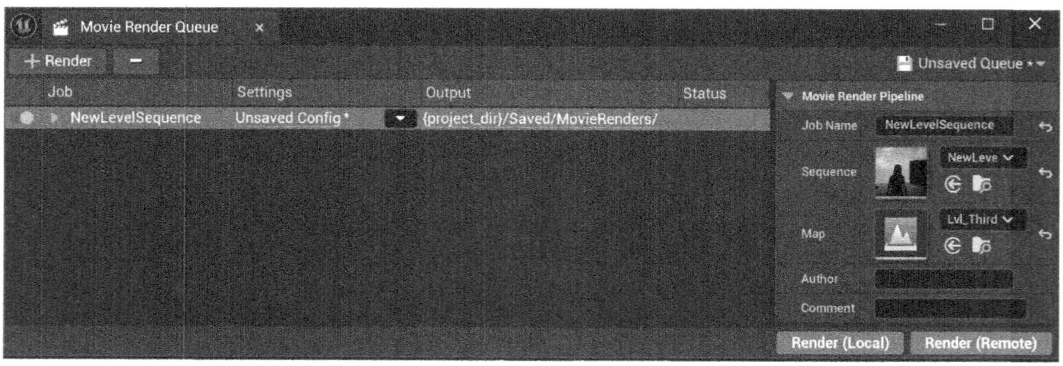

Figure 11.23: Opening the Movie Render Queue

The **+ Render** button in green is for determining which sequence to render. Initializing the **Movie Render Queue** will assign the current **Level Sequencer** for rendering. However, should you have multiple **Level Sequencer**s in your project, you can add them to the **Render Queue** using the **+ Render** button. In this dialog box, you'll see three columns:

- Job
- Settings
- Output

Let's go through each of these columns.

Job

Job is the sequencer name that has been chosen for rendering. By default, it will be titled **New Level Sequence**. Keep in mind that parameters such as **Range** (how long the animation is) and **Frame Rate** are determined in the **Level Sequencer**.

Should you have more than one **Level Sequencer** in your project, they would be available under **Job**, and you can select which **Level Sequencer** you want to render.

Settings

Settings refer to which render settings you want to apply to your sequence.

Output

The **Output** area displays the folder directory where your images or videos will be rendered, as set in the output settings.

There are quite a lot of options to choose from when it comes to rendering settings. Ultimately, if you are already committed to rendering a movie out of Unreal using a **Level Sequencer**, then you are not likely to be concerned with the real-time rendering capabilities of Unreal and are planning to do more work on the rendered sequence in post-production.

The file type, be it a movie file or an image sequence, is an important setting to consider. For example, should you plan to do additional post-production such as advanced color grading, then you should opt for an image sequence setting such as **Open EXR** that provides higher color fidelity. If you plan to just do a test render or commit a final render directly from Unreal, then a movie file such as a **Quicktime ProRes** would suffice.

Let's look at the default settings, as shown in *Figure 11.24*:

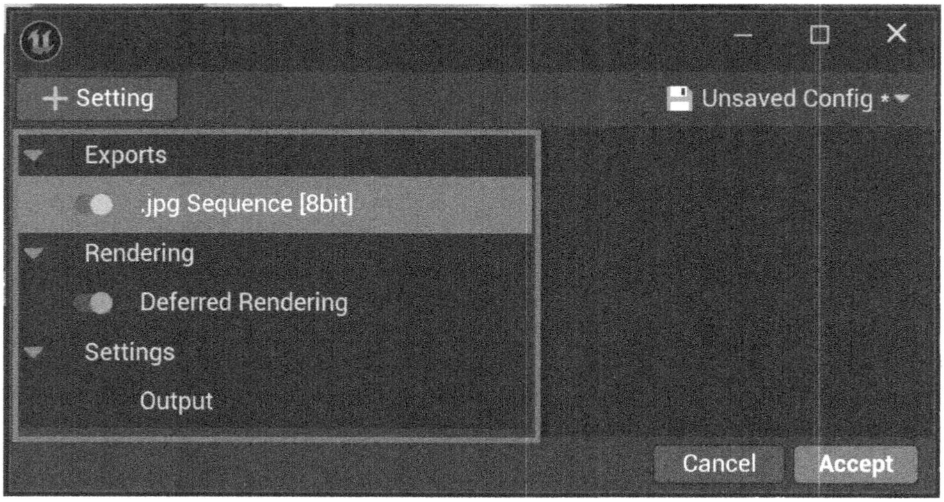

Figure 11.24: The Default Setting of Movie Render Queue

There are three types of default settings:

- **Exports (jpg Sequence 8bit)**: Exports allows us to choose what file format options we want, from low-fidelity and compressed formats (such as JPGs, which are only 8-bit) to high-fidelity Open EXR, which are floating-point 16-bit.
- **Rendering (Deferred Rendering)**: Deferred rendering is an optimized and default way of rendering a scene in Unreal. It renders in two passes. The primary pass includes calculations such as z depth and ambient occlusion. From the primary (base) pass, deductions can be made from the second pass regarding what needs to be calculated on a per-object basis in terms of shaders. This is to reduce processing time.

- **Settings (Output)**: When you click on **+ Setting**, you will see that there are more settings to choose from:

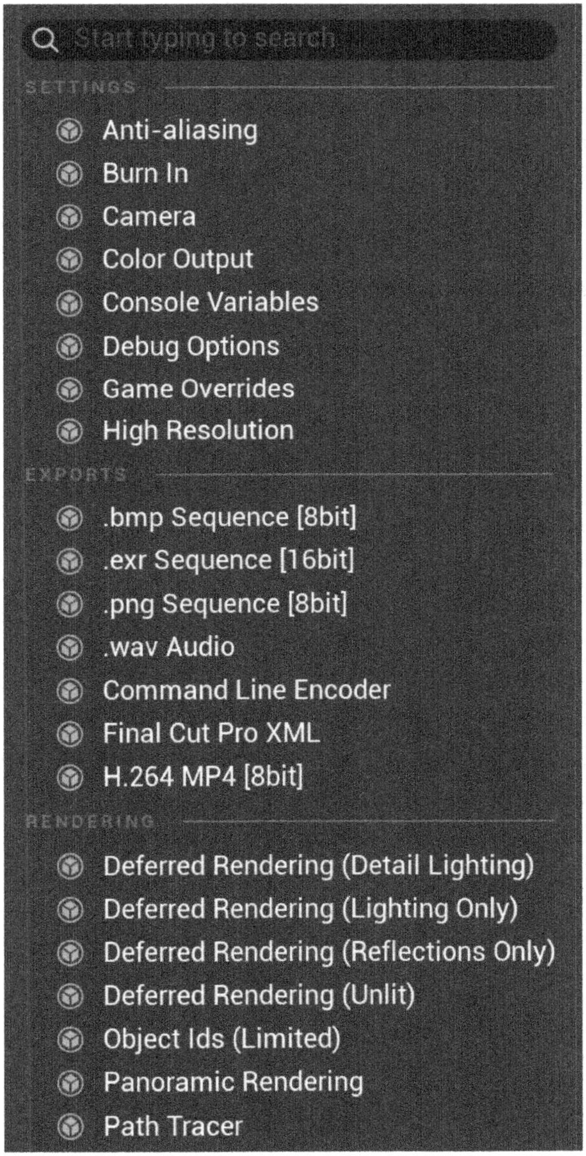

Figure 11.25: Available Settings in Movie Render Queue

When rendering the **Level Sequencer** to a hard drive, we have various options to choose from to improve its quality:

- **Settings**: From this list, you can pick multiple options at once. For this book, I'm going to add **Anti-Aliasing** so that I can improve the quality of the motion blur.
- **Exports**: I'm going to replace **.jpg sequence [8bit]** with **.exr Sequence [16bit]**; this will significantly improve the quality of the render, particularly to refine the picture later in a video editing package. **.exr Sequence [16bit]** is exported in an **Open EXR** format; it gives us far greater ability to control what is over and under-exposed in the application, such as After Effects, Nuke, or DaVinci Resolve. Open EXR is the global visual effects standard for movies and television because it stores much more color information than other formats and also stores metadata.
- **Rendering**: Let's look at some of the rendering options available:
    - **Deferred Rendering**: This is the standard cinematic rendering method in Unreal Engine. Rather than calculating the final image in one step, Unreal first renders information such as lighting, depth, and surface properties before combining them into the finished image. For filmmakers, you can simply think of this as Unreal's normal high-quality render mode.
    - **Deferred Rendering (Reflections Only)**: This rendering option only renders out the reflections. This is handy if we want to control the intensity of reflections in a compositing application such as Nuke. Typically, you would choose this option as an addition to **Deferred Rendering**.
    - **Object Ids (Limited)**: Each object is given an object ID, which is represented by a unique color. When we have this option enabled, we will get an object ID video channel as part of the EXR file. When compositing in an application such as Nuke, we can then manipulate objects separately using the object ID by selecting the color associated with it. This is convenient if we want to change an object's color in Nuke without having to make changes in Unreal.

You can see the settings I have selected in *Figure 11.26*:

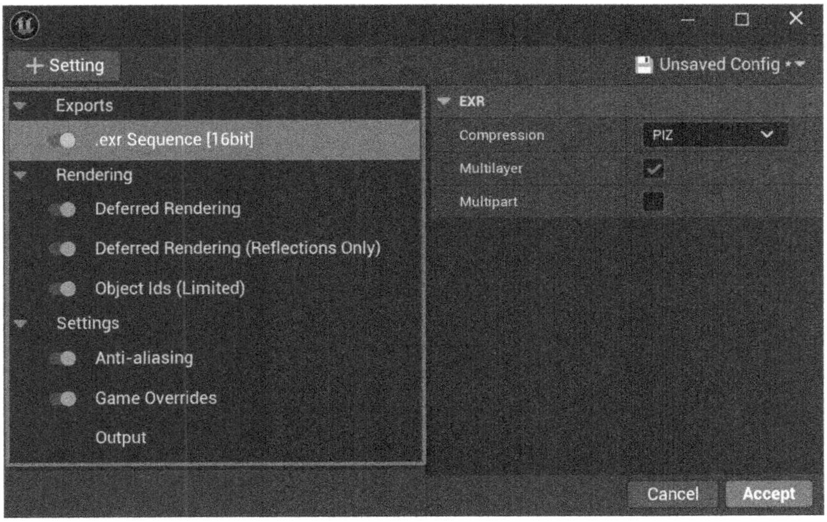

Figure 11.26: Common settings for cinematic productions

Note

The EXR file format is capable of storing multiple channels.

Most image files, such as JPEG files, store just three channels: red, green, and blue.

PNG files can store four channels: red, green, blue, and an alpha channel for transparency.

Settings (Output)

Your default **Output** settings will match your **Level Sequencer**'s default settings. However, the **Output** column is a means to override them, allowing you to control the final resolution and frame rate.

In *Figure 11.26*, I have used three render settings that will render out into one single EXR image sequence as separate channels, one channel for each of the following:

- Deferred Rendering
- Deferred Rendering (Reflections Only)
- Object Ids (Limited)

You can see the result of that render in *Figure 11.26*. This figure represents the three extra channels that have been rendered and stored in the EXR file: the top left is **Deferred Rendering**, which appears normal, the top right is **Reflections Only**, and the bottom left is **Object Ids (Limited)** (in a compositing program, I can make further adjustments by manipulating these extra channels):

Figure 11.27: Example of multi-layer EXR rendering: (a) Deferred Rendering, (b) Reflections Only, (c) Object IDs

The render settings in Movie Render Queue provide artists with a great deal of control over final image quality and remain a widely used cinematic workflow.

For larger productions, Unreal Engine also offers **Movie Render Graph**, a node-based rendering system that extends Movie Render Queue with more advanced automation and pipeline control. The rendering principles covered in this chapter apply equally to both workflows.

This aligns with the results expected from traditional 3D animation productions, where compositors are given the same or more control over the 3D renders. As developments progress in Unreal, we expect that more and more 3D animation studios will adopt Unreal into their pipelines.

In the next section, we will look at some of the professional color standards that now ship with Unreal, which allow MetaHumans to work within a professional studio environment.

ACES and color grading

As mentioned in the previous section, Open EXR is the professional industry standard file format used by visual effects and 3D animation studios for 3D rendering and compositing. One reason for this is that it can store a huge amount of pixel data, particularly color.

The default export image sequence is **.jpeg sequence [8 bit]**. Well, that just doesn't cut it in the professional world simply because it doesn't represent even half of what the human eyes can see. An 8-bit image can only store 256 shades of red, green, and blue, respectively. In total, that amounts to just over 16 million colors versus the 280 trillion-plus colors in a 16-bit image.

If you take a look at *Figure 11.28*, where the widest area of color is represented by the ACES color space, you'll see the significant difference when compared to sRGB. The JPEG format of 8-bit is only capable of working within a small color space such as sRGB. Therefore, utilizing the enormous data space of the EXR file format and the enormous color space of ACES, Unreal Engine is capable of incredibly photorealistic renders, which is why choosing **.exr Sequence [16bit]** is preferable:

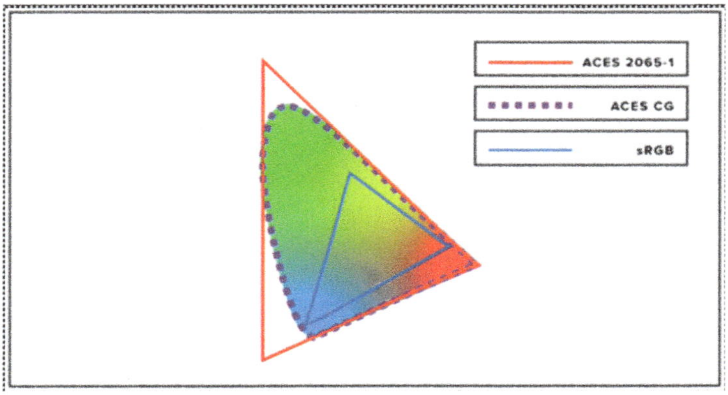

Figure 11.28: ACES versus sRGB color space

> **Note**
>
> For further reading on the ACES color space, go to `https://acescolorspace.com/`.

Summary

In this chapter, we got the opportunity to revise some key elements of bringing a MetaHuman to life by applying both body and face motion capture to the **Level Sequencer**. We looked at alternative ways to edit movement and fix common movement issues, such as fixing the position of a character when looping an animation. We also learned how to use **Transform**, **Location**, and **Show Skeleton** to help with creating longer animations using looped tracks.

After that, we covered cameras, lights, and **Post-Process Volumes**, reviewing some of the very powerful and professional rendering capabilities of Unreal Engine.

In the next chapter, we will take a look at a new feature (at the time of writing) that allows us to use our likeness or someone else's to fashion a MetaHuman around a real human!

Part 4

Advanced MetaHuman Workflows

In this final part of the book, you'll explore advanced workflows that extend the capabilities of MetaHumans beyond the tools available inside Unreal Engine. You'll learn how to create MetaHumans from custom meshes, integrate external sculpting and grooming workflows using Blender, and apply professional tools and plugins to enhance character creation, animation, and production pipelines.

By the end of this part of the book, you'll understand how to incorporate industry-standard applications into your MetaHuman workflow, giving you the flexibility to create more unique, production-ready digital characters.

This part of the book includes the following chapters:

- *Chapter 12, Using the Mesh to MetaHuman Plugin*
- *Chapter 13, Applying Hair Grooms*
- *Chapter 14, External Tools and Plugins for MetaHuman Workflows*

12

Using the Mesh to MetaHuman Plugin

In *Chapter 11*, we revised how to bring in animation and work with the Level Sequencer and then explored some fundamental lighting, camera, and rendering principles. In this chapter, we are going to revisit the MetaHuman Identity from *Chapter 9* with the view to creating a MetaHuman in our likeness.

In *Chapter 9*, the by-product of the MetaHuman Identity was a **Face Skeletal Mesh** of the user's face that we can repurpose to make our own MetaHuman via the **MetaHuman Creator**, which we will explore in depth in this chapter. In addition, we will explore bringing in third-party face meshes.

In the previous edition of this book, Epic Games had just released a groundbreaking plugin that allows users to use custom meshes of faces to be used as the face of their MetaHuman. The free plugin is called **Mesh to MetaHuman** and at its core is the **MetaHuman Identity Asset**. It is now embedded into the MetaHuman Core, which was enabled in *Chapter 1* of this book.

This feature opens the additional opportunity for artists to use all the great MetaHuman-related tools and functionality on custom face sculpts or digital scans of real people. Because we can use digital scans of real people, it gives artists the ability to create MetaHumans that have an incredible likeness to actors and artists.

In this chapter, we will focus on a very streamlined workflow of getting your own face and applying it to a MetaHuman. We will also look at production techniques for getting custom face meshes from a third-party application like Blender and turning them into a MetaHuman.

We will cover the following topics:

- Repurposing the MetaHuman Identity
- Conforming a MetaHuman to a MetaHuman Identity
- Exporting a MetaHuman base mesh for sculpting
- Importing and sculpting the mesh in Blender
- Conforming third-party mesh to MetaHuman

Technical requirements

In terms of computer power, you will need to meet the technical requirements detailed in *Chapter 9*.

You will also need:

- An iPhone or Android phone with at least 200 MB of free space (if you haven't completed *Chapter 9*)
- A stable internet connection as you will be downloading a plugin and uploading data to a server
- Access to the Epic Games Launcher used to install Unreal Engine
- Blender 4.6x

> **Note**
>
> You will need to be familiar with the MetaHuman Identity used in *Chapter 9*, and preferably have a MetaHuman Identity already created.

Repurposing the MetaHuman identity

In *Chapter 9*, the MetaHuman Identity was used for the sole purpose of calibrating the motion capture data to the performer during processing. The byproduct of this was both a skeletal mesh and the MetaHuman Identity itself. We are going to focus on the MetaHuman Identity in this chapter. Unlike the motion capture process, we now need to pay particular attention to accuracy. For the most part, the workflow remains unchanged. However, in the next section we'll discuss how to improve accuracy for a better result.

To get started, open up the project you used for completing the steps in *Chapter 9*.

Open up the MetaHuman Identity to make sure everything is intact. For instance, when you click on the neutral pose, do you see the correct **Capture Data** asset loaded with a corresponding video clip in the viewport? If you do see the video loaded, you can judge the accuracy of your MetaHuman Identity by using the **A/B Wipe** mode that I've highlighted in red in *Figure 12.1*.

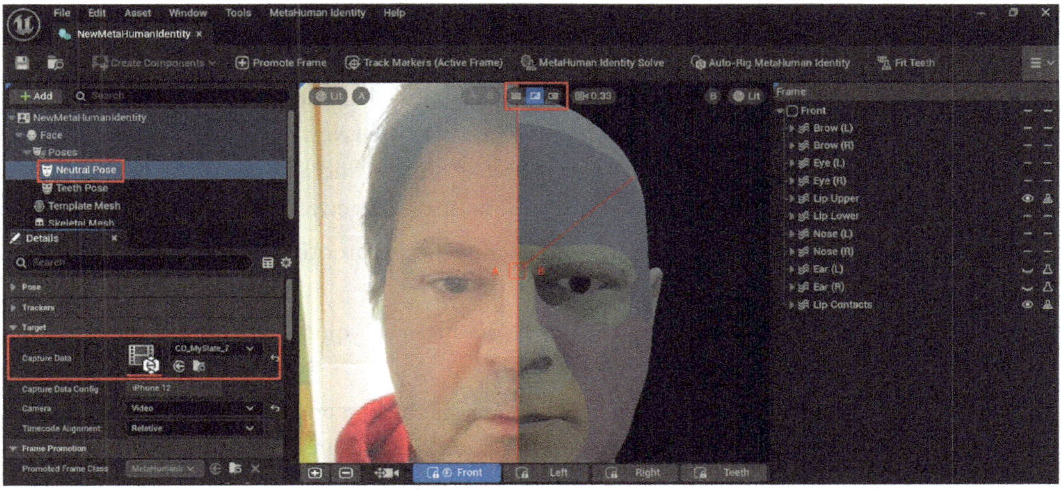

Figure 12.1: Opening up MetaHuman Identity

You can also use the **A/B Dual** mode option to the right of the **A/B Wipe** mode, which will show the video on the left and your mesh on the right. If you're not happy with the result and you think you could do a better job, you can always revert back to editing the green splines. When you've made some tweaks, run the **MetaHuman Identity Solve** and **Auto-Rig MetaHuman Identity** and check your results again with the A/B modes mentioned above.

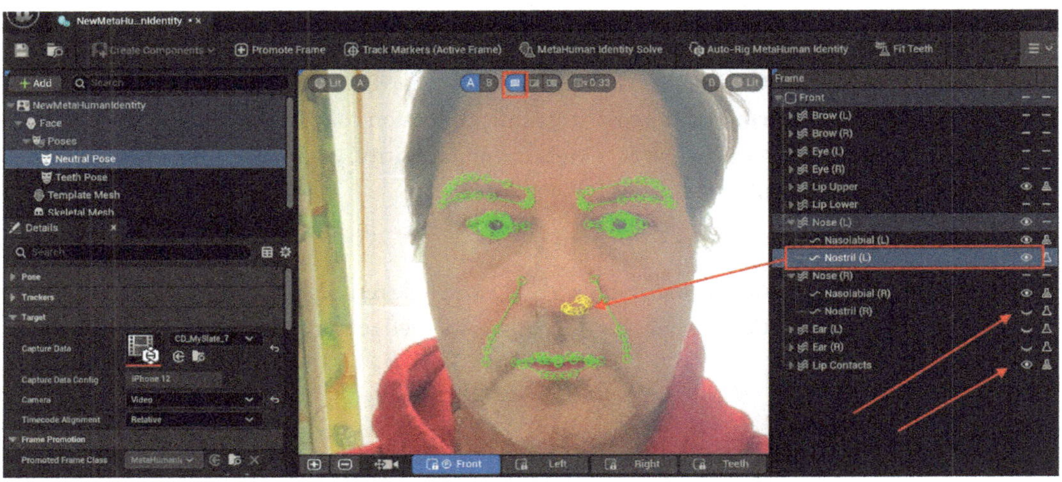

Figure 12.2: Editing and unhiding splines for detailed fine tuning

On the right-hand side of *Figure 12.2*, you can see I've unhidden a spline for a nostril. If you aren't getting a reasonable result, there are a few things to consider:

- You should get a good result if your smartphone capture is adequate. So, prioritize recapturing versus tweaking splines, utilizing the auto track feature.
- It's best to focus on promoting a frame that tracks well enough so that you need little to no editing. For example, if you promote a frame for the Front pose and it requires editing of the green spline position, it is better to try to find a better frame to promote that automatically tracks and positions the splines correctly.
- Usually, just three promoted frames are enough and promoting more than four usually adds no extra value.
- If everything is perfectly tracked but some details aren't quite right, unhide additional features for advanced editing.

As soon as you're happy with the result, and it resembles the person in the smartphone footage, all you need to do is save your MetaHuman Identity. We are now going to conform a MetaHuman's face to the face of our MetaHuman identity.

Conforming a MetaHuman to a MetaHuman identity

In *Chapter 1*, you've seen how we can edit the proportions of a MetaHuman face using the following techniques:

- Blend
- Sculpt
- Transform

I intentionally left out the **Conform** technique in order to cover it in this chapter. **MetaHuman Creator** uses the **Conform** technique to distort the proportions of the MetaHuman face to match that of an incoming asset such as a MetaHuman Identity, which is the cleanest method for creating likeness within Unreal.

You'll be pleased to know the process is simple.

Just open up the **MetaHuman Creator**, pick a body and face template that resembles you, and you're done. I'm kidding. It's not that simple, but we do need to make sure the proportions are close.

So, jump back into **MetaHuman Creator** and pick a template that is close enough.

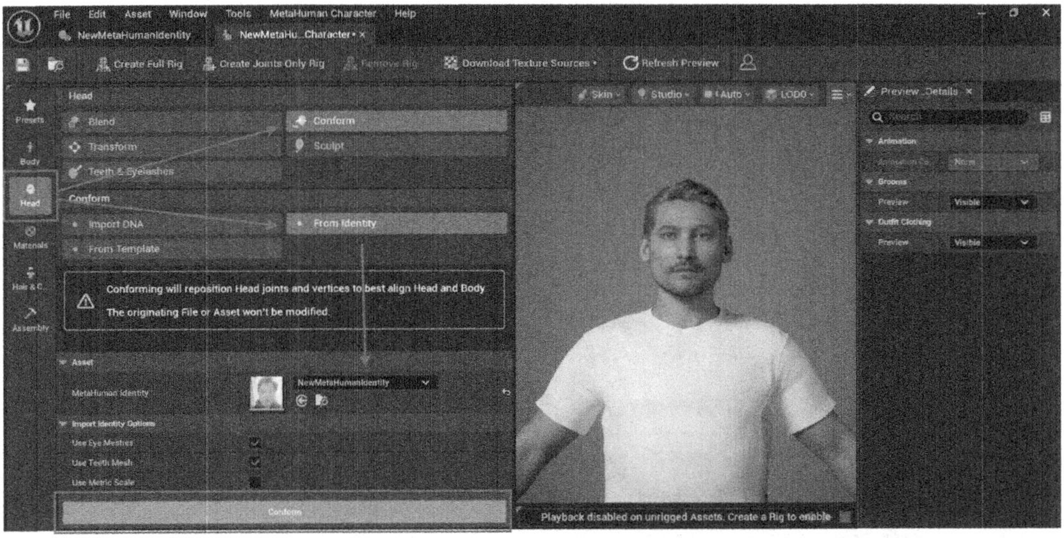

Figure 12.3: Choosing a similar Template and Conform

In *Figure 12.3*, I have started by choosing a template that had proportions close enough to me: similar build and similar face shape. It just so happened to have a similar hairstyle. After selecting **Head**, I chose the **Conform** option and chose **MetaHuman Identity**. You can see I've drawn an arrow down to our next step, which is to choose which **MetaHuman Identity** to use. The list should provide thumbnails to make it easier. Once your MetaHuman Identity is selected, click on the green **Conform** button.

When you hit **Deform**, the facial features will match the MetaHuman Identity proportions. However, because I have the material of the preset, it is a little tricky to see the resemblance. I'm at least 10 years older than the preset, for example. I also have lighter skin, and, in my video, I have less facial hair. So, if we were both compared to each other side by side, the resemblance would be weak until you review the result in **Clay** mode and hide groom because the hair and facial hair are very misleading if they don't match the user. I have switched to **Clay** mode in *Figure 12.4* so that I can objectively review the result without the distraction of the template material and grooms.

The next step is to use the **Sculpt** tool to make any changes. For instance, despite my best efforts, the result on one of the eyelids was a little higher than the original. So, I used the sculpt tool to make a slight adjustment with the **Symmetric Manipulation** turned off.

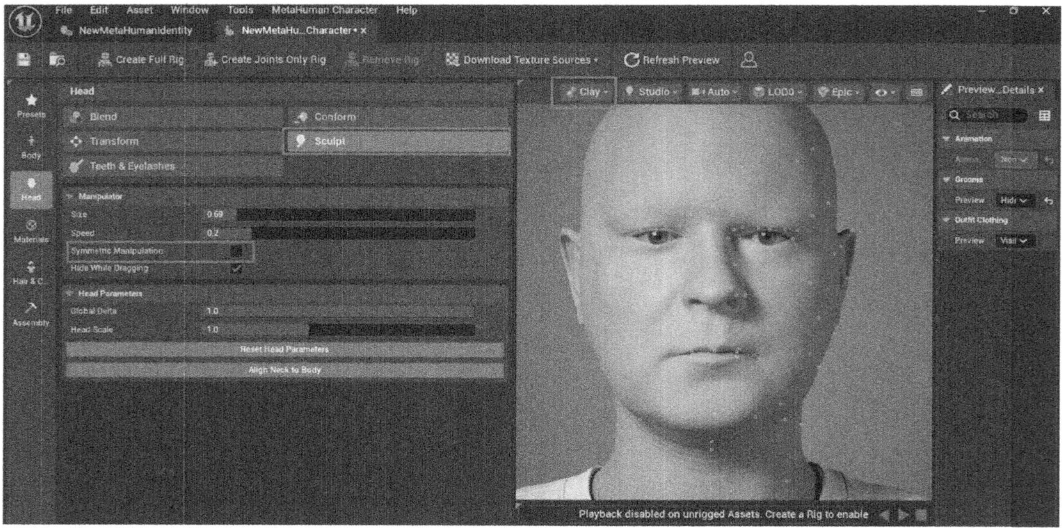

Figure 12.4: Reviewing the Conform result

I was pleasantly surprised with how accurate the mouth and overall proportions came out.

So, you can see that proportionally, the result is close but only visible in **Clay** mode. Unfortunately, there isn't a conform technique for materials, but we can do a really good job by going into the Materials editor and eyeballing a solution.

For my example, I don't have any freckles or blemishes, but I'm old enough to have lines and creases in my skin. These details are too fine for the **MetaHuman Identity** to pick up. To create details such as fine or thick lines in the skin, the **MetaHuman Creator** utilizes normal and cavity maps, which are textures that react to light and shadow. So, depending on the viewing angle of a MetaHuman, those lines will become less or more prominent depending on where and how intense the light source is.

Where do we get these normal and cavity maps, you may ask. Well, the **MetaHuman Creator** has 152 of them. In *Figure 12.5*, you can see that I've resized the **MetaHuman Creator** window so that I can see the **MetaHuman Identity** for comparison. I'm in the **Material** mode and editing **Skin**. You can see that I've matched the skin tone to close to my own. To get access to the texture maps, you can use the **Face Texture Index** slider, which I've highlighted in red under **Skin Tone** in *Figure 12.5*. Currently, it is set to 134. One drawback with the **Face Texture Index** slider is that it contains 152 normal maps for all the available face types. Ideally, they would be categorized into age and gender, so choosing the suitable one for your skin type can be time-consuming.

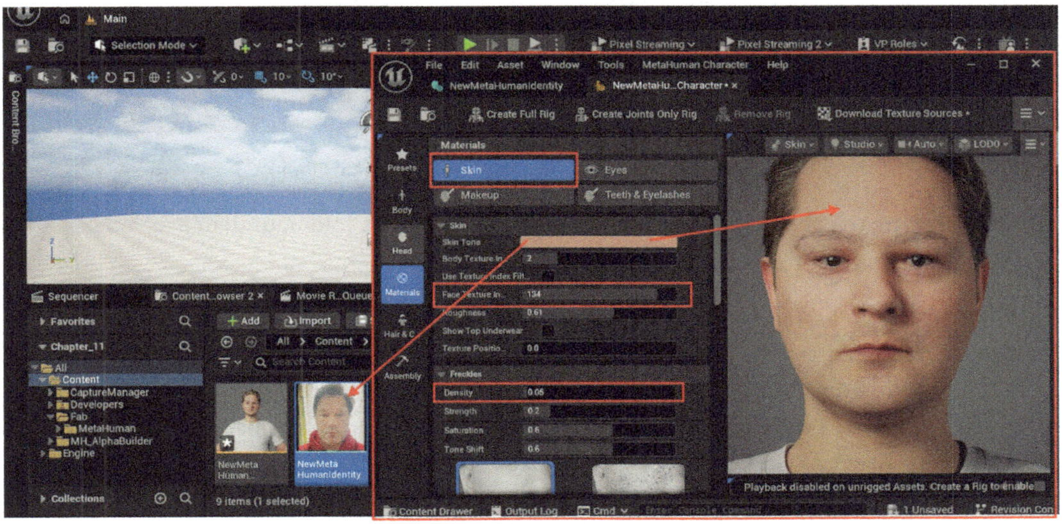

Figure 12.5: Matching by eye

Another fallback is that the **Face Texture Index** doesn't just contain normal and cavity maps for faking details like thin and thick lines; it also contains textures for blemishes and stubble. This can be a little frustrating when you've got a good normal map, but you've got too many blemishes or not enough.

The good news is that you can always edit these texture maps to remove blemishes. So, if you're happy with the normal map for the skin texture (lines on the faces), keep it. Assemble the character and locate the face material.

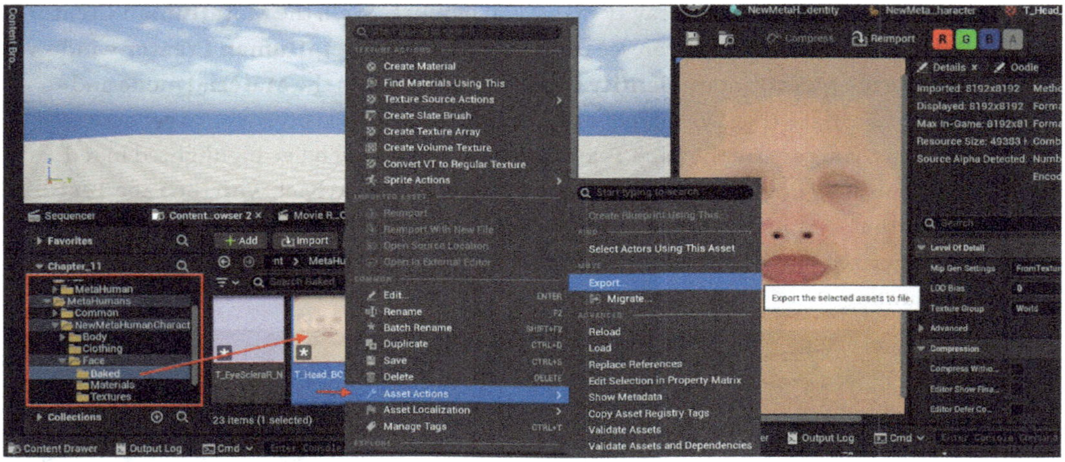

Figure 12.6: Locating the face texture map and exporting

After assembling the character, when you go to the `MetaHumans` folder, under `Face` you can locate the face texture map in the `Baked` folder.

Usually, it will be called something like `T_Head_BC`. The `BC` stands for `Base Color`, also known as **Albedo**. This will have the blemishes. It will only have freckles if you chose to add freckles before assembling the character, which will bake them into the albedo map. If you want to make changes to the Base Color, you can do this by right clicking on the Base Color texture map, choosing **Asset Actions**, and clicking on **Export**. This will bring up a dialog box, allowing you to export it as an image such as PNG where you can paint out or paint in any blemishes, scars, or even tattoos that you wish.

Photoshop or other image editing tools are fine for this. When saving it from Photoshop etc., if you overwrite the original, it will update in your MetaHuman without any need to search for the edited version.

> Note
>
> **Third-party MetaHuman Identity**
>
> Those who don't have access or time to create their own bespoke MetaHuman Identity, yet want to base their character on a real person, can acquire premade MetaHuman Identities based on scans that include the acquired base color texture maps and derived normal and cavity maps by visiting **3Dscanstore.com**. You can also get access to a free asset for testing at `https://www.3dscanstore.com/blog/Free-MetaHuman-Identity`.

As we don't have time to go in depth in texture map editing, we will move onto the next section, where we will prepare a mesh of a MetaHuman as a base mesh for editing in a third-party application such as Blender. We will focus on making significant proportional changes that wouldn't be possible with the **Sculpt** and **Transform** tools within the **MetaHuman Creator**.

Exporting a MetaHuman base mesh for sculpting

In this section, we're going to take a face skeletal of a MetaHuman and export it for use in Blender so that we can add significant deformations to it in Blender's **Sculpt** tool.

If you've already assembled your MetaHuman, navigate to the `MetaHumans` | `Face` folder and *right-click* on the **Skeletal Mesh**, then go to **Asset Actions**, and click on **Export**. This is the same export process as the texture map from earlier. Instead of looking for an image file, you can use FBX or if you have a personal preference for use in another DCC, there are other formats to choose from such as USD, Alembic, and OBJ.

Ultimately, we are only concerned with getting a MetaHuman facial geometry into another DCC for sculpting. So as long as you can export it from Unreal Engine and import it into Blender or whatever you prefer to work with, it will do.

Let's stick to FBX though. Be sure to disable **Level of Detail** as we only want one mesh to be exported and enabling **Level of Detail** will export multiple meshes. Choose **Simple** for **Bake Material Inputs**.

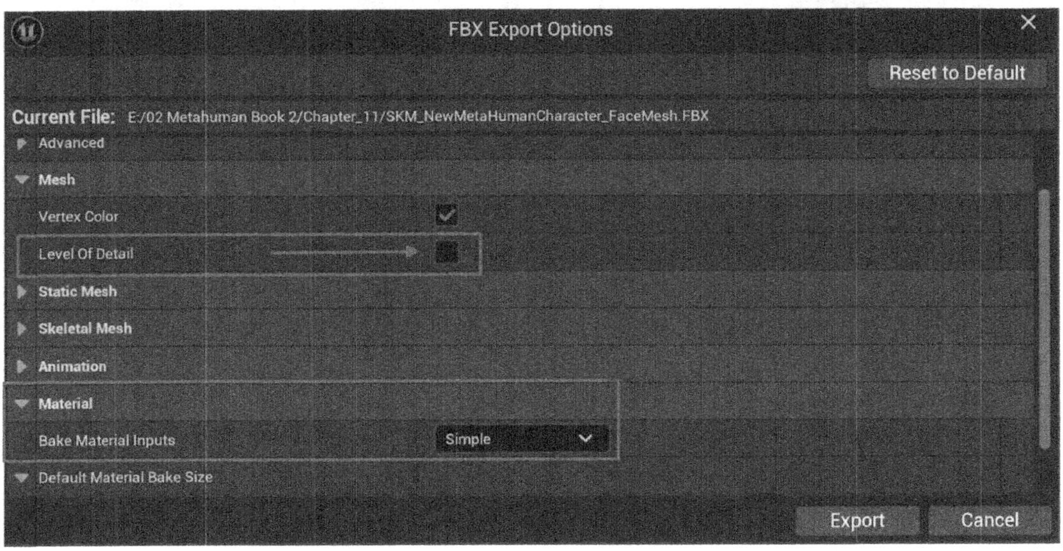

Figure 12.7: FBX export settings

Before moving into Blender, it is worth noting a key limitation of the **MetaHuman Creator**. The conform process is designed to interpret and transfer subtle sculptural changes within a fixed facial topology. It is not intended to support major structural additions or non-human features.

As a result, while proportion changes and surface refinements will transfer successfully, more extreme modifications such as horns or other added geometry will not carry through when the mesh is reprocessed.

For this reason, any non-human elements should be treated as separate assets and integrated later, rather than relying on the MetaHuman Identity workflow to preserve them.

Importing and sculpting the mesh in Blender

It's time to head on over to Blender. If you don't have Blender installed, navigate to `Blender.org` to get your free copy.

With Blender open, go to **File** | **Import** | **FBX** and import the skeletal face mesh you just exported from Unreal.

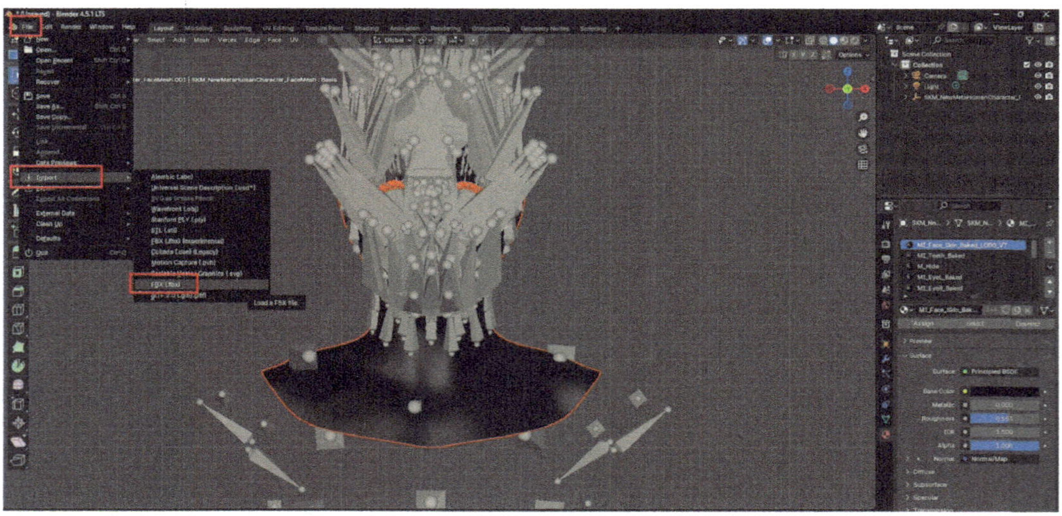

Figure 12.8: Blender FBX import

You'll need to hide the bones as they'll get in the way when we sculpt. You can do this in the Blender viewport, but let's go to the **Shader** viewport by selecting the **Shader** tab at the top of the screen.

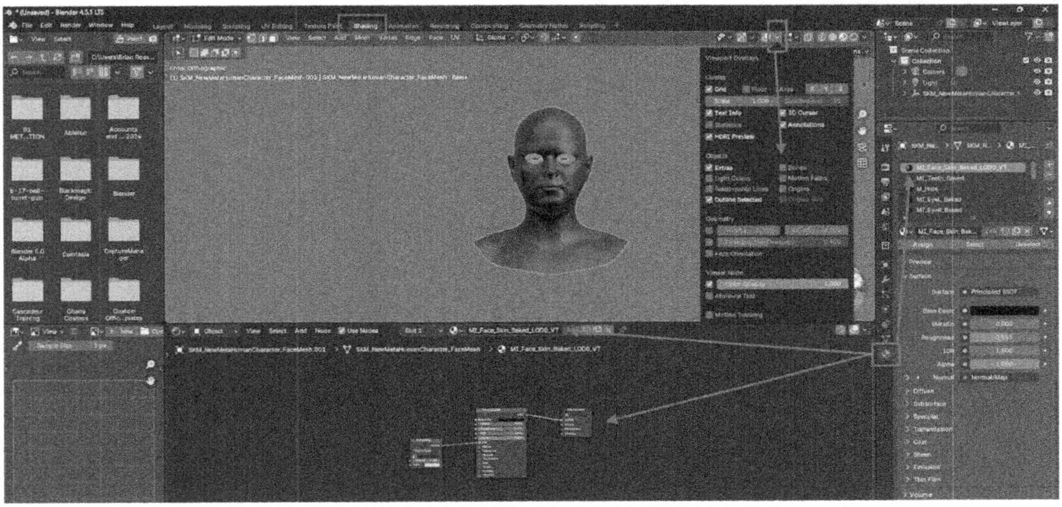

Figure 12.9: Hiding Bones in the Shader viewport

I've highlighted the **Shader** tab in *Figure 12.9* at the top. If you're not used to Blender, the tabs at the top dictate which viewport is active. You can also see that I've clicked on the **Overlays** button, which gives me the **Overlay Options**. I don't want the bones overlaid over the mesh, so I've disabled that feature.

Also note that on the right-hand side, I've clicked the **Material** tab. The arrow pointing to the top shows me the first material slot of that mesh, which happens to be for the face. The arrows pointing to the bottom viewport indicate the shader network of that material slot. The upper arrow demonstrates that it is the exact name as the material slot on the left because we are looking at the shader network of that material slot.

There are also two small issues we can see.

- The eyelashes, eyes, teeth, and tongue were imported too
- The mesh has no texture map assigned to it, which is why it is black in the viewport and the thumbnails in the material slots are also black to reflect that

We want to hide everything we don't need, but the mesh is all connected. We need to separate the mesh into different components and hide the ones we don't want. Fortunately, this is easy to do in Blender.

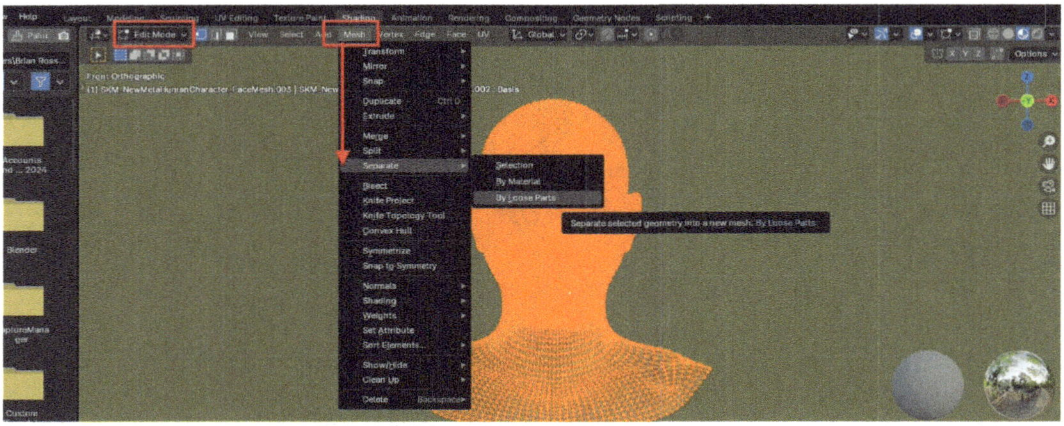

Figure 12.10: Changing the mode and separating the mesh by loose parts

While still in the **Shader** tab, click in the main viewport and hit the *1* key. Alternatively, go to the mode box and choose **Edit** mode from the drop-down menu. I've highlighted this in red in *Figure 12.10*. This is the shortcut to the **Edit** mode in Blender. Now you can edit the mesh. Select all by clicking *Shift + A*. Go to the top menu and click on **Mesh** | **Separate** | **By Loose Parts**, just like I have done in *Figure 12.10*.

Note

Depending on your PC power, it could take a while for the separation to complete.

When the separation is complete, change the mode back to **Object** mode, which is the default. Hit *Ctrl + Shift + A* to deselect everything. In the viewport, click on the head and nothing else.

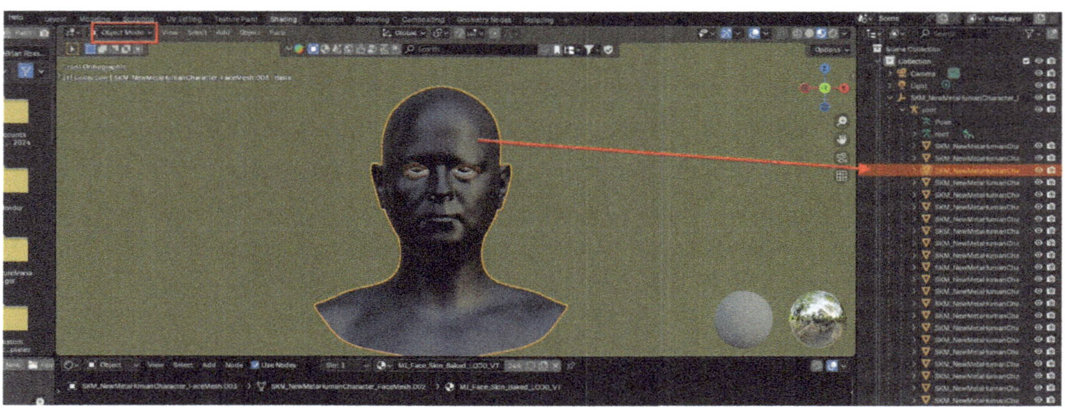

Figure 12.11: Changing the mode and selecting just the head

Clicking on the forehead is your safest bet. With the head selected, you could name it something like `Head`. That is all we want to concern ourselves with in Blender. Hit *Shift + H* to hide everything else. You can always manually unhide items such as the teeth in the **Outliner** to the right. It works just like the **Outliner** in Unreal Engine.

So, the scene has been simplified, no pesky eyelashes or eyeballs to ruin our day, but having a texture map assigned to the face is ideal as it gives us a better reference when sculpting.

Let's fix the texture map issue. You may recall locating the texture map of the face earlier in this chapter. Make sure you have located that in **Windows Explorer**. Because we already have the `Face` material slot active in the **Shader** viewport, you can drag and drop that texture map from **Windows Explorer** directly into the shader network viewport.

In *Figure 12.12*, I've positioned **Windows Explorer** to the left of Blender so that I can easily drag the image directly into the shader network. Once dragged over, the image turns into a **Texture Map** node. This will have no effect until you drag a noodle from the **Color Out** of the **Texture Map** node and into the **Color Input** of the **Principled BDSF** node. The illustration may be difficult to read but on the **Texture Map** node, it is the very top pin on the right to be connected to the very top pin on the **Principled BDSD** node. Dragging from the output automatically creates a wire that needs to be dragged into the target pin. As soon as you let go, the viewport will update with a texture.

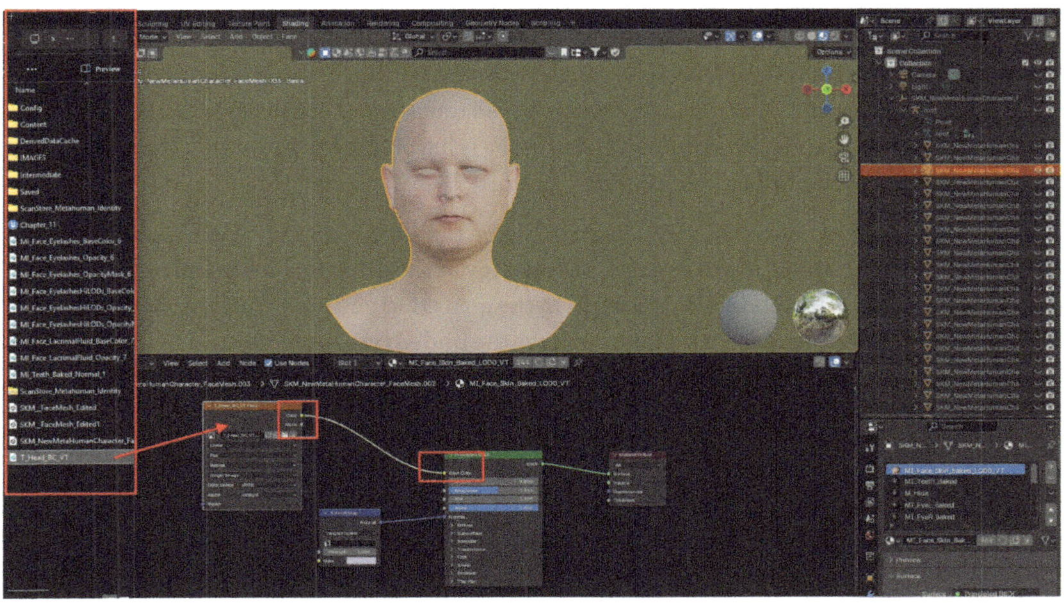

Figure 12.12: Dragging the texture map from Windows Explorer into the shader network

The next step is to change the viewport into the **Sculpt** viewport. Once you've done that, you might find the viewport is a little dark by default, so we just need to change how the mesh is being displayed by changing the viewport shading into **Material** viewport. I've highlighted this in red in *Figure 12.13*. Now you're ready to sculpt away. You can still rotate in the viewport to get a good idea of how to sculpt.

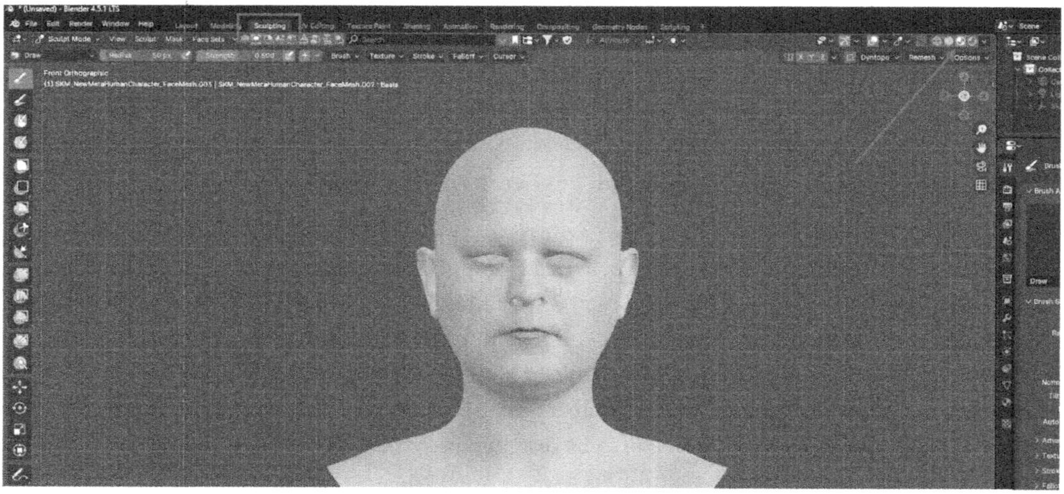

Figure 12.13: Changing to the Sculpting viewport

There are quite a lot of different sculpting brushes at the bottom of the viewport, and it takes time to experiment with them. Like any brush-based tool set, the brush of choice is usually a personal preference, and going through the brushes is beyond the scope of this book. There are a couple of things you need to know before you start.

The most important thing is that **Dynotop** should be turned off. Dyntopo is short for **Dynamic Topology**. When enabled, it will change the topology of the mesh to allow extra detail while brushing. Effectively, it subdivides the mesh in the areas that you are painting to increase detail. Unfortunately, enabling Dyntopo changes the underlying topology by dynamically adding and removing vertices while sculpting.

Although recent versions of Unreal Engine provide a more flexible conform workflow based on UV-space correspondence, preserving the original MetaHuman topology remains the safest and most predictable approach when creating meshes intended for the MetaHuman Identity workflow.

For that reason, Dyntopo should remain disabled throughout this chapter.

Additionally, I've also enabled symmetry on the X axis. For the most part, keeping symmetry off works fine, but the mouth and eye areas need to be symmetrical. While MetaHuman won't reject nonsymmetrical meshes, eye mismatches need to be determined in the MetaHuman sculpting and transformation tools. In short, if you want a lopsided MetaHuman, make it lopsided inside MetaHuman before you assemble and export it from the **MetaHuman Creator**.

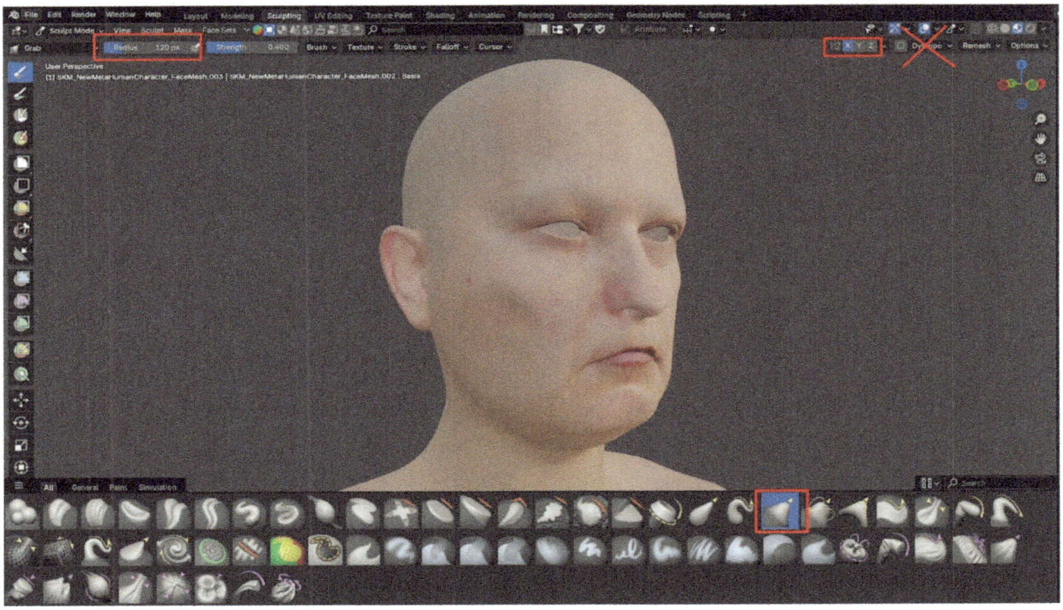

Figure 12.14: Sculpting settings

Effectively, I'm using the MetaHuman as a starting point. Because I've hidden everything but the main head mesh, I can't see the teeth. You can always unhide the teeth to make sure the teeth aren't protruding if you plan to sculpt a thinner face.

I'm going to sculpt thinner and gaunt features into the mesh. I advise you to get familiar with the mask brush in Blender as it can protect areas you don't want to affect.

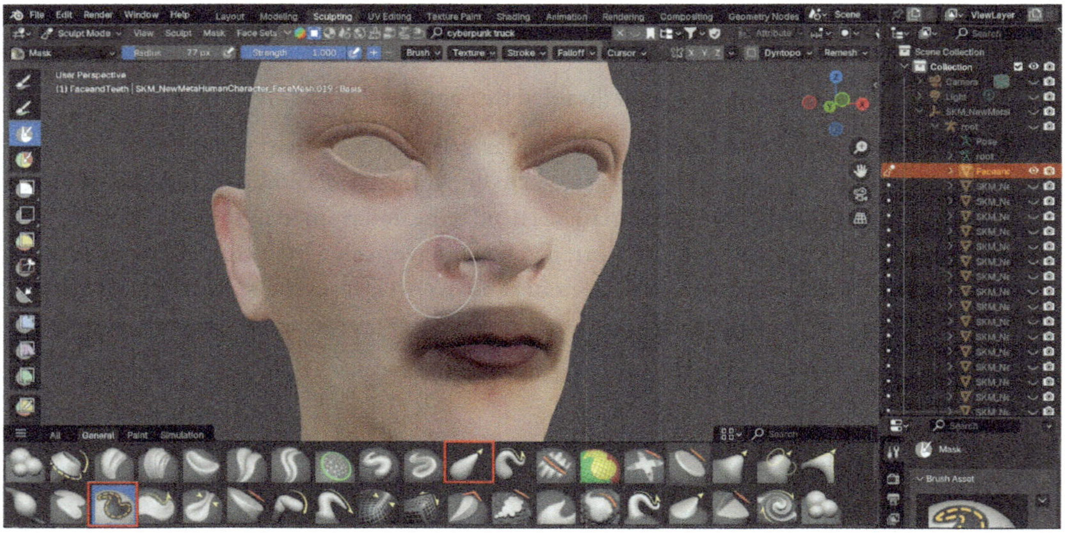

Figure 12.15: Sculpting brushes

You can see in *Figure 12.15* that my sculpt is considerably different from the original. I've used a mask on the mouth by selecting the Mask Brush, highlighted at the bottom. My go-to brush is the **Elastic Grab** brush, highlighted in red in *Figure 12.15*. Getting to this result would have been entirely feasible to do in **MetaHuman Creator**, but some users prefer to use sculpting brush tools like those available in Blender or ZBrush.

Once you're happy with the result, export the mesh as an FBX and import it back into Unreal Engine using the default FBX import settings. The mesh should retain its original scale and orientation, and no additional import scaling should be applied.

Before continuing, quickly compare the imported mesh with the original MetaHuman face to confirm that the proportions and alignment match.

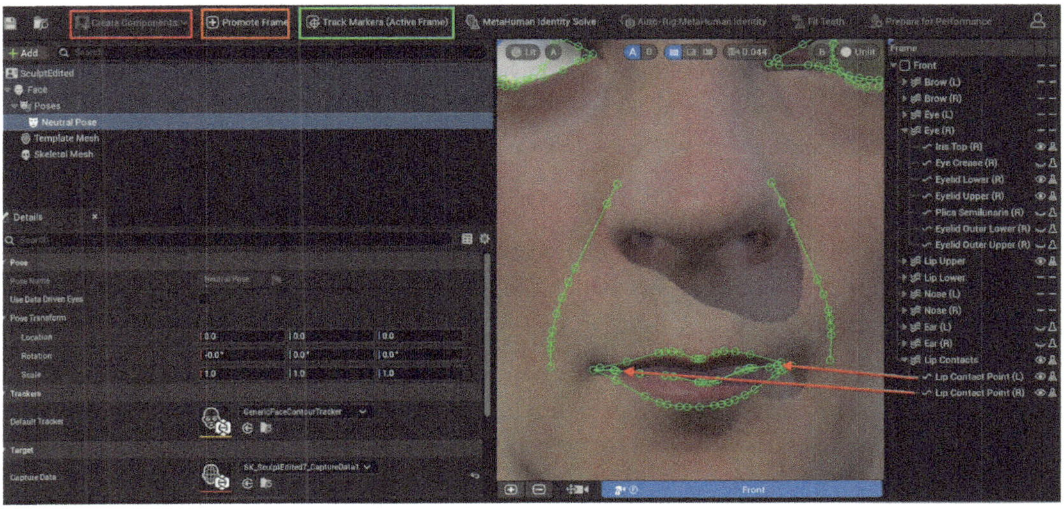

Figure 12.16: Creating a Mesh component and choosing your Blender mesh

You'll already be familiar with the MetaHuman Identity workflow. The main difference is we choose **Mesh** when we create a component. Instead of advancing along a timeline to find the best frame to promote, we just rotate our view around the mesh. Once you promote to frame, click the **Track Markers (Active Frame)** button. The green splines will appear.

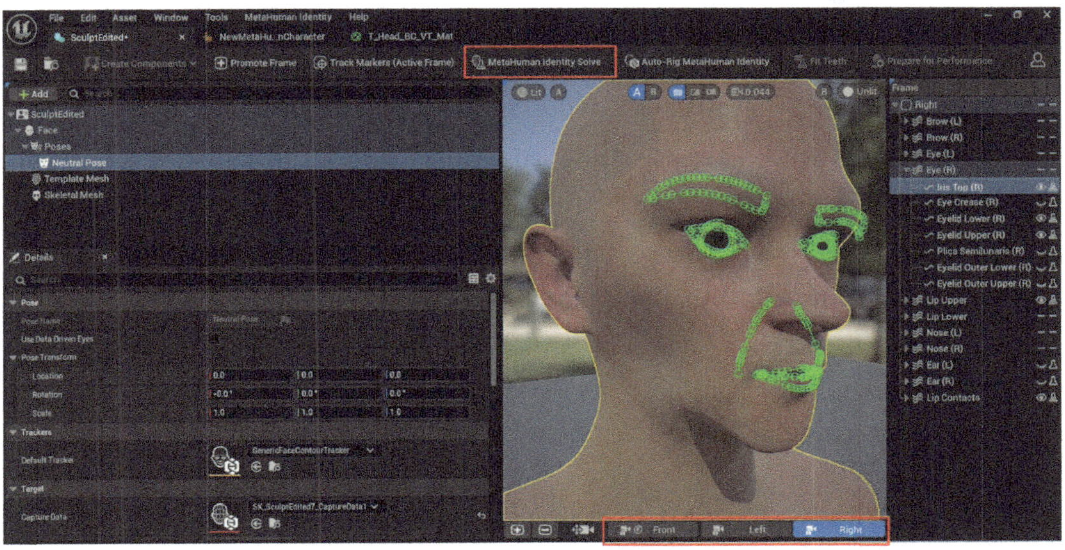

Figure 12.17: MetaHuman Identity Solve

> **Tip**
>
> Before you use the **Promote to Frame** button, be sure to have zoomed in as close as possible so that eyebrows to chin are fully in shot with a small room for extra. This will make it easier for us to see what we are doing when we edit splines.

You do need to be much more careful when tweaking the green splines. One common issue is the placement of the lip contact points, which can sometimes end up in the center of the lips instead of at the mouth corners.

If this happens, simply reposition the contact points so that they sit exactly where the upper and lower lips meet at each corner of the mouth before running **MetaHuman Identity Solve** again. Small adjustments usually produce better results than large movements.

Once you're happy, click on the **MetaHuman Identity Solve** button. You still need to save this **MetaHuman Identity** before closing. Hit save and open **MetaHuman Creator**. You can use the same one you used to export the `Head` or a new one. Be sure to keep the **MetaHuman Identity** open as you will need to go back and forth between the **MetaHuman Identity** and the **MetaHuman Creator** to fix any issues.

Conforming third-party mesh to MetaHuman

In the previous section, we updated the **MetaHuman Identity** with our sculpted mesh. Now, we want to conform the MetaHuman to the **MetaHuman Identity**. You will need to de-rig the character first before moving to the next step.

Next, go to `Head` and under the **Head Setting** and click on **Conform**. Because we're going to use the **MetaHuman Identity**, click on the **Identity** button under **Conform**.

Under **Assets**, choose the MetaHuman Identity that you saved in the previous section.

Under **Import Identity**, untick the following three options:

- **Use Eye Meshes**
- **Use Teeth Mesh**
- **Use Mesh Scale**

This allows the eyes to conform naturally to the incoming mesh shape, ignores the imported teeth geometry, and preserves the proportions created during sculpting rather than applying an additional scale adjustment.

Click on the green **Conform** button to see the results.

Don't be alarmed by any little errors. You can go back to the **MetaHuman Identity** and tweak the spline positions and hit solve again. Go straight back to the **MetaHuman Character**.

It's very useful to have both the **MetaHuman Identity** and **MetaHuman Character** tabbed next to each other, as tweaking can often require back and forth. You can see I've created a tab setup in *Figure 12.18:*

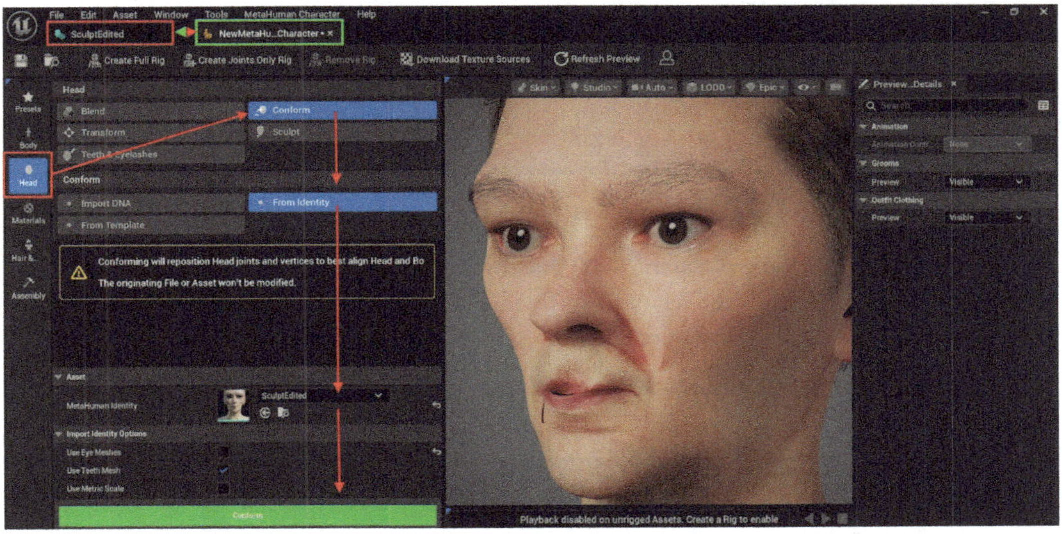

Figure 12.18: Conforming the MetaHuman to the MetaHuman Identity

Notice that the lips aren't quite right but the proportions of the rest of the face match the original Blender sculpt.

Rather than going back and forth to make tweaks, you can stay inside the **MetaHuman Identity** and view the results in A/B mode.

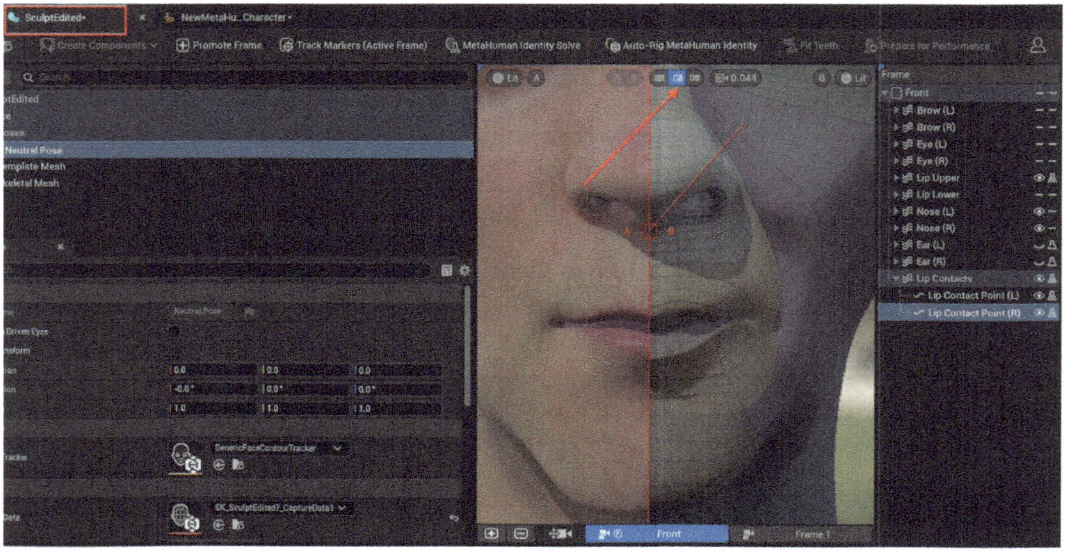

Figure 12.19: A/B mode for quickly testing results

As soon as you've done some tweaking and gone through the solve process a couple of times, you may get to a point where the result looks fine. This is most likely the case, but you may want to do an animation test to be sure.

In this case, with the **MetaHuman Creator** still open, select **Create Full Rig** and then choose **Face ROM** from the **Face Animation** selection, which I've highlighted in red in *Figure 12.20*:

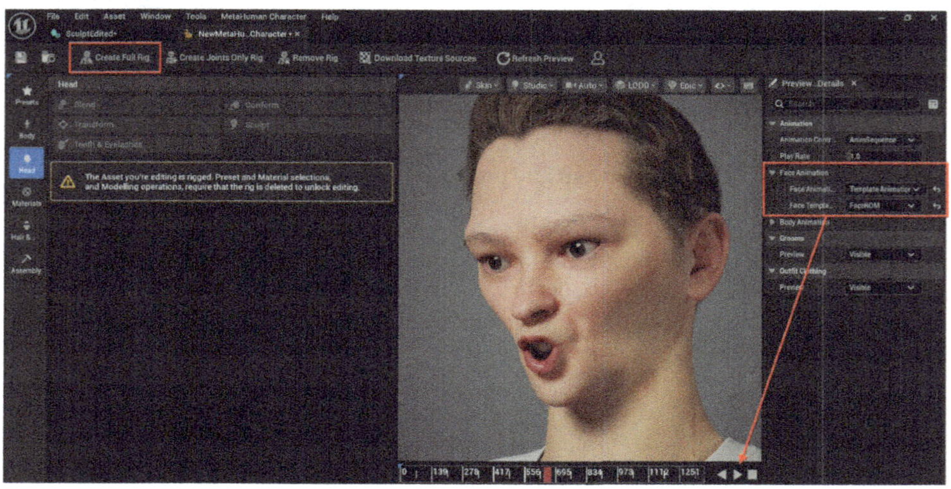

Figure 12.20: Testing with Face ROM animation

In most cases, if the result looks okay in the A/B mode of the **MetaHuman Identity**, it will animate fine with a Face ROM test.

> **Note**
>
> Promoting more frames than three to get more accuracy generally doesn't work. In fact, it will most likely get you a poorer result. So, it is worth trying with two or three frame promotions only.

Just like before, if you're happy with the MetaHuman as it is, you can always assemble it to see how it looks in your scene.

Summary

In this chapter, we explored the whole process of using the Mesh to MetaHuman workflow inside the **MetaHuman Identity** and the **MetaHuman Creator**. We went through the export process for the mesh along with texture map considerations. We then dived into Blender to not only get to grips with the workflow but to get a taste of the sculpting possibilities that high-end sculpting tools can offer. We then came back to Unreal to conform our MetaHuman into our sculpted mesh using the most efficient method and some troubleshooting tips.

In the next chapter, we will focus exclusively on hair grooms, but we will use Blender's built-in hair groom authoring tools.

13

Applying Hair Grooms

In *Chapter 12*, we looked at customizing a mesh using tools outside of Unreal Engine, namely Blender. We learned some exporting techniques and reimporting techniques that allowed us to use external assets on our MetaHuman.

In *Chapters 2* and *3*, when we first looked at editing a MetaHuman, we came across the presets for hair. At the time of writing, there are about 50 hair presets. While that may seem like a lot, you'll quickly start to recognize those MetaHuman hairstyles in games and short films online. Even though there are many things you can do in terms of coloring, the hairstyle remains the same.

It can be a little frustrating because taking one of those 50+ hairstyles and amending them to be shorter or longer and with or without waves, curls, etc. would increase the variety exponentially. Then again, maybe I'm just spending too much time looking at MetaHumans. Regardless, we're going to focus on how we can use Blender as a hair groom companion to Unreal Engine so we can set the MetaHumans you create apart.

Before we start, there is something we need to consider. Hair grooms are simply splines that begin from a surface and, with a physics gravity component, end up behaving like hair. The surface they begin from, from a character's perspective, is the scalp. The scalp is a surface area and shape specific to the character we are creating. We can't expect a groom designed for a tiny scalp to work on a huge scalp without problems or workarounds. You've probably guessed it by now: we're going to have to export another skeletal face mesh for Blender to use as the scalp or just use the one you made in the last chapter.

This is all good because you're now familiar with about half of what we're about to cover.

So, in this chapter, we will cover the following topics:

- Exporting a MetaHuman base mesh for Blender
- Preparing the scalp
- Introducing Blender Hair Curves
- Styling the hair
- Exporting the grooms in Unreal Engine
- Adding the Groom to the MetaHuman
- Applying a Hair Shader
- Editing Simulation Parameters
- Testing the groom in animation

Technical requirements

In terms of computer power, you will need to meet the same technical requirements detailed in *Chapter 9*.

You will also need:

- Access to the Epic Games Launcher used to install Unreal Engine
- Blender 4.6x
- A MetaHuman in your project

If you are new to Blender, I recommend enabling the **Industry Compatible** keymap (**Edit** | **Preferences** | **Keymap** | **Industry Compatible**), as all keyboard shortcuts used throughout this chapter assume that layout

> **Note**
>
> You will need to be familiar with the MetaHuman Identity used in *Chapter 9*, and preferably have a MetaHuman Identity already created.

Exporting a MetaHuman base mesh for Blender

In *Chapter 12*, you gained experience getting a MetaHuman Face Skeletal Mesh out of Unreal Engine and into Blender. For this chapter, you can continue with the Skeletal Mesh you have or create a new MetaHuman Character and use the **Export Face Skeletal Mesh** option at the top of the **MetaHuman Creator** menu.

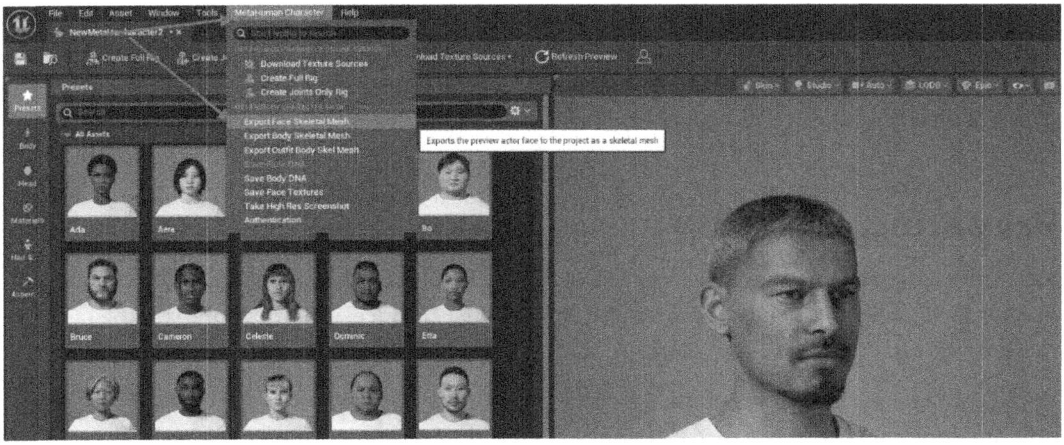

Figure 13.1: Exporting a MetaHuman Face Skeletal Mesh

Just like in *Chapter 12*, locate where you've exported your Skeletal Face mesh to within your Unreal Project, *right-click* on it, and choose **Asset Actions | Export**. This will prompt for the location target. In the FBX export settings, use the exact same settings as detailed in the previous chapter but most importantly, untick **Level of Detail**, otherwise the **Groom** tool won't know which mesh to work on and it will fail

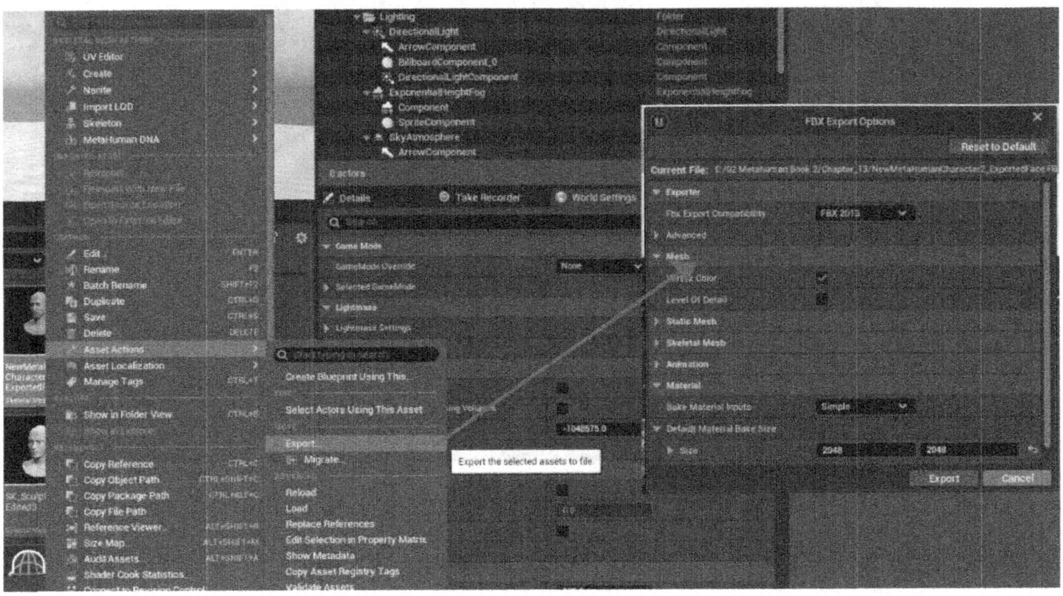

Figure 13.2: Export settings

Next, we will go into Blender and import the mesh we just exported. The steps for importing a mesh into Blender are the same as those described in *Chapter 12*. You will also need to hide the bones, separate the mesh into loose geometry, and hide everything other than the face mesh. Please follow the steps from the *Importing and sculpting the mesh in Blender* section of *Chapter 12*.

Preparing the scalp

Assuming you have followed the steps in the *Importing and sculpting the mesh in Blender* section in *Chapter 12*, where you hid the bones and isolated just the face, we'll now prepare the face mesh so we can use the top as a scalp.

We're going to select the area of the head that we want to be the scalp and then duplicate that area and hide the rest. To do the selection, we'll use the **Lasso** tool so we can simply draw what we want as the scalp. First, we need to view the mesh directly from the side. That will require the *F1* or *F2* key depending on which way your mesh is oriented. Or you can click on the direction widget in the top right of the viewport to cycle through the views.

Equally important is setting the view mode to **Xray**, so that your selection will be both sides of the head, not just the one you can see.

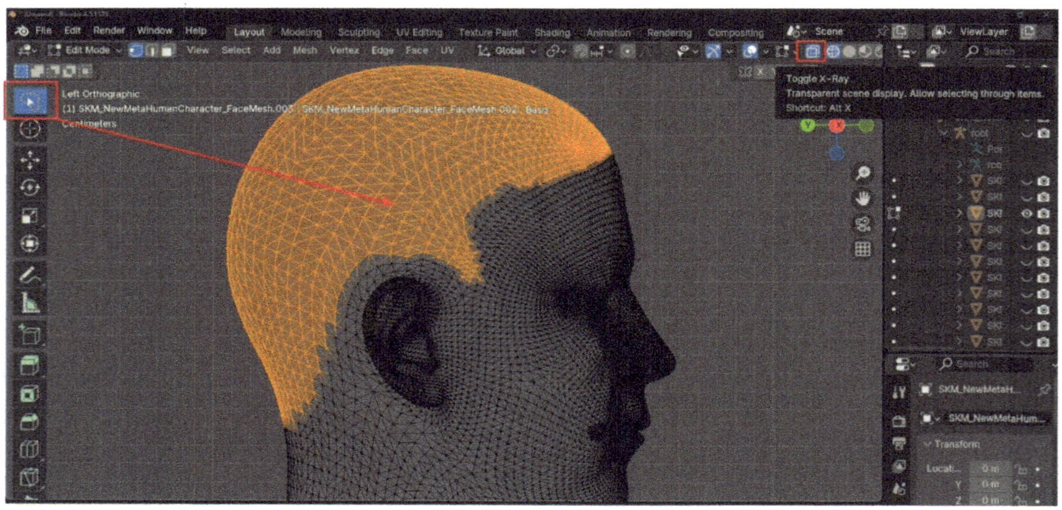

Figure 13.3: Drawing a selection with the Lasso tool in X ray mode

In *Figure 13.3*, I've highlighted in red the **Lasso** tool on the left and the **Xray** viewing mode on the right. You can use the *Alt+X* key to enable the X-ray viewing mode, as it is a common view to use. If you're new to Blender, this could take some getting used to.

If the shortcut keys aren't working for you, you can fix that from **Preferences** | **Keymap** and choosing **Industry Compatible** from the very top dropdown list.

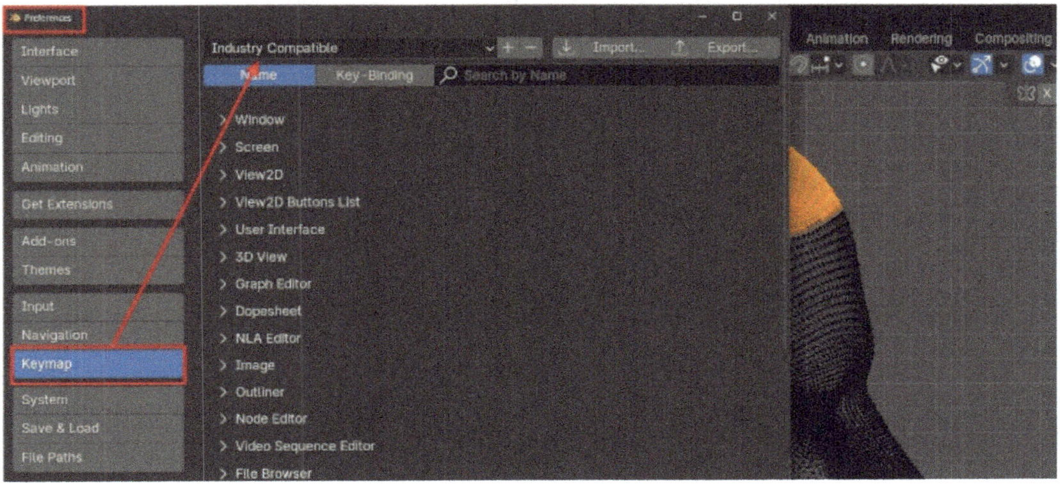

Figure 13.4: Preferences | Keymap | Industry Compatible

Let's get back to the selection. We want to duplicate the scalp and then separate it from the face mesh. Duplicate it first just so we have the original for safety. Go to **Mesh** and select **Duplicate**, as shown in *Figure 13.5*:

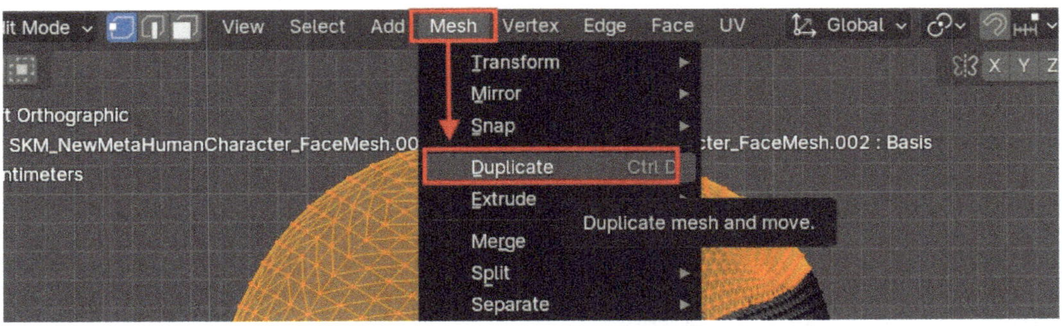

Figure 13.5: Duplicating the scalp selection

With the selection intact, go back up to **Mesh** again and this time choose **Separate** | **Separate by Selection**.

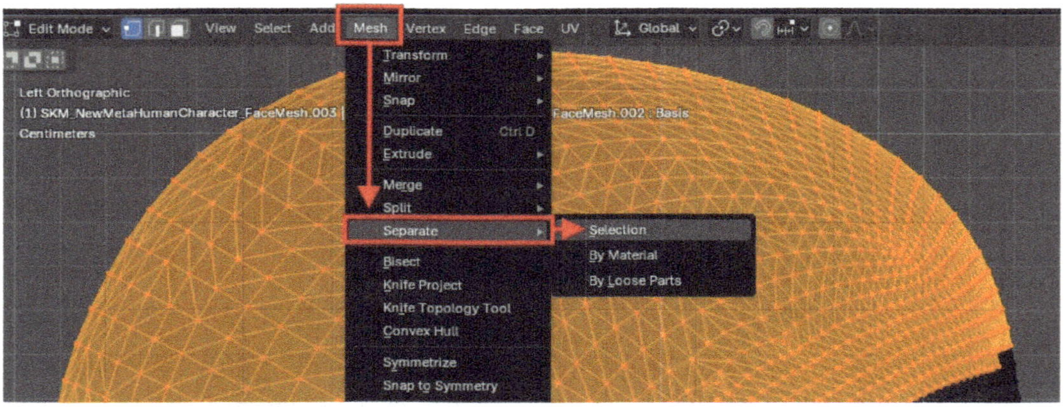

Figure 13.6: Separating the scalp selection

Introducing Blender hair curves

Now that we have a scalp to work with, we can start creating the hair itself.

In Blender, hair is created using curves. These are not individual strands of hair but guide curves that tell Blender how the hair should flow. Blender then uses those guides to generate the rest of the strands.

To begin, make sure your scalp mesh is selected. Then go to **Add** | **Curve** | **Empty Hair**.

You should now see a small set of curves appear on the scalp. These are your starting guides.

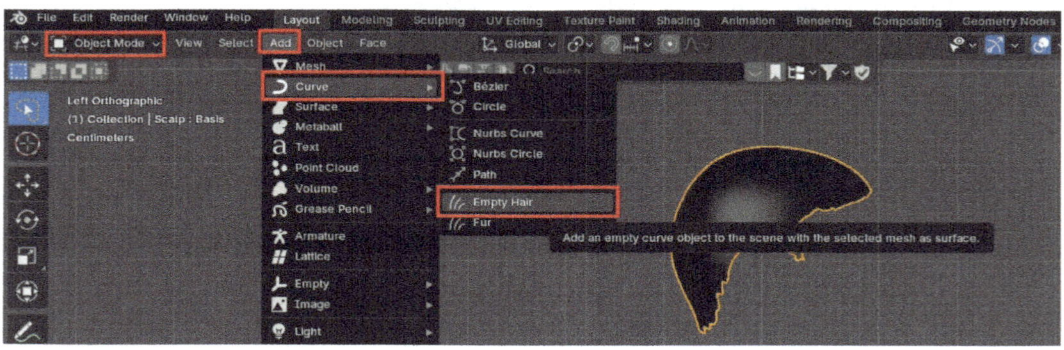

Figure 13.7: Adding an empty curve

It's a good idea at this point to rename the curve object to something more meaningful like `Hair_Guides`. Press *F2* to rename it.

Next, switch from **Object** mode to **Sculpt** mode.

Sculpt mode for grooms

Much of Blender's menu system is contextual, and a special **Sculpt** mode becomes available once you've created an empty hair Curve. It is not the same **Sculpt** mode you use for geometry, but a groom-specific sculpt mode.

Before doing anything else, look for the option called **Use Collision Distance** on the top right and make sure it is enabled.

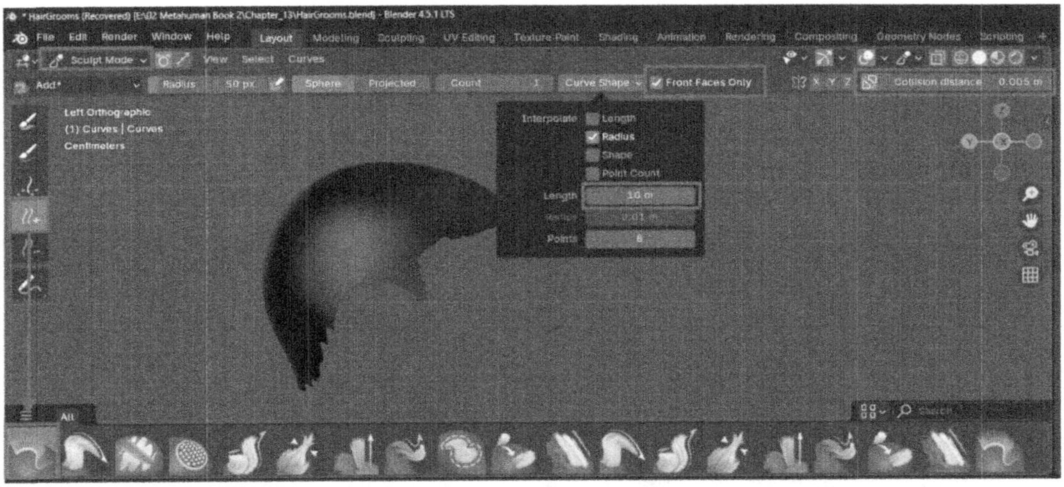

Figure 13.8: Adding curves in Sculpt mode

This is important. Without it, the curves can pass straight through the head mesh, which will cause problems later. You can see in *Figure 13.8*, I've enabled it and given it a **Collision Distance** of 0.0005 meters. Note that **Collision Distance** becomes available depending on which tool you're using. For instance, I've used the **Add Curve** tool seen on the far left. Both of those icons represent the same tool. The menu on the left is for adding and subtracting hair, while the icons at the bottom are all the styling tools.

With the curves selected and Sculpt Mode active, we can begin shaping the hairstyle.

Styling the hair

Start by selecting the **Add Hair** brush. This allows you to place guide curves directly onto the scalp. Think of these as directional strokes rather than finished hair.

There are a few settings worth adjusting:

- **Radius** controls the size of the brush
- **Count** determines how many curves are added per stroke
- **Length** controls how long the hair is and can be edited later

If you increase the **Count**, you'll get a denser result. If you reduce the **Radius**, you can place curves more precisely.

Go ahead and click on the scalp a few times to add some curves.

At this stage, don't worry about making it perfect. You're just blocking out the general direction of the hair.

To speed things up, you can use the **Symmetry** tool to mirror the result on the other side of the head. I've used this in *Figure 13.8*. I've also used just one curve for the **Add Hair** brush.

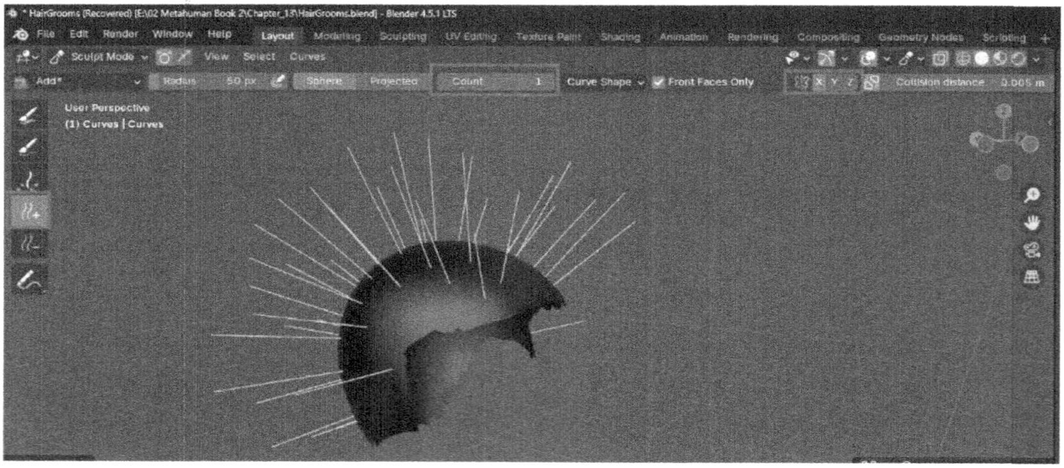

Figure 13.9: Using the Symmetry tool for adding hair

Hair density

Generally, 20 or 30 curves are enough to develop a rough hair style. A high density will cause performance issues. Once you have several curves in place, switch to the **Comb** tool.

This is where things start to take shape.

Use a larger radius to push large sections of hair into place. You can then reduce the radius for smaller adjustments. In *Figure 13.10*, I'm using the comb tool, but I've left the Symmetry on X on as a personal preference.

As you comb the hair, try not to push it directly into the scalp. Keep it slightly lifted. If the curves go into the head mesh, it will cause issues later when we bring it into Unreal Engine.

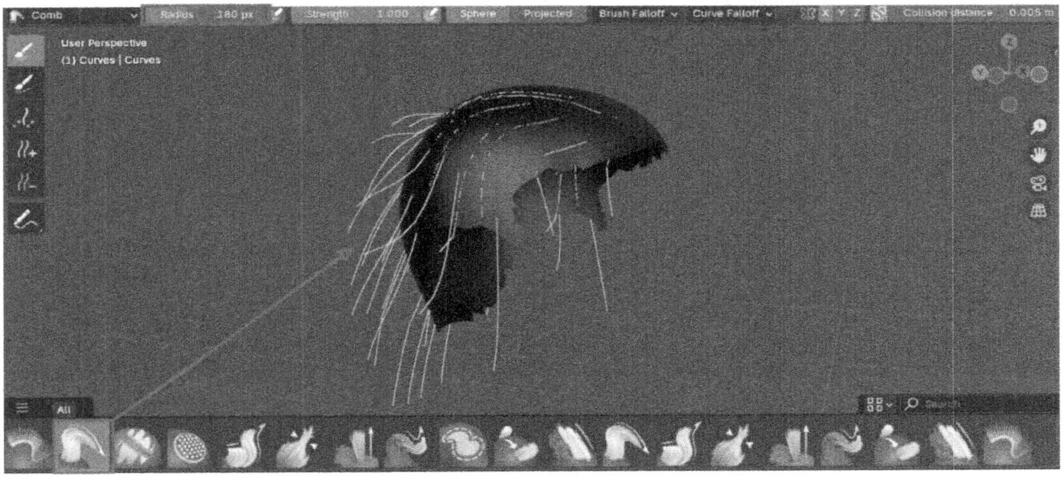

Figure 13.10: Combing with a large brush

You'll notice that even with a small number of curves, Blender starts to give a good sense of the overall hairstyle. That's because these are only guides. We don't need a huge number of them.

It's also worth mentioning that hair is often created in sections. For example, you might do the front, sides, and back separately.

For now, we'll keep things simple and focus on a single section. Once you're happy with the general shape, we can use modifiers to turn these guide curves into a full hairstyle.

Building density with modifiers

Select your hair curve object and go to the **Modifiers** tab.

The first modifier to add is **Interpolate Hair Curves**. You can find it by going into the **Asset Browser** tab, indicated by the icon on the far left of *Figure 13.11*. Then, drag and drop the modifier icon from the **Asset Browser** onto the guide curves in the viewport. Alternatively, you can go to the **Modifier** tab using the **Wrench** icon and click **Add Modifier | Hair | Generation | Interpolate Hair Curve**.

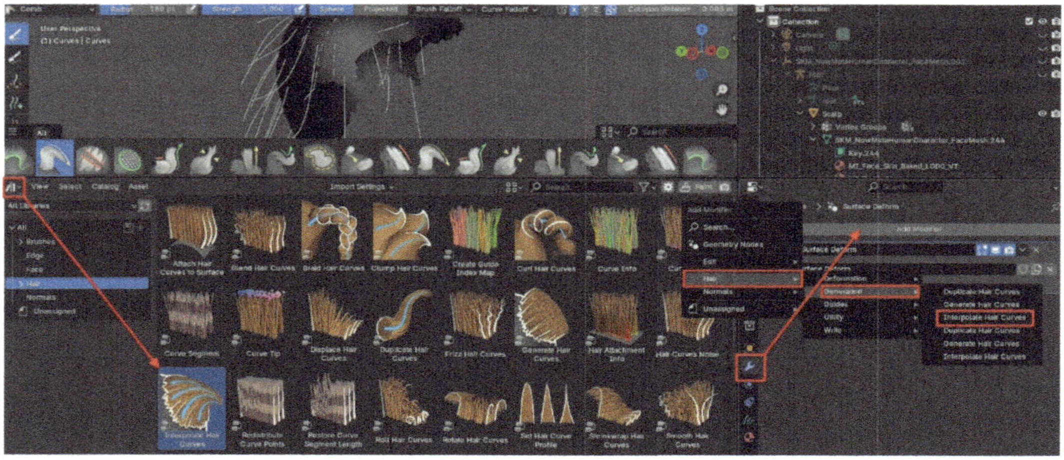

Figure 13.11: Add Modifier | Hair | Generation | Interpolate Hair Curves

This takes your guide curves and generates additional strands between them. At first, it may look a bit strange. That's normal.

Adjust the **Distance to Guides** until the density looks more natural.

Make sure that the **Surface** is set to your `Scalp` mesh. If it isn't, the modifier won't behave correctly. This feature is at the top of the **Modifier** tab, as shown in *Figure 13.12*. If your system is struggling, you can always reduce the density or just the density in the viewport.

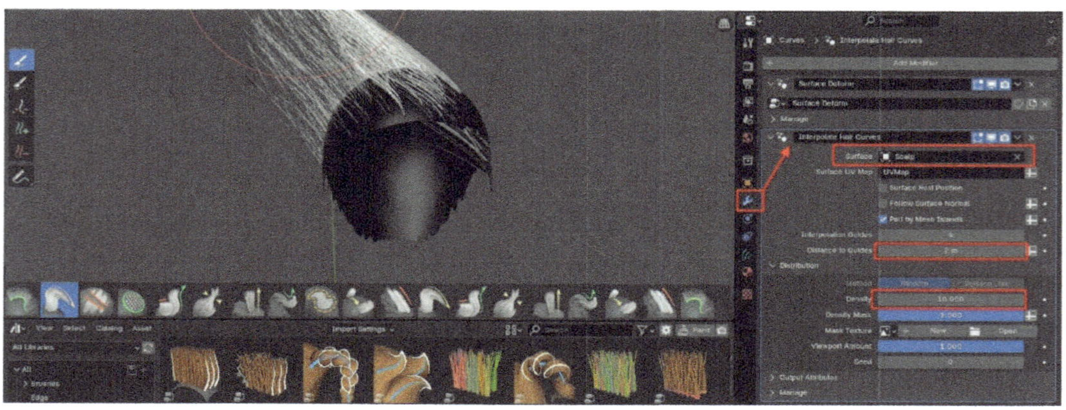

Figure 13.12: Interpolate Hair Curves Modifier

Next, add a **Clump Hair Curves** modifier.

Real hair tends to group together rather than sitting as perfectly separate strands. This modifier helps create that effect.

Use it carefully. Too much clumping will look unnatural. Small adjustments usually work best.

At this point, your hair should start to look more complete. To make quick adjustments and see the results, get in the habit of toggling the viewport visibility of your modifiers between brushing the curves. Doing so will quickly train you to understand what the result will look like without the need to visualize the full final density. In *Figure 13.13*, I've highlighted the viewport icons for both the **Interpolate Hair Curves** and **Clump Hair Curve** modifiers.

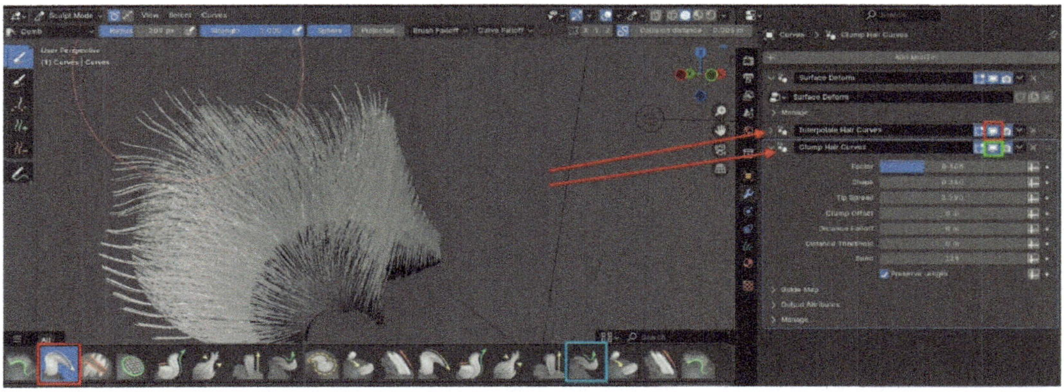

Figure 13.13: Toggling modifiers off when styling

You may have noticed that I've given the groom a shorter fringe. There isn't a scissors function in the style tools. However, there is a better tool called **Pull Tips**, highlighted in blue in *Figure 13.13*, which gives you more control than just cutting.

When you're happy with the hairstyle, the next step is to export it so we can bring it into Unreal Engine.

Exporting the grooms in Unreal Engine

Blender uses the Alembic format for the following.

Exporting the Alembic grooms

Before exporting, make sure that:

- Your scalp mesh is still in the scene
- Your hair curves are selected
- Everything is clearly named

Then, select both the scalp and the hair curves, and then export the file.

1. Go to **File** | **Export** | **Alembic (.abc)**
2. In the export settings:
    a. Enable **Selected Only (General)**
    b. Enable **Flatten Hierarchy (Scene)**
    c. Disable **Export Particles (Particle System)**

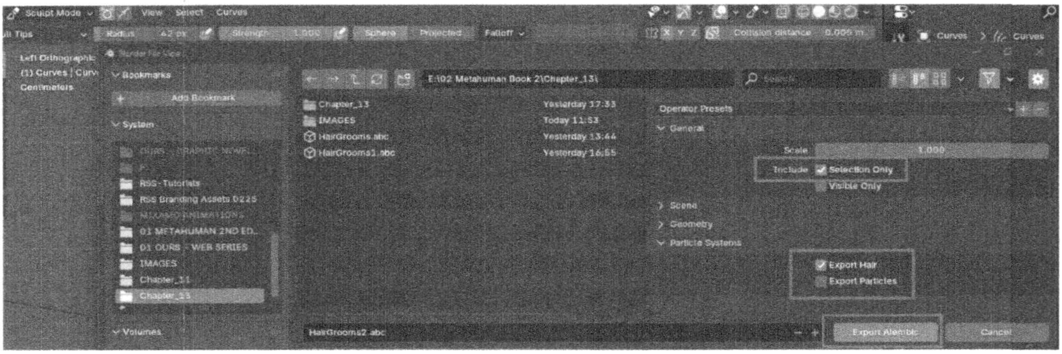

Figure 13.14: Exporting the Alembic file

Enabling the Alembic Grooms Export plugin

Before importing the groom into Unreal Engine, we need to make sure the correct plugin is enabled. Open Unreal Engine and go to **Edit** | **Plugins**.

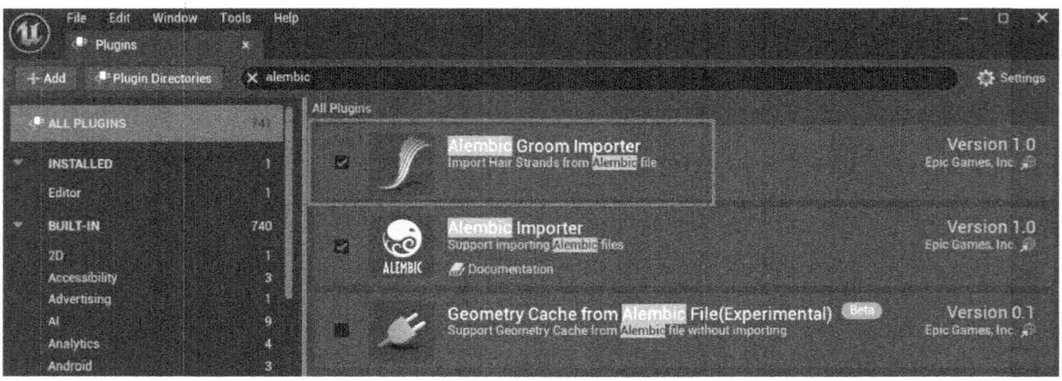

Figure 13.15: Enabling the Alembic Groom Importer plugin

Search for `Alembic`. Enable the **Alembic Groom Importer** plugin if it is not already active. You may be prompted to restart the engine. Without this plugin, Unreal will not recognize Alembic groom files correctly.

Importing the Alembic groom and creating a groom binding

Once Unreal has restarted, import your Alembic file into the **Content Browser**.

During import, you'll see a **Groom Import Options** dialog box. This confirms that Unreal has correctly recognized the Alembic file as a groom.

If the **Groom Import Options** dialog does not appear, the export has not been recognized as a groom. In most cases this is because:

- The hair curves were not selected during export,
- The scalp mesh and curves were not exported together, or
- The **Alembic Groom Importer** plugin has not been enabled.

Return to Blender, verify the export settings, and export the Alembic file again before retrying the import.

Conversion

Because Blender and Unreal Engine are different systems, they work with units and scaling in different ways. This is a common occurrence between **Digital Content Creation** tools. We need to tackle this conversion during the **Alembic Import** stage.

When we import, we get a dialog box with a conversion. In the **Rotations** for X, Y, and Z, we need to ensure the following applies:

Blender and Unreal Engine use different coordinate systems and axis orientations. These conversion values compensate for those differences so that the groom imports with the correct orientation and scale.

Use the following values:

- **Rotation**:
  - X = 90.0
  - Y = 0.0
  - Z = -180
- **Scale**:
  - X = -1.0
  - Y = 1.0
  - Z = 1.0

If your groom imports rotated or mirrored incorrectly, these are the first settings to verify

There is no need for any **Transformation** conversion, which is why it is left out of the import options, as you can see from *Figure 13.16*:

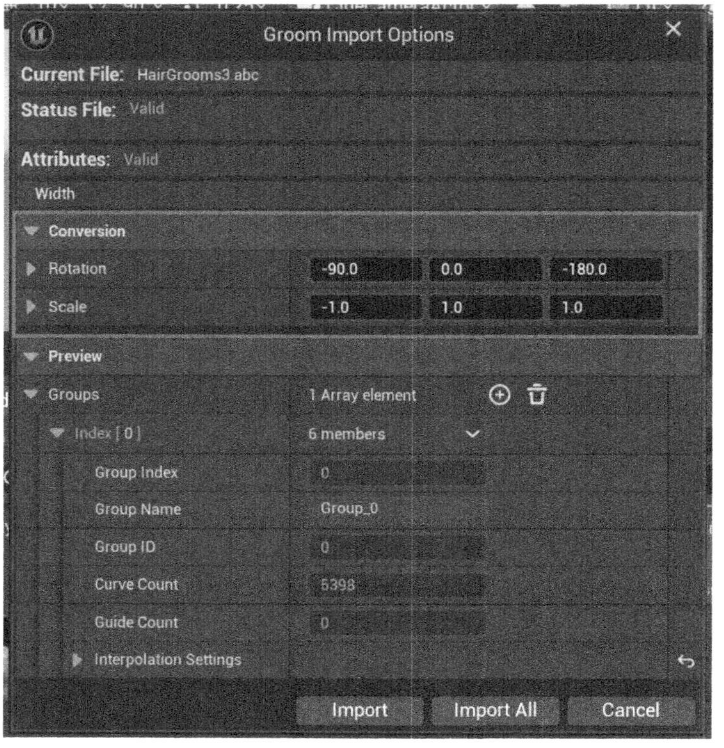

Figure 13.16: Groom Import Options dialog box

If you have exported correctly, you just need to click the **Import** button.

Next, we need to bind this groom to the MetaHuman. Typically, we don't want to simply attach it to the MetaHuman's head bone. Instead, we want to use a binding asset that will recognize the face mesh of the MetaHuman. Locate the groom asset you just imported.

Binding the groom to the head bone

Attaching a groom to the head socket works for wider shots, but it treats the hair as rigid and can cause slipping around the hairline during facial animation. Groom binding instead follows the underlying mesh deformation, keeping the hair properly aligned. This becomes important in close-ups where small errors are more visible.

Right-click the **Groom Asset** and create a **Groom Binding Asset**.

When prompted, select the MetaHuman face skeletal mesh, the one you exported into Blender.

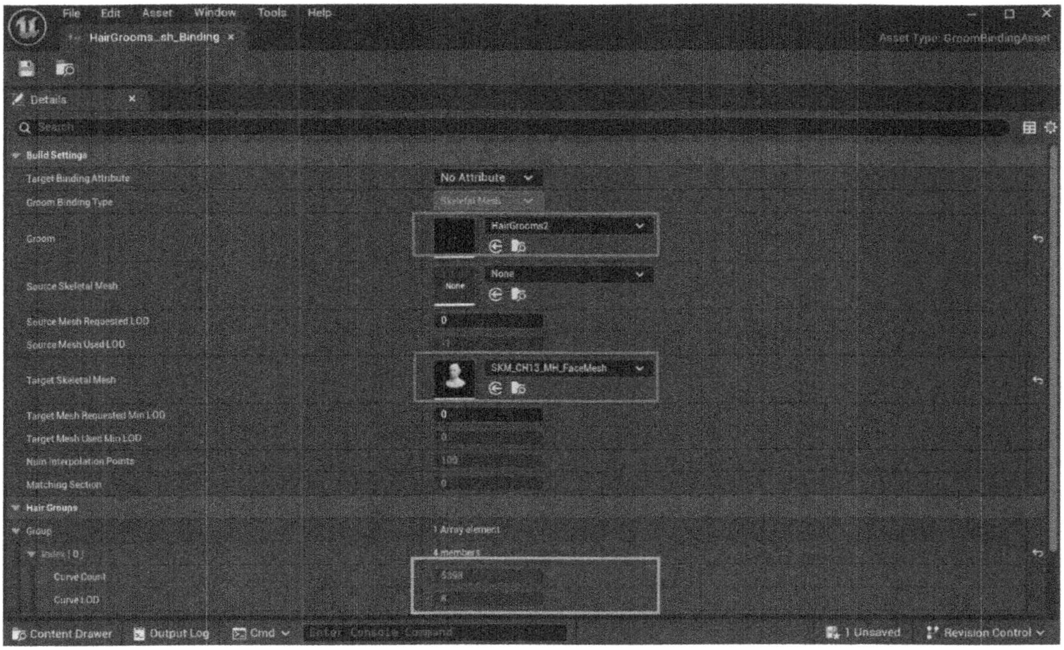

Figure 13.17: Checking the Hair Groom Binding asset

Feel free to *double-click* the binding asset once it's created to inspect it. You can see from *Figure 13.17* that my Blender Exported Groom is present in the groom slot. It also has the MetaHuman Skeletal Face Mesh as the Target Skeletal Mesh. Highlighted in green is the curve count. With just this information, we know it should work. This step ensures that the hair follows the character's movement correctly. The next step is attaching the groom to our **MetaHuman**.

Adding the groom to the MetaHuman

Open your MetaHuman Blueprint.

Locate the existing hair component and either disable it or remove it.

Add a new groom component by going to the **Component** section and clicking on the **+Add** button and searching for `Groom`.

It's likely that when you add a groom asset, it will be incorrectly placed in the hierarchy unless you selected **Face** before clicking on the **+Add** button. We need it to be within the **Face** hierarchy. So just drag the **Groom** asset into the **Face** in the **Component** tab, as shown in *Figure 13.18*:

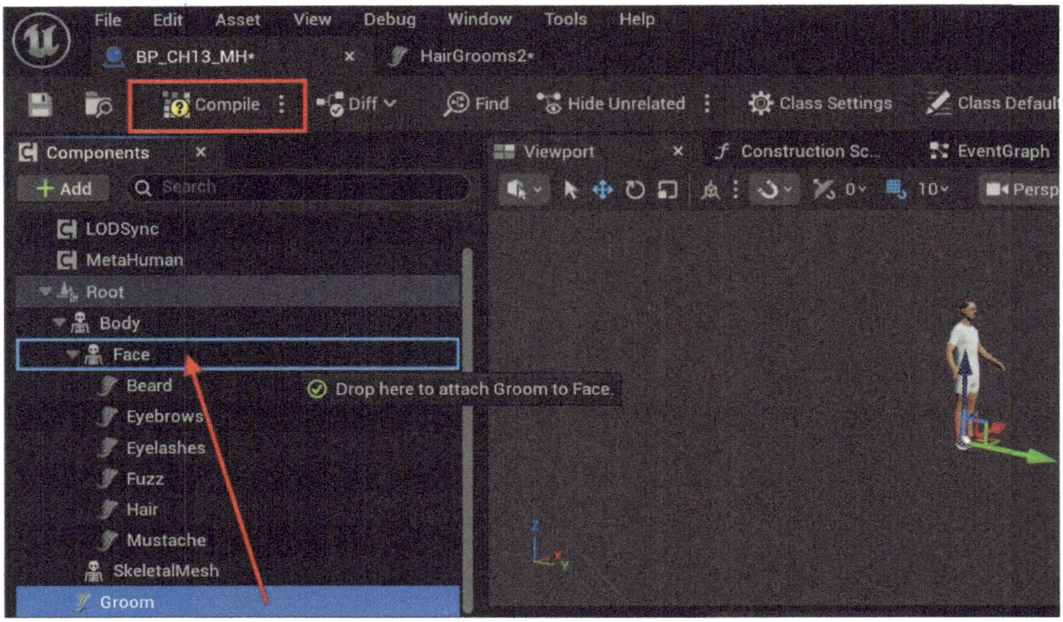

Figure 13.18: Adding the Groom to the Face hierarchy

Once your new **Groom** asset is in place, go to the **Details** panel and assign your **Groom** asset and the **Groom Binding** asset.

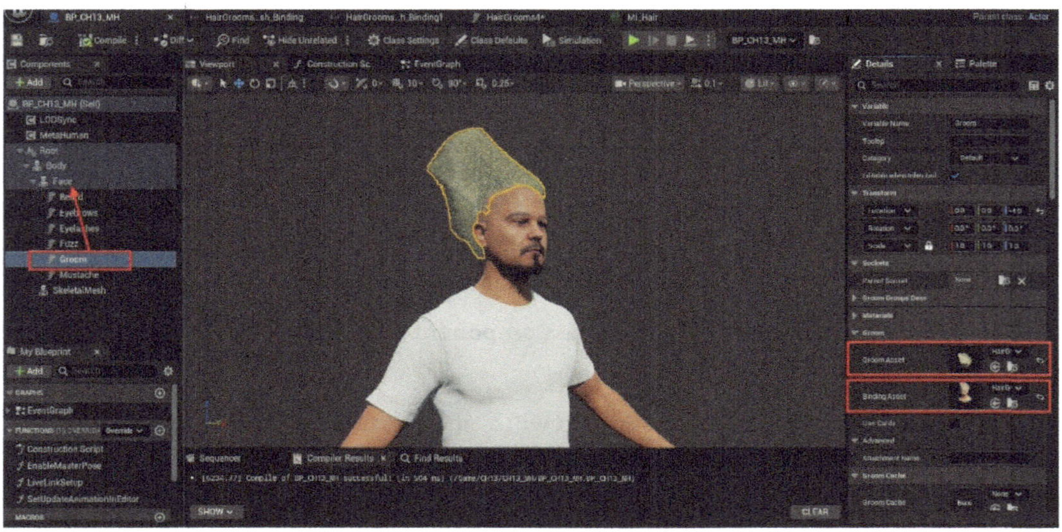

Figure 13.19: Adding the Groom binding

If everything has been exported correctly, the hair should appear in the correct position automatically, but if it appears in the wrong position and/or wrong scale, we can easily fix it by reimporting the Alembic file and changing the conversion transform parameters.

Applying a hair shader

In *Figure 13.17*, you can see the strange Mohawk kind of hairstyle I've fashioned. I'm not gonna lie, I'm no hairdresser. One important thing to note is that the display isn't great. We have grooms but grooms need a particular hair shader to look good. As it happens, a hair shader becomes available when you assemble a MetaHuman in your project. We're going to repurpose it for our bespoke grooms.

To use it, *double-click* on the groom asset to open it. You'll see a number of tabs to the right. Click on the **Materials** tab. You will have to click on the **+** icon to add a **Material** slot. In the **Material** slot, type `MI_Hair` and apply that material. You'll see a dramatically improved result as that hair shader responds to light in a more realistic way.

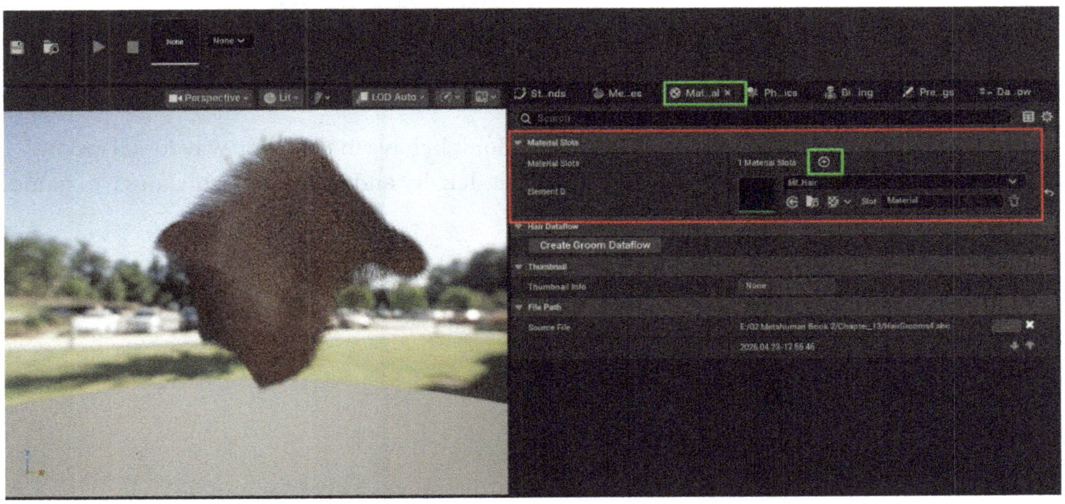

Figure 13.20: Adding the MetaHuman MI_Hair material

Just to note, you're looking at the hair shader that was assigned to the MetaHuman.

Editing simulation parameters

Different hairstyles will behave differently in terms of physics. While I'm happy with the starchy behavior, I can make it flop around much more if I like by going into the **Physics** tab.

All I want to do is reduce how stiff the hairstyle behaves, particularly to gravity. By default, the setting is a little high for my liking. So, I'm going to reduce it slightly.

You can see from *Figure 13.21* that there is a **Bend Stiffness** parameter, and by reducing it from 0.005 to 0.001, it gets me the floppy result I want.

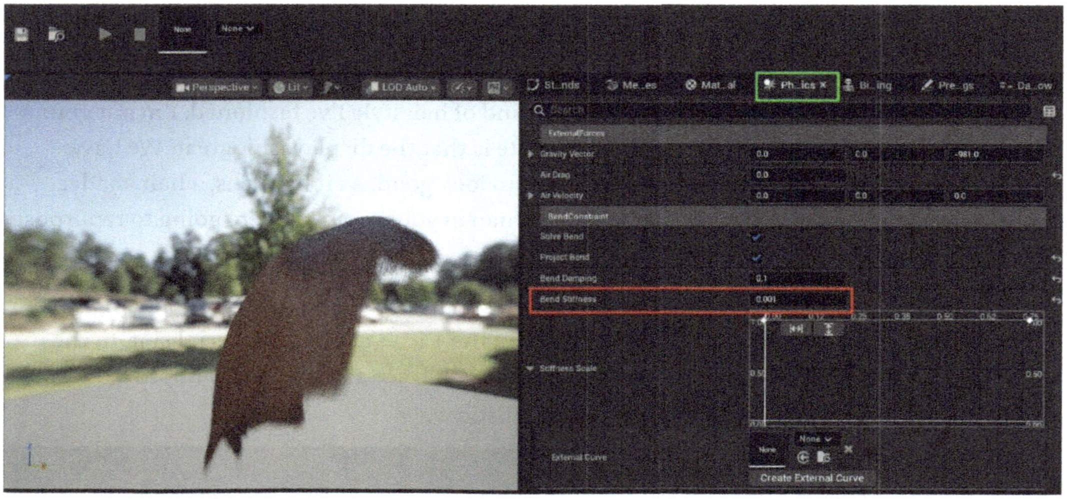

Figure 13.21: Reducing Bend Stiffness in the Physics tab

Just to reiterate, the physics behavior parameters don't behave in the same way for all grooms as there are many factors involved, particularly hair density and hair strand thickness, to name but a few.

I suggest you play around with the **Physics** tab with various groom types to get a better understanding. As we're only covering the Blender to Unreal Engine grooms pipeline broadly, we can't explore that section thoroughly.

Testing the groom in animation

The final step is to test the hair in motion.

Apply a simple animation to the body of your MetaHuman in a **Level Sequencer**.

Watch how the hair behaves. If needed, open the **Groom Asset** and adjust the physics settings, such as stiffness and damping.

Small changes can make a big difference here. Hair that is too stiff will look unnatural, while hair that is too loose can feel weightless.

Take a bit of time to test and refine it until it behaves in a way that feels believable.

Summary

In this chapter, we focused on creating and integrating hair grooms for MetaHumans using a third-party application. We began by exporting a base mesh into Blender, preparing it for modification, and building a scalp to support hair generation. From there, we introduced Blender's hair curves system and worked through the process of shaping and styling the groom. We moved into Unreal Engine, covering Alembic export, enabling the required plugins, importing the groom, creating a binding, and attaching it to the MetaHuman. Finally, we applied the MetaHuman hair shader and made a quick yet effective change to the physics.

In the next and final chapter, we will introduce external tools and plugins that support MetaHuman production. Rather than focusing on a single task, we will look at how different applications fit into a wider pipeline, including animation in Autodesk Maya and Houdini, character development with Character Creator, very efficient animation controls for MetaHuman and more.

14

External Tools and Plugins for MetaHuman Workflows

In *Chapter 13*, we focused on creating and integrating hair grooms for MetaHumans. This included building a scalp in Blender, styling hair using curves, exporting Alembic grooms, and binding them correctly inside Unreal Engine so they deform with the character.

That process highlighted an important limitation. While Unreal Engine provides a strong real-time environment, many key stages of character production rely on external tools.

This chapter expands the workflow beyond a single task. Instead, we look at a range of tools and plugins that support MetaHuman production across animation, asset creation, facial performance, and clothing. Each one plays a specific role within a broader pipeline.

In this chapter we will cover:

- Maya plugin support for MetaHumans
- Houdini plugins and procedural workflows
- Character Creator integration
- Wrap for mesh and scan processing
- MataHuman Animation Tool for animation control
- MetaTailor for clothing creation
- ZenBlink for facial workflows
- Fab as a growing resource platform

MetaHuman for Maya

Autodesk Maya is a core tool in most professional animation pipelines. Its MetaHuman integration allows you to bring fully rigged characters into a more traditional animation environment.

> **Note**
>
> At the time of writing, MetaHuman for Maya supported Autodesk Maya 2023 through 2026. As both Autodesk and Epic regularly update their software, it is always worth checking the latest compatibility information on Fab before installing.

This is where animators typically refine performances. While Unreal Engine supports animation, Maya provides deeper control, particularly for facial work and detailed timing.

With MetaHuman for Maya you can:

- Use the **Character Assembler** tool to assemble any MetaHuman Character asset exported from Unreal Engine using the DCC Export assembly pipeline as a rigged and textured character ready to animate
- Export MetaHuman-compatible grooms created with legacy **XGen Descriptions** to Unreal Engine using the **Groom Exporter** so they can be worn by your character
- Apply minor technical fixes, creative modifications of expressions, or pseudo-human features to the character's head using **Expression Editor** and advanced rigging tools
- Modify a character's body using Pose Editor to apply technical fixes or create new kinds of human, humanoid, or fantasy characters by authoring the secondary deformations using **RBF** (**radial basis function**) and **SwingTwist** solvers

You can work with layered animation, adjust curves precisely, and fine-tune expressions in a way that is difficult to achieve in real time.

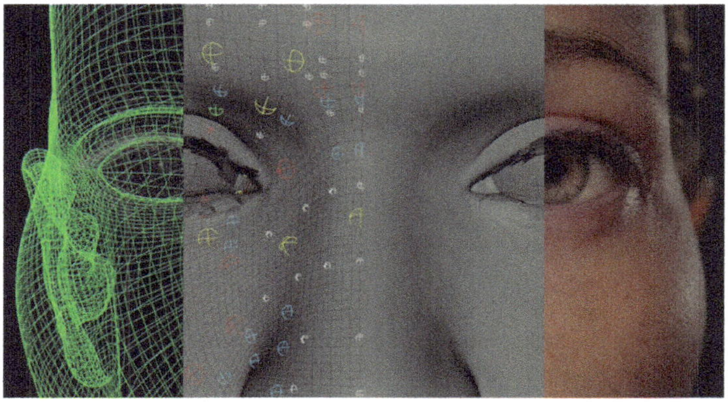

Figure 14.1: MetaHuman for Maya plugin

For Maya users, having access to MetaHumans directly inside Maya without relying on bridging tools is a massive time saver and it opens up access to other rendering solutions.

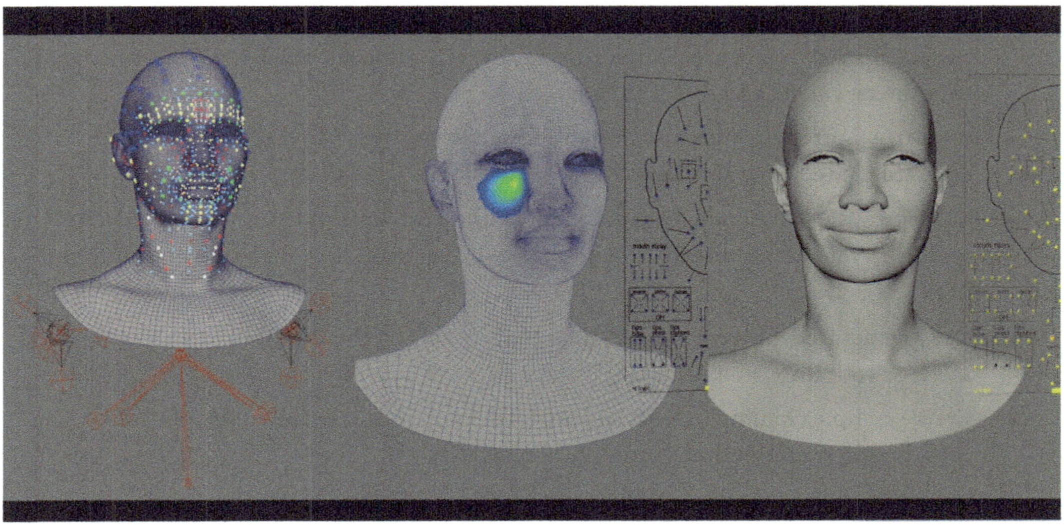

Figure 14.2: MetaHuman control board inside Maya

In most pipelines, Maya sits between capture and final rendering, acting as the primary space for animation polish.

You can get the MetaHuman for Maya plugin at `Fab.com`.

Houdini plugins

Houdini is built around procedural workflows.

Instead of manually creating assets, you define systems that generate them.

When connected to Unreal Engine through the Houdini Engine plugin, these systems can be used to drive content directly inside your scene.

> **Note**
>
> At the time of writing, the MetaHuman for Houdini tools supported Houdini 19.5 and later. As with all external plugins, always confirm the latest supported versions on Fab before installation.

With MetaHuman for Houdini you can:

- Use the **MetaHuman Character Rig HDA** to assemble any MetaHuman Character asset exported from Unreal Engine using the DCC Export assembly pipeline as a ready-to-animate rigged and textured character
- Import/export MetaHuman-compatible animation from Unreal Engine onto an assembled MetaHuman character
- Take advantage of parametric groom tools using the **Hairstyle Generator HDA** to rapidly iterate new hairstyles using a guide-driven workflow based on pre-authored data
- Use a structured, procedural workflow to style hair on the standard MetaHuman head mesh or your imported character
- Create complex hairstyles such as ponytails, knots, buns, braids, and donuts, in conjunction with Houdini's procedural toolset
- Export MetaHuman-compatible grooms to Unreal Engine

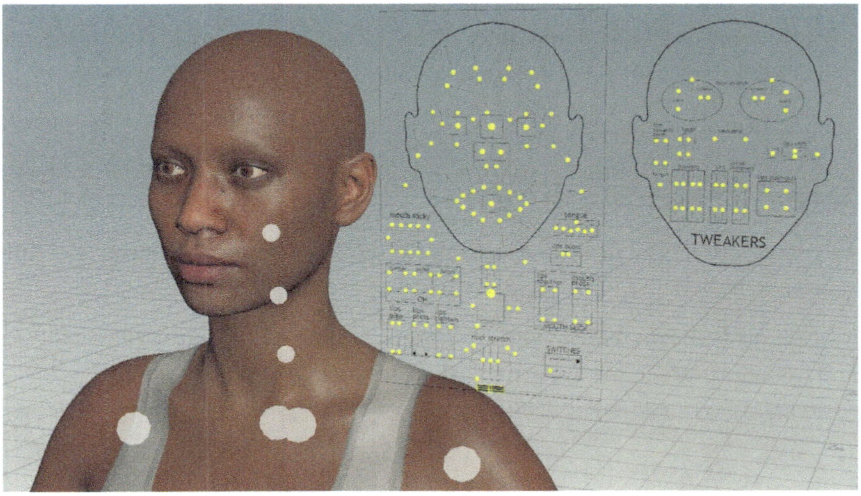

Figure 14.3: MetaHuman control board inside Houdini

In MetaHuman workflows, Houdini is often used to support environments, props, and simulations rather than the character itself. Its value lies in scalability and iteration.

Figure 14.4: Complex hairstyling on a MetaHuman in Houdini

Houdini users know only too well just how complex and powerful Houdini is for handling complex environments and crowds procedurally, so closer integration between Houdini and Unreal Engine through this plug-in is a significant development from Epic Games.

You can also get this plugin at `Fab.com`.

Character Creator plugin

Character Creator provides a flexible approach to character creation that complements MetaHumans.

While MetaHumans focus on realism and consistency, Character Creator allows for rapid iteration and detailed surface work, particularly through its **SkinGen** system.

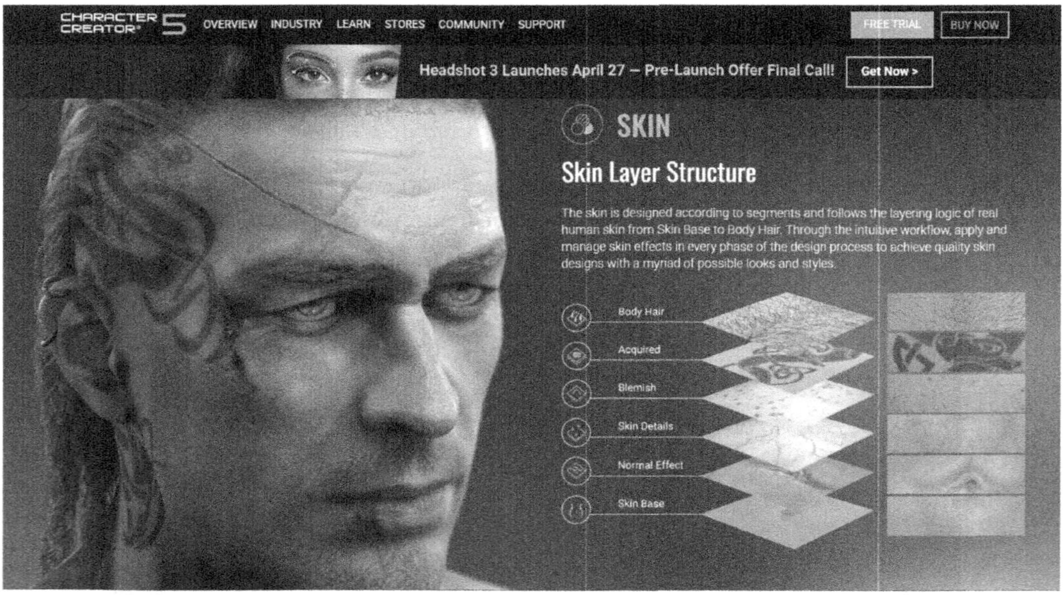

Figure 14.5: Character Creator SkinGen features

SkinGen allows you to build up realistic skin using layers, including pores, blemishes, and micro detail. In many cases, this level of control exceeds what is directly available in Unreal Engine.

The tool also integrates with Unreal, allowing characters and assets to be transferred into a MetaHuman-based pipeline.

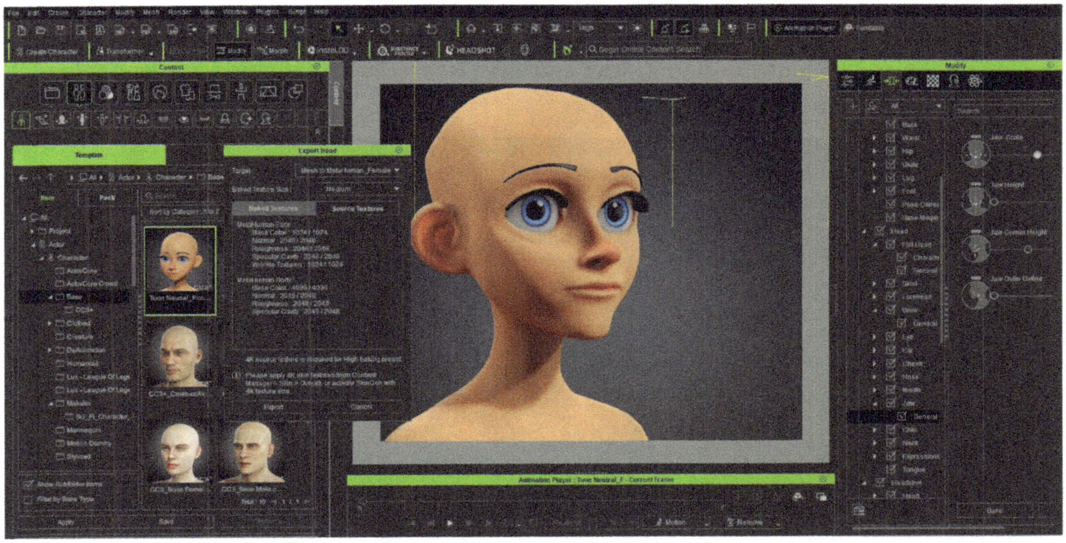

Figure 14.6: Transferring Character Creator heads to MetaHumans

The MetaHuman head export tool, using the Mesh to MetaHuman tool detailed in *Chapter 12*, allows for more toon-like characters with all the benefits of the MetaHuman expression and animation tools, including motion capture.

Note that **iClone** can transfer full characters to Unreal using the Live Link bridge between both applications.

You can get more information from `realusion.com` for both **Character Creator** and **iClone**. Both packages are not free but now have subscription packages as well as perpetual licenses.

Wrap

Wrap is used for transferring geometry between meshes, most commonly in scan-based workflows.

It allows you to take a high-resolution scan and align it to a clean, animation-ready topology such as a MetaHuman base mesh.

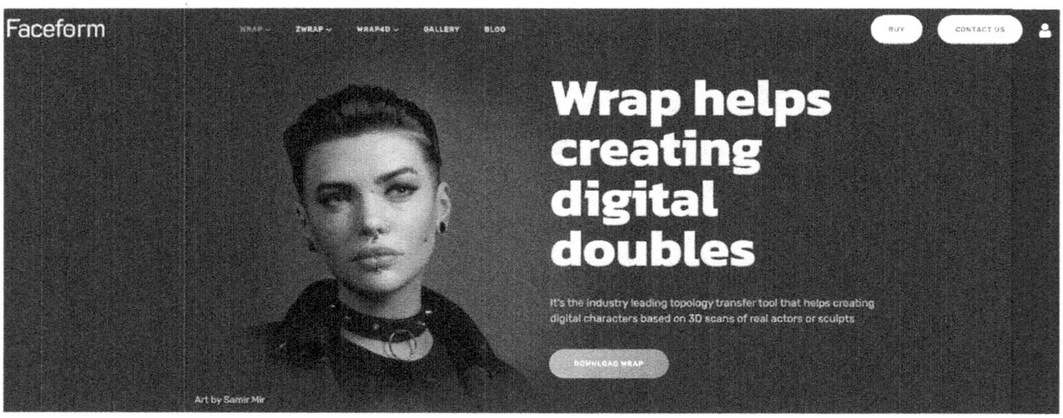

Figure 14.7: Faceform Wrap

This process preserves detail while ensuring compatibility with existing rigs. This comes in really useful not just for detailing but for allowing non-human scans or models to be retopologized to that of a MetaHuman-compatible retopology. This means creatures and animals can be brought into the MetaHuman pipelines effectively.

Note

There are many tutorials on the Faceform website covering MetaHuman workflows. One of the best demonstrations of non-human retopology is the Charlie Driscoll demo, which can be found on both the Faceform website and the official Faceform YouTube channel.

`https://www.faceform.com`

`https://www.youtube.com/@FaceformWrap`

Figure 14.8: Faceform Wrap Charlie Driscoll Demo

While this tool may not appeal to readers starting their MetaHuman journey, it will certainly appeal to more seasoned artists for advanced workflows.

MetaHuman Animation Tool (MAT)

Developed by Locodrome, the **MetaHuman Animation Tool** is designed to simplify interaction with complex rigs.

MetaHumans contain a large number of controls, especially for facial animation. Navigating these directly in the viewport can slow down the animation process. In fact, not using this tool for MetaHuman character animation is borderline prohibitive, and it would be rare to find seasoned professionals without this in their toolbox.

Figure 14.9: MetaHuman Animation Tool (MAT)

The picker provides a visual layout of controls, allowing animators to select and manipulate them more efficiently. In addition, you can mirror poses as well as copy and paste poses for the body.

Also from Locodrome and available on Fab is the **Face** version of the same plugin. It has the same functionality as the Body version but for the face. It's also keyboard friendly with a WASD game control system allowing for rapid adjustment.

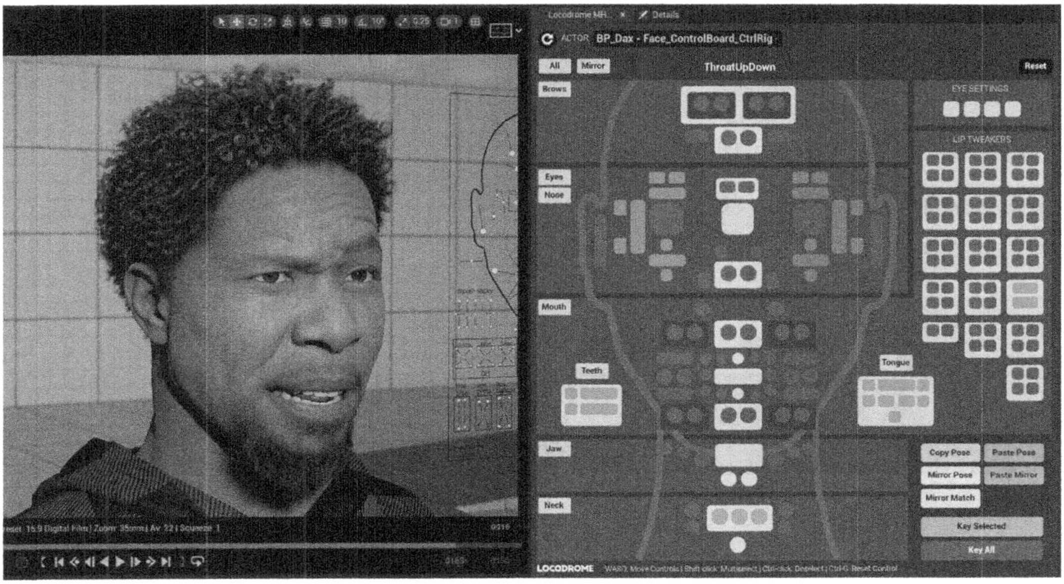

Figure 14.10: Face Animation Tool (FAT)

Both the body and face animation tools drastically speed up the control rig-based workflow, allowing seasoned animators who aren't familiar with MetaHumans to get to work quickly.

MetaTailor

It was very tempting to introduce **MetaTailor** in *Chapter 5* as a clothing solution just because of its sheer ease of use. MetaTailor is focused on simplifying clothing creation for MetaHumans. Unlike Marvelous Designer, which is the definitive professional solution, it comes with the caveat of being hard to use.

There are some limitations as the results are of game quality. So, if you're expecting the assets to hold up for feature film close-ups, this may not be the right solution, although the application continues to improve.

> **Note**
>
> At the time of writing, MetaTailor was available for Windows and operated on a subscription model, so Mac users, and those evaluating costs should keep this in mind before committing to the workflow.

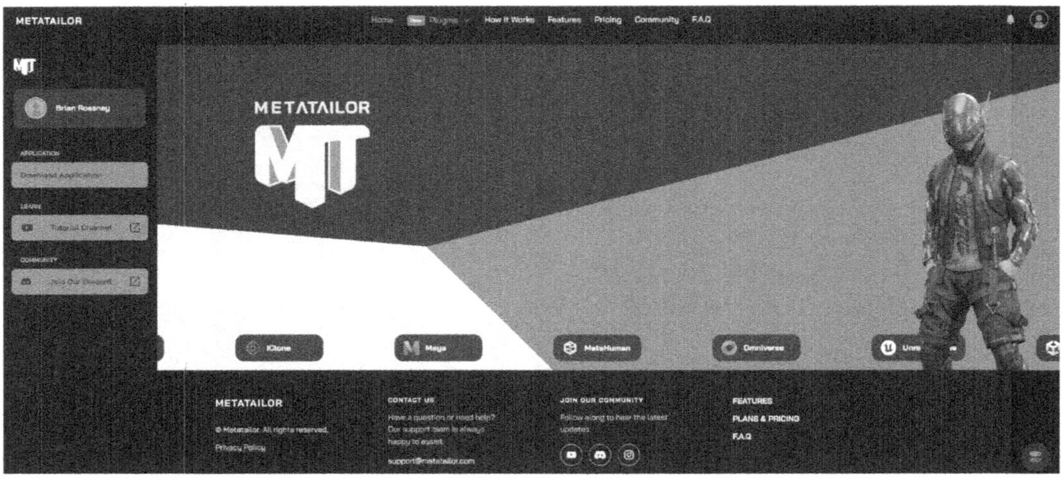

Figure 14.11: MetaTailor

Clothing can then be exported into Unreal Engine using a dedicated bridge.

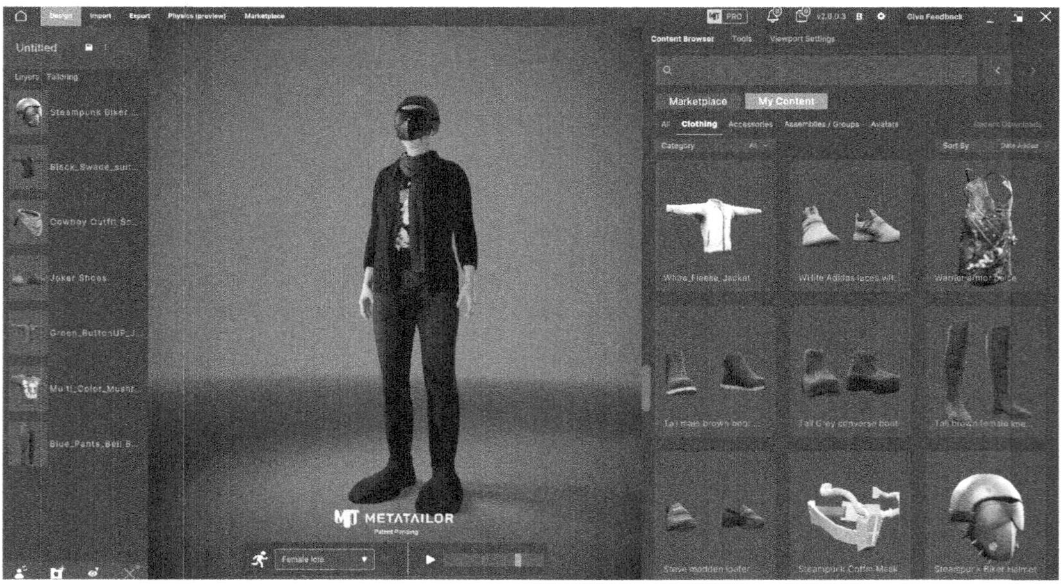

Figure 14.12: Completed clothing applied to a MetaHuman inside Unreal Engine

This makes it particularly useful for rapid iteration and character development.

ZenBlink

ZenBlink focuses on refining facial animation and performance.

Even when using captured data, additional work is often required to clean up and enhance the result.

Figure 14.13: ZenBlink

ZenBlink allows you to adjust timing, smooth motion, and improve expression quality. It also allows you to add these performance enhancers directly into the timeline, which is very time consuming. Key features include blinking, iris dilation, eye following, breathing, and many more. This tool works as an excellent companion tool when using just audio, which I featured in *Chapter 10*. So, if you're working in previz or games, this would be a valuable tool. It's published by Jobutsu and available on `Fab.com`.

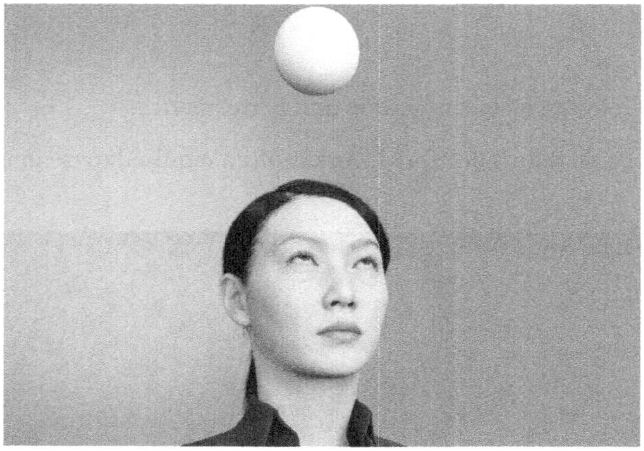

Figure 14.14: ZenBlink Follow target feature

Fab

I'm mentioning **Fab** as it is an incredible resource for assets but also plug-ins. Many assets are paid for, but some are free, and there are also monthly free items. If you are working full time in Unreal or are a passionate hobbyist and working with MetaHumans, this is the place to go.

Its support for MetaHuman content has grown significantly, making it a useful resource for production.

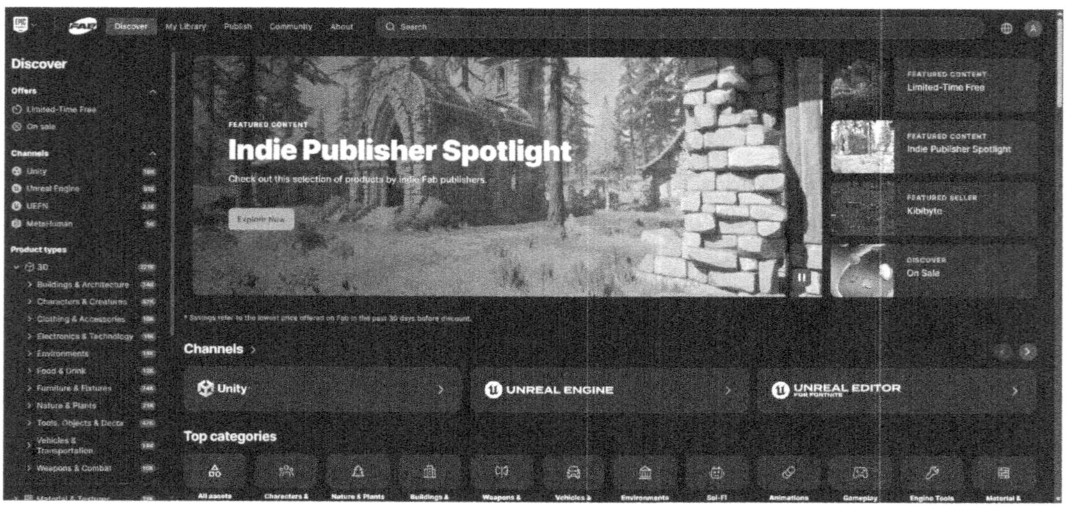

Figure 14.15: Fab, a fabulous resource

Rather than building everything from scratch, you can source assets that are already designed to integrate with your workflow. For new problems that require new solutions, it is always best to see if someone else has developed a Blueprint, a widget, or a plugin that could save you days if not weeks across a long project.

At the time I'm writing this last chapter, there are over 4.5 thousand accessories for MetaHumans, ranging from characters and creatures to clothing and accessories, tools, weapons, and animations.

I'm very sure that this figure was a lot smaller when I started writing this second edition, and it was in fact empty when I wrote the first edition.

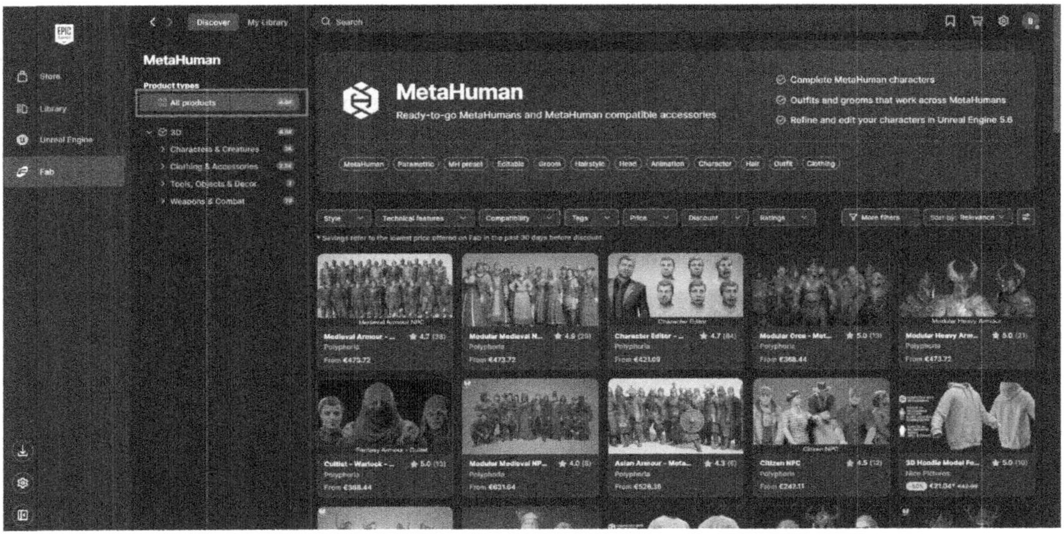

Figure 14.16: MetaHuman-compatible accessories on Fab

Summary

You have now moved beyond working purely inside Unreal Engine and into a broader workflow.

In practice, that is where most real projects sit. You use Unreal as the hub, but you are not limited to it. When you need more control, more flexibility, or a different approach, you bring in the right tool and keep moving.

You are not expected to use everything covered in this chapter. Most people won't. In many cases, a small, reliable setup is far more useful than a complicated one. The value here is simply knowing what exists, so when you do hit a limitation, you are not stuck guessing.

Final words...

So, at this point, there isn't really a next chapter. What you have now is a complete way of working.

MetaHumans, even in the short time they've been around, have come a long way. They started out as a browser-based tool, which at the time felt impressive enough. Now they sit fully inside Unreal Engine, faster, more responsive, and far more capable. The workflow is tighter, the features are deeper, and more and more industry professionals are starting to rely on them as part of real production pipelines.

At the same time, the barrier to entry is dropping. The learning curve is still there, but it is far more manageable than it used to be. The community around MetaHumans is growing quickly, and so is the number of compatible assets: hair, clothing, tools, plugins, entire workflows. You are no longer building everything from scratch unless you choose to.

Right now, if you lined up a group of digital humans, you might still be able to pick out a MetaHuman. But equally, with a bit of care and the techniques covered in this book, you could place one into a live-action scene and most people would not question it. Whether that is for a game, an animated project, or a digital double in a film, that level of realism being available in real time is a fairly significant shift.

It is also worth stepping back for a second and recognizing what that means.

Tools that would have required entire teams not that long ago are now sitting on a single machine. Real-time rendering, high-end facial rigs, photoreal skin—all working together in a way that is actually usable.

As someone who works with MetaHumans on a regular basis, it is still hard not to be a bit surprised by how quickly things are moving. There is a sense that this is not the finished version of anything, just the early stage of something that is going to keep improving.

And that is probably the best place to leave it.

Not at the end of a process, but somewhere in the middle of it, with the tools in place and plenty more still to come.

15

Unlock Your Exclusive Benefits

Your copy of this book includes the following exclusive benefits:

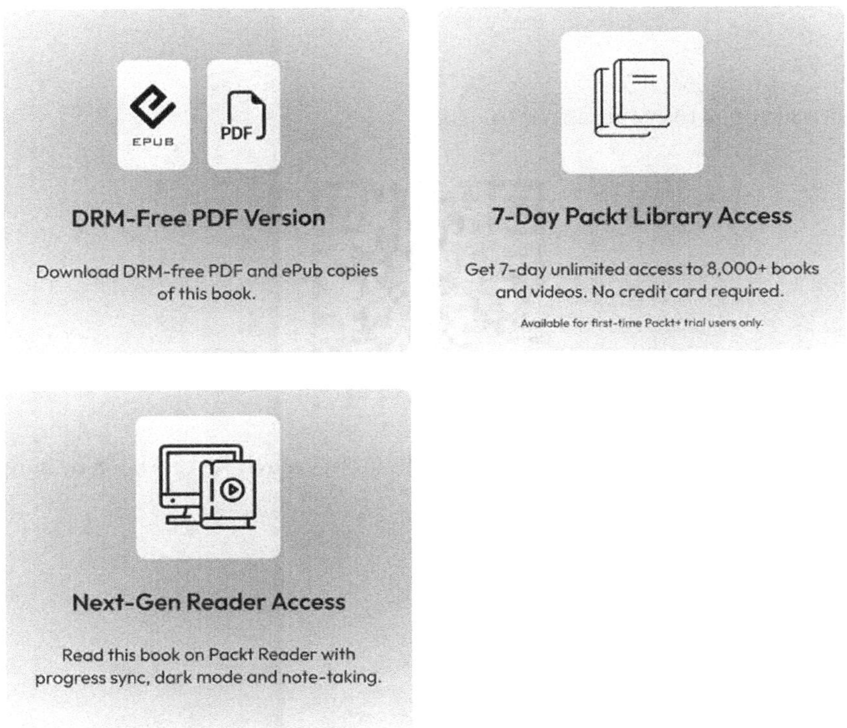

Follow the guide below to unlock them. The process takes only a few minutes and needs to be completed once.

Unlock this Book's Free Benefits in 3 Easy Steps

Step 1

Keep your purchase invoice ready for *Step 3*. If you have a physical copy, scan it using your phone and save it as a PDF, JPG, or PNG.

For more help on finding your invoice, visit `https://www.packtpub.com/en-us/unlock?step=1`.

> Note
>
> **Note**: If you bought this book directly from Packt, no invoice is required. After *Step 2*, you can access your exclusive content right away.

Step 2

Scan the QR code or go to `packtpub.com/unlock`.

On the page that opens (similar to *Figure 15.1* on desktop), search for this book by name and select the correct edition.

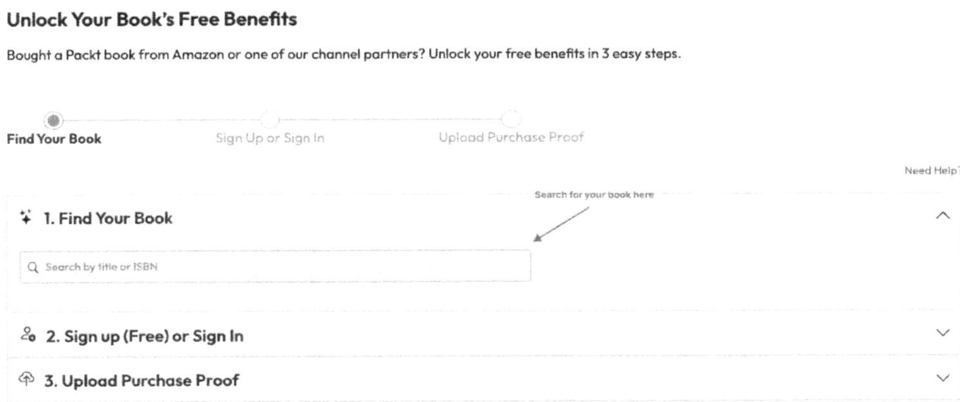

Figure 15.1: Packt unlock landing page on desktop

Step 3

After selecting your book, sign in to your Packt account or create one for free. Then upload your invoice (PDF, PNG, or JPG, up to 10 MB). Follow the on-screen instructions to finish the process.

Need Help

If you get stuck and need help, visit `https://www.packtpub.com/unlock-benefits/help` for a detailed FAQ on how to find your invoices and more. This QR code will take you to the help page.

> Note
>
> **Note**: If you are still facing issues, reach out to `customercare@packt.com`.

packtpub.com

Subscribe to our online digital library for full access to over 7,000 books and videos, as well as industry leading tools to help you plan your personal development and advance your career. For more information, please visit our website.

Why subscribe?

- Spend less time learning and more time coding with practical eBooks and Videos from over 4,000 industry professionals
- Improve your learning with Skill Plans built especially for you
- Get a free eBook or video every month
- Fully searchable for easy access to vital information
- Copy and paste, print, and bookmark content

At www.packtpub.com, you can also read a collection of free technical articles, sign up for a range of free newsletters, and receive exclusive discounts and offers on Packt books and eBooks.

Other Books You May Enjoy

If you enjoyed this book, you may be interested in these other books by Packt:

Unreal Engine 5 Best Practices

Tyson Butler-Boschma

ISBN: 9781836205654

- Explore advanced lighting techniques to create dynamic, realistic lighting using Lumen
- Build and edit assets directly inside Unreal with its built-in modeling tools
- Craft compelling cinematic sequences with cameras and storytelling
- Design stunning, immersive worlds through layout and composition design
- Add destruction and realism with Chaos integration
- Profile and boost efficiency across your projects
- Solve real-world development challenges with tested UE5 strategies

Mastering Unreal Engine 5 Game Development with C++ Scripting

Marco Secchi

ISBN: 9781806665938

- Write clean, optimized C++ code for Unreal Engine 5
- Work with Unreal Engine architecture for scalable systems
- Use pointers efficiently to improve runtime performance
- Apply event-driven programming with C++ and Blueprints
- Use Unreal Engine macros to extend gameplay systems
- Build Blueprint-accessible, optimized C++ components
- Implement data-driven gameplay systems in real projects

Packt is searching for authors like you

If you're interested in becoming an author for Packt, please visit `authors.packt.com` and apply today. We have worked with thousands of developers and tech professionals, just like you, to help them share their insight with the global tech community. You can make a general application, apply for a specific hot topic that we are recruiting an author for, or submit your own idea.

Share your thoughts

Now that you've finished *Reimagining Characters with Unreal Engine MetaHuman Creator, Second Edition*, we'd love to hear your thoughts! Scan the QR code below to go straight to the Amazon review page for this book and share your feedback or leave a review on the site that you purchased it from.

https://packt.link/r/1806024691

Your review is important to us and the tech community and will help us make sure we're delivering excellent quality content.

Index

H

I

L

M

Made in the USA
Monee, IL
15 September 2026

63035030R00216